A Bicentennial Publication of the Colby Museum of Art

MAINE FORMS

OF

AMERICAN

ARCHITECTURE

BELFAST, *James P. White House, by Calvin A. Ryder (1840)*
Photo: Richard Cheek

MAINE FORMS

OF

AMERICAN

ARCHITECTURE

DEBORAH THOMPSON

EDITOR

Published under the auspices of the COLBY MUSEUM OF ART,

Waterville, Maine

DOWNEAST MAGAZINE

Camden, Maine

CONTENTS

List of Figures

FOREWORD

Tʜɪs ʙᴏᴏᴋ ᴀɴᴅ ᴛʜᴇ ᴄᴏᴍᴘᴀɴɪᴏɴ ᴇxʜɪʙɪᴛɪᴏɴ ɪɴ ᴛʜᴇ Cᴏʟʙʏ Mᴜsᴇᴜᴍ ᴏꜰ Art were originally conceived by the late Willard W. Cummings. He directed much of his characteristic energy toward the organization of the project and he generated interest in it by his equally characteristic enthusiasm. It is the hope of all who have worked on either the book or the exhibition that both will be of the quality that would have pleased him.

From the beginning, Bill Cummings' idea of a project devoted to Maine architecture involved a feeling for the people and the land. In the course of one of the early discussions concerning the nature of the exhibition he used the phrase, "man's urge to build," and it has been frequently apparent in the course of planning that interest has focused on those kinds of buildings in Maine which are not products of the most prestigious architects but have rather been the natural outcome of a desire to erect an appropriate structure and to employ available talent. Hence we include reconstructions of native American settlements, examples of the vernacular architecture of the European colonists (and many of their descendants), and the unpretentious buildings of the Shakers. Another facet of Bill Cummings' talent was his ability to re-shape the natural environment so that its beauty was enhanced. He was a portrait painter by profession, not a landscapist, but he virtually created landscape art out of the real environment of his "Red Farm" just north of Skowhegan. It is therefore appropriate that one chapter of this book be devoted to the designing of landscape in the Maine environment. It was also typical of Bill Cummings that his interest in art extended from the past to the immediate present. (His art collection consisted largely of 19th-century works but the art school he directed for so many years was for the nurturing of contemporary talents.) Hence it is also appropriate that contemporary buildings of quality are included here along with those which have passed the test of time.

There have been many architects of wider repute who have designed buildings in Maine during every period since architecture was a profession in America. These provide a significant part of this study. It is hoped that by including buildings and environments that reflect the diversity of life in Maine a sense of the uniqueness of our part of the world will be revealed. No other state had exactly the sequence of development and the combination of interests that are found in Maine. For instance the parallel development of lumbering and ship building produced some fine mansions as well as many more modest dwellings, both coastal and inland. Farming, especially in the first half of the 19th century, was attractive enough to produce a wide scattering of white houses and their impressive barns throughout much of the state. The rivers worked harder than ever for man in the second half of the century and many new mills for the manufacture of cloth and paper were the result. From early times through the present, education was important and it was important to house it well and sometimes handsomely. Government buildings attracted good architects or builders: there are courthouses, city halls, and even jails that we can take pride in. As summer homes multiplied toward the end of the last century and into the present one there was much imaginative designing—and this has continued in recent times as "vacation homes" reflect an interest in all four seasons.

These are a few instances of the relation between living in Maine and building here. Many others will be discussed by the ten authors of the chapters which follow. Each of these authors has a special claim to expertness in the field about which he or she has written. We are most grateful to them for undertaking this project and for working so well as a team. For this latter achievement we are especially indebted to Deborah Thompson, coordinator of the project and editor of the book. Her command of the whole scope of the project and her ability to work effectively at the center of it held it together even when there seemed to be an excess of problems.

An obvious objective of this exhibition and book is to make us more aware of our architectural heritage. Another purpose, equal in importance, is to make us more conscious of our own responsibilities as we build for the present and the future—responsibilities that include a new awareness of the fragility of our natural environment. Because these two aims seemed to us very much in the spirit of the American Bicentennial we made application to the Maine Bicentennial Commission and received from them a generous grant. We are grateful to the Commission and to the Friends of Art at Colby who helped provide the matching funds. For special assistance in the mounting of the exhibition we thank the Maine State Commission on the Arts and Humanities.

It is with affection that we dedicate this book and the exhibition which accompanies it to the memory of Willard W. Cummings.

JAMES M. CARPENTER
Chairman, Department of Art, Colby College

HUGH J. GOURLEY III
Director, Colby Museum of Art

ACKNOWLEDGMENTS

MUCH OF THE SUCCESS OF *Maine Forms of American Architecture* and the exhibition accompanying its publication has been due to the generosity of the many individuals and business organizations whose help was asked during its preparation. The most generous single grant to the exhibition, in the amount of $12,500, was awarded by the Maine Bicentennial Commission. This has been matched by funds from the Colby Museum of Art, Colby College and Mr. and Mrs. Thomas J. Watson III.

So many people have helped the authors of the book and organizers of the project that it has been necessary to list them first of all according to the historical periods or chapters in which their help was relevant. Because of the scope of the undertaking, some names may appear more than once in the following paragraphs.

CHAPTER 1. THE EARLIEST SETTLEMENTS. David Sanger is grateful to the following sponsors of research: The National Museums of Canada; The Province of New Brunswick; the National Science Foundation; The Natonal Geographic Society; the Hazel Smith Fund; the University of Maine at Orono. Other assistance was provided by the Maine State Museum, in the form of photographs and floor plans of the Turner Farm site; the Trustees of the British Museum, for permission to use an old photograph; and Dr. Alvin Morrison, State University College, Fredonia, New York, for information on ethnohistory. Connie Crosby, Colby '76, was responsible for the construction under Dr. Sanger's supervision of a typological model of an Indian wigwam for the exhibition.

CHAPTER 2. THE ARCHITECTURE OF MAINE'S SETTLEMENT. For assistance in studying houses and obtaining research materials and photographs, Richard M. Candee thanks: Professor James S. Leamon, Bates College; John L. Cotter, National Park Service, Philadelphia; Mrs. Helen Camp, Round Pond, Maine; Edwin A. Churchill, Maine State Museum; Robert E. Moody, Boston, Mass.; Dr. Bernard H. Leonard, York Harbor; Thomas W. Eastwood, York; Mrs. Elizabeth S. Winton, York Gaol Museum, York; Mr. and Mrs. Robert M. David, York; Joseph W. P. Frost,

Eliot; Daniel Lohnes, Society for the Preservation of New England Antiquities, Boston; Dr. Helen Wallis, British Library, London; Thomas Gaffney and Gerald Morris, Maine Historical Society, Portland; and J. A. Parsons, Eliot. A typographical model according to Historic American Buildings drawings and research by Candee, of a garrison of the Junkins or McIntire form, was constructed for the exhibition by Joseph L. Alex, Jr., Waterville, Colby, '75.

CHAPTER 3. COLONIAL ARCHITECTURE *and* CHAPTER 4, PART 2. THE GREEK REVIVAL. Denys Peter Myers thanks Miss Christine St. Lawrence, Historic American Buildings Survey; Mrs. Mary Ison, Prints and Photographs Division, Library of Congress; Mrs. Willard Clinton Warren II; Mrs. Barbara Matlock Warren; the Portland Museum of Art; James B. Vickery; and Mrs. Steven Hammond, for assistance with photographs. For help in obtaining research information he thanks Richard M. Candee, Old Sturbridge Village; Mrs. Donald M. Kimball, Brick Store Museum, Kennebunk; and Earle G. Shettleworth, Jr., Maine Historic Preservation Commission. He is grateful also to the following owners of homes for allowing him to visit: Mrs. Francis O'Brien, John Watson House, Hiram; Dr. and Mrs. John Rice, Jr., Second Isaac Parsons House, New Gloucester; Dr. and Mrs. Henry K. Woodbrey, Gov. Washburn House, Orono; Mr. Douglas Corson, Gov. Abner Coburn House, Skowhegan; Mr. and Mrs. Charles Gatchell, Capt. Abraham Thing House, Hallowell; Mrs. Frederick Palmer, Connor-Bovie House, Fairfield; Dr. William J. Deighan, Kent-Cutting House, Bangor; Mrs. Alyce D. Prescott, Nathaniel Treat House, Orono; Mr. and Mrs. Earl L. M. Beard, Shaw-Chick House, Winterport; Mrs. Hugh McC. Marshall, Hugh McCulloch House, Kennebunk; Mr. Booth Hemingway, William Pepperrell House, Kittery; Mrs. Elizabeth Kiralis, East Vassalboro. His thanks also go to the following curators of houses maintained by the Society for the Preservation of New England Antiquities for allowing him to visit after their seasonal closings: Mrs. Andrew Ladygo, the Daniel Marrett House; Miss Elizabeth Goodwin, Sarah Orne Jewett House; Mrs. Larry Kilbourne, Lady Pepperrell House; Mr. and Mrs. Marlin E. Trafton, Jonathan Hamilton House; Mr. Thomas Peterson, Parson Smith House.

CHAPTER 4, PART I. THE FEDERAL STYLE. William D. Shipman thanks Denys Peter Myers and Earle G. Shettleworth, Jr. for their help during the preparation of the text. For permitting him to visit houses he acknowledges the kindness of Capt. and Mrs. Elmer Hill, Benjamin Porter House; Mr. and Mrs. Joseph Marcus, Ebenezer Alden House; Mr. and Mrs. Charles Dodge, Spite House; Miss Margaret Richards, Kavanagh House; and Mr. and Mrs. William Curtis Pierce, West Baldwin. Additional assistance in research and photographic matters was provided by: the Portland Museum of Art; Greater Portland Landmarks, Inc.; Maine Historical Society; Bowdoin College Library; Lafayette French, Knox Memorial Association; Mary Farrell, Historic American Buildings Survey; Jerry Kearns, Library of Congress.

A miniature replica of the Spite House parlor was built for the exhibition through the kindness of Mr. and Mrs. Harry N. Smith, Camden.

CHAPTER 4, PART 3. THE ARCHITECTURE OF THE MAINE SHAKERS. Marius B. Péladeau acknowledges the help of Sister R. Mildred Barker and the other members of the Shaker Community at Sabbathday Lake, New Gloucester. Dr. Theodore E. Johnson has been generous with his assistance and cooperation both in the preparation of the text and in making loan arrangements for the exhibition. Photographic assistance was provided through the skill of Mr. David Serette.

CHAPTER 5, PART 1. REVIVAL STYLES OF ARCHITECTURE. William B. Miller thanks the following owners and guardians of historic buildings: Dr. and Mrs. Robert O. Kellogg, Bangor; Mr. and Mrs. Arthur J. Thomas, Bangor; Col. and Mrs. Gordon Wildes, Winterport; Mr. George D. Carlisle, Bangor; Dr. and Mrs. Charles D. McEvoy, Jr., Bangor; Dean Milton Lindholm, Bates College, Lewiston; Mrs. Curtis Hutchins. He also acknowledges the generous assistance of Earle G. Shettleworth, Jr. and Denys Peter Myers in the preparation of the text, and that of Thomas Gaffney, Maine Historical Society, Portland, and Dr. Adolf Placzek, Avery Architectural Library, Columbia University, in obtaining illustrative material.

CHAPTER 5, PART 2. TURN-OF-THE-CENTURY ARCHITECTURE. For assistance in the preparation of the text, Earle G. Shettleworth, Jr. acknowledges the kindness of John Calvin Stevens II, Cape Elizabeth; Mark M. Wilcox, Portland; Frank A. Beard, Historic Preservation Commission; Linda P. Howe, Historic Preservation Commission. Illustrative material for the book and exhibition was offered through the generosity of: the Maine Historical Society, Portland; Lithgow Library, Augusta; City of Portland; College of the Atlantic, Bar Harbor; Camden-Rockport Historical Society; Christopher P. Monkhouse, Portland; Alonzo Harriman and Associates, Auburn; Judge and Mrs. Benjamin Butler, Farmington; Gary W. Woolson, Bangor.

CHAPTER 5, PART 3. INDUSTRIAL AND COMMERCIAL ARCHITECTURE. Marius B. Péladeau acknowledges the assistance of Earle G. Shettleworth, Jr. in sharing his knowledge of the industrial and commercial architecture of Maine.

CHAPTER 6. THE DEVELOPMENT OF MODERN STYLES OF ARCHITECTURE. In the preparation of this chapter, Philip Isaacson was greatly helped by a survey of Maine architects conducted by Nicholas Holt, A.I.A., president of the Maine Chapter of the American Institute of Architects. Architects who provided information and generous help with illustrative material are: Gridley Barrows, A.I.A., Lewiston (who made two renderings of earlier buildings for the exhibition); Eaton W. Tarbell, A.I.A., Bangor; Robert Adams, Deer Isle; The Architects Collaborative, Cambridge, Mass.; Edward Larrabee Barnes, F.A.I.A., New York City; Benjamin Thompson Associates, Cambridge, Mass.; Howard Barnstone, Houston, Texas; Stephen Blatt, Auburn; Camp Dresser and McKee, Cambridge, Mass.; Cooper Milliken, Old Town; John B. Scholz, Searsmont; Hugh Stubbins and Associates, Inc., Cambridge, Mass.; Scott Teas, Portland; John Weinrich and Steven Moore, Rumford Point; and Deane W. Woodward, Auburn. Information that contributed to the preparation of the text was also provided by: Professor Grant Hildebrand, Seattle, Washington; Bernard Carpenter, Lewiston; and Edwin Fitzpatrick, Portland. Illustrative material was generously contributed by: Casco Bank and Trust Company, Portland; R. Bruce Huntingdon; Miss Frances Mawn of the Ogunquit Museum of Art; Merchants National Bank, Bangor; Dr. M. Peter Mooz, Brunswick; College of the Atlantic; and Dr. Arthur Buswell, University of Maine at Machias. He is further grateful to the following for permitting him to study their houses: the Misses Marion C. and Winifred Gallagher, Blue Hill; Dr. and Mrs. Robert O. Kellogg, Bangor; Mr. and Mrs. August Heckscher, New York and Mount Desert; Mr. and Mrs. Mark A. Willis, New Haven, Connecticut; Francis Merritt, Deer Isle; Ms. Dorothy Livada, Cape Elizabeth.

CHAPTER 7. THE ARCHITECTURE OF MAINE'S SCHOOLS. Janet Hansen acknowledges the help of the following in the preparation of the text: William B. Miller; Judge and Mrs. Ben Butler; Nicholas Holt, A.I.A.; R. Bruce Huntingdon; Mrs. Ruth G. Bennoch; and Deborah Thompson. Illustrative material was provided through the kindness of Judge and Mrs. Ben Butler; Maine Historic Preservation Commission; John Bapst High School, Bangor; George W. Stearns High School, Millinocket; Earle G. Shettleworth, Jr.; Kent's Hill School, Readfield; Normand C. Dubé of the Title VII ESEA (bilingual) program, Madawaska; Denys Peter Myers; Krumbhaar and Holt Associated Architects; John B. Scholz; Jon F. Hall, Waterville; Charles H. Merrill, Portland.

CHAPTER 8. MAINE'S LANDSCAPES. Harriet Pattison acknowledges the help of the following who provided information, in personal and telephone conversations, and illustrative material, in the preparation of the text: Keith Miller, Acadia National Park, Bar Harbor; Wolcott Andrews, F.A.S.L.A., Wiscasset; Mrs. Su Patterson, Aroostock Arts Council, Caribou; Jack Maniglia, Bangor Planning Commission; Madge Baker, Southern Maine Regional Planing Commission, Alfred; Professor Charles Beveridge, American University, Washington, D.C.; Mrs. Olive Bragazzi, Curator, David Rockefeller Collections, New York City; Mrs. Doris Pitcher, Joseph Badger, Samuel Hamilton, Camden Public Library; William Reed, South Gardiner, of the Center for Natural Areas, Northeast Office; Vincent Cerasi, Katonah, New York; Domenico Annese of

Clarke and Rapuano Landscape Architects, New York City; Dr. JoAnne Carpenter, College of the Atlantic, Bar Harbor; Elmer Crockett, Camden; Duane Doolittle, Down East Magazine, Camden; Charles W. Eliot II, Cambridge, Mass.; Mrs. Pierre Fraley, Rockport; Mrs. Thomas S. Hall, Northeast Harbor; Angela Giral and Christopher Hail of the Frances Loeb Library, Harvard University; Philip Isaacson, Lewiston; Mrs. G. H. Kononen, Rockport; Myron Lamb, Limerick; Carl Laws, Saco River Corridor Commission, Cornish; William Ginn of the Maine Audobon Society, Portland; George W. Hannum and Norman Manwell, Maine Department of Conservation, Bureau of Parks and Recreation; Theodore Stone, Maine Department of Transportation, Bureau of Highways; Land Use Regulation Commission of the Maine Department of Conservation; H. S. Burrill, Jr. of the Mount Hope Cemetery Corporation; Richard Berman and Terry Dewan of Moriece and Gary, Portland; Christian Herter III of the Natural Resources Council of Maine; Robert Pyle of Northeast Harbor Library; Artemas P. Richardson of Olmsted Associates, Inc., Brookline, Mass.; Richard Anderson of the Portland Department of Parks and Recreation; Robert W. Patterson, Mount Desert; Thomas Savage, Northeast Harbor; Earle G. Shettleworth, Jr. of the Maine Historic Preservation Commission; Skowhegan Town Office, Skowhegan; Alexandra Tyng, Philadelphia, Pa.; Professors Roger Clapp, Alan Lewis, James Swazey and David C. Smith, University of Maine at Orono; Gerry Wolff, A.S.L.A., Atherton, California; Alexander Goriansky, Northeast Harbor; Thomas Paine, Boston, Mass. Other illustrative material was provided by: Nicholas Barth, Delmar, New York; Paul A. Knaut, Dover-Foxcroft; George Pohl, Philadelphia, Pa.; Denys Peter Myers; Heather Lyttle of Sasaki Associates, Watertown, Mass.; Lolly McDonnell-Mitchell of The Architects Collaborative, Cambridge, Mass.; George Taloumis, Peabody, Mass.; John Graves of the Department of Landscape Architecture, University of California at Berkeley; Mrs. Frances Hartgen, Special Collections, Fogler Library, University of Maine at Orono; and William D. Shipman. Permission to visit gardens was kindly given by: Robert Hallowell Gardiner, Gardiner; Mrs. Roger Milliken, Northeast Harbor; and Mr. Gerrish Milliken, Northeast Harbor.

In addition to the above, the following individuals and institutions were helpful in permitting material from their collections to appear in the exhibition, in supplying general information about architectural ornament, and in supplying other help: Ron Kley, Jane Radcliffe and Dora Sheldon, Maine State Museum; J. Gary Nichols, Maine State Library; Dr. Roger Howell, Jr., Bowdoin College; Dr. Howard Neville, University of Maine at Orono; Samuel Silsby, Maine State Archives; Bowdoin College Art Museum; Dyer-York Library, Museum, Saco; Farmington Historical Society; Kennebec Historical Society; Maine Historical Society; Mrs. John Hill, Joseph Downs Manuscript and Microfilm Collection, Henry F. DuPont Museum, Winterthur, Delaware; Prentiss and Carlisle Company, Bangor; Philip Conroy, Portland; Canal National Bank, Portland; Mrs. Arthur Tilley, Bangor; Mr. and Mrs. Earl L. M. Beard, Winterport; Mrs. Philip R. Christmas, Brewer; Wendell S. Hadlock, Farnsworth Library and Museum, Rockland; Mr. and Mrs. Ray Kononen, Rockport; Bangor-Brewer Y.W.C.A., Isaac Farrar Mansion; Professor Thomas J. Morrione, Winslow; Mrs. Ambrose C. Cramer, Rockport; Jon F. Hall, Waterville; Bingham Union Church Association; Head Tide Church Association; Mrs. Richard Price Dunn, Brooklin and Washington, D.C.; Richard Nylander and Daniel Lohnes, Society for the Preservation of New England Antiquities; Mrs. Elain Evans Dee, Cooper-Hewitt Museum of Design, New York; Dr. and Mrs. Robert O. Kellogg, Bangor; Colby College Library; Portland Museum of Art; Fogg Art Museum, Harvard University; Mr. and Mrs. Bertram K. Little; Mr. and Mrs. Joseph Marcus; Mrs. Elizabeth Webb, Bangor Daily News; Michael Thom, Kingfield; Marius B. Péladeau; Earle G. Shettleworth, Jr.; Denys Peter Myers; Thomas Gaffney, Maine Historical Society; The Silent Woman, Waterville; Mr. and Mrs. Marshall L. Stone; Mr. and Mrs. Nicholas Kuhn. Mr. Kuhn was responsible for the capable design of the exhibition.

Students who were particularly helpful in research towards the preparation of the exhibition were Shelby Moravec and Jennifer Frutchy. Other student helpers were: Rebecca Guild; John LoConte; Jonathan Smith and Pat Trunzo. Other volunteers who contributed time and effort to the preparation of the exhibition were Mrs. Sam Pachowsky, Mrs. Hazel Longley and Jonathan Smith.

A special project, to build a replica of an historical gazebo for the exhibition, was carried out by students of the Waterville Regional Technical-Vocational Center, under the direction of Frank FitzGerald. We are grateful to Mrs. Buxton Warren for allowing her gazebo to be duplicated. Students who worked on the project were: Ken Theriault, Paul Boulette, Eric Marden, Bob Gagne, and Wayne King. Another exhibition project, "The Growth of A Typical Maine House," was carried out under the direction of Steve Jolicoeur by these students of the Technical-Vocational Center: Jeff Spencer, Clinton; Chris Hood, Benton; Dan Hudson, Oakland; Ray Breton, Vassalboro; Cindy Willey, Winslow. Information and photographs of this Bingham house were provided through the courtesy of Mr. and Mrs. Richard N. Hall, Jon F. Hall, and R. Bruce Huntingdon. The direction of both of these projects at the Waterville Regional Technical-Vocational Center was assisted by Mrs. Deborah Carroll.

The preliminary planning of the entire project was undertaken by the Advisory Committee for the Exhibition, whose members include: Mrs. Thomas J. Watson III; Gridley Barrows; James M. Carpenter; Mrs.

William Carpenter; Abbott Lowell Cummings; †Willard W. Cummings; Hugh J. Gourley III; Bronson W. Griscom; Nicholas Holt; Mr. and Mrs. Ellerton M. Jetté; E. Verner Johnson; James H. Mundy; David C. Smith; John Calvin Stevens II; Edward H. Turner; James B. Vickery.

A special sub-exhibit devoted to historical preservation was prepared by Christopher Glass through the courtesy of the Citizens for Historic Preservation.

Finally, the editor wishes to thank personally for their unfailing patience and help in the preparation of this book: Margaret G. Nutting, all of the authors, and my husband.

INTRODUCTION

THE HISTORY OF THE ART AND ARCHITECTURE OF MAINE HAS BEEN A
continuing source of study for many years at Colby College. In the
1940's, a series of four exhibitions was devoted to art in Maine, and the
last of these, *Exhibition of Maine Architecture from the 17th Century to
the Civil War,* consisted of the first important exhibition to survey the
architecture of the state. It was arranged by the Art Department of the
college, under the direction of Professor Samuel M. Green, and thus preceded the establishment of the Colby Museum of Art by several years. The
1945-46 exhibition, coming as it did when there had been relatively little
work by architectural historians in Maine, was limited in scope—much of
the interesting corpus of buildings now known in the various styles had
scarcely been documented or methodically studied. The show, therefore,
was not large and was able to travel, particularly since it consisted of large
panels with applied photographs. It did in fact appear at these institutions
after its début at Colby: Phillips Academy, Sweat Memorial Art Museum
(now the Portland Museum of Art), Bowdoin College, Smith College,
and the Bangor Public Library. The size of the exhibition, *Maine Forms
of American Architecture* (July 3–October 1, 1976) which accompanies
the publication of this book, is a testimony to the work that has been done
since then in the architectural history of Maine.

Those who read this written account while the exhibition is still on
view will recognize that the buildings in the exhibition have been
chosen by the authors of each chapter to amplify their texts. Since all the
buildings discussed could not be illustrated in the book, those that had to
be omitted are mostly to be found in the exhibition. Naturally, the proto-
typical buildings discussed and illustrated in the text are also featured in
the exhibition.

Another way in which *Maine Forms of American Architecture*
differs from its 1945 predecessor is in its broader range. In its planning by
the Advisory Committee on Maine Architecture of the Museum, it was
felt that a full history of architecture in the state should include its prehistory, or Indian settlements, and carry the story up to the present day.
In addition, the special aspects of landscape architecture and the architec-

tural history of schools, have been treated separately. The first would otherwise not have received the attention that it merits, and the second is of such interest to the public that the social changes underlying the development of different kinds of schools seemed to call for separate treatment.[1]

Colby's contribution to the study of Maine art and architecture has not been restricted to its exhibitions of the 1940's. The faculty of the Art Department and the museum (which opened in 1960) continued to give attention and study to the work of local artists and architects. In 1963, the museum published the book, *Maine and Its Role in American Art, 1740–1963* (Gertrud A. Mellon, coordinating editor, Elizabeth F. Wilder, editor, New York: The Viking Press).[2] Like the present volume, it was coordinated with a major exhibition *(Maine and Its Artists, 1710–1963),* which later traveled to the Whitney Museum of Art in New York, Museum of Fine Arts, Boston, and the Portland Museum of Art. Both exhibition and book marked the observance of the Colby College Sesquicentennial in 1963. The two parts of *Maine Forms of American Architecture,* as explained in the Acknowledgments, represent the National Bicentennial project of the Colby Museum of Art, and have been in the planning stages since the 1963 exhibition and book. Another important exhibition devoted to a Maine subject was *Landscape in Maine, 1820–1970,* sponsored by the Maine Federation of Women's Clubs, through a grant from the Sears Roebuck Foundation and the Maine State Commission on the Arts and Humanities. It appeared at Bowdoin College and the University of Maine at Orono, after its opening at Colby. The editor of the catalogue of the same title was James M. Carpenter, Chairman of the Department of Art at Colby, a chapter-author and organizer of the 1963 exhibition and book, *Maine and Its Role in American Art,* and author of the Foreword to the present volume.[3]

In the latter part of the 1960's and early 70's, a survey of Maine buildings on a county basis was undertaken. In 1965, Harry Greaver of the University of Maine worked on this project, funded by a grant from the Friends of Art of the Colby Museum. This work was continued by Sandra K. Sylvester in 1968, with funds granted by the Friends of Art and Maine State Commission on the Arts and Humanities. Descriptive material relating to Maine buildings, many previously unrecorded in a systematic way, began to accumulate in the architectural files of the museum.

A little earlier, the attention of a larger public was focused on Maine architecture by Oliver W. Larkin, who in his book, *Art and Life in America,* revised edition (New York, 1960), devoted a portion of the text to the architecture of the state. Joseph Coburn Smith, then director of development at Colby, was a dedicated amateur photographer of Maine architecture, many of whose photographs were used by Samuel Green in the 1945 show; one of them appeared in the Larkin book. In the 1960's, Bronson Griscom, an active member of the Museum Committee, and Christopher Huntingdon, Curator of the museum (1963–66) kept alive the plans for an exhibition devoted to the architecture of Maine. Another interested friend of the museum, the late Ambrose C. Cramer, Historic Preservation Officer of the Maine Chapter of the American Institute of Architects, contributed to the groundwork for this project by his assistance in the preparation of the *Maine Catalog* (see below).

Started under the direction of James H. Mundy, a major process of architectural inventorying by the Architectural Historian of the Historic Preservation Commission, Earle G. Shettleworth, Jr., has led so far to the listing of more than 900 buildings of importance in the state. There are other links to the Historic Preservation Commission (founded in 1971) among the authors of this book. William B. Miller has been a Commissioner since its foundation, and only recently relinquished the duties of Vice Chairman. Another chapter-author, David Sanger, is the present archaeologist-member of the Historic Preservation Commission and is also its Vice Chairman. The volume of work performed by the Commission and number of important Maine buildings inventoried and now listed on the National Register of Historic Places are outstanding. There are more than 230 individual entries, 30 Historic Districts and 25 National Historic Landmarks, and at this time, Maine leads the nation in the number of designated Historic Districts. All of this has been accomplished with a much smaller budget and staff than in other states, an indication of the high capacity for efficiency of Maine's civil servants.

All of the authors and organizers of the exhibition and book are indebted to the work of the Historical Preservation Commission in making known this corpus of buildings in the different styles and periods. We are also in debt to the groundwork laid by the Historic American Buildings Survey (HABS) of the National Park Service, and to the author of the *Maine Catalog*, Historic American Buildings Survey (Augusta: Maine State Museum, 1974), Denys Peter Myers. Myers, who is the author of Chapters 3 and 4, Part 2 in this book, like Shettleworth, has been open to all inquiries and requests during the preparation of the book and exhibition. The HABS program was first established in 1933, "under a Civil Works appropriation both to produce accurate records of significant American buildings and to provide employment for architects and draftsmen during the economic crisis of the Great Depression," (Myers, *Maine Catalog*, iii).

While an architectural survey written by several authors is bound to present different, sometimes inconsistent, approaches to the material, the present volume now stands as the fullest architectural history of our state. It is in the very nature of such a survey to be selective. The authors have had to omit many buildings of interest of which they were aware in order to produce a readable and instructive text. Although they have had the advantage of the groundwork prepared by the Historic American Buildings Survey and the Historic Preservation Commission, some of the buildings mentioned below are not listed by either source. It is natural that in this relatively new field of research, more buildings of merit in the different styles remain to be documented, and that future studies will reveal new aspects of certain buildings that are known or discussed.

In the division of the material, it was felt better to deal with the various aspects of the 19th century in different parts of Chapters 4 and 5, rather than by breaking up this material, which is part of the same complex story, into separate chapters. Such a division would have given a false impression of sequence, when the actuality is one of co-existence and inter-relationships, as well as of stylistic progression.

The architectural history of Maine is only a chapter in the architectural history of the United States, more specifically of New England. In their chapters, the authors have tried as much as possible to call attention to such differences, historical, climatic, economic, and social, that make the architecture of Maine distinctive in certain ways. For in the last analysis, it is not local patriotism, but these differences (even the lack of them sometimes) that justify a regional approach to architectural history.

It is the hope of authors and editor alike that *Maine Forms of American Architecture* will help its readers wherever they are to cultivate new levels of awareness to the buildings around them, both in calling their attention to unknown buildings of merit, and in stimulating them to find out more about buildings of recognized interest. We further hope that this awareness will make itself felt in the sensitive preservation, adaptation and use of older buildings, and in informed choices in the planning and design of modern buildings and landscapes.

Deborah Thompson

MAINE FORMS

OF

AMERICAN

ARCHITECTURE

———

1

The Earliest Settlements:

9000 B.C. to A.D. 1600

David Sanger

INTRODUCTION

THIS CHAPTER IS CONCERNED WITH THE HOUS-
ing and settlements of the first inhabitants of Maine—the prehistoric Indians. The
prehistoric period encompasses close to 11,000
years, closing with the arrival of Europeans and
written records in the 16th century A.D.[1] The
term "settlements" in this chapter refers to
houses, to village composition, and to the utilization of the landscape. Such a broad definition
recognizes the integration of housing into the
broader patterns of the prehistoric cultures.

There are two main lines of evidence that bear
on the question of prehistoric settlement. Foremost is the archaeological evidence derived from
the excavation and interpretation of the remains.
Unfortunately, the archaeological record has a
great many gaps, a circumstance related to lack
of work in Maine and the fragile nature of a
record that is easily destroyed by "progress" and

expanding civilization. In the name of progress
we dam up rivers and lakes, and bulldoze over
and through the historical heritage—the archaeological sites. A second line of evidence is the
historical, or written record. Early explorers,
traders, and religious zealots left accounts of
their contacts with the Indians. Many of these
were made nearly one hundred years after initial
contact, so that our most complete records, those
commencing after A.D. 1600, do not describe a
truly aboriginal way of life. The historic records
can be used to supplement the archaeological
evidence, but not without appropriate caution.

Before discussing the archaeological record, it
is important to note that up until around A.D.
1000 the inhabitants of Maine depended exclusively on hunting, fishing, and gathering for
their existence. Agriculture was restricted to the
western part of the State by historic times (17th

century).[2] Hunters and gatherers, the Indians of Maine scheduled their activities according to the resource base and the seasonal availability of certain staples, such as the anadromous, or sea-run, fish. In order to understand the Indian pattern of settlement, it becomes necessary to appreciate the restrictions and pressures exerted by the environment and resources of Maine. This apparently obvious point is frequently overlooked by those who judge the quality of housing by their own bias in regard to what constitutes "decent housing." That the Indian technology was in many ways well suited to the local environments is attested by the adoption of many Indian traits by successful European colonists.

THE ARCHAEOLOGICAL EVIDENCE

For most people the American Revolution happened a long time ago, and in this bicentennial period it is important to keep in perspective the full extent of the historical record of America. Man has been in North America at least 30,000 years and possibly longer,[3] spreading into the New World via the Bering Straits region during the last period of glacial advance. During that period sea levels stood about three hundred feet lower than at present, resulting in a land bridge, over 1000 miles wide, connecting Alaska with Siberia. Until perhaps 12,000 B.C., Maine was covered with a mile-thick ice sheet that effectively excluded man from the area. As the ice sheet began to disintegrate a complex series of events occurred about which we have only limited information. It would seem, however, that by 10,000 B.C. the landscape had recovered sufficiently for plants, animals, and perhaps man to colonize the state. At that time, Maine looked quite different. In place of the mixed conifer-hardwood forest of recent times, Maine was predominantly tundra, much like the Arctic regions today.[4]

There is no evidence of man in Maine until about 9000 B.C. The evidence is in the form of a handful of highly diagnostic spear points with distinctive basal thinning, or fluting. While no site in Maine capable of being excavated has yet been found, very similar spear points have been excavated in Nova Scotia and dated to between 8,000 and 9,000 B.C. At the Debert site, archaeologists uncovered firehearths surrounded by many artifacts and debris from manufacturing items. In the estimation of the excavator, the inhabitants lived in tents much like the historic wigwams, but there is no solid evidence of this. Because of the prevalent tundra conditions it seems likely that caribou constituted the principal prey of the Debert hunters, but they may also have taken migratory nesting birds, fish, and perhaps other mammals. A migratory way of life is probably indicated if for no other reason than that animals such as caribou move on a seasonal basis.[5]

Following this early period, there appears to be a lengthy hiatus in the cultural record in Maine. To what extent this is a reflection of the primitive state of our knowledge is not clear. In southern New England there is increasing evidence for occupation around 6000 B.C., and it is possible that Maine was also inhabited, even if sparsely. At the Hirundo site in Alton there is an occupation level on top of glacial till; below are deposits dated to around 2500 B.C. Some spear points from the early level are reminiscent of those found further to the south.[6] Another site in the pre-3000 B.C. period is the Turner Farm site on North Haven Island.[7]

In summary, there is some evidence to suggest the presence of man in Maine between 8000 and 3000 B.C., but the details are lacking. It may be

FIGURE 1. *Laurentian Tradition artifacts from Maine burial and habitation sites. Photo: University of Maine at Orono*

that the environment of Maine at that time played a role. According to the palynological studies, central Maine was dominated by a pine forest that may have been relatively unproductive for man (see note 4). On the other hand, it may be that rising sea levels in the Gulf of Maine have washed out sites of this period that were located in the littoral zone, while inland sites have been buried or eroded due to changing river and lake regimes.[8]

From around 3000 B.C. to recent times, the evidence for man in Maine becomes substantially greater. At 3000 B.C. there is a close resemblance between artifacts in Maine and specimens from the St. Lawrence Valley where the culture is known as the Laurentian Tradition[9] (see Figure 1). The Indians of the Laurentian Tradition spread into the Northeast from a yet unknown homeland, carrying with them a distinctive tool-kit and a way of life adapted to a mixed hardwood-conifer forest. At this time in Maine the forests had a great diversity of hardwoods, and central Maine looked like the forest of western Massachusetts, with very little spruce and practically no fir (see note 4). Although these Indians were adapted to the forests, lakes, and rivers, in time they developed techniques which allowed them to utilize the considerable marine resources.

In Maine it is possible to enjoy the benefits of marine species far above the head of tide by catching any one of a number of anadromous species, such as salmon, shad, and alewife. In fact, given the spearing and trapping techniques of the Indians, it is only really possible to systematically exploit these species out of the salt water zone. Such a fishing locality is the Hirundo site on the Penobscot River system (see note 6). Similar sites existed throughout the State, wherever rapids or other features favored the Indian fishing techniques.

A different kind of marine adaptation by these same people occurred along the coast. At several sites archaeologists have found abundant evidence for the catching of swordfish, a formidable animal whose capture implies a specialized knowledge of fishing and seamanship. The highest concentration of these sites occurs from Monhegan Island to Frenchman Bay. At some sites, such as the Stanley site on Monhegan Island, swordfishing and small species fishing would appear to represent the major economic activity (see note 8). Situated in a less open marine setting, the Turner Farm site on North Haven Island reflects evidence of a more mixed economy (see note 7). Because swordfish enter the Gulf of Maine during the summer only, the presence of these remains in high numbers indicates summer residence along the coast.[10]

Unfortunately, our research to date has not revealed any unequivocal houses for these Indians. It is safe to infer that they had shelters of some sort, but the physical remains of them have not been recognized at any of the excavated sites.

The Indians of the Laurentian Tradition are perhaps best known to the general public as the "Red Paint Indians" because of the practice of burying their dead after smearing them with a powdered, iron-rich mixture known as red ochre. A number of the red ochre cemeteries have been excavated and destroyed in the search for the finely fashioned artifacts[11] (see Figure 2).

Around 1750 B.C., the Laurentian Tradition in Maine was replaced abruptly by a culture that had its origin in southern New England. With the coming of the Susquehanna Tradition there are numerous and significant changes in all aspects of the culture that archaeologists can examine. Traits which characterize the Laurentian, such as plummets, ground slate points, special gouges, and red ochre burials disappear from the scene. There are changes in food procurement techniques reflecting greater utilization of estuaries and terrestrial resources. At Turner Farm, large "living floors" have been found with possible house remains (see note 7). Typical artifacts include stemmed points, drills, and distinctive celts. Susquehanna burials are cremations.

Between 1700 B.C. and A.D. 1 the archaeological record is again incomplete. The period is represented at Hirundo, at Moose Island near Eastport,[12] and elsewhere. Curiously, a number of these sites, although located in the marine zone, lack shellfish. Associated artifacts include contracting stemmed points, large scrapers, and chipped and ground celts. Similar sites have yet to be described from western Maine although they undoubtedly exist.

Ceramics are introduced into Maine during the first millennium B.C. In New York, it is known as Vinette I. This pottery is thick, with coarse sand temper. The introduction of ceramics probably resulted in little change in the overall life style of Maine Indians, but it does form a useful horizon marker for the period of prehistory, known as the ceramic period[13] (see Figure 3).

For the ceramic period we have numerous sites from which to reconstruct the culture. However, detailed excavation and analysis has occurred only in a few restricted areas, (for example see Figure 4). The central Maine coast from Frenchman Bay to Penobscot Bay is quite well known as is the eastern Maine coast in the Passamaquoddy-Cobscook Bay region.[14] Inland, the Hirundo site stands as the single, extensively excavated site of the ceramic period.

It is during this period that the first good archaeological evidence for housing is found, although the earlier inhabitants must have had shelters. The best documented dwellings come from a series of excavations in Passamaquoddy Bay where semi-subterranean houses are found in shell middens, (see Figure 5 for an example of the floor plan of such a house). These midden sites are composed of thousands of shellfish, mostly the soft-shelled clam, whose presence neutralizes the otherwise acid soil of Maine. The neutral, or even slightly basic nature of the middens results in the preservation of food bones, and from these, archaeologists have determined that the sites were used as winter villages. The presence of winter-killed animals in the houses confirms that they were winter dwellings.[15]

FIGURE 2. *Artifacts from the Turner Farm Site. Photo: Maine State Museum*

FIGURE 3. *Ceramic period artifacts. Photo: University of Maine at Orono*

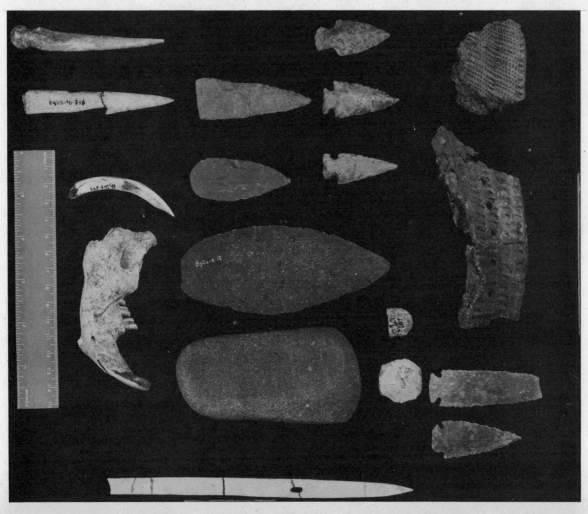

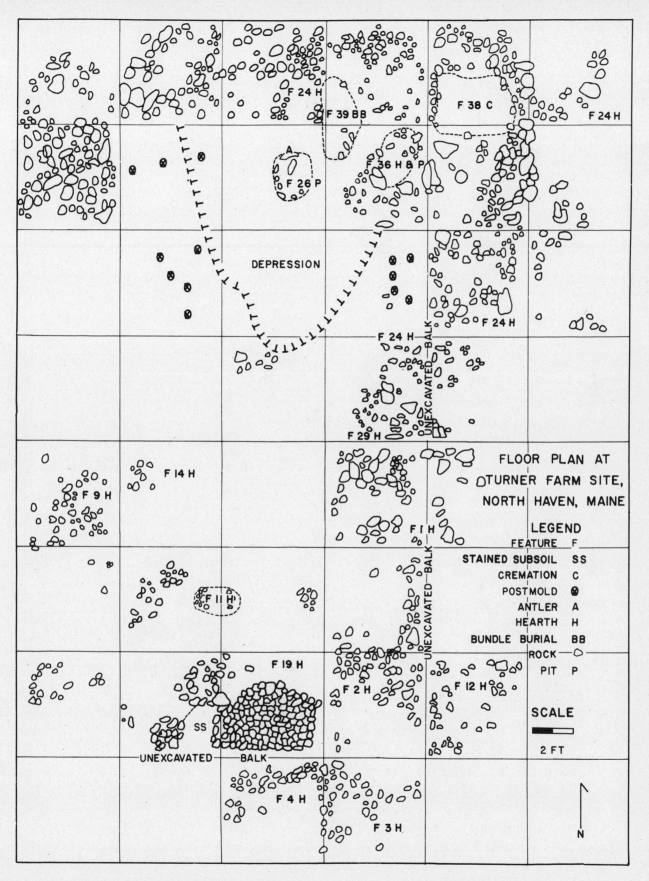

Within the figure:

F 24 H

F 39 BB

F 38 C

F 24 H

A
F 26 P

F 36 H & P

DEPRESSION

F 24 H

F 24 H

F 29 H

F 14 H

F 9 H

F 1 H

FLOOR PLAN AT
TURNER FARM SITE,
NORTH HAVEN, MAINE

LEGEND

FEATURE   F
STAINED SUBSOIL SS
CREMATION   C
POSTMOLD   ⊗
ANTLER   A
HEARTH   H
BUNDLE BURIAL   BB
ROCK   ⌀
PIT   P

F 11 H

UNEXCAVATED — BALK

SCALE

2 FT

F 19 H

F 2 H

F 12 H

SS

UNEXCAVATED — BALK

F 4 H

F 3 H

N

FIGURE 4. *Excavation at the Turner Farm Site, North Haven Island. Photo: Maine State Museum*

FIGURE 5. *Floor plan at the Turner Farm site. Courtesy of the Maine State Museum*

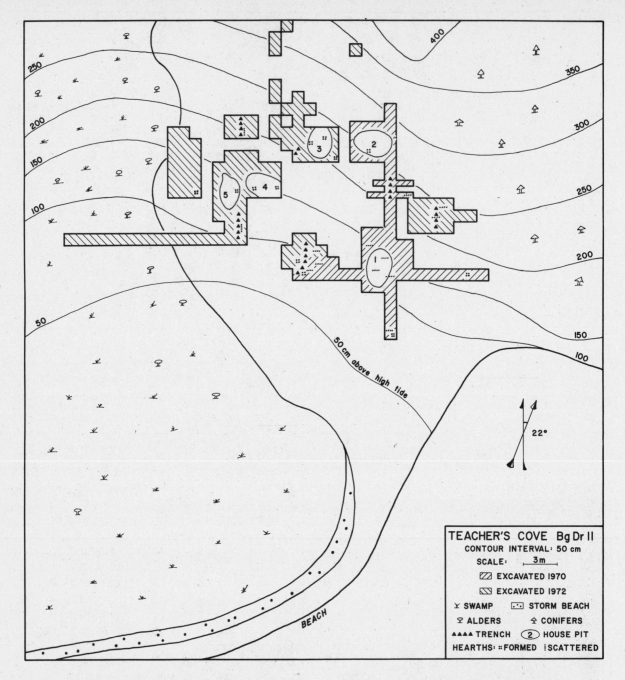

FIGURE 6. *Map of Teacher's Cove Site, Passamaquoddy Bay. Courtesy of David Sanger*

The houses in the Passamaquoddy Bay sites are remarkable for their uniformity. To date, they are known to exist in six sites ranging in age from approximately A.D. 1 to A.D. 1500. The first description is in the 1883 report of G. F. Mathew who dug in an unplowed field where depressions could be seen. More recent excavations, in the 1970's, indicate that a nearly conical structure was erected over a depression. The depressions are quite consistent in size, averaging

4 meters (13 ft.) by 3.5 meters (11.5 ft.) and are always oval. Depth of excavation below ground level ranges from 25 cm. (less than 1 ft.) to 50 cm. (1.5 ft.). Disintegrated remains of posts around the outer perimeter indicate a nearly conical arrangement of poles supported by strategically placed rocks. Sometimes, an entrance

way is observed and this is oriented away from the beach (see Figure 6). At one site in Passamaquoddy Bay, crushed shell was placed around the base of the tent or wigwam, presumably to prevent drafts. No trace of covering has been found to date, but it seems likely that bark or hides were in use. Inside the houses there is evidence of considerable activity. As many as twelve layers of charcoal-stained gravel and other living debris have been recognized in one house (see the excavation of a house at the Sand Point site in Figure 7). Hearths, some rather scattered, are present in all houses. Also indicative of activity in the dwellings is the presence of many artifacts, some broken. Unfortunately, analysis of the spatial distribution of artifacts and hearths has yet to reveal any specialized areas of activity, such as women's tasks (see Figure 8, A and B, showing the stratigraphy of a house at Sand Point). Considering the climate, the raw materials available, and the mobile way

of life of the Indians, a more perfect form of housing is hard to imagine.

The form of these dwellings is basically similar to those described in the early 17th century by the Jesuit Pierre Biard, and others, except that these accounts do not mention the oval floor plan or the semi-subterranean nature. A photograph taken in 1873 of a Nova Scotia Micmac wigwam shows a steeply rising front with an entrance way and a more gently sloping back (Figure 9). Such a shape would result in an oval floor plan very similar to those witnessed archaeologically. Nowhere in the archaeological record to date is there good evidence of the summer houses, nor is there any indication of the spacious buildings said to contain "fully eighty people."[16]

In addition to the advantages of the housing form described above, there is a matter of tools needed to erect this structure. While excavation for the "central depression" could pose problems in frozen soil, it would be relatively easy to dig into the loose shell of a coastal site, once some midden had been established. No clearly

FIGURE 7. *Excavation of House 2 at Sand Point Site, Passamaquoddy Bay. Courtesy of David Sanger*

defined digging implements have been identified, but a sharpened stick has proven adequate for many cultures. The supporting poles for the covering are of sapling size and are easily cut and trimmed by the ground stone axes which are found in the sites. Similarly, the bark and hide coverings require no elaborate manufacturing technology.

In the Passamaquoddy Bay sites a pattern is observable in which dwellings are arranged at the rear of the sites, whereas their seaward portions are reserved for dumping refuse. As might be expected of winter villages, the coastal shell middens are located on southern and southeasterly exposures close to clam flats and fresh water. During the warmer months the coastal sites were apparently abandoned as the Indians travelled to the interior lakes and rivers in pursuit of anadromous fish.

The summer-interior, winter-coast pattern described above is the opposite of that commonly attributed to the Maine Indians.[17] It must be remembered, however, that nearly one hundred years of European contact had occurred prior to

the first complete descriptions of the early 17th century. During that one hundred years, a trade pattern became established in which Europeans arrived on the coasts of North America during the summer, in search of furs taken in the interior during the winter. It seems that the trade relationships may have been sufficient to result in a rescheduling of the aboriginal seasonal patterns of movement.

A different settlement pattern is described for western Maine by Champlain in 1604 (see note 2). At the mouth of the Saco River, Champlain saw palisaded villages consisting of dwellings, some of which were of the conical wigwam pat-

FIGURE 8, A. *Stratigraphy of House 2, Sand Point Site. Courtesy of David Sanger*

FIGURE 8, B. *Stratigraphy of House 2, Sand Point Site, profile view. Courtesy of David Sanger*

FIGURE 9. *Micmac Wigwam, near Halifax, Nova Scotia. Old photograph taken in 1870's, courtesy of the Trustees of the British Museum*

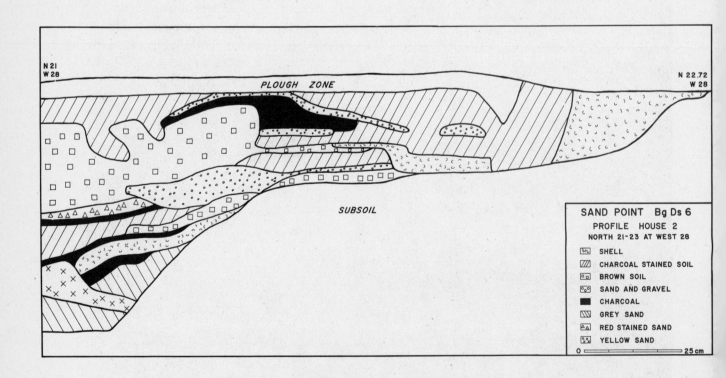

N 21
W 28

PLOUGH ZONE

N 22.72
W 28

SUBSOIL

SAND POINT Bg Ds 6
PROFILE HOUSE 2
NORTH 21-23 AT WEST 28

SHELL
CHARCOAL STAINED SOIL
BROWN SOIL
SAND AND GRAVEL
CHARCOAL
GREY SAND
RED STAINED SAND
YELLOW SAND

0 ———————— 25 cm

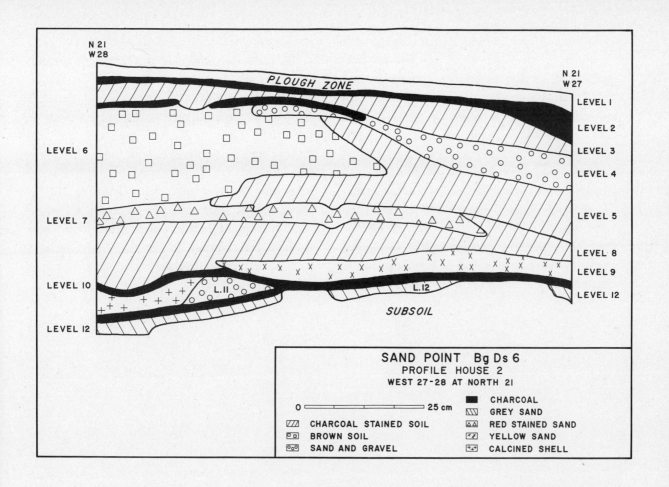

N 21
W 28

PLOUGH ZONE

N 21
W 27

LEVEL 1

LEVEL 2

LEVEL 6

LEVEL 3

LEVEL 4

LEVEL 5

LEVEL 7

LEVEL 8

LEVEL 9

LEVEL 10

L.11

L.12

LEVEL 12

LEVEL 12

SUBSOIL

SAND POINT Bg Ds 6
PROFILE HOUSE 2
WEST 27-28 AT NORTH 21

0 _____ 25 cm

▨ CHARCOAL STAINED SOIL
▨ BROWN SOIL
▨ SAND AND GRAVEL

■ CHARCOAL
▨ GREY SAND
▨ RED STAINED SAND
▨ YELLOW SAND
▨ CALCINED SHELL

tern, while others appear from the drawing to be elongate dwellings in the "Quonset hut" style. Surrounding these were fields of corn, beans, and squash planted together. Some time in the last 1000 years before European contact, these Indians had learned of agriculture, presumably from their neighbors to the south. A need to tend the fields and to protect the crops from marauders may have led to the acceptance of a settlement pattern common to the south and west. On the other hand, it has been suggested that the palisaded villages represent a response made in the historic period to European-stimulated trade.[18] Archaeological research in western Maine would clarify the situation.

In conclusion, it can be seen that the dearth of information on the settlement patterns of Maine's Indians over the past 11,000 years is due in part to the embryonic nature of research in this field. Even in the late shell midden sites where preservation is excellent, the evidence for dwellings is hard to see, and many sites have been dug without any report of houses. In the final analysis, our ability to reconstruct aboriginal settlement patterns will depend on their state of preservation, and on the skill of archaeologists in piecing together such clues as do exist.

2

The Architecture of Maine's Settlement:

Vernacular Architecture to About 1720

Richard M. Candee

AMONG THE MANY TEMPORARY SETTLEMENTS which dotted the seacoast of Maine in the 17th century, the earliest attempt at colonization was not English. Instead, the first recorded colony was established by the French at Saint Croix Island in Passamaquoddy Bay. In June, 1604, DeMont and Champlain, who had been commissioned to record the French exploration, began the settlement of the island. From Champlain's narrative and illustrations of the village erected during the summer and fall of that year, much is known of this first settlement. Over the winter almost half of the seventy-six colonists on St. Croix died of scurvy and in the spring of 1605 the site was abandoned. According to Champlain all the buildings, except a large storehouse, were disassembled and transported across the Bay to Port Royal.[1] But in 1607 a visitor to the island "found there the buildings which had been left all entire, except the storehouse which was uncovered on one side."[2] Six years later Capt. Samuel Argall, on a voyage from Virginia to destroy French "interlopers,"

stopped on St. Croix and "burned the settlement, and destroyed all traces and claims of France, as he had been commanded to do."[3]

Champlain's plan or view of DeMont's colony on St. Croix, published in 1613, shows the long storehouse at the northeast corner of a well planned village of houses and gardens. Recent archaeological investigation of the island has located two not quite parallel foundations of nearly sixty-six feet in length, thought to be the foundations of that storehouse. Other apparently domestic sites were also discovered, but these were closer to the storehouse than Champlain's plan would suggest. It now appears that the published illustrations of DeMont's colony at St. Croix are at least suggestive of the plan of the settlement. Since the wooden frames of the structures were either removed in 1605 or burned by Captain Argall in 1613, there is no way to determine the accuracy of the elevations presented in the plan. The lack of both wood and water, which caused many of the deaths during the winter of 1604, may suggest a less ambitious complex of buildings.[4] The remains at St. Croix are, however, far more complete than those of the comparable English attempt at settlement in northern New England.

Information about Sir John Popham's colony at the mouth of the Sagadahoc River derives from two contemporary manuscripts, a later published account and one purported illustration of the site[5] (see Figure 10). From these sources comes a picture of a somewhat formally planned settlement very similar to St. Croix. Two ships, the *Gift of God* under the command of Capt. John Popham and the *Mary and John* under Capt. Raleigh Gilbert, sailed from different English ports and met at Saint Georges Island in August, 1607. On August 18th the parties "mad[e] Choies of a place for our plantation whch ys at the very mouth or entry of the Ryver of Sagadehocke on the West Syd of the Ryver beinge almoste an Illand. . . ."[6]

The next several months were spent in building fortifications of trenches and a storehouse for goods which the ships unloaded in September. The *Mary and John* set sail for England with a load of masts in October, but the *Gift of God* remained to protect the settlement from French attack. This delay endangered the ship, which was damaged by floe ice in the river during the unusually early and severe winter. When it left in December, it carried barely enough supplies to support its crew of fifty men and boys for an estimated six weeks. The local president, John Popham, and the council of Sagadahoc provided orders in English and Spanish so that the ship might sail to the Azores and sell its cargo if supplies ran short. The manuscript account states that the orders were made in the "House of Capt. Raleigh Gilbert," admiral of the colony.[7]

From these materials, only the general fortification, the storehouse, and Gilbert's house can be firmly documented. Each may be located on a plan dated October 8, 1607. This view, "taken out by John Hunt" a few days before the *Mary and John* sailed, purports to show the colony

16

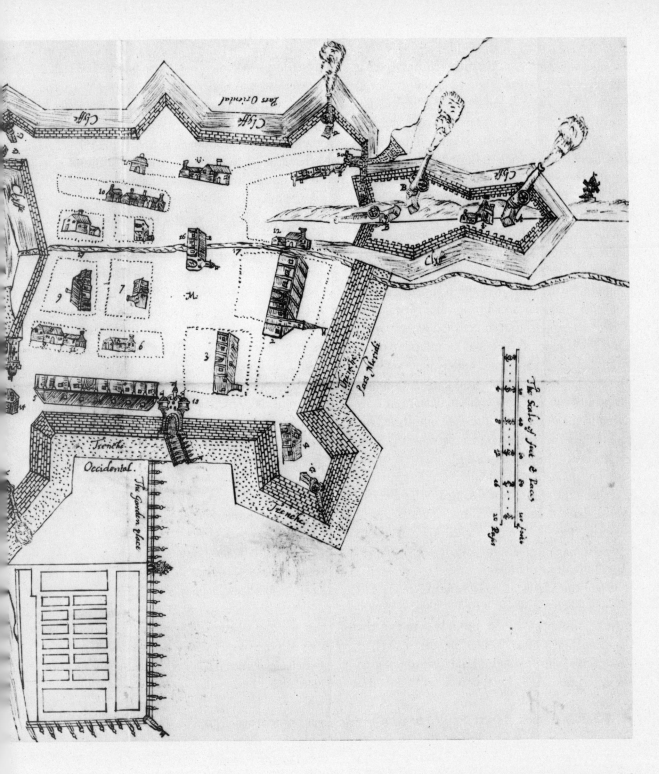

FIGURE 10.   *Plan of St. George's Fort, erected by Capt. George Popham on the Sagadahoc River, October, 1607. Original in Archivo General of Simancas, Spain. Photograph of facsimile courtesy of the Maine Historical Society, copy by Del Cargill*

after two and a half months of building! Rather than assume that its architecture represents what had been built in that time by a few hundred men at most, it may be understood as representative of an ideal plan laid out once the site had been chosen. Nonetheless, it should be noted that the buildings, such as Capt. Gilbert's house, are all low single-story buildings of a far more believable size than those pictured in Champlain's drawing.

The discovery of this plan of "Georges fort" elicited speculation in 1891 that the entire area portrayed by the plan still existed on Point Popham, at the mouth of the Kennebec River. However, modern archaeological investigation of the site suggests that soil erosion has removed a large portion of the original location. No physical traces of the short-lived colony have yet been found. Without archaeological corroboration of the Hunt view, it is impossible to determine how much of the initial layout was accomplished before the plan was made. The most recent investigation concludes that Hunt's plan is an accurate representation of the colonists' aspiration for a fort, with the walls drawn to scale where earthworks had been thrown up. The building sketches, however, do not appear to be drawn to scale but may represent the location of structures actually built or planned.[8]

When the *Mary and John* returned in the fall of 1608 "laden full of vitualls, armes, instruments and tools,"[9] it also brought word of the death of Capt. Gilbert's elder brother, as well as that of Sir John Popham, the major investor in the expedition. At Sagadahoc, it found Popham's kinsman and namesake dead with others of the small colony. When Gilbert decided to return to claim his inheritance in England, the remainder of the company decided to leave also.

Wherefore they all ymbarqued in this new arrived shipp . . . and set saile for England. And this was the end of that northerne colony uppon the river Sachadehoc.[10]

This end was only temporary; within a few decades English fishing vessels once more began to settle the Maine coast. Coordination of these new efforts was under the Council for New England, a royally chartered land-granting agency composed of men who faced America from England's western shore. By the 1630's Council patents to "merchant adventurers" stimulated a series of small trading and fishing settlements on the mainland and offshore islands.

The most complete record of one of these small "plantations" or trading colonies is found in the correspondence between Robert Trelawney, a Plymouth merchant with a patent from the Council for New England to himself and Moses Goodyear granted in 1631, and John Winter, Trelawney's agent at Richmond Island in Maine after July, 1632. This patent and other grants to Trelawney on the mainland gave him title to much of the land between Cape Elizabeth and modern South Portland. The principal settlement was on Richmond Island and was designed both for fishing and trade with Indians or Englishmen, although its location made it unfavorable for much Indian trade. In June, 1634, Winter wrote Trelawney a long letter describing the state of "our buildinge":

I haue built a house heare at Richmon Island that is 40 foote in length & 18 foot broad within the sides, besides the Chimnay & the Chimnay is large with an oven in each end of him, & he is so large that we Can place our Chittle [kettle] within the Clavell pece. We can brew & bake and boyle our Cyttell all at once in him with the help of another house that I have built under the side of our house, where we sett our Ceves & mill & morter In to breake our Corne & malt & to dress our meall in, & I have 2 Chambers in him, and all our men lies in on[e] of them, & every man hath his Close borded Cabbin: and I have Rome Inough to make a dozen Close borded Cabbins more, yf I have need of them, & in the other Chamber I have Rome Inough to put the ships sailes into and all our dry goods which is in Caske, and I have a store house in him that will hold 18 or 20 tonnes of Caske Underneath: & underneath

I have a Citchin for our men to eat and drinke in, & a steward Rome that will hold 2 tonnes of Caske which we put our bread & beare into, and every one of these romes ar[e] Close[d] with loockes & keyes unto them.[11]

It is difficult to picture Winter's house on Richmond Island from this description. It would seem, however, that what he suggests was a building with a chimney at one end, and possibly a lean-to or a small building adjacent in which grain was ground by a hand mill. In plan, the description seems to indicate two chambers, one for sleeping and another for the storage of ships' sails and dry goods. Winter describes "Close[d] boarded Cabbins" in which the men slept. These wooden bunks were occasionally mentioned as being in the earliest houses of the other New England colonies, like the "cabbin bedstead" sold with a house in Duxbury, Massachusetts in 1642.[12] The house appears to have had a large cellar or storeroom, a first floor with a kitchen at one end and a steward's room at the other, with a similar division of the chambers above.

It is interesting that two men employed by Winter at Richmond Island in 1636, the fisherman John Billine, and the sailor John Lander, shared a very similar house plan in Kittery, Maine, in 1639, when they made an agreement over the division of their jointly owned house:

John Billine is to have [that part of] the House wch hath the Chimney in it being the Western End of the House & the Loft over it And John Lander is to have the Chamber being the Easterne End of the House & Lofte over it. . . . And the said John Lander is to have free Egresse & Regresse to come to the Fire for his Uses so often as Occasion shall need. . . .[13]

Winter also maintained a house on the Maine coast, part of the Trelawney grant previously occupied by George Cleeves before he was forced to move to the present site of Portland.

At the maine we have built no house, but our men lives in the house that the Old Cleves built, but that we have fitted him som what better, and we have built a house for our pigs. We have paled . . . a pece of ground Close to the house for to set Corne in, about 4 or 5 akers as neare as we Can Judge, with pales of 6 fote heigh, except the pales that the old Cleves did sett up, which is but 4 foote & 1/2; he had paled of yt about an aker & 1/4 before we Came their, & now yt is all sett with Corne and pumkins.[14]

In December, 1634, Winter informed Trelawney that he had built a similar pallisado "about our house" on Richmond Island "15 foote high & mounted our ordinance in platt formes within our pallastho for our defence."[15] "I want nailes very much," Winter wrote:

& the[y] are scant to be gotten about these parts, & very deare, & so is any Iron worke that I make heare: . . . Our old booths & repairing & building of houses doth use nailes every day, & I deliver them all with myne owne hand.[16]

Even the simplest hardware had to be ordered in this manner from England. "Pray send by our next supply" he wrote, "hookes & twists to hang a double doore for a barn."[17] Over its first decade the small colony, which ranged between forty-five and sixty-seven as ships came and went, remained only a cluster of "housing and several Buildings." In this, Richmond Island was typical of the small trading and fishing settlements which increasingly populated the coastline of Maine during the 17th century. Certainly the small cluster of buildings excavated at Pemaquid and Arrowsic, both dating from the mid-century, suggest that fishing and trading plantations continued to be erected throughout the period.

Undoubtedly the most famous were those in which Sir Ferdinando Gorges and Capt. John Mason participated. Both were leading members of the Council for New England and investors with other merchants in a series of patents to lands which they helped settle during the decade of the Great Migration to Massachusetts Bay. The settlement of their Maine land grants was central to the history of the colony in the 17th century.

Until a division of December, 1633, all the lands on both sides of the Piscataqua River were held in common by Mason, Gorges and seven other men. Their principal settlement was at Newichawannock (now South Berwick) where by 1631 the company (known as the Laconia Company) employed an agent, Ambrose Gibbons, who had emigrated earlier under a former patent. Gibbons lived with his wife and several servants in a company-owned house and bartered the company's Indian trade goods for beaver skins to be sent back to England. With an undersupply of both food and indentured labor, Gibbons hired his few neighbors, "to pale in ground for corne and garden" and wrote, "I have digged a well within the palizado, where is good water, and I have that to close with timber."[18]

The main building is known by a household inventory taken in 1633. Above the ground floor was a "garrett" in which were three beds, (apparently without bedsteads but with sheets and bed-rugs) as well as carpentry tools and a herring net. Below this was "the Middle Chamber" which would appear to have been the major bed room. "In the Great House" (a common English term for the major "hall") were listed all the trade goods and supplies of the company, while "in the Little Roome" were the cooking utensils, arms, and other miscellaneous items.[19] This inventory and list of rooms may not have been entirely complete. However, it is comparable in several respects to the type of interior division at Richmond Island and Kittery. As there are no other "chambers" but the middle one listed, it may be that the house was a single-story building consisting of these three rooms, with a garret in which the servants slept.

In 1635 Gorges became Governor of New England and the land between the Piscataqua and Kennebec Rivers was named New Somersetshire; in 1639 a new charter further enlarged his holdings. The next year he sent his nephew, Thomas Gorges, as Deputy Governor to occupy a house which had been built for him, perhaps as early as 1634, at Agamenticus (York). Of this and other buildings erected here in the 1630's and 40's almost nothing is known, although one local historian has suggested that Edward Godfrey's house of about 1630 "was undoubtedly a rough log cabin, which cannot be glorified into an elaborately finished structure, with glazed windows . . . ."[20] While it was long ago recognized that none of the early homes of the first English settlers were rough log cabins, the house built for Sir Ferdinando Gorges was certainly not of monumental scale. The manuscripts of the letters written by Thomas Gorges to his father contain a description of the building as he discovered it upon taking up residence in 1640:

I have now been these three weeks at Acomenticus where I was a welcome guest to all sorts of people. I found Sr Fard: house much like your barne, only one pretty handsome roome of studdy without glasse windowes which I reserved for myself. . . .[21]

Patented as a borough, and later as a city, "Gorgeana" (York) was merely a rural agricultural village of simple English timber-framed houses during its early decades of settlement. Gorges' reference to unglazed windows, a dying practice in new construction in many parts of contemporary England, is matched by another traditional practice recorded in Saco a decade later. A buyer there was granted by deed "all the doors and windows" of a house,[22] continuing earlier English practice which considered such improvements the property of a former owner. A 1648 description of the York parsonage, moreover, suggests that these earliest post-mediaeval Maine dwellings were also built with framed (rather than masonry) chimneys like those in many new buildings in rural England of the late 16th and early 17th century.

Mr. Godfry whear he lives keeps a very good howes and if we will goe thither, a hows with 3 chimneys hee promiseth, if 2 of them blowe not down this winter, wich may be feard, being but the parsons howes.[23]

These two poles of commercial settlement, the trading house of the Laconia Patentees (which, after Mason's death, left their employees and neighbors to settle the land as they could) and Gorges' grand legal design had little observable effect upon the geographic development of Kittery and York. Both contained scattered farms of large acreage, a few trading posts, and clusters of fishing shanties along the waterways. Many houses were only one- or one-and-a-half-story structures, as is demonstrated dramatically in a map of Piscataqua of about 1655 (see Figure 11). It illustrates a region in which low houses, with either end or central chimneys and a variety of appendages, predominate over larger domestic buildings. Thus, the socio-economic factors which helped create the pattern of small rural farmhouses or clusters of fishermen's cottages,

so typical of Maine in later centuries, were already visible in its earliest permanent settlements by the mid-17th century.

It was here, too, that one of Maine's earliest industries began. While the locus of the lumbering industry shifted north over succeeding centuries, opening new lands to settlement, its origins were in the earlier trading posts along the river-highways running inland from the southern Maine coast. Moreover, it was in rural water-powered sawmills that new building skills and construction practices were developed and taught.

As the principal supplier of raw materials for building, not only locally (as in southern New England colonies) but for the heavily populated North American English colonies and the tree-less islands of the Atlantic, the sawmill is central to the understanding of Maine's economic and architectural development. That it also contributed to new methods of building in northern New England testifies to the complex relationship between English building technology and the environment of the New World.

LUMBERING AND BUILDING MATERIALS

The history of American lumbering may begin with a 1631 letter from Thomas Eyre, an English merchant-partner of Mason, to Ambrose Gibbons, agent for the Laconia Company's trading settlement at Newichawannock. "I like it well that your Governor will have a stock of bords at all times readie. . . . I will now put on the sending of you the modell of a saw-mill that you may have one going."[24] This model of a sawmill sent to the Piscataqua (it was most likely a drawing rather than a working model) is especially interesting because of the sawmill later erected there after John Mason received the tract in a general division of land among the merchant owners. In March 1633/34, Mason contracted with three carpenters, James Wall,

William Chadbourne, and John Goddard, "to goe over unto the said lands" and:

make and build such howses Two mills and other frames and things. . . . Thone of wch mills to be a sawe Mill wch shal be made and sette uppon good sufficient and workmanlike sort and manner. . . . and thother of the said Mills shal be a water Corne Mill. . . .[25]

Less than twenty years later, when Mason's heirs tried to gain title to land across the Piscataqua, James Wall testified that this contract for a sawmill had been fulfilled. The three carpenters had been brought to Mason's plantation by "Captaine Mason's agente," and there did builde upp at the fall there (called by the Indian name Asbendeick) for the use of Captaine Mason & ourselves one sawe mill and one stampings mill for corne wch we did keep the space of three or foure years next after. . . .[26]

John Mason was not the only patentee who contracted with English millwrights to build sawmills in New England. Ferdinando Gorges "sent over for my Son, my Nephew Captain William Gorges . . . with some other Craftsmen for the building of houses, and erecting of Saw-Mill . . ."[27] in Massachusetts. While this sawmill seems never to have succeeded, Gorges did finance another when Mason sent over his carpenters. Winthrop noted in his *Diary* on July 9, 1634 that Sir Ferdinando Gorges and Captain Mason had sent carpenters "to Pascataquack and Agumenticus, with two sawmills, to be erected in each place one."[28]

The manuscript letters between 1640 and 1643 from Thomas Gorges to his uncle, Sir Ferdinando, provide a unique and intimate account of the trials met by the young Governor and a local millwright in trying to keep their sawmill operating. The millwright appears in the nearly illegible manuscripts as "the carp: Barret or Barnat," probably Bartholomew Barnard, a London-born carpenter living in York until 1647.[29] It appears that Sir Ferdinando had continually to finance him, as his debt is a constant theme. At one point Thomas Gorges suggests that the carpenter would "gladly be rid" of the mills, "notwithstanding before I came he had the profit of the whole to himselfe and hath bin her I take it some 8 years. . . ."[30] In what appears to be among the earliest letters, Gorges writes his uncle:

I have procured the advice of all the millwrights in these parts & all conclude that ther must be a good som of moneys beestowed on them for the foundations being soe ill the worke is sunke, the wheels lye soe low in the backe water that the corne mill at ther best grinds not half her tyme, the saw mill break saws, & all iron & carpenters worke that is about her.[31]

Barnard's problems seem to have begun with the poorly laid foundation, and were complicated by the expense involved in constantly repairing the mills. A letter of 1641 indicates that Sir Ferdinando was making suggestions for another mill, and telling his nephew how to manage the operation. "For another saw mill above Mr. Vines his house, I have not the means to accomplish it, if I had, this mill would be fitted which being completed would furnish more [of the] province with boards."[32]

In describing alterations to his uncle's mill, Thomas Gorges writes, "We are now about putting in 2 new saws into her." With two saws, as another letter reports, the mill "cuts sometimes 400 some 5 or 600 ft a tide according to the water . . . ."[33] In 1642, Gorges informed his uncle that the court had finally taken over the disposition of Barnard's many debts, apparently naming Sir Ferdinando "Cheifest Creditor." With Thomas Gorges' departure from York in the summer of 1643 the manuscripts come to an end, leaving in doubt whether these mills continued to operate beyond his tenure.

As with their other colonial speculations, too much rested upon the personal activities of Gorges and Mason in supplying the fledgling sawmills at Berwick and York. After the deaths of these proprietors, the right to grant timber lands and the privilege of erecting sawmills was assumed by each town. It is difficult to determine whether any other mill grants were made prior to the mid-1640's. In all probability there were none, as the small labor force was matched by a lack of capital. However, what could be foreseen by the English patentees was not lost upon some ambitious Englishmen of Massachusetts Bay in the 1650's.

Richard Leader was the agent of the Saugus, Massachusetts iron works from 1645 to 1650, a manufactory promoted and partially owned by John Winthrop, Jr. with various English and local shareholders. Caught between the interference of the English investors and the local problems of an infant industry in the Puritan state, Leader gave up his post for other occupations. By Christmas of 1650, some idea of Leader's new interest was reported to John Winthrop:

I suppose you have heard how mr Ledder Late left the Ironworks, and lives at prsent in Boston, he is about erecting a sawmill at a place nere pascattaway that shall work wth nere 20 sawes at once . . .[34]

By March, Richard Leader was in Kittery, Maine, where he made "sertaine propositions" to the Court "for the Erectinge of a Mille or Milles for the improvement of these parts and the advancement of trade here amongst us."[35]

The site granted by the Maine Court in 1651 included the abandoned mills of Captain John Mason. Soon Mason's heirs brought suit against Leader for trespassing and building houses, as well as cutting timber to erect a sawmill "in or Antient possessed place whereon wee formerly began & do intend to pceed in ye like work imeadiately."[36] The suit was referred to the Massachusetts General Court (once Maine had submitted to that government) and little action was taken for some years.

If Leader's mills were being erected in 1652, he must have had immediate financial problems. In 1653 Leader sold three-quarters of the mills to John Becx, Richard Hutchinson, and others. Becx and Hutchinson were London merchants with considerable interest in the Saugus ironworks, and their backing may have been arranged the previous winter when Leader appears to have made a voyage to London as an agent of the province of Maine. Despite new English capital, the venture proved unsuccessful and he was forced to mortgage the remaining quarter-share in the mills to secure an appearance in London to account to Becx and Company. The London backers made Edward Rishworth, Court Recorder of Maine, their agent to lease the mills. By 1669, when an inventory

of the mills was taken at Rishworth's request, the site contained:

A broaken dwelling house ready to fall, & a barne much out of repayre, Two orchards without fence. . . . The broaken Mill with the Iron & Utensills . . .[37]

as well as blacksmith's shop, meadows, falls and timber grant.

While Leader's "great Works" never returned the profits which Becx and Company must have desired, especially after the expensive bankruptcy of the Saugus ironworks, New England merchants and millwrights soon cooperated on dozens of sawmills in the Piscataqua region. When the anonymous "I.S." prepared a map of the "Pascatway River in New England" its purpose was to "Declare (by Mapp) how Englands strength doth lye/Unseene in *Rivers* of the New Plantations"[38] (see Figure 11). Carefully noted are no less than fifteen mills along the inland river systems. To these may be added the sawmills built on other rivers of the Maine coast; more than half a dozen can be identified prior to 1660 in York, Wells and Saco alone. William Hubbard, historian of the New England Indian wars, writing in 1677 is quite explicit:

All or most of the forementioned [Maine] towns and Plantations are seated upon or near some greater or lesser river whose streams are principally improved for driving of saw mills those late inventions so usefull for the destruction of wood and timber, especially of firr trees, which do so abound in these coasts, that there is scarse a river or creek in these parts that hath not some of those engines erected upon them.[39]

The bulk of the financial support for most of these mills took the form of partnerships between a millwright or carpenter and a merchant from Boston, Salem, or Ipswich. In return, a local mill owner might enter into an agreement such as that written in 1656 with Capt. Thomas Clark and William Paddy of Boston "concern-

ing ye Enacting of a Trade in Pascataqua River
. . . ." By the terms of this contract, Clark and
Paddy supplied "such suteable goods as may be
for ye use for ye people of ye sd River" for three
years. The mill owner acted as their agent, buy-
ing whatever "goods as the River affords, as
boards planke pipestave hogh staves trunells &
ye like,"[40] and taking one third of the clear
profit from both the imports and exports. Clark
was a part owner of two sawmills in York, while
Paddy soon became a partner with Richard
Leader in a mill across the Piscataqua in 1657.
Such business contracts provided profits for each
of the partners. The owner provided the mer-
chantable lumber to the trading firm and maintained his own third of the profit in the sale of
both goods and product. The merchant, on the
other hand, had a monopoly in the importation
of goods and may have acted as the sole supplier
to the community which developed about the
mills.

The success of the lumber economy in Maine
has obscured the contrast between the use of
waterpower for sawing and contemporary English technology. The sending of a sawmill
model to Gibbons in 1631, followed by the erection of Mason's and Gorges' mills in 1634, illustrate the interest of English merchants in water-
powered sawmills and a familiarity with their
construction. Yet only two experimental attempts at water-powered sawmilling in England
prior to the 1630's are known.

A 1604 letter to the Earl of Shrewsbury describes an experimental water-powered sawmill
in the West Riding village of Emsley Park,
Yorkshire. The earliest published description
would appear to be Rowland Vaugh's reference
in *Most Approved and Long Experienced Water
Works* (London, 1610) of a sawmill in the
Golden Valley, Herefordshire, where, "those
that are desirous to see a mill sawing timber,
there shall there desires bee fully satisfied, seeing
a mill by watercourse keep a dozen sawes on
work together."[41]

The paucity of waterpower sawing in England
throughout the 17th century, in a period of

active trade and communication with the conti-
nent where it was common, suggests that social
reasons prevented the adoption of power sawing
rather than a simple lag in technology. In fact,
the application of power milling was actively
opposed in England for more than a century by
hand sawyers, who felt endangered by this form
of automation. A Welshman wrote from Ham-
burg in 1623 that he "would recommend the use
of mills to saw timber [as was common in Ger-
many], were it not that it would hinder the employment of poor men."[42]

English merchants such as Eyre, Mason,
Gorges and Becx realized that conditions in the
New World were exactly the reverse of those in
England. Rather than possessing an abundant
labor supply based upon traditional pit sawing,
by hand, the colonies had neither an organized
body of sawyers nor an abundance of labor. Reports of navigable rivers with many tributaries,
each containing several waterfalls in the midst
of virgin forests, obviously interested these mer-
chant-capitalists. The very absence of the factors
which hindered England's technological advance in sawing provided the incentive.

Mills with one to four saws, producing hundreds of thousands of feet of sawn lumber an-
nually, could not but affect the building trades of
the region. In Kittery, when Nicholas Shapleigh
dammed Sturgeon Creek for a sawmill in 1652,
he signed an agreement with the inhabitants
promising "what boards the sd inhabitants of
sturgion Cricke shall want for their necessary
building, I promisse them and theires to deliver
them at Three shillings per hundred."[43] Similarly, the price for half a sawmill in Wells,
which Thomas Paty sold to Henry Sayword in
1670, was the right to bring logs to be sawn for
one year and free boards from these logs. Paty
was also granted the right to cut pine logs:

FIGURE 11. *"Piscatway River in New England by
I.S. Americanus," c. 1655–60, dedicated to James,
Duke of York (whose abandoned claims to Maine
lands were taken over by Massachusetts in 1674)
to "declare (by Mapp) how Englands strength
doth lye Unseen, in Rivers of the New Plantations,"
with key to sawmill locations. Photo of facsimile,
by permission of the British Library Board*

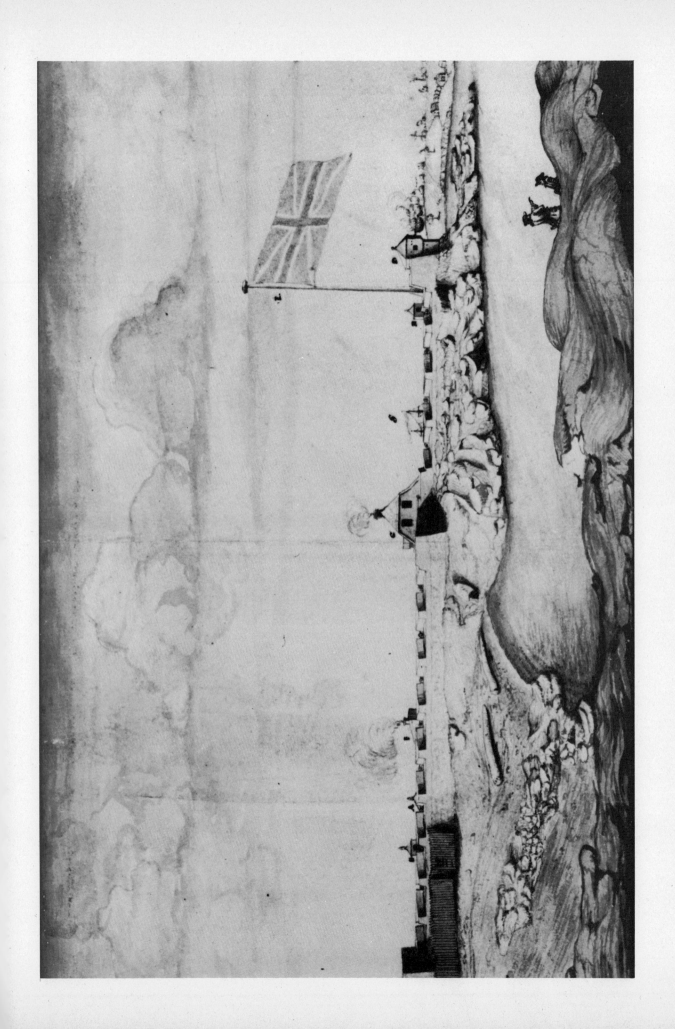

for all tyme afterwards . . . & the sd Sayword to saw them or cause them bee sawn . . . & the boards soe sawn of such Loggs or planke or slit worke, to be equally divided. . . .[44]

Milled lumber, indeed, created a minor revolution in vernacular construction practices. "Loggs or planke" as well as boards, joists and "slit work" were the major products of this extractive industry and provided the Maine house carpenter with every part of the frame except the hewn posts and beams. While every element of the timber buildings of England and those of the first colonial settlements required hand hewing and sawing, during the second half of the 17th century, New Englanders could substitute the products of the sawmill.

Moreover, the training given native-born carpenters provided an opportunity to combine the talents of the housewright and millwright. Thus, when young John Loverell was apprenticed by his parents to "house carpenter and millwright" Abraham Tilton of Wells, it was to learn "the secreats & Mistery of his art in building houses & Mills, teaching or causing him in all poynts to be taught his aforesd Calling."[45]

TIMBER-FRAMED CONSTRUCTION

With no examples of timber-framed buildings of the 17th century surviving in Maine, it is impossible to compare buildings of the initial settlement with those constructed of mill-sawn lumber. However, one can reasonably suppose that houses of the first generation of Maine settlers, like those in other English colonies, contained roof bays of principal rafters between which smaller common rafters were backed in their midst by a single purlin. Over this frame, thatch or horizontal roof boards for shingles could be laid. By the 1660's, in neighboring colonies, the hewn roof frame was altered by the elimination of common rafters and the adoption of multiple purlins to support sawn roof boards laid vertically from ridge to plate.

Similarly, the earliest method of framing exterior walls involved hewn corner posts and studs interlaced with small branches or sticks (wattles) and covered with mud (daub). Plastered on the interior, the wattle and daub was often covered on the exterior by clapboards nailed directly to the closely spaced studs. By the second half of the century, this English building tradition was commonly replaced by a covering of mill-sawn sheathing between the sawn studs and the clapboards.

Alternatively, the studding between the hewn upright posts could be eliminated altogether and replaced by thick boards or planks nailed to the top plate and bottom sill. On some buildings the narrow spaces between this vertical sheathing were battened by thin strips of wood and left exposed to the weather. In cases where the exterior was to be clapboarded the interior wall might be battened or plastered.

One specific example of these changes is a 1665 building contract for the erection of a new meetinghouse in York. The carpenter was Henry Sayword, the York saw mill operator, who engaged himself to "inclose the sayd Meeting house with good sound plank Slabs three Inches Thicke, & to Batten Sd planke sufficiently on the outside" by May, 1667. However, the completion date was later extended another year and Sayword indicated then, that "for feare of the want of Nayls . . . the house must be done in Stoods."[46] Reverting to studs morticed into the frame, which could be accomplished with greater labor but without the expense of the nails or spikes needed for planks and exterior battens, suggests both the continuing scarcity of iron and the ability of carpenters to practice both methods of wall construction as required.

While the major members of a house and roof frame were of hand-hewn oak or hard woods difficult to saw, the floor joists running between a large, hewn, carrying timber in the middle of each ceiling (known as a "summer" beam) changed from hand-sawn oak to mill-sawn pine sticks on this side of the Atlantic (see Figure 12, Page 42). An interior finish of soft woods for sheathed walls, doors, and partitions was more easily constructed of mill-sawn boards than by the handsawing of English oaks. Once these subtle alterations to traditional English timber architecture had evolved in New England, a development that probably dates to the 1660's in Maine, an Anglo-American tradition of timber frame construction emerged that continued to be the primary building method for two cen-

turies. Details of trim, such as the change from diamond-paned casement windows in horizontal or square frames (or smaller attic windows in large protruding gables in the front roof) to new sash, might alter the external visual appearance, but the system of building beneath the clapboards remained essentially the same.

Only a handful of Maine buildings survive for the period between 1700 and the advent of the Georgian style in the 1720's. Each illustrates these later 17th-century changes in construction. By this period, double sash may already have replaced the casement window, leaving only the outline of the earlier house form. Thus, the Joan Deering house in Kittery, for example, may be seen either as a late example of post-mediaeval English architecture, or as the beginning of the traditional combination of this house form with Georgian decoration that has become an enduring symbol of rural New England.

LOG BUILDING AND DEFENSIVE ARCHITECTURE

While the tradition of English timber framing continued to evolve, a second, nearly unique, method of construction developed around the region's sawmills which was of far more limited duration and function. This is the "log house," built of horizontal timber walls, often with an overhanging second story projecting on all four sides. Although there were variations in corner framing, jettying, and form, certain features may be said to typify those log buildings and differentiate them from the later "log cabins," which were the product of central European migration to Pennsylvania. Most importantly the walls of New England log houses (in contrast to the log cabin) are constructed of *sawn* timbers between six and ten inches thick, often more than eighteen inches high, some running the entire length of the wall. These "logs" or timbers

are set on edge, directly upon one another, and are joined at the corner of the building in such a way as to leave no space between the logs.

The earliest detailed architectural description of this type of log building was published by Edward E. Bourne in 1876. It appears to be an accurate account of an early 18th-century "garrison house" built "at the eastern end of the lower bridge over the Cape Neddock [*sic*] river" and provides an excellent narrative description of this special building type.

It was about forty feet long and twenty-two wide; to this main body, was built out the western end a kitchen. It was constructed entirely of timber, or as we might at the present time say, of deals. These were sawed about twenty inches wide and about five inches thick, or sufficiently so to be impenetratable to bullets, muskets being then the only guns of which the Indian could avail themselves. They were sawn out as thin as they could be with safety, for convenience in raising them to their positions. These were placed on their edges, and were all dovetailed at the corners, so that they could not be started from their places. . . . The door posts were of stout white oak, and so grooved to receive the door, that nothing could penetrate from the outside. The doors were made of thick heavy wood. The house was of two stories, the upper projecting on each side and end twenty inches beyond the lower. . . . At each corner of the second story were built what was termed sentry boxes, sustained by three braces from the walls of the main building. These projected about six feet and were made large enough to accomodate six men . . . Small openings were made in the walls from which they could discharge their guns in any needed direction.[47]

However, the context of this description in an article entitled "The Garrison Houses of York County" has given rise to a number of misconceptions as to the origins and use of this method of construction. Bourne's fascination with functional logic also helped to create or foster a myth about 17th-century buildings, in describing the supposed function of the overhang:

The projection of the second story over the first was for two special purposes; to turn down hot water on any assailants, and to extinguish fire if they should attempt to burn the garrison. I do not remember any instance from books or tradition in which the former mode of defence was resorted to.[48]

Despite this disclaimer and the known use of the overhang or "jetty" in England (where the threat of Indian attack was minimal), this romantic explanation was soon attached to any and all such buildings in New England and persists as part of our architectural mythology.

Every writer who has attempted to describe or explain the presence of these log buildings in New England has begun with an implicit assumption that all log buildings were built as "garrisons," or that the method of construction was synonymous with defensive building. The term "garrison" (properly applied to any structure housing soldiers) has been carelessly used to differentiate this type of log construction from timber-framed building. Yet 17th-century writers were specific in their terminology: "log house" referred both to the method of construction and the building's primary function as a residence. "Garrison," on the other hand, had a purely military connotation without reference to the size, shape, or method of building involved.

There were, in fact, two forms of military defense in the region throughout most of the 17th century and the Indian wars of the 18th century. First, there were the military forts of the colonial governments. Fortunately, a great deal of information is preserved in English archives as to the nature of these fortifications. Plans and elevations dated 1699 survive for Saco Fort, as does a 1705 view of Casco Bay Fort. There are also plans of the ruins at Pemaquid destroyed by the French by 1690. These military installations were designed along European lines for the protection of a river mouth from foreign vessels. Their walls of masonry and earthworks protected a wide range of timber buildings within. At Saco and Pemaquid, soldiers' quarters lined one wall, while a section of the Casco fortification illustrates framed pitched- and shed-roofed freestanding buildings in the enclosure. A 1705 elevation of Fort William and Mary in Newcastle, New Hampshire illustrates an even more elaborate complex built to house the military (see Figure 13).

Of greatest interest in this "Prospect Draft," however, is the detail of "Justice Peperils Gareson hous[e]" across the Piscataqua in Kittery. Within its palisade wall can be seen the first William Pepperrell house, built on land granted by his father-in-law in 1682. It was listed as a garrison in 1690 and as "Pepperrell's Fort at Kittery Point" in 1704.[49] What is most striking about the watercolor drawing of 1705 is that it shows

FIGURE 13. "*Prospect Draft of Fort William and Mary*," *Newcastle, New Hampshire, Col. W. W. Romer, 1705. British Library, London, by permission of the British Library Board. Photo: R. B. Fleming and Co., London.*

none of the log-building features such as the four-sided overhang and very small windows that one would expect, but rather a two-and-a-half-story central-chimney frame house with triple facade roof gables.

Similar features may be seen in a series of land plats of other buildings in Kittery drawn by that town's surveyor, William Godsoe. From 1689 to 1715 the town records contained surveys illustrated with drawings of the buildings upon, or adjacent to, the measured lands. Among these are several labeled or otherwise identified as "garrisons." Godsoe surveyed one property in 1698 and his drawing was later copied into the town records by the clerk, Maj. Joseph Hammond, whose own house is labeled "Majr Hammonds Garison" (see Figure 14). His house, with multi-banked casement windows and pedimented first-story fenestrations, was surrounded by a palisade. This was mentioned after an Indian attack in 1695 when one man "in the garison . . . put his gunn throw a Litle Craues of the pallosadoes, there being but fower menn in the garison at that time. . . ."[50]

The Godsoe drawing of a subdivision of Elihu Gunnison's land about his sawmill on Goose Creek, records it as adjacent to "Mr Wilsons Garrison." Like the Pepperrell and Hammond garrisons, this seems to have consisted of a palisade, large casement windows, and what may represent triple facade gables. This 1696 survey is supplemented by another in 1703 showing "Sargent Wilson's Home Lot." The location of the house partially on the Gunnison sawmill lands may be correct, for Sargent Joseph Wilson died in 1710 owning half the sawmills, logs and sawn timber, as well as various "Arms and Ammunition."[51]

Garrisons in the lower part of Kittery often contained no soldiers but were defended by their inhabitants while those in less populated areas usually had troops stationed in them. Each of these "garrisons" appears to have been the home of a leading citizen, of military or civil rank, fortified by palisade and force of arms rather than by the features characteristic of defensive buildings of log.

On the other hand, certain log buildings contain architectural features which leave no doubt that they were either built or used as private garrisons. The door jambs grooved for a sliding portcullis, previously described in the 1876 account of the Cape Neddick garrison, were not unique; similar evidence survives in the Gilman log house in Exeter, New Hampshire. Other log buildings can also be identified from contemporary records as having been built for defensive purposes, or as having been adapted to this use some years after their construction.

Nevertheless, there are many other log structures surviving or known through other sources which were neither built nor used as garrison houses. These include a log church, a prison, and several houses on both sides of the Piscataqua. The so-called McIntire "garrison" and Junkins "garrison" in York, appear to have been merely log homes, for another building adjoining both properties (long ago destroyed) was regularly listed as the only garrison in that section of town.

Log building, rather than being a product of military design should be seen as merely one alternative construction method which appeared shortly after the mid-17th century. Despite the traditionally early dates of log houses in Maine, those surviving today or illustrated before their destruction were apparently all built after the third quarter of the 17th century. On the other hand, it is possible to determine the period in which log building first occurred in Maine from references to log houses in the colonial records. These are most numerous in the late 1650's and early 1660's, although other scattered references to log building occur during the decades at the turn of the century when those log houses surviving today were first built.

The earliest appearance of the log house occurred simultaneously with the development of a commercial lumbering industry and well before the earliest Indian War. This mid-17th-century period also encompasses a brief experimen-

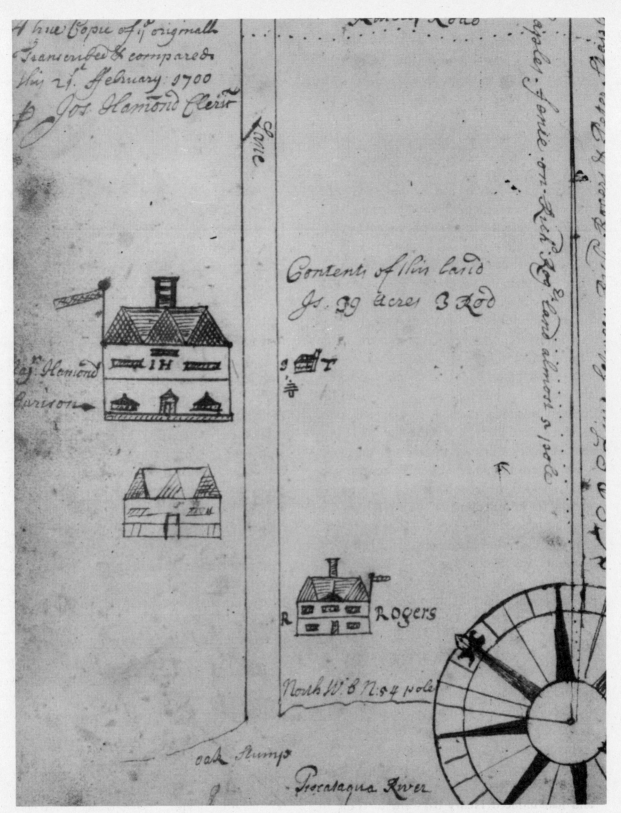

FIGURE 14. *Kittery, Joseph Hammond Garrison House and Richard Rogers House, 1698. William Godsoe survey, Kittery Town Records, vol. II, p. 140. Photo: Douglas Armsden*

tation with indentured Scottish soldiers exiled from Great Britain to New England after the Cromwellian revolution. A number of these Scottish exiles were indentured to sawmill owners on both sides of the Piscataqua during this decade and accounted for a large part of the population steadily employed in lumbering.

One argument as to the origins of log building can be based on the speculation that some of the Scots were soldiers who had occupied the Northumberland border lands before their capture. It is possible that the remnants of an ancient log building tradition may still have survived in the British border country. Whether or not this can serve to explain the use of sawn logs as an alternative to conventional timber framing remains hypothetical for lack of any surviving evidence.

What is certain, however, is that several of the earliest references to log houses in Maine indicate that they were built near sawmills. Whether the idea of log building was derived from the memory of similar methods used elsewhere or, as seems more likely, it was the innovative product of the first British emigrants to engage in large scale water-powered lumbering, the sawmill provided the technology and the training ground for its dissemination.

Thus, in 1667 when Edward Rishworth sold thirty acres of land to Richard Hardy of York, the land was described as being between the mouth of the Old Mill Creek and the site of the old 1633 Gorges sawmill, running back from the creek "towards Capt Clarkes Logg house."[52] Captain Clark, as has been noted, was the Boston owner and trading partner of two sawmills in York. Another reference to log building on Old Mill Creek in York, Maine appears in 1678. In that year Rishworth sold four acres on the west side of the northwest branch of the creek where "sometymes Jere: Mowlton built his logg house when he logged for Henery Sayword."[53] Rishworth was a partner with Clark in his York mills and had induced Henry Sayward to come to York and erect a sawmill in that town in 1658 just as the Scots would have been finishing their

indentures in other mills. Sayword is also known to have employed two Scots in his mills in York and Wells as loggers and sawyers.

One building of log that partially survives today is the so-called Whipple Garrison, traditionally thought to have been erected during the 1660's by Captain Robert Cutt. The land was originally granted by the town of Kittery to "Richard Leader & friends," who forfeited it when Leader left New England. It was regranted to Cutt, who returned from Barbadoes in the early 1660's. He died in 1674 and his inventory lists a house with parlor and kitchen, upper chambers, a shop (which may have been in the house) and a brewhouse.[54]

The present building was greatly altered in 1859, at which time it was noted that a log section apparently thirty-four feet square with a second story projecting eight to ten inches on each side had been incorporated into a larger house. Whether this building could have been the Cutts house is difficult to determine, as the 19th-century alterations have completely obscured all but an overhang on one end. It is equally likely that the log portion was erected by a subsequent owner. There is no mention in any of the physical descriptions of protruding beams supporting the overhang, and one writer describes the corner framing as dovetailed. Since most examples of dovetailing occur in log buildings erected after the turn of the 18th century in both Maine and New Hampshire, it may be prudent to assign an early 18th-century date to whatever portion may survive within its walls.

With the outbreak of the Indian wars after 1675, the need for defense was obvious, especially near the sawmills in less settled parts of the area. On September 9, 1685 Samuel Sewall recorded in his diary:

Mr. Hutchinson shewed me his Letter concerning his Mill at Piscataqua, wherein is sollicited to build a Fort, lest the Indians burn it. When came home heard about a Body of Indians near Chelmsford, 3 or

400. The Rumors and Fears concerning them do much increase.[55]

Whether the "fort" about the Great Works which Sewall described was a palisaded wall or some form of log building can only be a matter of speculation. However, in 1709 when Timothy Wentworth purchased a half-right to land on "Worster's River" a few miles above the Great Works in present-day Berwick, it was agreed:

a Saw Mill [is] to be erected built and finished by the sd Timothy Wentworth . . . further Said Wentworth is to build a Logg house twenty foot long and sixteen foot wide by the Mill for her more Safety. . . .[56]

While no log houses survive in this Maine town today, it is interesting to note Williamson's description of Berwick in his 1832 *History of the State of Maine.*

All [the houses], which were built here, between 1690 and 1745, were of hewed [*sic*] logs, sufficient to oppose the force of small arms. There was a block house on the western side of Salmon Falls brook, a mile above Quampeagan, where William Gerrish lived; a mile higher, was Key's garrison; —next were Wentworth's and Goodwin's block houses.[57]

Only the Dennett house (c.1710–20) in Eliot and a smaller log cottage in Kittery survive as remnants of log construction along the Maine side of the Piscataqua. Both, like all other log homes of the period, moreover, were sawn rather than "hewn"—a false assumption Williamson may have derived from later military log building practices.

BUILDING FORMS OF THE 17TH AND EARLY 18TH CENTURIES

While log houses in traditional one- and two-story forms continued to be built during the first half of the 18th century, some houses combined structural methods of both log- and timber-framed building. Two examples existed in that part of York known as Scotland Parish. These were the so-called Junkins and McIntire "garrisons," of which only the McIntire log house survives today (see Figure 15). From the pictorial record, however, it is clear that both buildings shared a nearly identical structural composition. Neither of these houses may be directly attributed to the first generation of Scots who settled this parish; nor from either documentary or physical evidence can it be argued that either was built or served as a "garrison house." The only garrison listed from 1690 to 1707 in this section of York was built and maintained by Alexander Maxwell, a Scot who purchased lands in this part of town in 1657/8 after completing his indenture to George Leader. In 1707 Maxwell sold to John McIntire, a son of the Scot exile Micom McIntire, three acres of empty land bounded on the southeast "by the orchard or garden of sd Maxwell where the garrison now stands."[58]

McIntire's post-1707 house is a central-chimney, two-story building with four-sided overhang. The sawn log walls are seven-and-a-half inches thick with individual logs slightly more than a foot in height and joined at the corners with several forms of dovetailing. In plan, it contains a narrow northwestern and a wider southeastern room now divided by a chimney "restored" in 1909.

The floor framing which forms the overhang of the second story in the larger room is not, however, composed of a series of squared beams such as are common to other log houses. Rather, a summer beam runs from the chimney girt to the top log of the first-story end wall and pro-

FIGURE 15. *York, John McIntire Log House, built c. 1707–10 with frame addition to the west end built c. 1740, removed 1908. Photo: Douglas Arms-den, 1975*

trudes beyond the wall to form a support for the end overhang. Into this summer beam are framed seven pair of joists which also protrude through the walls beneath the front and rear overhang. Second-story room measurements are increased by the eleven-inch overhang on the front and rear, and the ten-inch side overhangs. In the larger upstairs room a tie beam runs in the opposite direction between front and rear walls, a practice common in New England tim-ber-framed houses. The use of timber-framed flooring techniques on both stories of this house is a marked departure in log construction.

FIGURE 16. *York, Junkins "Garrison," post-1607, now destroyed. Steropticon view c. 1870, courtesy of the Society for the Preservation of New En-gland Antiquities*

34

Detail of Frost Garrison interior showing heavy timber framing and flush plank panelling.

The counterpart to this house, the so-called Junkins "garrison," was across the road from it; this log house was burned in 1889, but its picturesque quality made it a subject for artists and photographers throughout its last twenty-five years. From these views, its physical features can be reconstructed and its decay marked. A sketch by H. Church in 1873 shows the house with its central chimney decorated with double pilasters. A photograph of a few years earlier, from a stereoptican view shows a nearly identical scene (see Figure 16). The roof had not yet begun to rot as it had by 1879 when Winslow Homer painted this "Garrison House." A sequence of illustrations showing the progressive decay of the roof, pilastered chimney and log walling also provides evidence of the protruding summer

FIGURE 17-B. *East Eliot, Maj. Charles Frost Garrison, c. 1732-38, restored 1974. Photo: Douglas Armsden.*

beam in the end wall of the larger room, projecting and supporting the overhanging second story. Where clapboards had fallen away, the log walls of the house are plainly visible and by the 1880's, several views show some fallen dovetailed logs stacked against the half-ruined building.

As in its surviving counterpart, floor joists protruded between the chimney and end girts of the larger room beneath the overhang. Like the McIntire house, too, the Junkins house had no protruding summer beam on the opposite end wall, but must have used a series of spanning beams across the narrower room for floor framing. It would appear that all the windows were once as small as that over the front doorway, since cuts for window sills at that level may be seen in the exposed logs. The log cornering appears to have been dovetailed, like the McIntire house, and the walling logs grooved into front door jambs, as elsewhere. It might also be noted that neither building displays any loopholes or other defensive features in the exposed logs.

Log buildings of the second quarter of the 18th century took on a formal or semi-formal military usage while domestic building increasingly turned away from log construction altogether. A military and utilitarian type of log structure is best illustrated by the Frost garrison (c.1736) in Eliot (see Figure 17). The building is constructed in the form of a barn with double doors at one end and a set of stairs to the attic loft near the opposite end. The floor of this single-story structure is of dirt. The walls are of logs seven inches thick and between twelve and eighteen inches in height. There are no windows, but two loop-holes for guns on each side of the building. The logs are grooved into door jambs, both at the end double doors and a side entrance near the stairs. The overhanging second story is supported by eight very heavy beams protruding front and rear, and smaller joists framed into the end beams and over the top logs of the end wall support the end overhangs. Each of the major spanning beams is reinforced with ship's

knees along the inside wall. Some yards away from this structure is a smaller (fifteen feet square) dovetailed log powder house or flanker, which was purportedly constructed without a door and originally entered from the Frost dwelling by an underground passage. The house is timber-framed and, although dated in the 1730's with other buildings on the site, has been much restored.

The Frost log garrison, which has obviously served as a barn as well as a defensive unit, is transitional between domestic log buildings and specifically military log structures. A series of fortifications erected in the 1750's also made use of log construction as in the blockhouse or flanker of Fort Halifax in Winslow (1754) which still survives. In Augusta, on the site of a trading post set up by men of Plymouth colony in 1627, the proprietors of the Plymouth Company erected Fort Western in 1754 on the basis of a plan by the builder Gershom Flagg of Boston. The exterior of the main block is one hundred by thirty-two feet, undoubtedly the largest surviving building of log construction in New England. Like the other log buildings in Maine, it is dovetailed at the corners, but the building contract specified that the wall should be constructed of "hewn Timber, the lower Story to be twelve Inches thick & the upper story ten Inches thick."[59] Unlike earlier log buildings the walls are not jettied and the logs are described as "hewn," the earliest use of this method in New England architecture and a movement away from the earlier traditions, perhaps for lack of an available sawmill. The use of spanning beams and floor joists suggests that the combined building techniques of the early 18th century were also adopted by military builders of the mid-century.

Both the paucity of 17th-century buildings and the few remaining early 18th-century structures in Maine reflect the upheaval of the Indian wars which erupted sporadically between the 1680's and 1713, and to which the log houses built during this period were one response. The almost complete lack of surviving secondary buildings, the nearly continual replacement of public buildings, and the selective survival of domestic architecture have left mere remnants of a wholly forgotten society, which cannot illustrate the variety of different ways in which these New Englanders adapted to their New World experience and restructured their natural environment. The fishing and trading settlement, the political domination of Massachusetts Bay Colony, the development and growth of the lumbering industry, the commercial activity along the coast, and the widespread destruction of the Indian wars, each played a part in determining Maine's building patterns.

In Kittery, for example, the population was initially concentrated in upper Kittery (present day South Berwick) around the site of Mason's mills and the Great Works. By the end of the century, however, the lower quarter of the town held almost three-quarters of its nearly 900 people. While upper Kittery remained primarily a lumbering area and the middle parish (Eliot) was largely agricultural, lower Kittery specialized in maritime and mercantile occupations. Differences of primary economic functions in widely separated parts of Maine towns resulted not only in eventual political sub-divisions, but recognizable differences in the architectural landscape. Where similar activities clustered, both on the mainland and the offshore islands, communities took on visual characteristics which reflected these practices. The sawmill and its hamlet, independent and separated farmsteads, wharves and warehouses along a river, or fishermen's shanties surrounded by fish flakes were as typical of the Maine landscape during its first century of settlement as they would be in more recently populated parts of the state during the 19th century.

Domestic architecture is one index to these economic differences. The largest homes were built for the lumber-merchant elite and a wider range of smaller homes for yeomen, many of whom mixed agriculture with a craft or trade, and for the maritime callings. Like their landed contemporaries, sea captains and lesser merchants often pursued a number of economic interests and modified their homes to accommodate their business interests over their lifetimes. The buildings which housed these varied activities, however, were products of their own time.

The building blocks of nearly all house forms derived ultimately from the construction elements of the English timber-framing tradition: a box of posts and beams combined in multiple bays beneath a pitched roof, the porch (a protruding single bay of two stories for an entry and staircase), the gabled ell, and the lean-to. These basic forms could be combined to erect one- or two-story domestic, public, or utilitarian buildings of greater or lesser complexity. But in contrast to the situation in later periods, the range of variation between buildings remained relatively narrow. After a period during which a number of building forms from disparate parts of England appear to have been utilized, certain types came to predominate in Maine as they did throughout New England. A further characteristic of the architecture of the period should also be mentioned. No matter which alternative method of construction or building material was chosen, buildings for similar strata of society tended to share certain characteristics of size and shape.

In the absence of the accumulated wealth of a fully settled society, few dwellings in Maine could compare in size to contemporary manor houses or even the elaborate framed homes of many yeomen in fertile southeastern England. Nevertheless, the records of one mid-17th-century lumber-merchant's home suggest a scale and complexity which may be favorably compared to those of the wealthier merchants of Massachusetts. Nicholas Shapleigh of Kittery was as much a merchant-mill owner and public officer as he was a successful yeoman. A major in the militia, he was among the town's earliest planters and held the office of selectman until disallowed by Massachusetts in 1669 for his Quaker sympathies. He continued to hold civil and military posts although his dislike of the Massachusetts government brought him to prison briefly in 1674. Lt. John Shapleigh, his nephew and heir to Nicholas' large estate, also held a variety of town and military offices before his death in 1707.

The Shapleigh house was a full two-story structure of ten rooms plus cellar and garret, as shown by the inventories and other documents of its successive owners. Maj. Nicholas Shapleigh's "homestall, dwelling outhouses grandings pastures fields . . . out lands" and a sawmill and gristmill were worth more than £800 at his death in 1682. He also owned a variety of carpenter's tools, logging implements, and a blacksmith shop as well as "one ould Li[gh]ter, one shallop" and "3 great hay conows [canoes] & a coasting canow." With "3 men one woman & one little" Negro slaves and "two Irish boys" with two or three years to serve out their indentures, the estate was obviously an extensive operation.[60]

The center of this estate was the large house, which may have been built in several stages. The "inner Rowme" and "hall" are listed so as to suggest that they were an integral unit, although each had a fireplace. The inner room, called the widow's "lodging Chamber" in 1684 and "Nicholas' Chamber" in 1707, was a sizeable bedroom, while the hall functioned as an eating area with "3 Tables & a carpet . . . [and] 12 chares" in 1682. In that year, another "lodging rowme" downstairs contained a bedstead, little table, court cupboard, two chairs, a settle, a "Spanish Chest," linens, a chamber pot, and an old Turkey carpet.[61]

Near the kitchen, a dairy and kitchen lean-to were the "leantows adjoyneing" widow Alice Shapleigh's two rooms, assigned in the household division of the estate. As no rooms above the kitchen are listed in any document the room was probably a single-story ell to which the lean-tos were joined. A projecting porch contained an entryway at ground level and at the second story "another little Rowme" (1682) or "portch Chamber" (1707). On the east of the house was the "Parlor Chamber" and on the west the "Hall Chamber," both primarily used as lesser bedrooms. Also recorded is "ye little Canopy Rowme over ye Hall" (1682) or simply the "canopee Chamber" (1707). No plausible explanation of this name has been found for this "little" bedroom containing only "bedding ruggs, blanketts with other things" in 1682 and "a fether Bed and Bolster and Larg Carpit" in 1707.[62]

Several alternative floor plans for this combination of rooms can be conjectured from the descriptions. Certainly the core was a two-story building, perhaps of central-chimney plan. If so, the Shapleigh house may have resembled that of New Hampshire's Governor Samuel Allen at Newcastle, an L-shaped form with two chimney stacks, but with a single-story ell and adjoining lean-to. Its protruding two-story porch may have resembled one illustrated in the 1705 view of Fort William and Mary on the house belonging to Mr. Atkinson (see Figure 13). On the other hand, rooms may have been combined in numerous other ways, including the use of end-chimney stacks as was common in Shapleigh's native Devon. If so, the house may have been a two-bay end-chimney house internally divided with an end lean-to (inner room) off the hall and rear kitchen ell with its own lean-tos.

Ten rooms between the cellar and attic appear to have been a maximum for solely domestic architecture well into the succeeding decades of the 18th century. Far more common among the lesser civil and military leaders in Maine communities was the two-story house with one room on either side of the central chimney and a lean-to at the back. Throughout most of the first part of the century the lean-to was simply abutted at slightly lower pitch than the main roof, but by the last decade it might be built as an integral part of the house and roof framing. By the first quarter of the 18th century this "salt box" form, as it was later called, might be built with Georgian interior and exterior decorative features. Yet, its plan reflected a popular form which evolved over the previous century and was a fully integrated part of the colony's timber-framed architectural tradition.

While none of their 17th-century subjects survive today, it is occasionally possible to link the drawings made by the Kittery surveyor, William Godsoe, to inventories which list the contents of each room after the house owner's death. Thus, Joseph Curtis' "garrison" is identified in documents of 1706–07 as having a parlor with "chamber and Garrit over it" as well as a hall, kitchen and chambers on the ground floor. Likewise Maj. Joseph Hammond's home, also identified as a garrison, contained a rear lean-to kitchen with service rooms and a small sleeping chamber not clearly identifiable from Godsoe's crude sketch[63] (see Figure 14).

On the other hand, documentary evidence suggests that Richard Roger's c. 1697 house across from Hammond's was a central-chimney house of four rooms without lean-to. As the McIntire and Junkins houses also illustrate, the full central-chimney plan continued to be built well into the 18th century and offered ample opportunity for a wide range of additions. A building contract for another house of this type provides a terse description of the major elements of interior and exterior finishing. Francis Moore in 1715 hired two Boston builders to proceed "with all convenient speed . . . to Arrowsick Island" and raise the house frame, sheath it with feather edge boards, and shingle the roof. They agreed to "lay the floors of the lower rooms & Chambers with plained boards, the garretts rough" and build "winding stairs from the lower room to the Garrett." On the outside there were to be "outside Cellar doors & stairs" and a total of four casement windows. Inside they were to make wooden partitions between rooms, "five plaine batten doors," "plaine boards" above the four fireplaces and closets.[64]

This house form was common not only to yeomen but was used by coastal merchants such

as Robert Cutt and Maj. Francis Hook. Like Andrew Searle, who had "his shop built in the garrison" where he lived in Berwick, Hook's mercantile activity was also carried on in his residence. His 1695 inventory and his widow's in 1706 both indicate that the central-chimney two-story house drawn by Godsoe in 1715 contained a hall and kitchen below, bedroom chambers above, as well as a kitchen chamber and shop. These appear to have occupied a small (perhaps lean-to) addition off one of the two lower rooms.[65]

A similar structure is recorded in the early Biddeford town records. From 1683 to 1686 the town tried to hire workmen to build a parsonage for their minister. Their first vote called for a one-room plan with loft, but was revised three years later to contain four fireplaces of brick in a full two-story central-chimney plan "with a Lintel [lean-to] at one eand."[66]

A house with nearly the same room pattern, but with the addition of a porch and porch chamber above, was the tavern of Kittery shipwright John Bray. From his will, however, it is apparent that the house did not originally take this form, but evolved over the last quarter of the 17th century for it refers specifically to "the new end" of his home.[67]

Additions which enlarged smaller houses seem to have been common, especially among innkeepers. Another Kittery shipwright, Peter Dixon, who served as a taverner and ferryman in 1695, died in 1718. His inventory describes not only an "old Bedroom" and "new Bedroom" but also an old and "new leanto." John Davis, a York taverner, also had enlarged his home of one room on each of two floors to a full central-chimney plan with a "new room" and chamber over it by the time of his death in 1691. Unfortunately, neither the Bray nor Davis taverns has survived, although the later houses now occupying their sites may have been erected with their reused lumber.[68]

The enlargement of these houses, furthermore, points out how common dwellings with

FIGURE 19. *York Gaol, detail showing sawmill blade reused as flashing in 18th-century chimney. Photo: Douglas Armsden*

FIGURE 18. *York, York Gaol, stone section built 1720–25 with later additions. Photo: Richard M. Candee*

a one-room plan once were. As the "I.S." map of the Piscataqua river illustrates (Figure 11), these lesser dwellings were for many years the most prevalent. Often the lower room was divided internally or a lean-to was appended. Some were one story tall with merely a loft above. Robert Gouch (or Gutch), for example, the minister on the Kennebec River opposite Bath, died in 1667 with an estate valued at little more than £95. His house contained only a kitchen with cooking and eating utensils, the "chamber Next the Kitchine" in which he slept, and "the loft above."[69] Nor did one have to be relatively poor to live in a single-story house with divided first-floor plan. When Nicholas Frost of Kittery died in 1663, his estate was valued at £665. This comparatively successful yeoman and mason lived in a house containing a kitchen, an "inner chamber" and "the upper chamber." Besides these rooms there was a cellar and storage in "the Darie," which may have been a separate building or connected with the house. Like other houses of this type, the cooking and eating was done in the kitchen, sleeping in the inner chamber, and the upper chamber was used for grain storage and other produce. Here among the sacks and barrels there was a canvas bed and bedstead which must have been for the "servant boy," who still had more than seven years to serve, perhaps as a mason's apprentice, when Frost died.[70]

Alternatively, a small house might be a full two stories tall. The 1660's homes of William Leighton and Capt. John Mitchell of Kittery were both of this sort with a hall or kitchen downstairs, a chamber over it, and a garret above. To this might commonly be appended a lean-to for parlor, kitchen or dairy. Thus when York built a new parsonage in 1698, it was to be only twenty by twenty-eight feet "two story high with three fiere pleses," the third of which to heat a "lentoe at on[e] end twelve fout wide."[71] The home of Thomas Spencer, late of Berwick in 1681, was nearly identical on the exterior al-

though it also had a "seller leanto." Inside, however, the main lower room seems to have been divided into a "lower chamber" and "hall."[72]

Interior room divisions of simple board partitions could also be found dividing the upper room into two or more small bed chambers. This is the case of the Richard Millbury house in York Harbor, now believed to have been built about 1715 (see Figure 12). It is one of the few surviving Maine examples of the two-story one-room plan although later additions have hidden the original early 18th-century core within a central-chimney plan.

A third variant of smaller domestic buildings in Maine's first century may be a distant ancestor to that form commonly called the "Cape Cod" house. The floor plan in one-story homes with a central chimney is unclear from the several Godsoe drawings of such houses. Thomas Hodson of Berwick, who died in 1717, had a hall, parlor, kitchen and dairy between the garret and cellar; others may have had simply one room on either side of the fireplace.[73] While several examples of both types may be found with relatively early traditional dates, few—if any—can be verified by their physical appearance to date before the second quarter of the 18th century; (see in this regard Myers, p. 53 below).

Nevertheless, one-story houses of several rooms were numerous not only among lesser farmers (as illustrated by the Kittery land plats) but for relatively prosperous fishing masters at the Isles of Shoals. William Sealy who died there in 1671 with an estate of over £600, lived in a "new dwelling house contayng 3 rowmes, and a Leantow adjoyneing."[74] The estate of Philip Babb, which Sealy had inventoried some months earlier was recorded as "one dwelling house with adjacent Rowmes."[75] Perhaps, like Francis Wainwright's home on Smuttynose Island (in 1686), it was a "house with two leantows" built of mainland timber imported to the nearly barren site.[76]

FIGURE 12. *York, Millbury House, interior (c. 1715). Courtesy of Dr. and Mrs. Bernard H. Leonard. Photo: Douglas Armsden*

The earliest decades of the 18th century were a period in which new ideas about domestic architecture made their first appearance in Maine. They were also linked to the local vernacular building traditions of the colony with its emphasis on practical innovation. These diverse elements, occurring at different levels of society simultaneously, are symbolized by the second William Pepperrell house in Kittery (see Figure 21 and Myers, p. 49 below), on the one hand, and the York Gaol on the other.

Long thought to be a mid-17th-century jail, the old York Gaol (Figure 18) has recently been the subject of more intensive investigation by several scholars. It now appears that the essential document in its history had been overlooked. This is a court order of 1719 authorizing a local building committee to erect a "County Gaol" which was to be "thirty foot long Eighteen foot wide & Eight foot wall [to] be built with Stone or Brick" near the "meeting house in York."[77] Although no evidence of the committee's building accounts has yet been discovered, the central and original core of the present structure corresponds to this description. Whether erected immediately or several years later (towns were often slow in accomplishing court-ordered activities), it is clear that York soon had a new jail by a sharp increase in the number of prisoners actually incarcerated.[78]

Unlike houses, jails were specialized structures erected only irregularly. Functional demands for security produced individual solutions which depended upon available building materials. Building stone was certainly plentiful, as was sawn plank from the local mills. Thus the walls, floors, doors, and internal partitions throughout the jail were heavily planked and fastened with massive iron spikes. Windows were barred with iron rods, perhaps worked from used saw blades like those reused as flashing in several parts of the building including the chimneys (see Figure 19).

It is difficult today to envision the jail without its later gambrel roof which encloses not only the jail but also the jailor's house—a one-story building set slightly off center in front of the jail under its own pitched roof, which was added by a court order of 1729.[79] Subsequent alterations and enlargements gave the building the form which made it so attractive in the 19th century to artists and photographers.

During the early 18th century, new architectural ideas also began to appear among the wealthiest merchants on both sides of the Piscataqua River. Rather than simply to combine available building materials in a traditional or functional manner, skilled and talented carpenters and joiners were importing new tools to elaborate beyond the simple finish of the most elegant houses of the previous century. Appropriately, the earliest example of this new style of ornamentation in Maine still survives in the William Pepperrell house at Kittery Point. Like the York jail, the Pepperrell mansion is a product of a long history of growth, change and even diminution.

Two evidences of early changes may be found within the present structure. The support between the front sill and western chimney base for the first-story floor is a reused 17th-century "summer" beam. Two stories above, in the western half of the attic, the principal rafters and collar beams attest to a pitched roof originally on only that end of the house. Thus, it would appear that at some date the present structure was extended and covered by a gambrel roof although a part of the original house has since been removed. Clearly an earlier house, perhaps that shown as Pepperrell's Garrison in the 1705 view, was removed (its materials partially re-used in the new building) and this house then grew in several subsequent stages throughout the 18th century.

Although documentation for the building of the original portion of the Pepperrell house is far from complete, a daybook and ledger of the two Williams kept between 1717 and 1721 provides a clue. In the hand of the younger William Pepperrell under the ledger account of "Robart Pearse" for June 1720 is a credit "Bye house fen-eshing at ye Point pr Agreemt . . ." and board for nine weeks through August 20, 1720. The account of "Mr. Samuel Huit" for September 8, 1720 also mentions "my new house at Kittery Point." [80]

Although the younger William had not yet inherited his father's property, as he would in 1733, he kept most of their accounts and it is un-clear to whom "my new house at Kittery Point" should properly refer. However, in association with the surviving physical evidence, it is fair to identify it as the earliest portion of the present dwelling. Certainly the detailing and composi-tion of the interior finish in the parlor or sitting room bear direct comparison with the raised bolection-molded paneling and arched door-ways of the Macpheadris house built in 1716 by the Boston ship-joiner John Drew across the river in Portsmouth, New Hampshire.[81] Both interiors bear witness to the introduction of aca-demic design concepts by people of the greatest wealth and standing.

Between 1716 and 1720 at least two men along the Piscataqua had acquired the tools and tech-niques to provide patrons with progressive archi-tectural living spaces, comparable in design and detail with Boston's newest merchant housing. Given a new technology and design ideas to meet the needs of increased wealth and social emulation, the carpenters and joiners of the Piscataqua entered a new phase of vernacular building. The central-chimney house plan, with or without lean-to, remained the most popular. The interior elements, however, received a new and more detailed finish, as Maine entered the new century as part of a wider, international culture.

3

Colonial Architecture:

from about 1725 to 1790

Denys Peter Myers

THE PERIOD FROM AROUND 1725 UNTIL THE close of the 1780's was, except for military matters, relatively static. The *pace* of change scarcely accelerated beyond what it had been in the previous century. During the 1720's almost all settlement in the District of Maine was confined to York County and, in what became Cumberland County, to the area around Portland, then called Falmouth. In 1713, when Queen Anne's War ended, all Maine settlements except Kittery, York, and Wells had been left desolate and uninhabited by Indian raids instigated by the French in Canada. The unsettled conditions resulting from the imperial rivalry of Britain and France account for the frequent occurrence of defensive construction as late as the 1700's in the vicinity of York. There was a respite from 1713 until the outbreak of King George's War in 1740, when moderate prosperity and welcome peace prevailed. By 1743 the District had a population of around 12,000. It was not, however, until the conclusion of the French and Indian War and the cession of Can-

ada by France to Great Britain by the Treaty of Paris in 1763 that peace seemed finally to have arrived. The central fact of all American history, as well as that of the District of Maine in the 18th century was, of course, that civil war between Englishmen commonly called the American Revolution. Between 1775 and 1781 Maine once again suffered the ravages of war and was partially occupied by enemy forces. Falmouth was burned in 1775, the Penobscot country was captive, and Indians were paid to serve as irregular allies by both sides. Thus, the later Colonial period may be said to have been a time of slow progress all too frequently enlivened, in Maine at least, by battle, murder, and sudden death.

While the construction of log "garrison" houses appears to have ceased in Maine by 1725, the structural method employed in them continued to be used for blockhouses throughout the 18th century and even well into the 19th century, whenever and wherever the need arose. Fort Kent, for instance, is a blockhouse erected as late as 1838–39 during a border dispute between the

United States and Canada called the "Aroostook War." One fine 18th-century blockhouse, the oldest surviving example in the United States, still commands the strategic confluence of the Kennebec and Sebasticook Rivers at Winslow. Fort Halifax, built in 1754 for the Plymouth Company from plans credited to General John Winslow and the engineer Capt. William Lithgow, was erected by the Falmouth (Portland) builder Isaac Ilsley. It is a log building with an overhanging second story and hipped roof, measuring a trifle over twenty feet square. Now a museum, this well-preserved example of wilderness defensive architecture belongs more to 17th-century building practice than to its actual mid-18th-century date.

Another building type that originated in 17th-century New England was the meetinghouse, as distinct from the church. That is, the church form, deriving ultimately from pre-Reformation liturgical practices, had its focal point, whether altar or pulpit, on the narrower wall of the interior, often with an entrance tower at the opposite end; in other words, the congregation was seated along the long axis of the building. The meetinghouse, on the other hand, was a rectangular preaching box with the pulpit centered on the long wall and the entrance, sometimes sheltered by a porch enclosing the gallery stairs, opposite. U-shaped galleries terminating where they abutted the pulpit wall were standard. High wineglass pulpits (so-called because of their tulip shape) with handsomely shaped sounding-board canopies were customarily placed in front of arched windows often flanked by fluted pilasters. Maine was slow to give up the meeting house form; one example, Porter Meetinghouse, dates from as late as 1824. As Calvinist doctrine rejected the concept of holy *places,* there was no bar to using the meetinghouses for all decent business requiring public assembly, as well as for worship.

The oldest remaining meetinghouse in Maine is that at Harpswell, built in 1757–59, probably by Elisha Eaton, a housewright who was the son of the first pastor. The building measures about forty by thirty-five feet and has, like all other Maine meetinghouses, a gable roof. The clapboarded exterior, with its two tiers of windows, and the relatively modest scale, give to this public building the decidedly domestic appearance common to all New England meetinghouses. At Harpswell, there is a projecting stair wing entered laterally at each short flank. The interior has the gallery and pulpit arrangement described above. Unfortunately, most of the pews have been removed but otherwise, the interior is little altered. Harpswell Meetinghouse served as both a church and place for town meetings until 1844, and still serves the latter purpose.

Lincoln County is fortunate in possessing four noteworthy 18th-century places of worship. Like its counterparts elsewhere, Walpole Meetinghouse has a five-bayed front and gabled roof, but it lacks the entrance element that forms so conspicuous a feature at Harpswell. Instead, it is entered from a particularly handsome doorway enframing paired eight-paneled doors and composed of Roman Doric pilasters supporting a pulvinated frieze, above which is a finely denticulated triangular pediment. The interior of Walpole Meetinghouse retains its original fittings of 1772; its austerity is, however, relieved by the enrichment of the pulpit composition placed against an arched window flanked by Roman Doric pilasters supporting an entablature below the suspended sounding board. The gallery rails and pew dividers are handsomely paneled. There are, in this Walpole example, two side entrances, one of which is as elaborately composed as the front entrance described above. The exterior is shingled, making the splendid entrance appear even more remarkable than it would if the building were clad in the rather more formal vesture of clapboards.

Harrington Meetinghouse at Pemaquid is in Bristol Township, like Walpole Meetinghouse. Completed in 1775, it very closely resembles the latter, except that the exterior is clapboard and has corner pilasters that appear to date from a

FIGURE 20. *Alna Meetinghouse, interior (1789). Photo: Historic American Buildings Survey, by Allen L. Hubbard*

very extensive renovation carried out by 1853. The interior was radically changed in the late 1840's, and the galleries were removed. Abandoned for about fifty years, the derelict building was thoroughly restored on the basis of physical evidence between 1960 and 1965 and now looks much as it did when new.

A variant from the meetinghouse type, astonishing for the period in Maine, is the German Lutheran Church at Waldoboro. As it is commonly supposed that pre-Revolutionary Maine was settled almost exclusively by Englishmen and Scots, it should be noted that Samuel Waldo enterprisingly achieved the settlement of a portion of his vast land grant by offering favorable terms to German Protestants, thereby inducing them to exchange the hardships of Europe for the perils of the wilderness. Their place of worship at Waldoboro, built in 1773 and moved and re-erected in 1795, has the pulpit at the end of the long axis opposite an enclosed entry housing the gallery stairs. Thus, unlike the standard meetinghouse arrangement, the entrance is at the gable end, as in a traditional church. This simple clapboarded building is also remarkable for its setting, the old German cemetery that surrounds it. Inside, there is a paneled gallery supported on square piers. Box pews and a wineglass pulpit complete the ensemble.

The last of this series of Lincoln County places of worship to be erected was Alna Meetinghouse, built in 1789 at the very end of the period under consideration. Measuring over fifty by forty feet, Alna Meetinghouse is the largest of its kind in Maine. The exterior, which has a stair pavilion like that at Harpswell, is clapboarded on the front and rear elevations and shingled on the sides. The fittings of the interior (Figure 20) are especially handsome. The panels of the gallery parapets and the pulpit are grained. The sounding board is hexagonal in shape and domed. Its handsomely paneled soffit is set above a pilaster-flanked arched window. The rails of the box pews are supported by turned balusters. Altogether, Alna has probably

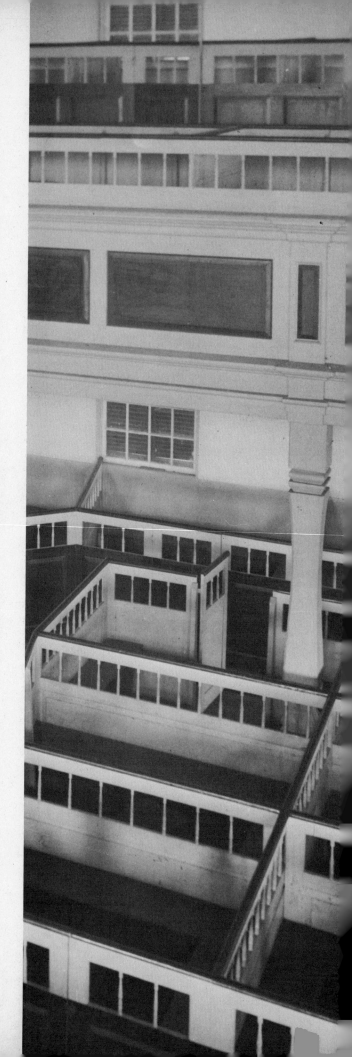

the best meetinghouse interior in Maine. The no-nonsense approach of its anonymous creator is amply demonstrated by the exposure of the structural elements. By 1789, a more self-conscious builder might well have been tempted to conceal the frame behind plaster and lath.

Among Colonial public buildings, the subsequent history of one previously mentioned, the York Gaol (Figure 18), deserves notice. It is now, as Candee observes (see p. 43 and chapter 2, note 77) well established by documentary evidence that the earliest, stone portion of the building was built in response to a court order of October 6, 1719.[1] That section, formerly thought to have been built in 1653, is nevertheless still the oldest stone building in Maine and, most probably, the *only* 18th-century building of that material in the state. The later additions (constructed in wood) that now give the building the appearance of a large gambrel-roofed frame structure with one exposed section of rear stone wall were built at various dates from about 1737 to 1806. Apart from the heavily plank-sheathed cells of the original stone section, perhaps the most interesting feature of the interior is to be found in the jailor's quarters. There the long west room can be subdivided into two chambers by the device of lowering a paneled wall that is hinged at the ceiling. It is possible that inns and taverns in the 18th century may have converted dormitory space into private rooms on occasion by means of a similar device. A set of moveable paneled walls dating from 1782 in a private house will be noted later in this chapter.

The one pre-Revolutionary courthouse remaining in Maine does not differ in any significant way from the larger sort of domestic structure of its period and will therefore be discussed with dwellings of its specific type. Since inns and taverns during this period did not differ from private dwelling houses in form or construction, there remain, after the meetinghouses and jail discussed above, no typological categories save the varying types of dwelling to be mentioned.

With only two exceptions, all the houses, whatever their form, were of frame construction. Basically, the method of assembling the framing members was the same, whether for one- or two-storied houses of any size. Pre-cut timbers, usually about ten inches square in section, were numbered and joined by mortise and tenon joints secured by treenails (often called trunnels.)[2] While the framing elements were heavy, the walls they supported were surprisingly light. Outside walls were clapboarded or shingled, their interior surfaces being sheathed with lime plaster over split lath. Interior partitions were often constructed of vertical beaded sheathing only an inch or so thick.

House and barn raisings were community undertakings. Putting together the previously prepared parts of the frame, rather like a huge puzzle, and then raising and securing the four wall frames called for united and neighborly effort. Not the least attraction of such events was the very considerable amount of potable spirits customarily supplied by the man whose house or barn was put up.

Although most houses built between 1725 or so and the late 1780's were merely later versions of basically 17th-century types, two newer house forms made their appearance in Maine during that time, the first around 1725, the second in the 1750's. The earlier of the two was the gambrel-roofed house. That roof form, with its steep lower slopes and rather flat upper slopes, gave much more attic space than a standard pitched roof. Another probable reason for its adoption in many 18th-century Maine houses was that it worked well for houses that were two rooms deep, as a gabled roof with a forty-five degree pitch had to be higher in such a case than when over a house only one room deep.

Possibly the first gambrel-roofed house in Maine is that built in Kittery by William Pepperrell. It is large for its time and place and, unlike most of its contemporaries, it has a central-hall plan. As early as 1683 Col. William Pepperrell, who died in 1733, had a house on the site. In 1720–23 the younger William Pepperrell, who later became Sir William, the first American-born baronet, either extensively altered or entirely rebuilt the house. The documentary and physical evidence seem somewhat to conflict, and precise dating is therefore difficult, if not impossible to achieve. The house (Figure 21) now measures forty-three feet in length, but it is said to have had an original length of fifty feet, later increased to eighty feet. It is stated that in 1848 fifteen feet were taken from one end and five feet from the other.[3] It is possible that the central hall and east portion of the house date from before 1750 but not as early as 1720. The physical evidence seems so to indicate. Originally, the house had a pitched roof of standard gable form. The two principal elevations do not correspond; the front has five bays, whereas the rear (street side) has four irregular bays. The exterior was formerly clapboarded and is now shingled. The cornices have been renewed, and the Greek Revival corner pilasters date probably from 1848. Interesting as is the exterior of this early, darkly hulking two-chimnied gambrel-roofed house, it is the interior that is its great glory. The parlor, apparently dating from 1720–23, is fully paneled in fielded paneling with heavy bolection moldings. The walls are articulated by compound stop-fluted pilasters on plinths. The cornice breaks forward over the pilasters, the keyblocks of the arches flanking the fireplace, and the windows, in a very baroque manner. The dining room across the hall is lighter in character, suggesting a somewhat later date. Doric pilasters flank the fireplace in this fully paneled room, and there is a shell-headed cupboard in the same wall. The chamber over the dining room is also fully paneled. That over the parlor has moldings of unconventional form and a low dado. The library behind the parlor was originally a kitchen. The hall contains a fine staircase with an unusually deep landing and boxed soffits under the short upper run. The balusters, most of them restorations, have three patterns of turnings. The angels

painted in the spandrels of the arch-headed landing window appear to be original. Photographs give a rather inaccurate impression of these splendid interiors, for the scale is, surprisingly, smaller than one would expect. The stair landing, for example, is less than six feet above the floor. In 1945 this extraordinarily fine house was painstakingly restored.

Another York County gambrel-roofed house, Leigh's Mill House in South Berwick was reputedly built as early as 1726. It is quite a large house, two-chimnied, with a five-bayed front. There is a good arched window above the quite simple transom-lit front entrance. The side wing at the right is clearly a later addition.

Until 1967 a really grand gambrel-roofed mansion, the Nathaniel Sparhawk House of circa 1742 stood in Kittery. It was built as a dower house for Sir William Pepperrell to present to his daughter Elizabeth upon her marriage to Sparhawk. The transom-lighted front doorway with its sixteen-paneled door was flanked by stop-fluted Roman Corinthian pilasters on plinths. Above was an entablature with pulvinated frieze crowned by a fine swan's neck pediment. The dormer windows of this two-chimnied five-bayed facade may have been later additions, as dormers rarely appear in combination with gambrel roofs in Maine until the 1780's. The parlor, or "banquet room," was paneled throughout. There were shell-headed cupboards in the reveals of the chimney, and the fireplace was flanked by stop-fluted Doric pilasters on plinths. Much of this trim, so convincingly 18th-century in appearance, was in point of fact, the work of John H. Bellamy (1836–1914), the noted ship carver. Bellamy signed his work and dated it 1867. It should therefore be noted as one of the very earliest really plausible examples of Colonial Revival work of which there is record.[4] The loss of the Sparhawk House was, to say the least, most unfortunate.

The house built in 1755 in Stroudwater (now a part of Portland) for the royal mast agent George Tate has the central-chimney plan more

FIGURE 21. *Kittery, William Pepperrell House (first built in 1683, either rebuilt or extensively altered 1720–23). Photo: Historic American Buildings Survey, by Jack E. Boucher*

common to Maine gambrel-roofed houses. The most noteworthy feature of the exterior is the highly unusual clerestory motif set vertically within the gambrel-shaped gables of the roof (Figure 22). This form, rare indeed, occurs in only one other Maine example, the Burnham Tavern of 1770 in Machias. The front elevation of the Tate House is five-bayed, the rear three-bayed. The entrance is dignified by pilasters and a triangular pediment and is lighted by a circular-headed fanlight. Within, the hall has an un-

usual coved cornice. The stairs rise rather steeply in three runs and have vase-turned balusters, two to each step. The parlor has fielded paneling and, beside the bolection-molded fireplace, Doric fluted pilasters. The dining room has a high paneled dado and, in one corner, a handsome shell-headed cupboard. The scale of this beautifully finished house is ample for the period; it measures a bit over thirty-six by twenty-eight feet. In 1952 it was restored by the architect Walter M. Macomber for the Maine Society

FIGURE 22. *Portland, Stroudwater, George Tate House, front (1755). Photo: Historic American Buildings Survey, by Jack E. Boucher*

of Colonial Dames, who maintain it as a museum.

The unpainted exterior of the George Tate House reminds us that, until well after the Revolutionary War, most Maine houses were not painted. Oil paint with a linseed oil base was practically unknown until the Federal period. In the Colonial era, when paint was used, it was frequently an amalgam of a local pigment called Indian Red (iron oxide) and fish oil. Interior plaster was usually whitewashed or covered with a tinted wash.

There can be no doubt that more simple story-and-a-half gambrel-roofed houses of central-chimney plan were built than large gambrel-roofed houses. The first frame house built in New Gloucester, the Isaac Parsons House of 1762, was a three-bayed story-and-a-half house of central-chimney plan with a gambrel roof. Unfortunately, it has been almost entirely rebuilt, using the original frame. At least twice moved, it now rests on a new site and has an extensive modern addition in the Colonial manner. The above-mentioned Burnham Tavern of 1770 in Machias is another story-and-a-half central-chimnied example. As already noted, it is remarkable for the rare "clerestory" treatment of its gambrel roof, as well as its historical significance as the place where the first sea battle of the Revolution, the seizure of the British armed cutter "Margaretta," was planned.

The largest house in the Stroudwater section of Portland, the Francis Waldo House (also known as the Daniel Dole House) of circa 1768–70, has the rather high-shouldered bulky look characteristic of its type. It is possible that it was built by Moses Pearson (1697–1778), a Falmouth (Portland) joiner who was Dole's father-in-law. The gambrel roof has no dormers. A more formal, or certainly a more elaborate, example than the Waldo, or Dole, House was built in Saco by four brothers named Moody for Col. Thomas Cutts in 1782. The five-bayed front had quoined corners (as does the Francis Waldo House), pedimented first-floor windows, dor-

mer windows, and an outstanding entrance with a swan's neck pediment. In an act of vandalism almost comparable to the destruction of the Sparhawk House, the Cutts House was moved in 1937, reduced to a story-and-a-half, stripped of its entrance pediment, and all but destroyed. Fortunately, this fine gambrel house was recorded by the Historic American Buildings Survey before disaster overwhelmed it. In the Kennebunk area there is only one example of the type, the house built in 1784 for Theodore Lyman but now called by the name of Henry Kingsbury, a later owner. This distinguished house is somewhat marred by the modern dormers added to the front.

"Cape Cod House," now often shortened to mere "Cape," has become so widespread a generic term as scarcely to require definition.[5] The term appears to have gained currency from Timothy Dwight's account of Cape Cod houses written in 1800. The cape was the most ubiquitous type of Maine farmhouse from around 1750 until about 1850. The major characteristics differentiating the cape from other house types are that it is invariably one-storied or has only a story and a half and that, in pre-Revolutionary Maine, it is always found with a central chimney. If one assumes the ascribed date of 1743–46 to be correct, the Joseph Small House in Stroudwater (Portland) is one of the earliest examples of the type in Maine. In 1842 it was moved from its original site. The present side-lighted entrance is 19th-century and may date from the time of the move. The house has modern sash and a relatively new roof covering of composition shingles. The Abner Perkins House in Kennebunkport, apparently built in 1750, has been similarly altered with respect to entrance, sash, and roof. Thus, neither cape now looks distinctively 18th-century. The Chapman-Hall House of 1754, the oldest house in Damariscotta, has been well restored and looks much as it doubtless did in the 18th century with its nine-over-six-light sash, entrance lit by a small rectangular transom, and wooden-shingled roof. The front is clapboarded, but the sides are shingled. The interior has a kitchen with vertical sheathing of 1754, a room paneled around 1790, and a room plastered about 1810, among other features.

On the west side of Route 88 in Falmouth Foreside there stands one of the handsomest capes in Maine (Figure 23). This beautifully maintained example may date from around 1760. The pilaster-flanked entrance has a rectangular four-light transom, the four front windows have nine-over-six-light sash, the roof has wooden shingles, and the large square central chimney appears to be original. As is almost without exception the case in Maine, the chimney is built of brick. Not all capes had five- or three-bayed fronts. The house in Camden built, it is believed in the 1770's, by Robert Thorndike and now known from the surname of a later owner as the Conway House, is an asymmetrical cape, having four bays. The exterior is shingled, and there is an early 19th-century addition at the rear, giving the house a lean-to form. The house measures twenty-two by thirty feet. The most remarkable interior element is the entry wall opposite the front door. It is curved in plan, suggesting the hand of a builder familiar with maritime building practice, and contains an inset cabinet termed a "parson's cupboard." The Conway House was saved when almost derelict and has been restored using old elements from other sources where certain original elements were missing.[6]

A house known as the Ward House on Route 1 in Searsport dates from 1794 and has a pilaster-flanked entrance crowned by a semicircular transom. In most capes, the stairs are placed in front of the central chimney in a shallow entry. In the Conway House, however, the stairs run from the kitchen and are set at the rear of the chimney. In the Searsport example, they are placed beside the chimney. It has been previously noted that inns and taverns did not differ from private houses. An illustration of that fact is to be seen in the Black Horse Tavern on Searsport Avenue in East Belfast. In appearance the tavern, built in 1800 for Jerome Stephenson, a tavern keeper, differs in no way from any farmhouse of the cape type, except, perhaps, for its small side ell. Until fairly recently, the setting of the Black Horse Tavern was made particularly picturesque by the presence of one of the few remaining well sweeps to be seen. Unfortunately, it rotted away and has not been replaced. The house itself has been recently refurbished, and new clapboarding and dormers have been added to the formerly shingled ell. Both the Black Horse Tavern and the James Winslow House of 1819–20 in New Gloucester show the persistence of the cape up to and well beyond the end of the 18th century. The latter is a typical cape with an extensive rear ell. As in many other cases, the roof has composition shingles, and the original sash has been replaced with two-over-two-light sash of later 19th-century design.

The cape is frequently, in northern New England, found with farm outbuildings attached. A quite large example, the Miles Cobb Farmhouse of 1788 in Warren, has a cape measuring over thirty-eight by thirty feet with an offset wing attached to the rear ell and extending out for nearly ninety-four feet (Figure 24). The wing is composed of a summer kitchen, sheds, and a large barn. These connected farm building complexes were necessary to give easy access to livestock during hard winters. The attached buildings of the Miles Cobb Farmhouse appear not to be coeval with the house and barn but to have been added later.[7]

Like the cape, the standard two-storied gable-roofed house of central-chimney plan had its origins in 17th-century building practice and remained common into the early 19th century. In many instances, gable-roofed houses one room in depth received one-storied rear additions, giving them the well-known "salt box" shape, i.e., a form where the eaves line in front was at second-story height but that in back was at first-floor level. The long unbroken rear slope of the roof was sometimes called a "cat slide." In some

FIGURE 23. *Falmouth Foreside, cape on Route 88,*
front (c. 1760). Photo: Richard Cheek

examples, there was a break in the rear slope at first-floor height, giving a variation termed the "lean-to" roof. One of the earliest salt box houses in Maine, the Benjamin Haley House at Biddeford Pool, has been so very much altered that little remains of its original aspect except the basic shape. Inside, the closed-string staircase, rising in three steep runs against the central chimney, and the paneled fireplace wall of the parlor, with its pilasters and bolection molding surrounding the fireplace opening, remain to at-

test to the earlier quality of this much mutilated house dating from the 1720's.

The Hugh Holmen House in York dates from 1727 and is, except for a later enclosed entrance vestibule of around 1800 and a rather too conspicuous exterior electric meter, a quite pristine example of the five-bayed salt box type. This

FIGURE 24. *Warren, Miles Cobb Farmhouse, plan (1788). Courtesy of the Historic American Buildings Survey, drawn by James M. Replogle*

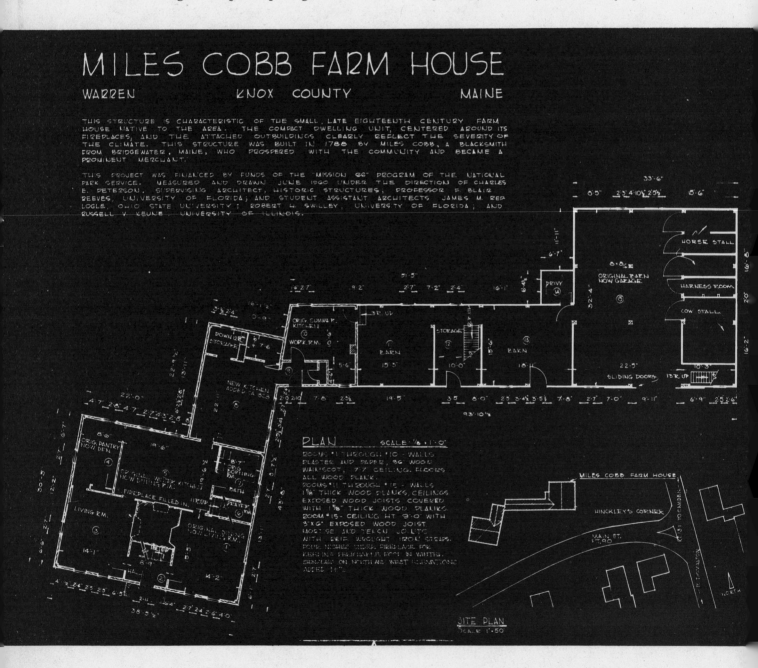

house is sometimes known as the Eastman House. One of the finest of the early Maine salt boxes is the three-bayed Tristram Perkins House built in Kennebunkport about 1730. The front and side entrances and the window architraves were altered during the Greek Revival, probably before 1850.

Certainly one of the least altered houses (except for the loss of its original chimney and fireplaces) of mid-18th-century date in Maine is the Greenfield Pote House, moved by Capt. Pote from Falmouth (Portland) to Freeport in 1765. Old views show the house to have been formerly clapboarded instead of shingled, as at present. It is an asymmetrical salt box, having four bays, and measures about forty-one by thirty-three feet. The front eaves are some sixteen feet above grade. Some of the fenestration has been altered, and none of the sash is original. In spite of these changes, however, the house retains an extraordinary amount of its untouched interior trim and even areas of original red and blue paint. The closed-string three-run staircase with heavily turned balusters and square newel posts is unchanged, as are the fielded paneling of the parlor fireplace wall and the bead and bevel vertical sheathing of the opposite wall. The doors, hardware, and interior trim are all untouched except by time. This fine salt-box farmhouse is now undergoing rehabilitation on the salt water farm site it has occupied since 1765.

In the Stroudwater section of Portland the Deacon John Bailey House, now a salt box, was, when it was built about 1750, a one-and-a-half-story cape. About 1807 the house was raised by inserting a new story below the original one. This method of enlarging a house was occasionally practiced in Maine. The rear wing of the Deacon Bailey House was added in 1967. The rear addition giving a salt box form to the Capt. James Hubbard House of 1751 in Kennebunk may be considerably later than the mid-18th century. This fine five-bayed example of its type appears to be quite pristine, except for an obviously rebuilt chimney and a Greek Revival

entrance dating from around 1850. The well-known Jefferds' Tavern in York is an example of the lean-to house shape. It was built in Wells around 1760 for Capt. Samuel Jefferds, a tavernkeeper and mill owner. After standing neglected and vandalized for some years, it was disassembled in 1939 and re-erected in York, where it now serves as a museum building.

In rural settings, the salt box remained popular to some extent, as is attested by the Pettengill Farm of about 1800 in Freeport and the Joseph Miller house of about the same date in the vicinity of Belfast. Unfortunately, the Pettengill Farmhouse, a four-bayed example, has now become so nearly a complete ruin that its survival is in doubt. Its fine setting, a salt water farm, remains unspoiled. Almost equally unfortunately, the Joseph Miller salt box is in poor condition and has been disfigured by asphalt shingles covering the walls.

In various areas of New England are found L-shaped houses with roofs that may be described as quarter-hipped (because a single hip is formed where two gable roofs intersect). The greatest concentration of this type in Maine is to be found in York, where most of the quarter-hipped houses appear to date from before about 1750. The Jeremiah Moulton House, for which a date of 1710 is claimed, and the Lt. Daniel Simpson House, said to date from 1720, both stand in a part of York called Scituate Men's Row after four settlers who left Scituate, Massachusetts for York in 1642. The Moulton House has a seven-bayed front with the quarter hip of the roof toward the right. The entrance is 19th-century, and the stairs are of the open string variety, suggesting a date several decades after 1710. The small size of the windows, however, argues for a date in the first half of the 18th century. The Daniel Simpson House is a five-bayed example of the same type. The front section has a central-chimney plan. Yet another handsome example of the quarter-hip type is the Emerson Wilcox Tavern of 1740, now a museum. Both main elevations are four-bayed. The Wilcox

Tavern, built for George Ingraham, has fully paneled fireplace walls, bolection moldings, and a fine corner cabinet, this last in the room to the left of the side entrance. Another York tavern, the Matthew Lindsay Tavern built in 1751, is also a building of the quarter-hip, or L-shaped, type. This excellent specimen of its kind is also known as the Stephen Lovejoy House. No definite explanation for the frequent occurrence of quarter-hipped house specifically in York has been adduced. The probability is that a builder, having demonstrated the feasibility of the L-shape for large houses, either received orders to duplicate his first house of the kind, or that several builders emulated the achievement of the first.

The standard two-storied gabled house without salt box, lean-to, or L-shaped form was, along with the cape, the house type most frequently to be found in Maine during the Colonial period. Like the cape and the salt box, it derived from 17th-century precedents. After the middle of the 18th century, the gable-roofed house appears in both central-chimnied and two-chimnied examples. Although 18th-century houses are, in an absolute sense, rare, there are nevertheless so many of the type now to be mentioned that time and space preclude extended discussion of more than a very few.

The Nicholas Sewell House in York is reputed to have been built as early as 1713 or 1719. The elevation facing the Green has four bays; the other front has five. The closed-string stairs with vase-turned balusters inside the house are an indication of fairly early date. The Isaiah Perkins House near the border of Wells in York dates from the first third of the 18th century and is of interest partly because, like the Deacon Bailey House in Stroudwater, it was originally a story-and-a-half house and was raised by the insertion of a new first floor in 1790, thus putting it in the category under discussion. The Elizabeth Perkins House, built for Capt. Joseph Holt, reputedly in 1730, in York has undergone major alterations. The two Palladian gables and sun

porch on the rear are 20th-century, and the Greek Revival corner pilasters are 19th-century. The house has, like many other 18th-century Maine houses, so-called "Indian shutters," i.e., paneled shutters that slide into the walls through the window reveals instead of being hinged and folding against the reveals. The James Merrill House in the vicinity of Falmouth was reputedly built in 1738. The front entrance certainly dates from after 1800, and many details, including neo-Colonial paneling of around 1930, are modern. There are extensive new additions at the rear of the Merrill House. In Kennebunk the Parson Daniel Little House was one of the first two-story houses built. It was completed in 1753 and was then remarkable for the amount of window glass it boasted. The enclosed entrance vestibule of this five-bayed house is a later addition.

The earliest of the two-chimnied gable-roofed houses to be noted is the Parson Smith House in South Windham. Now a property of the Society for the Preservation of New England Antiquities, the house was built in 1764 for the Reverend Peter Thatcher Smith. The side-lighted entrance of this clapboarded house is 19th-century. Otherwise, except for the later rear ell, the exterior is unaltered. The first-floor has twelve-over-twelve-light sash, the second twelve-over-eight lights. The windows have "Indian shutters." The plan, of course, is the expected central-hall one, with two rooms at either side. The lefthand chimney may have been rebuilt, as the parlor fireplace has a mantelpiece of Federal design, and the chamber above the parlor has Greek Revival trim. The dining room has a fireplace wall with fielded paneling and a bolection fireplace surround. Curiously, there is no dado in that room. The room over the dining room has a paneled chimney wall. In the kitchen there is a very large fireplace with ovens at one side. These brick ovens have no doors, as they were never supplied with the later cast-iron doors seen on so many early ovens. They are closed with wooden covers propped against them in the 18th-century way. The front stairs have well turned balusters and newel posts; the back stairs are simpler. In the library is an unusual feature, a bed enclosed in a paneled cupboard.

A central-chimnied example, the John Hunter Tavern, was built in Topsham before 1770 and was believed to have been the oldest building in the Brunswick-Topsham area. Abandoned for years, this plain "country" structure was demollished about 1964, but not before it had been measured, drawn (and photographed) by the Historic American Buildings Survey.

New Gloucester, first settled in the late 1730's and abandoned because of Indian raids in the mid-1740's, was resettled in 1753. In 1762, as noted above, this inland settlement had its first framed dwelling, the first Isaac Parsons House, a gambrel. Only three years later an astonishingly large and elegant parsonage, the Reverend Samuel Foxcroft House, was built. This two-chimnied two-and-a-half-storied house has a five-bayed front with quoined corners and a beautifully proportioned entrance with fluted pilasters, a rectangular transom, and a modillioned triangular pediment. The Foxcroft House is as refined in design as any of its contemporaries in long settled parts of New England. An almost identical New Gloucester house with a very similar doorway, the Jonathan Rowe House, dates from the late 18th century. Unlike the Foxcroft House, it has a central chimney. The Bell Tavern, a New Gloucester hostelry possibly dating from 1782, has been so greatly altered that it no longer retains a validly 18th-century appearance. Double houses are rare anywhere in America in the 18th century and are certainly so in Maine, yet New Gloucester had a fine example (in rather poor condition) dating from 1785. An eight-bayed building apparently one room deep, the house lacked its chimneys and had a tarpaper roof. The two doorways are handsome examples of the pedimented type. It seems probable that this double house was built for two households related to each other. It has been recently sawn apart and moved.

The second house Isaac Parsons built in New Gloucester (in 1781) far surpassed his first one, the small gambrel. The newer Parsons House is a large two-chimnied residence with both front and side entrances. The two doorways have pilaster-supported triangular pediments of the locally popular pattern. The windows have twelve-over-twelve-light sash (Figure 25). The stairs ascend in two runs with a landing two-thirds of the way up. The side entrance stairs rise in two runs against a chimney and are enclosed by unbeaded vertical sheathing. The windows have Indian shutters. The interior trim in the front hall, side hall, parlor, dining room, and library (formerly one of two original kitchens) is original. The finish of the front hall, and the dining room and parlor is of outstanding quality. Both rooms have fully paneled fireplace walls with Doric pilasters and bolection fireplace surrounds. The cornices break forward over the architectural elements. The excellence of the second Isaac Parsons House amply witnesses to the skill and taste of its builder. It is clear from the remarkable group of 18th-century dwellings in New Gloucester that fine building was not confined to the coastal area of Maine. Houses of the utmost distinction were to be found in at least some inland settlements as well.

So many houses of the simple gable-roofed type were built in the 1780's and 1790's, as compared with earlier decades, that it seems evident that a kind of building boom followed upon the cessation of military operations in 1781. The Archelaus Lewis House of 1783 in Stroudwater (Portland), originally a central-chimney house, has since been altered and now has two small chimneys. The nearby Jesse Partridge House, built three years later, has kept its original big central chimney. The entrance vestibule, side porch, and side entrance are, of course, later additions. The interior of the Partridge House has fine original paneling. In 1784 the Daniel Walker House was built in Kennebunkport. Another of the central-chimney type, it has quoined corners and highly unusual compound

FIGURE 25. *New Gloucester, second Isaac Parsons House (1781). Photo: Maine Historic Preservation Commission, by Earle G. Shettleworth, Jr.*

lintel and keyblock motifs over the windows. These, like the front entrance, may be later alterations. The Henry Hodge House in Wiscasset, dating from 1787, is an asymmetrical example of the two-chimnied variety. This six-bayed house, the main block of which measures about forty-two by twenty-nine feet, has both offset side and rear two-storied ells.

Another of the central-chimnied gable-roofed houses, the Daniel Marrett House, was built in Standish in 1789. The original owner was Benjamin Titcomb, but the house now bears the name of its best-known occupant, the Reverend Daniel Marrett. It is now a property of the Society for the Preservation of New England Antiquities. The exterior of the Marret House, except for such tell-tale elements as the large central chimney and the Federal detailing of the entrance vestibule, now looks like a mid-19th-century building. Greek Revival trim, a side porch, and the large barn connected to the house by a rear ell and wing of sheds all give the complex the aspect of a farmhouse around 1850. The interior has numerous original features and furnishings of various periods. It is precisely this lived-in look with no attempt at backdating to an arbitrarily selected time that gives the house its admirable air of authenticity, rather than the artificial museum-like appearance found in too many historic houses. The brick oven beside the kitchen fireplace has an early 19th-century cast-iron door marked "Jacob Kimball, Portland, Me."

The Moody Homestead in York, a two-chimnied example built in 1790, incorporates in a rear ell an earlier structure believed to date from the last decade of the 17th century. The homestead is now a typical connected complex with barn attached to the ell. It is not astonishing to find that the large central-chimnied Bucknam House built in 1792 in the remote reaches of Washington County at Columbia Falls is somewhat *retardataire* in its details. The exterior is severely plain. The great square chimney, as in most cases, is supported on brick arches. The

rather heavy stair balusters, fielded paneling, and bolection moldings of the fireplace walls, were already old-fashioned in urban areas. The cast-iron door of the kitchen oven is very similar to the one in the Marrett House, if, indeed, it is not identical.

If the year 1797 is indeed the correct date for the General Ichabod Goodwin House in South Berwick, that house must be the most *retardataire* building in Maine. It is a gable-roofed house with a central chimney. The windows of the five-bayed front are small for the 1790's, and the arched pediment of the front doorway looks like examples dating from the 1730's. In fact, the Goodwin House facade looks more like that of the Short House of around 1732 in Newburyport, Massachusetts and the John Kingsbury House in York, built around 1730, than it does a work of 1797. Usually, the problem of dating Maine houses arises from the natural desire on the part of local citizens to claim very early dates on the basis of old records. Too often, the records actually refer to structures later replaced by others on the sites in question. Where documentary and physical evidence conflict, it is wise to base one's conclusions on the latter. Dating houses from stylistic evidence alone, however, does not work well where vernacular examples are concerned, as the same trim was frequently used over a long span of time. Be that as it may, it is somewhat refreshing to find an example like the Goodwin House that may well, for a change, be *earlier* than the date given for it.

It was remarked above that two newer forms, not deriving from 17th-century precedents, appeared during the later Colonial period, one around 1725, the other around 1750. The first, the gambrel, has already been discussed. The second, the hip-roofed house, remains to be considered. With few exceptions, the hip-roofed houses were major dwellings with central-hall plans. After about 1760 members of the squire-archy seem to have favored this house type above all others. One public building, the only courthouse in Maine antedating the Revolution, so nearly resembles a hip-roofed residence (except that it has three stories) that it merits discussion here. Pownalborough Courthouse was commenced in 1761 in what is now Dresden but was not completed for some years. Gershom Flagg (1705–1771), supervised by Maj. Samuel Goodwin, was the builder. (Flagg was also the builder of Fort Western at Augusta.) Pownalborough Courthouse is approximately forty-five feet square and housed a tavern and living quarters as well as a court room. The original court arrangements no longer exist. Aside from its important historical associations, the building, a plain country edifice, is unremarkable except for its unusual height.

Gershom Flagg also built the Bowman-Carney House in Dresden in about 1761. The main block measures approximately forty-three by thirty-nine feet, and, except for a later side ell, the house is virtually all original. The pediment above the front entrance is a restoration. A plain country house on the outside, the Bowman-Carney House has particularly fine interiors. The exterior depends upon good proportions rather than rich detail for its handsome effect. The central hall has a spacious and dignified staircase and fine paneled dadoes. The principal rooms have fully paneled chimney walls, dadoes, and cornices of the best quality. This particularly satisfactory house has been excellently restored and maintained.

What is now the rear wing of the William Lord-Jonas Clark Mansion in Kennebunk was built in 1760 for Jonathan Banks, apparently as a hip-roofed house. It is now overshadowed by the splendid front block erected in the Federal style in 1804 from designs by Thomas Eaton. Not all hip-roofed houses had central-hall plans. In North Edgecomb the Decker-Clough House of around 1774 has a five-bayed front and a hipped roof, but that roof terminates against a large central chimney. Another coastal example is to be found in Riggs Cove at Robinhood. Built about 1792–94, this three-bayed house was erected for Benjamin Riggs and measures only

around thirty-two feet square. Inland, in Oxford County, another hip-roofed house of the central-chimney type stands in Hiram. Built in 1785, the John Watson House is a remarkable backwoods version of a squire's mansion. Originally called Intervale Farm, the house now appears rather grander that it should, since modern arcaded flankers in the Federal manner have been added to the main block. The doorway of the five-bayed facade is probably a 19th-century alteration of about 1825. The louvered fan and sidelight arrangement was certainly not current very much before that time. The interior trim is very simple, much use being made of feather-edged vertical sheathing. The cellar contains a most surprising construction—the great central chimney is supported, not on brick arches as one would expect, but on timber cribbing much like wharf pier construction. The under sides of the first floor joists are half-round logs. The aesthetic quality of the John Watson House has been singularly well described by Earle G. Shettleworth, Jr. as "the embodiment of eighteenth century Georgian architectural ideals expressed in the forthright terms of rural New England. The artful simplicity of its rational design continues to please the eye after the passage of nearly two hundred years."

The grandest of all the hip-roofed mansions were those with four chimneys. The Lady Pepperrell House at Kittery appears to have been the earliest example of this mansion type in Maine, having been built in 1760. By any standard, it is one of the most suavely sophisticated Georgian houses in America (Figure 26). Now a property of the Society for the Preservation of New England Antiquities, the house is particularly noteworthy for the design of its facade. Measuring almost fifty feet across, this facade has quoined corners and a slightly projecting central pavilion flanked by Roman Ionic pilasters with entablature blocks bearing sections of pulvinated frieze. The whole is crowned by a low pediment forming a subsidiary gable against the hipped roof. A modillioned cornice termi-

FIGURE 26. *Kittery, Lady Pepperrell House (1760).*
Photo: Douglas Armsden

nates the walls. The pavilion is most effectively set off by the use of smooth vertical sheathing contrasting with the clapboarding of the rest of the house. The remaining side porch, or "piazza," is one of two added by John Mead Howells in 1923. Otherwise, except for restored sash and the second story added to the rear ell around 1900, the exterior is unaltered. The interior trim is as advanced for the time and place as is the facade. Denticulated cornices, eared overmantel panels, and broad expanses of plastered wall characterize the rooms. A fire in 1945 unfortunately did considerable damage and destroyed the front stairs, now represented by an excellent replica of the original. This truly elegant house may be counted as one of the very finest Colonial mansions ever built in Maine.

The McCobb-Hill-Minott House of 1773–74 in Phippsburg was built by the housewright Isaac Packard.[8] It has two chimneys and is unusual in that the roof terminates in a tall square cupola. Although the cupola may not date from the building of the house, it was certainly in place by 1794, for it is seen on a map of that date. The ceilings of this Phippsburg house are a bit lower than the proportions of the house would suggest, being only eight feet and nine inches or so above the floor. The interior trim is up-to-date for its period, but the front stairs were replaced in the 19th century. The large offset ell and connected barn, now so conspicuous an element of the exterior, were added in 1870. In spite of changes and additions, the McCobb-Hill-Minott House remains a fine, slightly rural, example of its type.

The Goddard-McCulloch House in Kennebunk, generally known as the Hugh McCulloch House, is too large and impressive an example of the hip-roofed central-chimney type to have been classed with those previously mentioned. A break at the eaves level of the dormers gives the roof a hip-upon-hip form. The five-bayed front has three dormers and a somewhat later enclosed vestibule. The house was built in 1782 for a Dr. Goddard but was soon acquired by the McCulloch family whose descendants still occupy it. The stairs ascend in three runs against the very large chimney. There are also back stairs. The rear portion of the house has been altered, but the main block is unchanged. Two interior features are worth special mention. In a closet of the parlor is a section of original wallpaper representing America (an Indian woman), Britannia (a Bellona-like personification), and a man on a pedestal (in contemporary dress of the 1770's) who holds a scroll dated July 4, 1776. The Indian America looks rather smug, and Britannia appears to be decidedly dejected. This repeat group is placed under an arch forming part of the continuous framework of the overall design. The other noteworthy interior feature is an arrangement of paneled walls that are hinged at the ceiling so that the three upstairs chambers to the right of the central chimney can be thrown into one large room. This area of the house was apparently used for large entertainments. One other analogous arrangement, the hinged partition in the York Gaol, has already been noted.

Considerable wealth had long been concentrated in the Piscataqua Valley area, so it is hardly surprising to find two of the major Maine mansions of the Colonial period (both owned by the Society for the Preservation of New England Antiquities) in South Berwick,

where the Salmon Falls River and the Piscataqua join. The house built in 1774 for John Haggens and now known by the name of its most famous occupant, the Sarah Orne Jewett House, is similar to several in Portsmouth, New Hampshire. (The flared eaves of the Jewett House are a Portsmouth mannerism.) The five-bayed front of this two-chimnied house has an especially well-proportioned Roman Doric entrance portico. The three pedimented dormers, however, are late 19th-century Colonial Revival additions. The corner post of the frame is boxed in the parlor and is treated as a fluted pier. The broad central hall has superlative joinery that is reputed to have required the work of two men for a hundred days. The trim was originally dark brown mahogany color.[9] The lefthand front chamber has light and delicate trim of the Federal period. It may fairly be said that the architectural merit of the Sarah Orne Jewett House equals the importance of its best known occupant in the history of American literature.

The Jonathan Hamilton House, the other great South Berwick mansion, was built in 1787–88 (Figure 27). The spacious setting overlooking a secluded reach of the Salmon Falls River is a beautiful one, fully worthy of the house itself. Except for the roofing material the exterior of the house is original and unaltered even to the window sash. The scale of the building (fifty by forty-seven feet in plan) is as large as in any Colonial house in Maine. The four tall chimneys, the dormers on all four slopes of the roof, and the general air of amplitude give to this splendid mansion an appearance of grandeur unsurpassed by any Maine house of its day. Only one significant alteration has occurred within; the dining room has been enlarged by the elimination of a secondary staircase. The central hall closely resembles the hall of the Jewett House, with its archway, dadoes, and wide staircase. Here, however, the soffit of the stairs is boxed instead of paneled, as in the slightly older house. A principal glory of the interior is the fireplace wall of the great drawing room. The fireplace,

FIGURE 27. *South Berwick, Jonathan Hamilton House (1787–88). Photo: Douglas Armsden*

with its crossetted overmantel panel, is flanked by alcoves the depth of the chimney. These windowed alcoves are entered under arches supported on Doric pilasters. The arches, elliptical in shape, have richly carved keyblocks and soffits ornamented with meander, or "Greek key," moldings. Colonial magnificence of this kind is rarely to be found north or east of Portsmouth. This house, built at the very end of the period that is the subject of this chapter, may be said to represent the very climax of Colonial architectural achievement in the District of Maine.

It is necessary, before closing, to mention two other Maine houses simply because they were built of brick and therefore represent the very beginning of an extensive use of that material in later times. The Hugh McClellan House in Gorham is the earliest known brick house in Maine. It is, because of its present condition, important only for that reason. The original roof has been replaced, and nothing original except the newel post and railing of the front stairs remains inside the house. The early date (for a brick house in Maine), 1773, and the segmental arches of the first-floor openings are the sole features of interest. It is a question whether alteration or vandalization is the correct word for what has happened to the Hugh McClellan House. The only other brick house in Maine antedating the Federal period is the Wadsworth-Longfellow House, now part of the Maine Historical Society, in Portland. It is the first brick house built in Portland itself and dates from 1785–86. Originally it was two-and-a-half stories high and had a gabled roof. The brick was, so it is said, brought from Philadelphia and was laid up in Flemish bond, the preferred bond in Colonial building practice. The present appearance of this house, now a three-storied building with a hipped roof, resulted from an addition made in 1815 after a fire destroyed the original roof. It is worth noting that the third story is laid up in common bond, the bond most used in the 19th century. The earlier segmental lintels of the first two stories gave way, on the later third floor, to flat-arch lintels. This Portland residence, important both for its construction and for its association with General Peleg Wadsworth and Henry Wadsworth Longfellow, points the way toward the future Federal style.

4

PART 1

The Federal Style:

from about 1790 to 1825

William D. Shipman

INTRODUCTION

THE FEDERAL PERIOD, EXTENDING ROUGHLY from 1790 to 1825, had an effect on Maine's architectural development in much the way that spring has an effect on her people. These years witnessed a proliferation of fine buildings, domestic and otherwise, which took advantage of the new architectural ideas emanating from Boston and Salem as well as the new-found prosperity begot by New England's position as neutral carrier during the Napoleonic Wars. The awakening of interest in design could be seen in virtually every village along the coast. The period therefore can be said to be the first, in Maine, in which architectural distinction became a dominant goal for large numbers of owners and builders.

In the context of architectural history, the Federal period is usually characterized by an evolution and refinement of earlier architectural forms rather than by a wholly new departure. Emphasis increasingly was placed on balance, proportion, regularity, and symmetry, and on a light and relatively delicate ornamentation in contrast with the heavier detail seen in earlier buildings. Somewhat greater use was made of classical motifs (particularly columns and arches) than was characteristic of most Colonial or early Georgian buildings, and many of the new examples had accentuated horizontal lines which helped to impart a "classical" emphasis on stability. Federal architecture is thus inherently neo-classical in its approach, albeit the most traditional of several variants of American neo-classical style.[1] And it borrowed freely from similar neo-classical ideas prevalent in 18th century England.

The period also is sometimes seen as a transition from the relatively functional and block-like architecture of the colonies to the more frankly revivalist designs of the mid-19th century. But, while Federal buildings clearly had a more academic character than did most Colonial architecture, and while the style sought some classical *objectives,* it did not, at least in New England, attempt to emulate in a literal manner the buildings of earlier centuries. The result was an evolved "Georgian" architecture in which very simple forms were employed in such a way as to emphasize their symmetry, horizontality, and proportions. On the more ambitious structures, a wealth of detail was effected by intricate and small-scale carving or molding, usually within a classical frame, as in mantels, door and window casings, panels, and cornices.

In Maine, as suggested, the Federal period coincided with the arrival of prosperity in a hitherto remote and relatively backward region. The scarcity of distinguished Colonial buildings, outside the extreme southern section, contrasts with the plethora of good Federal examples and testifies to the District's late development. (The British bombardment of Falmouth [Portland] in 1775 and other wartime depredations also contributed to the scarcity of good Colonial examples.) The emergence of shipping and shipbuilding as major—and highly profitable—industries after 1790 helped to create small pools of wealth along the Maine coast. While this wealth was hardly comparable to that of the Boston-Salem or New York areas, it was nevertheless sufficient to bring about a wave of building activity at, architecturally speaking, just the right time. Importation of the ideas of Bulfinch and McIntire (together with some of their English antecedents) resulted in a series of buildings whose elegance and restrained classicism make them unusually good examples of their period.

Even so, application of these ideas continued to be limited in some degree by the character of the region. Most, though not all, Federal buildings in Maine were smaller, more functional, and less ambitious with respect to detail than their counterparts in the shipping centers of southern New England and the Middle Atlantic states. Outside of Portland itself, there were probably not more than a dozen fully elaborated churches and residences erected along the coast. But there were (and are) many substantial buildings which embodied the essence of Federal design. The *characteristic* Federal house in Maine is thus one which adopts the general form of the period (a rectangular block, typically two or three stories, with either hipped or gabled roof, central hall, and from two to five chimneys) but depends for its architectural appeal more on careful attention to proportion than to ornamentation or overall scale. This emphasis on proportion, as opposed to detail, is also characteristic of many Maine churches and public buildings of the period, and it further applies to smaller homes; it is not unusual to find symmetrical, well-proportioned "capes" dating from 1800–1820 in which the only ornamentation is an elegant front entrance.

The following paragraphs, describing a number of Federal buildings in Maine, are organized by functional types. We begin with a discussion of residences, and later take up public, educational, and religious buildings, commercial structures, and civil and military works, in that order. Our reasons for choosing this approach are two. First, the period under review is really a rather brief one. Only about thirty years separate the first examples of Federal architecture in Maine from the emergence of Greek Revival. A strictly chronological approach therefore would seem to miss the point. (The evolution of doorways, staircases, and room layout constituted the only important stylistic progression within this period, and is given some consideration in the discussion below.) Second, differences in geographic location within the District of Maine do not appear to be fundamental in tracing the evolution of architectural design. Which is to say that most towns along the coast, except possibly the east of Penobscot Bay, benefited from the new-found affluence and ideas in much the same way and at the same time.

There is one exception to this assumption of geographic neutrality—Portland. For Portland was clearly the major city in the District and the scene of much the greatest number and variety of Federal buildings. It is not true that other towns on the coast were dependencies of Portland, either economically or architecturally. Most of them had direct access to Boston and points south, and it is untenable to argue that builders had to go to Portland for their ideas rather than, say, to Boston or Salem. Nevertheless, Portland is strategic as the major coastal city whose excellent harbor enabled it to compete effectively with Salem, Newburyport, and Ports-

mouth, and whose wealth was sufficient to justify the construction of numerous large buildings. By 1800 there probably were more than a dozen Portland merchants willing and able to sink some $10,000 or more into a suitable residence.[2] Not many of these buildings have survived. Some fell victims to the great fire of 1866, a larger number have been displaced by age or a location inhibiting growth, and a few have been denatured almost beyond recognition. But there are several good examples still intact, and old photographs convey a reasonably accurate impression of some that have disappeared. Portland, then, becomes a convenient starting point for a discussion of Federal buildings.

RESIDENTIAL STRUCTURES

Residences of the period can be classified roughly into three groups: the mansions built by the leading merchants and shipbuilders (and an occasional retired military officer or land proprietor); the somewhat smaller and usually plainer houses of an "upper middle class" of professional men, lesser merchants, ship captains, and a few farmers; and the very large number of small residences built for (and frequently by) farmers, tradesmen, fishermen, and artisans. While the categories are defined primarily by a combination of scale and ornamentation, the divisions are not always distinct. A few of the smaller houses, for example, have unusually good details, and the appropriate scale of the "leading" house in, say, Machias, is quite different from its counterpart in Portland, Wiscasset, or Kennebunk. The following discussion concentrates on a limited number of examples in order to emphasize the basic types and to provide an opportunity for drawing similarities and contrasts.

A study of old maps and views of Portland suggests that there were upwards of twenty three-storied mansions built in that city between

1800 and 1820. Most of these had the rectangular "block" form of the period, with hipped roof, central hall and entrance, and small-scale windows on the third floor. Beyond these basic similarities, however, there were notable variations in ornamentation and interior detail.

The houses built in 1800 and 1801 for merchant-shipowners Hugh and Stephen McClellan by the local housewright, John Kimball, Sr. (now the Museum of Art Annex and the Cumberland Club, respectively), were of brick construction, one painted and one natural brick. The exterior walls consisted of single planes broken only by the numerous windows (with molded frames and projecting caps) and surmounted by modillion cornices and finely wrought balustrades. Each of the facades is five bays wide—the almost universal choice—and has a highly detailed portico with its own balustrade, which in turn forms a base for the Palladian window immediately above. While the scale and elevation of these windows are somewhat inadequate to their position on the facade, they serve to carry the ornamentation to the second floor and provide an effective focal point for the central hall and staircase. The lengthened windows on the first floor fronts of both houses, and (probably) the heavier portico of the Stephen McClellan House, were subsequent modifications. The fence and balustrades of the Hugh McClellan House (Figure 28), on the other hand, appear to have been integral parts of the original design.[3] A third, similar house also was built about this time (probably by Kimball) for Ebenezer Storer at the corner of High and Danforth streets. It served for many years as the Children's Hospital and was only recently taken down.

Quite apart from their architectural detail, these houses demonstrate in their very simple lines, their mass, and their subtle proportions, the basic strength of Federal architecture. They consist essentially of a single block (with only minor appendages originally), surmounted by a low roof and tall chimneys, and having only selective and restrained embellishment. Indeed, it is at least partly their economy of form that makes them so pleasing and so durable, architecturally speaking.

Their interiors also reflect a direct approach to the requirements of lighting and heating. The numerous and amply-scaled windows provide an abundance of light (too much for some later tastes), and the placement of chimneys on outside walls reduces somewhat the extent of cold surfaces while bringing the hearth close to the center of each room. The interiors are also characterized by finely detailed woodwork in the fireplace frames, the door and window frames, the cornices and wainscoting, and of course in the formal and elegant staircases. This detail is largely a reflection of the Adam influence, relayed to builders through the carpenters' manuals circulating at the time and through the famous intermediaries Bulfinch and McIntire. Since the detail required many hours of skilled labor, it also was a convenient yet tasteful indulgence whereby the very wealthy families distinguished themselves from the not-so-wealthy.

A few of the Portland mansions built at this time revealed, at least in their exterior aspect,

somewhat greater architectural sophistication than the preceding. These were the houses designed by Alexander Parris, who is sometimes said to have been the only true "architect" in Maine at the time, and who acquired a considerable reputation for his buildings in the Boston area a few years later. He left Maine about 1812 and for a time worked in the offices of Charles Bulfinch, a man whom he greatly admired and who apparently exercised considerable influence over even his (Parris's) Maine buildings.[4] While not all of Parris's work has been identified (he is believed to be responsible for certain features of houses built by others), there were at least three Portland residences which showed the influence of a professional. These were the mansions of Matthew Cobb (corner of High and Free Streets, Figure 29) and Joseph Ingraham (51 State Street) both built in 1801, and the residence of Richard Hunnewell (156 State Street, now the Portland Club), built about 1805. It is somewhat ironic that, while the McClellan houses have survived almost intact, the best of the above mentioned Parris houses was demolished and the other two have been substantially altered.

In the Matthew Cobb House, now removed, Parris utilized a set of arches on the lower part of the facade, supporting and integrated with four wooden pilasters extending the full height of the building and having Corinthian capitals, all applied against flush wood sheathing and surmounted by an elaborate cornice and frieze board (Figure 29). This general design was similar to several used by Bulfinch in the Boston-Salem area between 1795 and 1800; for example, the Franklin Place group and the house built for Ezekiel Hersey Derby in Salem.[5] The flush sheathing, whose purpose was to suggest stucco or smooth masonry, became widely used in the more elegant wooden houses built in Maine during the Federal Period. (It has the disadvantage, for present day viewers, of losing its smooth appearance from the effects of age and moisture.) Parris apparently did not favor Palladian windows; the rectangular fenestration

FIGURE 28. *Portland, Hugh McClellan House, by John Kimball, Sr. (1800). Photo: Historic American Buildings Survey, by Jack E. Boucher*

FIGURE 29. *Portland, Matthew Cobb House, corner of High and Free Streets, possibly by Alexander Parris (1801). Photograph courtesy of the Maine Historical Society, copy by Del Cargill*

is continued across the second story, but the central window is divided into three sections and has small brackets supporting a projecting lintel. The front entrance shown in Figure 29 is a mid-19th-century addition. Matthew "King" Cobb was a prominent merchant and shipowner whose fortune (along with that of his partner, Asa Clapp, and unlike those of the McClellans) survived both the Embargo and the War of 1812.[6] The house was taken down in 1895 at the time the present Libby Building was erected.

In the house built for Joseph Ingraham, Parris again utilized wooden pilasters the length of the second and third stories, this time rising from a slender belt course above the ground floor windows (but with no arches below) and supporting a well detailed entablature. Once again there is a rectangular, three-sectioned window in the center of the second story, this time with a semicircular window on the third story directly above. Slender portico columns set off a finely detailed, elliptical fanlight and horizontally reeded door frame. The house has passed through the hands of many owners, including the redoubtable William Pitt Preble in the mid-19th century. Unfortunately, much of its architectural distinction has been lost in its 20th-century conversion to apartments.[7]

Parris was also responsible for the house built for Richard Hunnewell in 1805, now the Portland Club, at 156 State Street. Interestingly, this house, except for its circular staircase, was markedly plainer than the preceding ones. (The present front entrance and Palladian window are the result of an early 20th-century "restoration.") While the ends are of brick, the original facade used ordinary clapboard and eschewed any but the simplest windows. The only exterior extravagance appears to have been a nicely detailed balustrade. The plan of the circular staircase, set off to one side of the central hall, again shows the influence of Bulfinch, who favored this scheme over the more conventional one.[8]

Portland also witnessed the building of a large number of two-storied "Federal" residences during the last years of the 18th and early years of the 19th century. While many of these were of wooden construction and were scaled down in degree from the largest mansions, they nevertheless exhibited an elegance and dignity that distinguished them from the average of the time. Good examples are (or were) the houses built for James Deering (c. 1804, now removed, along with its fine barn), Samuel McClellan (c. 1813, 57 Park Street), and, in Stroudwater, the James Means House (1797). The last named building, while quite plain on the exterior, has particularly fine interior wood and composition moldings, strongly reminiscent of the better houses of Salem, which may well have been the work of an important or itinerant craftsman. On a slightly smaller scale, the Daniel How House (c. 1799, 23 Danforth Street, Figure 30) offers a good example of the middle-class residence of the time. (It must be remembered that the "middle class" was, proportionately, a much smaller group in 1800 than now.) Recently restored, this building is notable for the good proportions achieved within an utterly simple form, and for its pleasing, classical front entrance. It demonstrates, once again, that the refinement and embellishment sometimes associated with Federal architecture are by no means its only virtues.

Before looking afield from Portland, it should be noted that the Federal period also produced a few interesting variations on the basic "foursquare" theme. There is, for example, the Prentiss Mellen House on Portland's State Street (1807, 166 State Street, later the home of William Pitt Fessenden) built next door to Richard Hunnewell's residence and offering a pleasing, yet formal contrast to it. Whoever designed the house was in advance of his time; he employed a plan that later became a convention of the Greek Revival by placing the entrance on one side and using a lateral hall, thus bringing together the two front parlors. Then there is the attractive, three-bayed house built for Zebulon Babson (c. 1827, 164 Danforth Street), with its off-center entrance and parlors on one side only.

FIGURE 30. *Portland, Daniel How House, 23 Danforth Street (c. 1799). Photo: William D. Shipman*

FIGURE 31. *Union, Ebenezer Alden House, exterior (1797–98). Photo: Joseph Marcus*

A number of double houses also may be seen, mostly dating from the decade 1825–35. Some Portland owners undertook to enlarge and modify their residences during this period, a practice that became common (some would say too common) as the 19th century progressed. A notable example was the Longfellow family, whose 1786 house (487 Congress Street—the first one in Portland to be built of brick) had a third story and hipped roof added in 1815 after a fire. The result in this case is a pleasing amalgam of the late Colonial and Federal, but with the former predominating (see Myers, p. 66 above).

Looking beyond Portland, one is impressed by the frequency with which distinguished examples of Federal architecture appear. There is hardly a coastal town of any size that does not have at least one very good Federal residence; some have several. Moreover, they come in all sizes, and many of them have a local, vernacular quality that gives them greater vitality than is possessed by the more strictly academic models. There are also a few inland towns having unusually good examples. Development of the District had not proceeded far enough by the early 1800's, however, to afford many opportunities for inland building on the Federal model—Paris Hill, Gorham, Hallowell, and a few of the western border villages being notable exceptions. While the distribution of Federal houses along the coast is fairly even, there are clusters evident in those towns which had achieved an exceptional degree of prosperity by or shortly after 1800. Wiscasset and Kennebunk are in this category. There was one Federal residence, moreover, which preceded most of the other good examples and dwarfed them in terms of both scale and elaboration. This was "Montpelier," built for General Henry Knox about 1795–97 in Thomaston.

Montpelier is a three-and-one-half-story building which originally stood on elevated ground facing south down the bay. (The present building is a c. 1930 reconstruction of the original edifice. The first location is easily identified by an existing two-storied, hipped-roof house which was one of the original outbuildings and later served as the railroad station.) The mansion has a brick basement set mostly above ground level, but partially hidden by supporting members of a balustraded porch extending around the entire structure. The formal rooms and entrances are thus on the "second" floor. The facade is seven bays wide, with a surface of matched wood sheathing and, most notably, a projecting, elliptical central section articulated by slender, engaged columns. The other sides have plain clapboards but retain the large corner quoins of the front. The building is surmounted by another balustrade, and also has a monitor extending between the chimneys with its own, third, balustrade. The design was unquestionably inspired by Bulfinch (it bears some resemblance to the house he built in Charlestown, Massachusetts for Joseph Barrell in 1792–93), but we do not know whether he was ever formally engaged by Knox. The house seems to have been assembled on site from sections, panels, pilasters, cornices, door and window frames, etc., made in the Boston shop of the Dunton Brothers.[9] This was much the largest residence built in Maine during the Federal period, and, indeed, was one of the largest in New England. The General's construction project in the then primitive area of Thomaston must have had an impact on local settlers comparable to that of Noah's.

Its impact, however, did not lead Maine builders to attempt similar examples elsewhere. While more modest variants of the curved bay appeared on the Lee-Tucker House in Wiscasset (1807) and the Reed House in Waldoboro (1814–16), the scale of Montpelier was probably too grand for even the wealthiest of Maine proprietors or merchants to contemplate adopting for their own use. Indeed, the house, and the style of living it implied, were too grand for General Knox; the building itself, as well as the estate of Mrs. Knox, who had inherited much of the original Waldo patent, were in ruins within a generation after his death (1806). Montpelier is thus in a class by itself. While it undoubtedly represents some of the best and most advanced ideas of the period, it is in no way characteristic of Maine architecture, then or since.

Perhaps the best examples of the more straightforward three-storied, hipped-roof mansions outside of Portland are to be found in the Kennebunk area and in Wiscasset. Both the Nathaniel Lord House in Kennebunkport and the Parsons-Bourne House in Kennebunk (both 1812) utilize this design and may have had a common builder. The Lord House demonstrates the simplest possible relation between height and mass (i.e., it resembles a square block) and benefits also from the relatively simple fenestration carried through at each floor level. The large rear ell was a late 19th-century addition. The house occupies a fine location, with its front lawn sloping down to the river, and is said to have been built during the years of distress (1812–14) by its owner in order to keep the local workmen employed. It also has a large octagonal cupola which is accessible directly by stairs entered from the side door and which, unlike most of the later examples, was actually used to sight incoming ships.

In Wiscasset, the Nickels-Sortwell House (1807–12) and the Abiel Wood House (1811–24) are also of this general type. The former is an unusually detailed version, in which the same combination of pilasters and arches used by Parris in Portland, and Bulfinch in Boston, is applied to a flush-sheathed wooden facade, this time with both a Palladian and a semi-circular window above the front entrance. While some of the details are nicely worked out, the facade seems a bit overwrought in contrast to the Portland mansions. (It is perhaps significant that both Alexander Parris and Samuel McIntire had reverted to more restrained, almost severe designs by 1805.) The Abiel Wood House on High Street is of the same general dimensions, but benefits from a somewhat plainer treatment of the front, and a fine, though not particularly

ornate, doorway and wooden fan. The twelve or more years required for its construction testify to the economic stresses experienced by Wiscasset during and after the War of 1812.

Wiscasset and Kennebunk were the only towns, outside of Portland, which could support any considerable number of these large, three-storied houses. There were a number of isolated examples in the smaller villages, however, at least three of which bear mentioning. The Holden-Frost House in Topsham (1806) has flush sheathing and a low hipped roof. It is very plain on the exterior (or was until the addition of a cupola in the mid-1800's and wings in this century), yet has a well-detailed interior including a ballroom in the rear part of the second and third floors. (The house was built partly to accommodate a Masonic lodge.) At the other end of our period, the Ellis Usher House in Bar Mills (c. 1830?) is of brick construction and has a gabled roof, with tall end chimneys and a fanlighted window on the third story directly above a similar, second-story, entrance. (This vertical repetition of the fan motif is also found on the John Ruggles House of similar vintage, c. 1827, in Thomaston and in the Tontine Hotel in Brunswick, 1828, see below.)

Probably the best example in brick, outside of Portland, of the three-storied mansion is the residence built for Samuel Rawson at Paris Hill in 1815. In scale the building is only slightly smaller than the McClellan houses, and the proportions are roughly similar. In this case, there is a minimum of exterior ornamentation, save for the balustrade and front entrance, with the result that the handsome appearance is a function almost exclusively of proportion and texture. The house complements other Federal and Greek Revival types in the village. Indeed, Paris Hill is perhaps the best example of the early 19th-century shire town in interior Maine. It is fortunate, in retrospect, that the village, seated as it was atop a hill, had no water power or other attributes that would attract "development" of any sort.

FIGURE 32. *Union, Ebenezer Alden House, parlor, showing carved woodwork.* Photo: William Cross

Although the three-storied town house is the model which we typically associate with Federal-period domestic architecture, examples of its two-storied counterpart are far more numerous, in Maine as elsewhere. Moreover, to the extent that "Federal" connotes an emphasis on proportion, symmetry, and fine detail, some of the middle-sized "country" houses of the period are every bit as representative of the style. Maine has some of the best two-storied examples to be found anywhere on the Eastern seaboard. Because of their large number and generally high quality, it is particularly difficult to choose among them in matters of architectural distinction. For present purposes, however, a somewhat arbitrary selection of six houses has been made, with a brief discussion of each. Most of the group have three or four outside chimneys, but in two of the earlier examples the chimneys

are paired, inside. Most of these buildings have a rectangular main block with the front and rear nearly one-third longer than the sides, and all but one have relatively flat hipped roofs. Except for the last one (1824), all have the customary Federal "four square" room arrangement and central hall extending from front to rear.

The earliest of these examples is the Silas Lee House in Wiscasset, built in 1792. This house, both chronologically and architecturally, belongs as much to the late Colonial as to the Federal period. It is a "brick-ender"—a not unusual choice of the period—but has a finely articulated facade of flush sheathing framed by Ionic pilasters and a cornice with both modillions and dentils. Unlike most of the flush sheathing of the

76

period, the boards in this case have uniform beveled edges which impart a horizontal accent to the structure similar to that of clapboard, while still retaining the elegance of matched siding. (The horizontal bevel was used in a number of Colonial designs.) A well-proportioned, elliptical porch with Ionic columns sets off a front entrance which, interestingly, eschews both overhead and sidelights. The hipped roof has a low monitor, a striking contrast to Montpelier, and a relatively flat pitch considering its early date. Although the large pilasters, set in from the ends and with their capitals well below the cornice, appear to lead a life of their own—again like those of a number of other late Colonial examples—the overall proportions and detail make this one of the best houses of its period in Maine.

The second example is the Ebenezer Alden House in Union, built by its owner in 1797-98. Alden was a Massachusetts craftsman who had come to Maine to work for General Knox on Montpelier. As the General's mansion was nearing completion, Alden chose an attractive inland site at the head of Seven Tree Pond in Union to build a home for himself. The result is an unusually well detailed, yet modestly scaled residence, again having a number of colonial as well as Federal attributes (Figure 31). The building has two and one-half stories and a gabled roof, and is of framed construction with brick filler between the vertical timbers; it has very narrow clapboards on the outside surface. Both north and west faces have central doorways framed by pilasters and attractive pediments over semi-circular fan lights. Prominent quoins, resembling those at Montpelier, mark the corners of the building, and there is a cornice surrounding the whole with finely detailed dentils. The interior parlors are marvels of carved woodwork (Figure 32). Many of the designs, for example in the door and fireplace frames, appear to have been taken from one of the widely used builders manuals of the period, William Pain's *The Practical House Carpenter* (London

1794, or Boston, 1796).[10] The house, which has been beautifully restored, testifies to the consummate skill and taste of this extraordinary craftsman.

The Benjamin Porter House in Topsham was built by the brothers Aaron and Samuel Melcher, III in 1802 (Figures 33 and 34). This is the largest of the houses in the present group, with a rectangular main section measuring fifty by forty feet, and two wings, one containing the original kitchen and pantry and the other, built somewhat later, used for servants' quarters. The house faces south across sloping lawns and, from a distance, almost resembles an English manor in its unusual setting. The facade has the usual five bays, with a three-sectioned central window on the second story complementing an unusually well-detailed front entrance with elliptical fan and sidelights. (There is some reason to believe these central features date from a slightly later period, perhaps the 1820's, but were also the work of Samuel Melcher, III[11]—whereas the small, bracketed roof over the front door is undoubtedly a late 19th-century addition.) Flush sheathing is used on the facade and is framed by very simple pilasters and a finely detailed modillion cornice. Slightly projecting entablatures surmount the first-story windows, giving them an elongated appearance, and the windows in the wings are scaled appropriately to the somewhat lower roof line.

The interior carving and composition moldings in the Porter House are perhaps the finest examples of the Adam influence in Maine. Several of the mantels are decorated with swags, urns, and cherubic figures, and framed by fluted bands (Figure 34). A number of door frames and cornices display unusual combinations of reeding, fluting, modillions, brackets, and even a rope molding. While it is known that the Melcher brothers were familiar with the carving and molding techniques employed by McIntire in Salem, there would appear to be no certain way of determining whether they were responsible for this extraordinary detail work. (Another

FIGURE 34. *Topsham, Benjamin Porter House,*
interior details. Photo: John McKee

FIGURE 33. *Topsham, Benjamin Porter House, by Aaron and Samuel Melcher III (1802). Photo: John McKee*

Topsham residence of the period, the Walker-Wilson House, has much the same type of detail, as does the Means House in Portland and a few others.) A final, interesting feature of the Porter House is the slightly off-center hallway—despite the door being centered on the facade—so designed as to permit a larger than usual (twenty-two by twenty-two foot) east parlor.

The last three of this group of six houses represent somewhat more formal variants of the Federal style, in which horizontal lines are emphasized even more than before, and rectangularity is accentuated by tall end-chimneys. The earliest of these is the Kavanaugh House, built in 1803 at Damariscotta Mills by the "imported" architect, Nicholas Codd. (There is continuing debate over Codd's origins: i.e., whether he came

from Ireland directly or simply down the coast from Boston.) James Kavanaugh, one of the wealthiest merchants of the area, chose a hilltop site overlooking both Damariscotta Lake and, at a distance, the river of the same name. And Codd proceeded to lay out a design of great charm and sophistication while still adhering to the "four-square" dictates of the period (see Figure 35).

Here both the facade facing east and the north side are of flush sheathing, with fluted Doric pilasters set in from the ends, a narrow belt course just above the first-floor windows, and a handsome modillion cornice. An amply scaled Palladian window is located immediately above, and effectively repeats, a simple but well-proportioned doorway with semi-circular fanlight. There are attractive balustrades over both the roof and the small portico, and the roof itself is

surmounted by a large octagonal cupola. An ell
and set of outbuildings admirably complement
the main block. Without question, this and the
Silas Lee House are Maine's most suave examples of the Federal, two-storied residence.

The interior of Kavanaugh has some particularly fine wood carving in its front parlors. Indeed, the northeast parlor, with its paneled fireplace wall and wainscoting, fluted pilasters enframing set-in shelves with arched openings and
an extremely intricate cornice, probably is
unique in Maine. While it is not wholly representative of the "Adam" style, it combines some
of the very best features of late Colonial and
early Federal woodworking. The main hall is
divided, front from back, and the front stairway
has a gracefully ascending U-shape. This divided
hall and turning staircase apparently was preferred by both Codd and Melcher to the full
length alternative, probably because it provided
a separation of functions (e.g., family and guests
vs. servants) and encouraged fewer drafts. The
interior of the Kavanaugh House, like most of
its contemporaries, becomes increasingly informal as one moves from front to rear, and the
kitchen and rooms in the ell are relatively simple, yet well proportioned and well lighted.

In 1806, Thomas McCobb had an unusually
fine house built in Phippsburg. Its construction
was aimed at least partly at spiting his step-
mother whom he felt had taken advantage of
an awkward family situation to preempt for her
own son what was, up to then, the most elegant
house in the immediate area. (This latter was
the McCobb-Hill-Minott House, built in 1774,
which is one of the best remaining examples of
the late Colonial style in Maine, see Myers, p. 63
above). Thus, the new residence came to be
called the "Spite House" (Figure 36). The
builder of the house is not known with cer-
tainty; it may have been one of the Melchers, or
possibly Nicholas Codd, or perhaps another
housewright brought in for the purpose. Whoever it was, created one of the finest pieces of
Federal architecture in New England. The

FIGURE 35. *Damariscotta Mills, James Kavanaugh
House, by Nicholas Codd (1803). Photo: Historic
American Buildings Survey, by Cervin Robinson*

house was moved by barge from Phippsburg to Rockport in 1925 by the late Donald Dodge. While the move meant leaving behind the original kitchen and outbuildings (not to mention the object of its original spite), it also meant restoration of a building that had deteriorated badly and might otherwise have been lost altogether.[12]

The builder approached the problem of designing this, a country facade, with determination to achieve classical objectives without excessive formality or simulated materials. He thus used a narrow clapboard throughout and limited himself to regular, six-over-six windows and a denticulated cornice. Since this might have resulted in too plain a design, he added a simple but elegant balustrade (the balusters are straight, square sticks, as they were in most of the staircases of the period), a well thought-out cupola whose scale is perfect for the house, and, most notably, a set of panels midway between first- and second-story windows, each with a carved, wooden swag. The front entrance is relatively plain, with a semi-circular transom and curved brackets supporting a small lintel. The fenestration is uniform throughout, although some changes in window placement on the sides were necessitated by the addition of wings after the 1925 move.

The interior of the "Spite House" is remarkable for its stately elegance without extensive detail. The main hall has a curved, flying staircase (which was reversed following the 1925 move) and a graceful arch separating the front two-thirds from the rear third. The more formal of the parlors, that on the southeast corner, has exceptionally good proportions but relatively restrained detailing. The double cornice is without modillions or dentils, and the wainscoting and chair rail make use of simple panels and only the periodic fluting of the Doric frieze. The fireplace frame consists mainly of a set of contrasting yet related panels without ornamentation. Indeed, the room is a study in how to achieve the balance and proportions that epitomize the Federal ideal without the use of extensive detail.

The last of the "country" examples is the Col. John Black House, built in Ellsworth in 1824–27 (Figure 37). This is without question one of the finest houses of the entire period and one whose beauty and refinement are enhanced by its woodland setting. The building is of red brick construction, with mostly white wood trim and details. While continuing a strong emphasis on the horizontal by the use of a low hipped roof and balustrade, the house departs from the Federal norm by having its front entrance in one of the wings and its hall running parallel to the long side of the main rectangle. This permitted the two front parlors to be joined and was to become a standard feature of many Greek Revival residences. The two wings are offset symmetrically and are only one story in height. There is a columned porch extending across the front, and both porch and wings have balustrades of a different design than that on the main roof. Although the builder of this house is not known, the basic design (except for the porch) appears to have been taken from Asher Benjamin's *The American Builder's Companion,* a manual which, along with those of William Pain, enjoyed wide circulation in New England in the early 19th century. The interior of the house is notable for its elegant woodwork details, spacious parlors, and for an elliptical flying staircase that was probably the finest in Maine up to that date.

While the preceding examples are chosen to illustrate the best features of Federal domestic architecture, "best" can, of course, be interpreted in more ways than one. Maine has so many excellent houses in the style that even a slight shift in criteria would produce a list of alternate examples as impressive as the foregoing. Moreover, the list would extend the distance of the entire coast, from "Coventry Hall" in York (1794) to the Brewer "Mansion House" in Robbinston (c. 1818). It would almost certainly include the Banks-Clark-Lord House in Kennebunk (front section built by Thomas Eaton c. 1803), the

FIGURE 36. *Originally Phippsburg, now Rockport, Thomas McCobb (Spite) House (1806). Photo: Historic American Buildings Survey, by Cervin Robinson*

Parker Cleaveland House in Brunswick (built by Samuel Melcher III in 1806), the Edward Robinson and John Ruggles Houses in Thomaston (the former by William Keith, 1825), the Benjamin Field and Thomas Whittier Houses in Belfast (c. 1801–1807), the Abbott and Johnston

Houses in Castine (c. 1800–1805), and the Thomas Ruggles House in Columbia Falls (Aaron Sherman, 1813).[18] And it would include any number of fine but less well known examples such as the Isaac Purinton House in Bowdoinham (c. 1800), the Vaughan Houses in Hallowell (c. 1797–1801), the Gates House in Machiasport (1807), and the several c. 1800–1820 residences in the Parsonsfield and Sheepscot-Alna areas. All of these conform to the "Federal" criteria for a distinctive residence: ample scale, economy of form, symmetry and regularity, low hipped roofs and other features emphasizing the horizontal, and just enough classical detail to lend touches of elegance.

In retrospect, there were perhaps two major drawbacks to these criteria in everyday use. First, the economy of form and some repeated classical details led to an absence of variety; many of the houses looked alike, and after about 1806 it was increasingly difficult in fact to build a "distinctive" residence. (This, of course, was and is a problem with many other building styles.) Second, the relatively low hipped roof, especially when bounded by a snow fence, was remarkably ill-suited to the Maine winter. One could be fairly certain that the more "classic" the house, the damper the interiors. Fortunately, advances in roof technology have recently provided these buildings with better protection than they had at the beginning.

But no advances in technology or in architectural practice have succeeded in improving their pleasing appearance, or their elegant and well lighted yet simply arranged interiors. Moreover, apart from their roofs they were surprisingly functional. For their block-like form, with a minimum of extensions and only moderately high ceilings (typically ten or eleven feet on the first story, eight to ten feet on the second) meant that relatively little heat or space was wasted, at least by comparison with some later 19th-century designs. While the presence of a central hall is sometimes thought to be inefficient on this score, it should be remembered that interior doors were generally kept closed during the winter months (as were the window blinds at night) and the fireplaces were designed and scaled to throw adequate heat. Indeed, the result was an early approach to zoned heating, with "individual" thermostats geared both to room temperature and to one's reluctance to go to the shed for firewood or more pressing needs.

The final category of domestic residence built during these years was the ubiquitous "cape" or "farmhouse." (But not all farmhouses were capes; many were two-storied, gabled roof structures, in effect stripped-down and usually smaller versions of the houses already discussed.) These must surely have outnumbered the larger, more formal houses many times over. They unfortunately do not figure in most works on architectural history, probably for two reasons. For one thing, they fit into a continuum of small-house construction extending all the way from the early 18th to the mid-19th century, with little that was unique to, or characteristic of, the "Federal" years. It is true there was a definite evolution in this design; by the 1820's, for example, the ceilings were higher, with correspondingly higher eaves and roof profiles, and end chimneys and modest central halls were not uncommon. For another thing, all but a few of these houses seem to have undergone continued "improvement," so that pure examples of the period are difficult to find.

There are, however, a few exceptions relevant to the present chapter. Here and there, mostly along the Maine coast, one comes upon small, story-and-a-half, houses with exceptionally attractive front entrances or unusual interior paneling and carving that can only date from the Federal years. Most have a few Greek touches as well, and some have had heavy hands laid upon them, but a few seem not to have enjoyed any face-lifting at all. There are several very good examples along U.S. Route 1 and 1A between Belfast and Bangor (Figure 38). Their histories are in most cases yet to be traced, awaiting the efforts of local historical groups or per·

FIGURE 37. *Ellsworth, Col. John Black House (1824–27). Photo: Deborah Thompson*

haps their owners. Another unusually good, but again unidentified, example of the Federal cape is in Columbia Falls, a few steps from the Ruggles House.

One other note is in order concerning the evolution of Federal design. By the 1820's increasing use was made of circular staircases in the larger houses, in place of the straight run with landing. While there were few which could match the beauty of the staircase in the Black House, there were many which utilized a tighter circle or ellipse to good effect. The 1820's also witnessed in some towns a new type of front entrance—one which was inset into the building a foot or two, usually in the form of an arch. This had the advantage of protecting the visitor from the elements, including rain or ice coming off the roof, but it was achieved at the cost of somewhat obscuring the then conventional fan and side lights,[14] and depriving them of the classical frame they enjoyed when mounted in line with the front wall. The inset doorway is particularly to be noted on a number of late Federal residences in Portland; the idea was then continued, usually with rectangular lights rather than a fan, well into the Greek Revival period.

FIGURE 38. *Searsport area, unidentified cape house.*
Photo: William D. Shipman

Apart from residences, most of the buildings erected in Maine during the period from 1790 to 1820 were devoted to community functions, either religious or civic. Commercial activity and primary education continued, for the most part, to be carried on in residences adapted or converted for the purpose. As in colonial times, the meetinghouse was a focal point for the community. It was customary, at least in the 1790's, for public business as well as religious services to take place in the local meetinghouse. Even so, these years can be said to mark an increasing differentiation of function in the larger communities of Maine, and it is not unusual for the single "public" place to be superseded by multiple structures, each with its own specific purpose, by the 1820's. Moreover, the years between 1815 and 1825 witnessed a considerable growth in mills and buildings devoted specifically to industrial pursuits.

Architecturally, the most interesting changes were the emergence of (1) "churches," with towers containing belfries and formal entrances, in place of the plainer meetinghouse, and (2) county and town buildings which served purely public needs such as the administration of justice. The new "church" form was perhaps a reflection more of increasing wealth than of religious sentiment; whatever the cause, it apparently was not difficult for parishioners to become enthusiastic over the erection of more monumental buildings. Thus, in the years following 1800, one community after another sought to create buildings which more properly symbolized the faith, and incidentally offered local builders an opportunity to display their talents to more than domestic advantage. (At least one city—Portland—enjoyed a meetinghouse that resembled a church well before 1800.) The result was a series of structures, usually though not always one to a town, reflecting the ambitions of the dominant local sect, typically Congregationalists. Within a few additional years, moreover, the growth of population, or simply an occasional wealthy patron, made it possible for rival groups to erect comparable edifices. While most of these buildings have been either demolished or adulterated by later 19th-century improvements, a few can still be considered to represent the best architectural style of the Federal years.

The first parish churches of Kennebunk and Belfast are notable examples. Parts of the Kennebunk structure actually date from the 1770's, but its present dimensions, tower, and belfry were determined shortly after 1800 by the local builder, Thomas Eaton. (The present front entrance, however, is a product of the 1830's.) The building is larger than most of its contemporaries, perhaps befitting the unusual affluence of its community, but it combines the essential features of the older, barn-like meetinghouse with the new emphasis on height and artistry in the form of elliptical and arched windows and clock faces in an octagonal belfry. The very tall, tapering spires frequently associated with early New England churches did not appear in Maine for another thirty years. The Federal model instead had a domed, usually octagonal, cupola set on a square base and topped by a spirelet with weathervane. The Kennebunk church was divided into two stories in the 1830's; hence most of the interior reflects a later style of church design.

The First Church in Belfast, built in 1818 by Samuel French, is a somewhat purer example of Federal style in that its tower is an integral part of the structure, rising, in front, from a projecting pavilion whose pedimented roof repeats the slope of the gable on the main building. This pavilion has a three-bayed front, with the central doorway slightly larger than those on the flanks (but all having later 19th-century door panels) and a Palladian window directly above. The other windows and shutters are rectangular but elongated in the manner of those on the first story of the Kennebunk church. The tower has a relatively wide, square base containing four clock faces and supporting a two-tiered, octagonal belfry plus a dome, spirelet, and weathervane (Figure 39). It is interesting to contrast the dimensions of this tower and front with the somewhat more attenuated proportions realized on a church of similar scale in Brunswick built by Samuel Melcher III in 1806–1807 (long since demolished).[15] The interior of the Belfast church is, like most of its contemporaries, barnlike and very well lighted, no doubt drafty, and has an attractive gallery around three sides. The present chancel is a later addition.

If the two foregoing examples of Federal period churches are characteristic of the general style, it is well to remember that there was also considerable variation. On the one hand, most Maine churches were smaller than these, and at least a few of the older style meetinghouses continued to be built. The Porter Meetinghouse, for example, was erected about 1818, the same year as the church in Belfast, yet it retained the stark simplicity of its 18th-century predecessors. Its remarkable state of preservation, in a rural area near the New Hampshire border, makes it one of the state's best examples of the older generation of meetinghouses. At the other extreme, there is the very fine First Parish (Unitarian) Church in Portland, built by John Mussey in 1825–26. This structure has the general shape of the period, but is built of granite ashlar. It reveals a consistent and tasteful use of arched doors and windows, extending even to the tower, and suggests an exceptional talent for employing stone contours for contrast and outline. Because of the rather drab appearance conveyed by the granite, it is all too easy to overlook the fine architectural details of this building.[16]

Most civic buildings of the period have not

FIGURE 39. *Belfast, First Church, by Samuel French (1818). Photo: Historic American Buildings Survey, by Cervin Robinson*

88

enjoyed the longevity even of the churches. Only a few of the early town buildings and court-houses remain, in part because local pride in civic improvements took the form of updating or replacing older structures, partly because the newer buildings were sometimes more economi-cal to operate; that process is, of course, still go-ing on. It is also true that many Maine communi-ties continued, at least until the 1820's, to use their meetinghouses for town functions (some still do) so that "town halls" were not a conven-tional building form until after the Federal pe-

FIGURE 40. *Wiscasset, Lincoln County Courthouse, by Tileston Cushing under the supervision of Nathaniel Coffin (1818–24). Photos Historic American Buildings Survey, by Cervin Robinson*

riod. It was otherwise with the county court-houses, however, for a safe, centrally located place for trials, deeds, and other public records was thought to be imperative even in these early years. The same was true for jails. The most obvious form of civic building, the state capitol, had to await the late 1820's in Maine's case, thus taking it out of our period.

County courthouses were, as a class, the most ambitious public buildings undertaken in Maine during the Federal period. Among these, the Cumberland County Courthouse, built in Portland in 1816 by or from the designs of John Kimball, Jr., was probably the largest and most refined, architecturally speaking. This building had two and one-half stories (with high ceilings), and was of brick construction, with a low hipped roof, balustrade, and a prominent open cupola. Its dominant architectural theme was strongly neo-classical: combinations of paired columns and pilasters extending the full two stories were spaced across the front, and the facade was broken by three projecting pavilions, the center one with a pediment. The columns and pilasters rested on large pedestals and had Ionic capitals which, in turn, "supported" an elegant entablature of a sort found ever after (at least through the 19th century) on courthouses across the land. Both the entrance and first-story windows were set into shallow, recessed arches, thus completing a sort of classical catalogue. This neo-classical design was, of course, a direct import from England, perhaps via Boston. But it gave Portland what must have been one of the finest public buildings of its size in New England. This particular building also housed the state legislature from the date of Maine's statehood (1820) to the completion of Bulfinch's capitol in Augusta in 1832. The Courthouse, which was located where the present City Hall stands, was taken down in 1858.

Among the smaller courthouses, the one built at Wiscasset (Lincoln County) in 1818–24 is particularly handsome (Figure 40). The builder was Tileston Cushing, working under the super-vision of Nathaniel Coffin.[17] This is a two-storied, brick example with pitched roof, pediment, and open belfry, and, as in the case of the churches, with the narrow side of the rectangle serving as the front. The first story of the Wiscasset courthouse has three arched bays centered on the main entrance which itself consists of an inset half dome. While the arch motif is repeated in the pediment, all of the windows are themselves rectangular and quite plain. The interior of the courthouse is well preserved, and the courtroom, with its wooden rails and fixtures and sharply outlined panels, is an exceptionally fine example of early 19th-century design.

The jails of the period were related to, though usually separate from, the courthouses. Two surviving examples are at Wiscasset (1809–11) and Paris Hill (1822–28). These are, respectively, three- and two-storied buildings of granite construction, with gabled roofs and small windows or apertures in their very thick walls. They now serve admirably as a museum (Wiscasset) and library (Paris Hill).

Another important class of buildings were those devoted to educational purposes. Since the evolution of this type of building is discussed separately in Chapter 7, a few comments on Federal period examples will suffice here. The group includes a series of "academies" established in several of the counties shortly after 1800, and Bowdoin College, founded in 1794 and located in Brunswick. Among the academies, the best architectural examples are probably those at Gorham (1805), Wiscasset (1807), and East Machias (Washington Academy, 1823). All are simple and relatively small in scale; only Wiscasset is of brick construction. Though simple in conception, the front elevations of both the Gorham and Washington (East Machias) academies evidence a combination of arches, pilasters and other classical details, all worked out in an appropriately academic manner; (see also Hansen, p. 257 below). The result is a rather nice complement to the Federal churches and residences of their respective villages. Some of the early academies were actually built as houses; the original building of Thornton Academy in Saco (c. 1811), for example, is virtually indistinguishable from the then popular three-storied, hipped-roof residence.

These academies typically were established by middle-class families desirous of obtaining a classical secondary education for their children. While there were a few genuine "schoolhouses" built during the period, most primary education continued to be carried out in local meeting-houses or in residences adapted to the purpose. And it is not unusual to find old and sometimes distinguished houses (for example, the Porter House in Topsham) which served for a time as boarding schools. One of the few early school-houses actually built for the purpose is that at Alna, dating from 1795. As befits its elementary function, it consists of one well-lighted room, with a hipped roof and a belfry; (also see Hansen, p. 256).

The earliest buildings put up by Bowdoin College were Massachusetts Hall (1799–1802), Maine Hall—then known as "the College" (1806–08), and the first chapel (1805), a wooden structure that served the purpose until the 1840's. All were designed and built by members of the Melcher family. Both Massachusetts and Maine

Halls are in existence today, but in somewhat modified form. The former is a severely plain, three-storied building with exceptionally pleasing proportions. Its roof originally had a lower pitch than at present, with very tall chimneys, and the only evidence of asymmetry was a one-story (now two-story) ell which served first as a kitchen and later as a laboratory (Figure 41). The building originally had a central hall with doorways at either end. The remaining (south) entrance is distinguished by a graceful door frame and fanlight whose beauty is an effective complement to the plain brick walls and windows. The interior has been largely rebuilt twice, once in 1873 and again in 1936.

The original Maine Hall was considerably more elegant than the present building and, indeed, probably was one of the more ambitious structures of its time in Maine. It shared with its successor four stories and a low, hipped roof. But the original building had a central, pedimented pavilion, a balustrade, and entrances on the front (long) sides. The structure was rebuilt in the plainer manner of Winthrop Hall (1821) after a fire in 1837. The 1805 chapel was a smaller version of the very fine church built by Samuel Melcher, III in 1806–07 just beyond the northwest corner of the campus (see above, p. 88)[18]

COMMERCIAL AND OTHER STRUCTURES

While commercial and industrial buildings were in common use during the Federal years, few examples remain. Most commercial activity took place in frame buildings that resembled the residences of the period (in some cases the functions were combined) and were located in what are now the older, central sections of our towns and villages, which sections have been largely rebuilt. The early industrial structures were apt to be larger than residences, though extremely plain and functional, and also of frame construction. Attrition by fire, remodeling, or demolition

was to be expected. The frame residence-shops of 1800–1820 were mostly replaced by improved, usually masonry, structures as the century wore on. Those that remain have been altered so many times that any resemblance to the original structures is improbable at best.

Outside the principal cities the older buildings which housed commercial enterprises have fared somewhat better. But these are (were) mostly taverns and inns whose form, once again, was identical to that of the residences of the time. To cite only two examples from the Federal years, the Peacock Tavern (c. 1790) on Route 201 south of Gardiner, and the Lindsey Tavern at Wells (1799), both served for many years as travelers' resting places. And the Whittier House in Belfast (1801, see above) also was built as a tavern.

Good examples are the Brick Store Museum in Kennebunk (1825) and the Tontine Hotel in Brunswick (1828)—the latter no longer standing. The former is a two and one-half storied, gabled-roof structure of brick construction, four bays wide, with off-center entrance, tall chim-

FIGURE 41. *Brunswick, Bowdoin College, Massachusetts Hall, by members of the Melcher family* (1799–1802). *Old photograph courtesy of Bowdoin College Archives, copy by James Pierce*

If examples are to be found of Federal-period commercial buildings having a non-domestic architecture—other than shipyards, sawmills, and textile mills, virtually all of whose pre-1825 models have long since disappeared—it is necessary to stretch somewhat the confines of the word "Federal" and examine what was being done in the mid- to late 1820's. Here one begins to see the emergence of brick structures that were meant to be stores, and hotels that could not be mistaken for residences.

neys, and prominent granite lintels and sills. The Tontine Hotel, built by Anthony Raymond, was considerably larger. It was of frame construction, with four stories, and exhibited the form of an oversized or extended Federal house, complete with shuttered windows, tall chimneys, and a second-floor doorway with fan and side-lights. Confirming its post-Federal vintage, a Gothic window appears in the Greek fourth-story pediment. A balustraded porch across the west and south fronts gave it some shaded bench space (as well as a viewing platform) and the general appearance that came to be associated with the 19th-century, small-town, hotel.

Other notable structures of the period included military buildings and lighthouses. Unfortunately, Maine's early forts appear mostly to have disappeared or been rebuilt later in the century. The old blockhouse at Fort Edgecomb, however, built in 1808–09 by Moses Porter, is a good example of the early yet relatively simple fortification put up at control points on the major rivers and estuaries. The building is of wood construction, hexagonal in shape (an advance over the earlier square structure), and the upper floor has the overhang inherited from the 17th century (see Candee above, pp. 27–33). A tall, narrow cupola affords the necessary observation post. The Old Powder House at nearby Wiscasset (c. 1813) is another example of the military or, better, "preparedness" genre—in this case a small cylindrical building of brick, with a single opening and conical roof. In Portland, a wooden observation tower was built atop Munjoy Hill in 1807 by Lemuel Moody. The building is eighty-six feet in height, octagonal and tapering toward the top, and shingled overall. The tower still commands a sweeping view of the harbor. It is historically significant as being one of the very few such towers remaining anywhere, and for having narrowly escaped the devastating fire of 1866.

Finally, there are the lighthouses of the period. Both Portland Head Light and the original light on Seguin Island (at the mouth of the Kennebec River) properly date from the 1790's, and a number of other towers were built for this purpose shortly before and during the 1820's. Again, most have been rebuilt; only the lower part of the tower (below the belt course) at Portland Head is original. These lighthouses were among the top priority projects of the new Federal government, and their construction was considered to be a matter calling for the utmost care in engineering and masonry execution. The several towers dating from the period 1820–30 (e.g., Owls Head, Pemaquid) and still standing after one hundred and fifty years of Atlantic weather, attest to the quality of that construction.

4

PART 2

The Greek Revival:

from about 1835 to 1850

Denys Peter Myers

THE PERIOD DURING WHICH THE GREEK RE-vival style flourished in Maine was one of rapid development and profound change. The peak years of the style were from around 1835 to about 1850, although there are both earlier and later buildings to be found in Maine that exhibit the characteristics of the Greek Revival. During those years the style so impressed itself upon the landscape of Maine that Greek Revival buildings (and those in the preceding Federal manner), rather than Colonial buildings, now seem to predominate, in spite of later structures. Much of Maine, particularly outside the cities, appears relatively unchanged since the first half of the 19th century.

The decades from 1820, toward the end of the Federal period, to 1860, when the Greek Revival had run its course, were, by and large, a time of economic boom. In 1820 Maine had a popula-tion of 298,335, but by 1860 the inhabitants num-bered 628,279. There was some decline in rural areas, although seven new counties were formed, but urban growth accelerated. Portland in-creased from 8,581 to 26,341 persons during those forty years. Augusta became the capital of the state in 1832, Bangor achieved city status in 1834, and, at the end of the era under discussion, the manufacturing town of Lewiston received its city charter in 1861. The general prosperity of the period was certainly not affected adversely by Maine's change from a district ruled from Massachusetts to an independent state in 1820. Another salutary factor was, of course, the peace that prevailed from 1815 until the outbreak of the War of the Rebellion in 1861. (The argu-ment with Great Britain over the Canadian border in 1838–39, called the "Aroostook War," resulted in little more than extravagant congressional appropriations for defense and the consequent building of Fort Knox and Fort Kent.)

Many of the traditional pursuits continued. For example, in 1848 over half the adult males in the coastal areas were employed in some phase of shipping, and in 1850 Bath ranked fifth among American ports in the amount of its trade. Lumbering and, to a lesser extent, farming retained their importance, but the trend toward urbanization, slight by modern standards though it was, and the rise of manufacturing and new forms of transportation produced building types hitherto unknown. The industrial complexes and their housing will be considered in a later chapter (see Péladeau, p. 214). The coming of steamboats and railroads, with the resulting increase in trade, demanded the construction not only of mills but also of warehouses, banks, commercial blocks of stores, and such civic monuments as the splendid Portland Merchants' Exchange. The first Boston to Portland steamboat service was inaugurated in 1823. The year 1836 saw the first rail line in Maine, and by 1842 Portland and Portsmouth and Boston were connected by rail. The 11 miles of Maine railroad in 1840 had risen to 472 miles by 1860. The travel stimulated by these events soon led to the replacement, in the cities and towns, of the old inns and taverns by the new form of accommodation for wayfarers, the hotel. The growth of the cities led to an increase in land values that may account for the popularity of double houses and houses sited with their narrow, or gable, ends toward the street.[1]

While this accelerated pace of change in general conditions certainly had its effect upon the building trades, changes in building materials and methods, not to mention a most significant development, the rise of architecture from a craft to a profession, had even more profound effects on the practice of building in Maine. The general changes produced new demands; the adoption of new materials and methods, and the appearance of professional architects for the first time, produced new forms. The extensive use of granite, and the widespread use of granite and brick in combination, as well as the greatly increased use of brick itself, utterly changed the appearance of the few urban centers in Maine. Toward the very end of the 1850's, the use of the new balloon frame wholly altered the method of erecting wooden frame buildings and rapidly replaced the less economical traditional heavy frame. The central manufacture of millwork and ornamental trim gradually arose and eventually replaced much work formerly performed on site. This latter situation contributed greatly to the use of stock trim over wide areas and the consequent decline in individual inventiveness and regional variations on basically similar themes.

The Greek Revival was, it cannot be too often emphasized, one among a number of "styles" used, sometimes quite superficially, for basically similar buildings. The romantic eclecticism of the age offered a choice of Greek, Gothic, or Italianate forms (to mention only the leading fashions) to be applied to more or less the same structure. It should be borne firmly in mind that, although the Greek Revival predominated, the first phase of the Gothic Revival and the Italianate Revival were contemporaneous with it. It is a vast oversimplification to say that Greek was followed by Gothic and Gothic by Italianate. One did not, in any strict sense, follow the other, although, by the 1850's the Italianate became the predominant mode. The previous Federal period had drawn upon a commonly accepted, if somewhat limited, vocabulary of form. The succeeding period saw the acceptance of connotative, literary values and romantically assigned symbolism in architecture. It is paradoxical that the Greek Revival, a "classical" style, was romantic in its inspiration and its attempted evocation of distant climes and times. It seems fair to set off the word "classical" in quotation marks, because in practice the style was used with great freedom and inventiveness. Greek precedents provided (in published form) certain basic proportions and accurately rendered details, but these details were varied and combined in wholly fresh ways. As the proportions did not differ significantly from those used during the Federal period, the new manner was very readily taken up by builders used to working in the older way. All a country carpenter-builder needed to produce an up-to-date look was to replace his more delicate Federal trim with heavier Greek Revival details. Surely this accounts in part for the readiness with which the new fashion found acceptance. The many plan books and pattern books published during this period were certainly a help to vernacular builders.[2] They served as books of etiquette for the polite use of Greek Revival manners.

Only one professional architect, Alexander Parris (1780–1852), appears to have worked in Maine (early in his career, at that) during the Federal period (see Shipman, p. 70 above). In the years after 1825 the situation changed radically. While most buildings, as had always been the case before, were built by carpenter-builders, most *important* buildings erected after 1830 were architect-designed. Evidence for Maine's prosperity during the three decades before the Civil War can be found (if evidence aside from the best buildings themselves is needed) in the fact that a number of nationally known architects were commissioned to design Greek Revival edifices there, not to mention those who designed Gothic Revival and Italianate structures.

Charles Bulfinch (1763–1844) was already Architect of the United States Capitol when he was asked to design the State House at Augusta. The design of the Tremont House in Boston by Isaiah Rogers (1800–1869), the leading hotel architect of his day, profoundly influenced the design of the Bangor House, although Rogers had no direct connection with that building. Ammi Burnham Young (1800–1874), while he was Supervising Architect of the Treasury Department, designed the United States Custom House in Bangor in the Greek Revival manner with Italianate touches, as well as other less Greek government buildings. While that curious character Orson Squire Fowler (1809–1887), a phrenologist and theorist rather than an architect, may not have designed anything in Maine, his book on octagons was certainly responsible for a number of Maine houses, including a few Greek Revival ones.[3] The slightly less famous architects Richard Bond (1797–1861) and William Washburn (1808–1890) also built Maine buildings. Bond was the designer of the Portland Merchants' Exchange and was based in Boston. Washburn, designer of several Maine hotels, was also based in Boston but maintained a Portland office in partnership with Edwin Lee Brown (1827–1891) in 1855. Brown is not known to have designed in the Greek Revival manner.[4]

The 1856 *Maine Business Directory* listed 10 architects distributed between Portland, Bangor and Bath, and 1,580 carpenters living in 340 communities. These men ranged in skill, apparently, from rather unsophisticated country carpenters to architects whose work fully equalled that of any out-of-state architect in quality. Charles G. Bryant (1803–1850) and his partner Lyman Seavey (1807–1886) were responsible for much of the finest Greek Revival work in Bangor. Col. Benjamin S. Deane (1790–1867), another Bangor architect, designed outstanding churches in Hancock County. The architect and builder Charles H. Pond (1802–1884) practiced in Bangor and vicinity, and the Skowhegan master carpenter, carver, and builder Joseph Bigelow worked both in Skowhegan and Bangor.

Calvin A. Ryder (1810–1890) was the designer of a fine church and the two most splendid Greek Revival houses in Belfast as well as other buildings in the Penobscot Valley and houses of later styles in Cambridge, Massachusetts (also see Miller, pp. 152 and 177). Anthony Coombs Raymond (1798–1879) built churches in Sagadahoc County and elsewhere that were an unorthodox blend of Greek and Gothic elements, although the basic proportions were more classical than otherwise. The Thomaston builder-architects William R. Keith (1799–c.

1875), Albert Morton (1820–?), and James Overlock (1813–?) built Greek Revival houses of specific local character. Thomas Lord (1806–1880) of Blue Hill listed 83 vessels, 84 dwellings, 12 schoolhouses, 14 meetinghouses, 15 barns and sheds, 10 stern moldings and figureheads, and 250 coffins among his works. John D. Lord (1797–1888) was the designer of the Hallowell House, a hotel now called the Worster House. In Fairfield, Charles D. Lawrence (1819–1907) built Greek Revival houses to which he often added other stylistic elements such as Gothic bargeboards. It is worth noting that later in his life Lawrence became a manufacturer of architectural millwork.[5] That shows quite clearly a trend of the times.

PUBLIC BUILDINGS

Because there are so many Greek Revival buildings deserving at the very least a passing mention, it has been found convenient to group them in categories and to discuss only major examples or single representatives of various types in detail while relegating others to brief references. The first category to be considered is public buildings erected under government auspices, whether federal, state, county, or local. The Greek Revival style was favored for public buildings as a suitably simple and practical mode.

During the years 1829–32 the first really major public building in Maine was constructed in Augusta from the plans of Charles Bulfinch. While the State House was still transitional rather than fully Greek Revival in design, its restrained, almost severe form and grey Hallowell granite material showed strong influence from the new, more strictly neo-classical trend. The order chosen was Roman Doric of a modified type, and the monolithic columns were set over the eight piers of a rusticated arcade. In spite of the use of arches on the first floor below the colonnade and above the second-floor windows, and the Roman order, one has only to compare this Bulfinch state house with his Massachusetts State House of 1798 (designed in 1787), which it so much resembles in general composition, to perceive the difference between the Federal style and that of the succeeding period. Instead of the red brick with white wooden trim of rather delicate character and elaborate detail, the newer building is monochromatic and eschews applied ornament. The one remaining portion of the original building is the facade, now a 146-foot central section of the present 319-foot-long front. The central eleven bays fronted by the pedimented octastyle colonnade set on its arcade have survived, but the comparatively low dome crowned by a domed cupola surrounded by an annular colonnade and set upon a square podium has been replaced by a new dome 185 feet high. The first exterior change occurred in 1891, when a west three-storied wing was added. Between 1901 and 1910 the rebuilding, from plans by G. Henri Desmond, took place. The old front (Figure 42), a masterly design, is now a gem reset in a newer matrix.[6]

Another granite public building in Augusta, the Kennebec County Courthouse, actually antedated the State House, having been designed in 1828 and completed in 1830. The pedimented portico of the Courthouse is therefore the first temple-fronted motif in the Greek Revival style erected in Maine. The architect, James Cochran, inset his hexastyle center capped by a rather unclassically high gable between two hip-roofed end pavilions. Hence, the facade is all in one plane. The first floor of the portico is treated in the most austere manner possible; it is composed of six perfectly plain square piers supporting un-

FIGURE 42. *Augusta, Maine State House, by Charles Bulfinch (1829-32). Old photograph courtesy of the Maine Historical Society*

molded lintels of the same dimensions. Upon this base, almost cyclopean in its effect, is an unfluted Doric colonnade that departs from Greek precedent only by the placement of the columns on bases. An elegant cast-iron railing between the columns contributes the only light touch to alleviate the forceful severity of the building. The wooden belfry on a square podium is not part of the original design but was apparently added within a few years after 1830. The belfry and end pavilion roofs were formerly crowned by crenelated parapets. The gable window is a later alteration, and the rear wing dates from 1851. Otherwise, this fine exterior is unchanged.

Norumbega Hall in Bangor, while not, strictly speaking, built under any government auspices, was authorized by legislative charter and erected as a civic enterprise. It was designed by William G. Morse and built in 1854–55 under the supervision of Leonard L. Morse. The building measured 58 feet wide and 165 long and rose about 60 feet from entrance level to eaves. The entire structure rested on granite piers in the Kenduskeag Stream between the bridges carrying Central Street at the front end and Franklin Street at the rear. The first floor had fourteen stalls for produce sellers and separate stairs to the concert hall above. The hall above the market was as wide as the building and 117 feet long with a 39-foot-high ceiling. The floor had a seating capacity of some fifteen hundred people, and about five hundred more could be seated in the galleries. Norumbega Hall had an admixture of Italianate elements, arched rusticated entrances and a broken pediment over the middle triple window among others, but the basic design, with its Doric pilasters and anthemion-ornamented triangular pediment panel, was still Greek Revival. This market hall was destroyed in the Bangor Fire of 1911.

The Spring Street Firehouse was built by the City of Portland in 1837. It is a granite-fronted brick building with its wooden gable end fronting the street. The three second-floor bays are articulated by four monolithic granite Doric pilasters. The central doorway rises above the belt course on which the pilasters rest. The rough surfaces of the Kennebunkport granite ashlar courses give the facade an appearance of rugged strength. This civic building is unusual in that it was built to serve two quite disparate purposes; it housed a volunteer fire company on the first floor and the West Female Grammar School on the second. There was also a wardroom at the rear of the first floor. The school room, later altered for firemen's quarters, measured forty by seventy feet. This multipurpose structure continued to serve as a firehouse until 1966 and is now a fire-fighting museum. Horse stalls and the vertical hose-drying room are still intact.

The United States Government did not undertake any significant building campaign, except for engineering works, until the 1850's in Maine. The custom houses and post offices then built were Italianate, but certain engineering works of the period erected by the national government show strong neo-classical influence. Fort Knox at Prospect, for which appropriations had been made in response to the so-called Aroostook War, was begun in 1846 and finished, insofar as it ever was finished, in 1864. Col. Reuben Staples Smart was the engineer-architect of that massive fort. Built of granite from nearby Mount Waldo, Fort Knox rests atop a steep promontory commanding a portion of the Penobscot River opposite Bucksport. The quarry-faced ashlar wall is pierced by a Doric pilaster-flanked gate with a triangular pediment. Aside from the simple granite trim of the gate, there is no stylistic detail, yet the beautifully cut stone work and the quality of the construction certainly merit recognition as architecture. Another great fort designed by Col. Smart, Fort Gorges, was built, beginning in 1858, on an island in Portland Harbor. It is a half octagon in plan, like Fort Sumter in Charleston Harbor, but it is built of granite, whereas the southern fort is brick. The entrance to Fort Gorges is like that at Fort Knox. These two granite forts were the largest

United States construction projects in Maine before the Civil War.

Major public works included lighthouses as well as forts. The light tower built, probably from the plans of Lt. W. B. Franklin, on Boon Island in 1854 was perhaps the finest of its day on the Atlantic coast. It is an octagonal granite tower with walls that batter from a base diameter of twenty-five feet to a diameter of twelve-and-a-half feet at the top. The total height of tower and lantern is 118 feet. A cavetto cornice (an Egyptian form) caps the tower below the lantern. Boon Island Light is a classic example (in both senses of the word) of its type. At the end of the breakwater that projects into the harbor from the South Portland shore stands a little light that is as overtly Greek Revival as can be, except that its order is Roman, not Greek, Corinthian. Portland Breakwater Light, first built in 1855 and re-erected in 1875, is a circular cast-iron structure backed with brick. The scale is small, the diameter being only eleven feet and eight inches. The design is based upon the most popular Greek Revival precedent for cupolas, the Choragic Monument of Lysicrates in Athens. The proportions of this delightful little building are rather more squat than those of the Athenian original, and the order does not, strictly speaking, correspond correctly with the original, but only a purist would wish to be strict or correct when looking at this most charming of all Maine lighthouses. The antefixes crowning the cornices of both drum and lantern fret the sky in an almost playful way. As all this classical detail is executed in that then most up-to-date of materials, cast iron, Portland Breakwater Light may be taken as typical of its time—a building using old forms but a new material.

The straightforward practicality of the Greek Revival style, in its simplified form, made it the most frequently chosen style for commercial buildings of all types, blocks of stores, banks, hotels, and so on, until about 1860 in Maine. Of all the Greek Revival buildings ever built in Maine, certainly the most magnificent was the Portland Merchants' Exchange. It was designed by Richard Bond and was built between 1835 and 1839 (Figure 43). This Kennebunk granite monument to commerce was 72 feet wide by 136 feet long and was fronted by a Greek Ionic octastyle colonnade of 26-foot-high monoliths weighing thirteen tons apiece. Square piers at the first-floor level supported the colonnade. Behind the parapet blocks with their acroteria rose a twenty-five-foot-high Pantheon dome sixty-three feet in diameter. Unfortunately, Portland could not afford masonry vaulting, so the building was not fireproof. On January 8, 1854, the splendid Portland Merchants' Exchange, the purest example of the Greek Revival style in the state, was gutted by fire and subsequently demolished.[7]

An equally unusual commercial building, Mercantile Row in Bangor, merits special notice. Attributed to Bryant and Seavey (Charles G. Bryant and Lyman Seavey), it was built in 1833–34 and was, after much deterioration, only recently demolished. Mercantile Row was a wedge-shaped group of three-storied brick stores with trabeated granite first floors. These were not in themselves remarkable, but the apex of the group, faced with granite ashlar, had an elliptical central bay crowned by a very richly ornamented blind cupola bearing a clock. The hipped roof of this front element had an elaborate cast-iron railing. The circular cupola had paneled pilasters, carved anthemion panels, a wreathed frieze, and an elaborately carved parapet. The building was so well esteemed that it was depicted on the cover of the sheet music for a composition by Oliver J. Shaw titled the "Bangor March" (Figure 44).

It was possible to achieve appropriately classical effects by the simplest means as well as by the elaborate enrichments used by the designers of Mercantile Row in Bangor. A modest little two-storied red brick bank built around 1840 in Topsham depends almost entirely upon its proportions to gain its effect. It stands with its gable end toward the street, and the gable is of the cor-

FIGURE 43. *Portland, Merchants Exchange, by Richard Bond (1835–39). Old photograph courtesy of the Maine Historical Society*

rect low pitch. Four plain brick pilaster strips with unmolded stone blocks for capitals articulate the three-bayed facade. Nothing could be simpler, yet this unassuming bank is quite as classical as its much grander contemporaries.

Granite was so highly regarded that it was occasionally used merely as a facing, a kind of stone veneer, so to speak. It was so used in the Bangor building just mentioned, and in Hallowell a brick three-storied three-bayed store built in 1809 was refaced with granite around 1846. It stands at 156 Water Street and is known simply as the Granite-Fronted Building. Adjacent three- and four-bayed three-storied stores on Main Street in Ellsworth probably date from around 1845. Their facades are quarry-faced and carry no moldings whatsoever. This trabeated design appears to be structural, but although it looks almost ponderously heavy and solid, it is actually only skin deep. Alterations to the first-floor shop fronts and a sharp look at the return of the right-hand wall just below the cornice reveal the deception. The third-floor windows of the left-hand store retain their six-over-six-light sash. A genuinely structural use of granite may be seen in the Granite Store, sometimes called the Old Salt Store, in Sullivan. The date of construction appears to have been some time between 1835 and 1855. The walls are composed of rough random-laid but coursed ashlar. Only the proportions of the three-bayed and gabled front show classical influence.

Granite construction, as has been already noted, took the form of a post and lintel (trabeated) system. By 1840 this was the common mode of building first-floor store fronts in commercial blocks. In some instances this structural system was used for the second story as well. In Saco a particularly fine example at 192–206 Main Street has beautifully finished granite panel infilling between the bearing members, thus producing a facade entirely of granite. The lefthand end of the block has a brick third story added about 1860 to the original part built, perhaps, as early as 1840. In Belfast there are two stores on

NORTH FRONT OF MERCANTILE ROW WITH A N.E. DISTANT FRONT OF THE BANGOR HOUSE

FIGURE 44. *Bangor, Mercantile Row, by Charles G. Bryant and Lyman Seavey (1833–34). Sheet music for the "Bangor March," courtesy of Earle G. Shettleworth, Jr., copy by Wendell A. Ray*

FIGURE 45. *Searsport, Business block (c. 1840). Photo: Richard Cheek*

FIGURE 46. *Portland, Mariners Church (1828–29).*
Photo: Historic American Buildings Survey, by
Jack E. Boucher

Main Street that appear to date from about 1830 and that are similar in construction to the Saco examples. A row of three stores of what may be termed this granite-frame type stands in Searsport and may date from around 1840 (Figure 45). In this instance, this very handsome row has brick infilling on the second floor instead of the granite to be seen in the Saco and Belfast stores just mentioned. As in a section of the Saco row, one of the Belfast stores has a later brick third story.

In most commercial buildings of the period, however, the granite post and lintel construction was confined to the first, or shop-front, floor with standard brick masonry used above. One of this type, a block on Fore Street near Center Street in Portland, appears to date from about 1845. It is two-and-a-half stories high and is worthy of notice because it is one of the few examples having the low rectangular entablature windows so characteristic of Greek Revival domestic work. Good, standard, three-storied examples are to be seen opposite the above-mentioned granite-framed stores on Main Street in Belfast. They may date from about 1840. The Johnson Block on High Street in Belfast has the usual trabeated granite first floor. The two brick upper floors, however, are treated a bit more elaborately than is usually the case. The seven bays (the center bay is blind above the first floor) are articulated by brick pilasters. A granite tablet centered on the upper facade bears a date of 1847. The Johnson Block is also worth notice because the pharmacy (Gould's) that occupies the righthand street floor has its original shelving and a stamped metal ceiling that is, although considerably later, also of interest. The Odd Fellows Block of about 1845 in South Berwick is another good example of the type. The first floor is substantially unchanged, and one second-floor window has its original twelve-over-twelve-light sash. Day's Block in Damariscotta is quite a large building, having ten bays and three and a half stories. It is dated 1850. Unlike the others in this group, it has a brick masonry first floor instead of the usual granite post and lintel system. The entrance of Day's Block is graced by a distyle Doric portico. In Rockland the Rankin Block of 1853 is one of the more usual type. It rather resembles the Odd Fellows Block in South Berwick. Business blocks of this period, when sited on corner lots, often effected the transition from one street front to the other by means of a curved bay at the corner. In Ellsworth there are two examples having rounded corner bays at the intersection of Main and Water Streets. They appear to date from around 1845. One last example of this type, the Glidden-Austin Block of 1845 or thereabout in Newcastle, may be mentioned as having quarry-faced granite on the first floor facade instead of the more frequently seen smoothly dressed stone. This three-storied block was built as a ship chandlery and a tenement for shipyard employees.

Another new commercial type of building, the hotel, also made its appearance in Maine during the 1830's. In 1828–29 the Tremont House by Isaiah Rogers, the prototype of the modern hotel as distinct from the inn, was built in Boston. In 1830 a full description of the Tremont House illustrated by many detailed plates was published.[8] The Bangor House of 1833–34, as originally designed by Charles G. Bryant and built by his partner Lyman Seavey, resembled Rogers's Tremont House rather closely, even to the trick of masking the angle where the Union Street and Main Street elevations join by using an elliptical bay on the Main Street side, so that the acute angle can be "read" as actually having the expected forty-five degrees. The distyle Greek Doric entrance portico (here carried out in wood instead of granite, as in the Boston example) is another point of resemblance. Most significant, however, is the interior distribution. The original plan was, in all essentials, a mirror image of Rogers's published Tremont House plan. The Boston facade was granite; the Bangor hotel is, except for the basement story, brick. The scale is quite large, the original Union

Street elevation running some 112 feet. Even in its much-altered present state, the Bangor House merits consideration as one of the very few surviving palace hotels of its period. Originally the basement story was concealed by a granite podium, or "piazza." When the grade of Union Street was lowered, the podium was removed, a rusticated arcade was inserted beneath the old Doric portico, and the basement became the entrance story. In 1869 the courtyard between the Main Street wing and the east wing was occupied by a new one-storied billiard hall. By 1872, when a portico was added to the Main Street entrance, the principal lobby had been moved from the Union Street side. In the following year a major addition, the mansard-roofed Shaw Wing, extended the building back to May Street. That wing burned down in 1954. In 1895–98 a new kitchen wing and the present wing extending east along Union Street were added. The final major change occurred in 1901, when the top floor of the original section was built.

Another brick hotel was built at the same time in Hallowell. Begun in 1832, a year earlier than the Bangor House, the Hallowell House (now called the Worster House) is less advanced in design than its Bangor counterpart. It, too, has been altered, although not as radically so as the Bangor House. The designer of the Hallowell hotel was John D. Lord. In Biddeford the Thatcher Hotel of about 1840 still stands. It is a brick building of three stories with a dormered slate roof. The exterior of the Thatcher Hotel is noteworthy for the fine sweeping curve that melds the two main elevations of its corner position. Bath once had a hotel whose facade was based closely on that of the Tremont House. Designed by William Washburn (who had already "cribbed" Rogers's Tremont House design and plan for his United States Hotel of 1840 in Boston), the Sagadahock House was built in 1848–49 by Isaiah Coombs from Washburn's plans. That Bath hotel burned in 1894.

Churches, as distinct from meetinghouses,

were already built in considerable numbers in Maine during the Federal period. In the ensuing Greek Revival times, churches were built in greater numbers and far more varied forms than previously. Churches were one of the building categories contributing most significantly to both townscape and landscape in 19th-century Maine. The Mariners' Church in Portland gives no visible hint of the religious use for which it was designed (Figure 46). It was built in 1828–29 for a total cost of $51,000, a rather considerable sum for that day. No record of the architect has so far come to light, but it should be noted that the granite front, with its arcuated second story sandwiched between two trabeated floors, quite closely resembles the facades of the warehouses designed by Alexander Parris to flank his Quincy Market of 1825 in Boston. The Mariners' Church is also not unlike East India Marine Hall in Salem, built in 1824 from designs by Thomas Waldron Sumner (1768–1849).[9] The church occupies a trapezoidal site on Fore Street between Moulton and Market Streets. The rounded corners of the granite front disguise the lack of forty-five-degree angles. The facade is about eighty-two feet wide and has a high gable above the third floor. The trabeated and arcuated granite construction allows the maximum amount of window area possible before the introduction of cast-iron fronts (very rare in Maine) in 1848. The sides of the building are of conventional brick masonry. This multi-purpose building is really a cross between a commercial structure and a church, as the first two floors were designed to produce rent from business premises to support the church that occupied the forty- by sixty-five-foot chapel on the third floor.

Masonry churches of whatever form are rare in Maine. (Only three of the twenty-six mentioned in this chapter are *not* built of wood.) The Falmouth Congregational Church, built in 1833, is a temple-fronted brick building with columns of stone. The gable is rather high, and the four fluted Greek Doric columns (the shafts are in two sections) are rather too widely spaced for a truly classical effect. The gable has a large louvered lunette. The relatively light trim of the two front entrances has an elongated meander (Greek key) pattern. The flanks of the building are treated as shallow brick arcades within which the arch-headed windows are set, rather in the Federal manner. The portico of this still transitional building seems added to, rather than integrated with, the overall design, since the arcade motif of the sides projects upward to the cornice, and the entablature of the temple-front ends abruptly at the front wall. Notwithstanding what must, from the strictly academic point of view, be seen as infelicities of design, this well constructed country church has considerable charm.

The Swedenborgian Church of 1843 in Bath (Figure 47) is correctly proportioned according to classical canons. No other church in Maine so accurately reflects the ancient temple form. As the temple was very rarely used in Maine as a precedent for church buildings, this handsome tetrastyle Greek Doric church must surely be deemed both atypical and extraordinarily classical. There are no windows in the entrance front, and the side windows are masked by free-standing square piers when viewed from most angles. Thus, the building appears as much like a windowless marble Greek temple as a fenestrated wooden building can. The original aspect, however, was slightly less strictly classical than at present, because a partial rebuilding after the roof fell in from an excessive accumulation of snow in 1920 changed the plane of the side walls to narrow the interior. The original pilasters of the flanks were thereupon altered to free-standing piers. This beautifully designed and skillfully altered church epitomizes the romantic longing for classical antiquity that so typified the cultivated taste of its time.

Most Maine churches of the time were far more naive in design than the Swedenborgian Church in Bath. The Congregational Church in Limerick, for instance, displays an artless combination of late Federal, Greek Revival, and

FIGURE 47. *Bath, Swedenborgian Church (1843).*
Photo: Anne W. Hammond

Gothic details. The three entrances have Gothic arches, the lunette in the pediment is typically Federal, and the belfry has Ionic columns. This innocent country church was built about 1835. The little church at Head Tide dates from 1830 and exhibits a similar combination—Gothic-arched windows and Greek Revival Doric pilasters all on the same building. Here the windows are actually rectangular but have Gothic-arched shutters applied to give the effect. The Congregational Church at Harpswell, built in 1843, has a Greek Revival body but pointed shutters above its rectangular windows. The doorway has an elaborate ogee arch with "Gothic" tracery. An attribution of this church to Anthony Coombs Raymond seems plausible from similarities with his known works. The Harpswell church is often called the Elijah Kellogg Church after the pastor who had it built, (also see Miller, p. 152 below). The churches at Head Tide, Harpswell, and Lincolnville, as well as almost innumerable other country churches of the period, have square wooden towers set athwart their gables. The towers have open belfrys and square spires. Often the spires are surrounded at their bases by four spirelets. Almost invariably these churches are three bays long. The Lincolnville example was built about 1835 and is called Bayshore Union Church. At Fryeburg the First Congregational Church of 1848 is another of these tower-athwart-gable examples. It has a fine *distyle in antis* front, but the spire seems under-scaled for the belfry below it. While there are no Gothic stylistic elements in this church, the sides of the building have board and batten sheathing, a wall treatment almost wholly confined to the Gothic Revival style.

The First Congregational Church in New Gloucester replaced the meetinghouse of 1771 on the same site in 1838. The building is most unorthodox in design, as the front columns rise only the height of one story and support an overhanging second floor whose pilasters continue the lines of the columns upward to the entablature. The gable is rather steep. A low square tower with clock faces rests athwart the gable and supports an open belfry with a domed roof. This curious front has a disconcertingly top-heavy effect. The much smaller Universalist Church in New Gloucester was built in the following year, 1839. As the church in North Yarmouth combines the front of the Universalist Church with the belfry design of the First Congregational Church, it seems probable that the same man designed all three. The small Universalist Church is as completely satisfactory in design as the other New Gloucester church is unsatisfactory. It is of the type aptly termed "stripped classic." All depends for success upon justly calculated proportions. Four wide pilaster strips support a broad plain entablature below a reasonably low paneled pediment. The two rectangular entrances have rectangular panels set above them, and there is a rectangular window in the middle bay. Nothing could be simpler, yet the subtle geometry of this facade renders it wholly pleasing. One hopes that eventually its authorship will come to light. Its anonymous builder surely merits praise.

The Damariscotta Baptist Church of 1843 is a considerably larger and rather more pretentious building than the Universalist Church in New Gloucester, yet it is not as pleasing to the eye. The four Greek Ionic columns of the portico that spans its front seem too widely spaced, and the vast blank expanse of the high pediment appears over-large for the square clock tower, enclosed belfry, and square spire that terminate the composition. The windows were altered to unclassical late-19th-century stained glass ones in 1891. The best thing about this really not very distinguished church is its site. It is placed at the top of a rise and dominates the main street of Damariscotta. The tower and spire are an impressive element of the local skyline.

The third and last of the three masonry churches of the Greek Revival style to be considered is the First Methodist Episcopal Church, commonly called the Pine Street Methodist Church, in Bangor. The church was built in

1836–37 from plans by Charles G. Bryant, all the joinery and carpentry being executed by Cyrus Brown and David Rice. The design is most unusual. A broad pavilion projects boldly before the building and carries a blind rectangular attic against which is set a shallow pediment. Above the attic block is a square enclosed belfry that was originally capped by a clock stage and cupola, now long missing. The corner pilasters and entablatures of the main block and pavilion, and the quoins of the attic block, were at one time painted white in contrast to the rest of the brick. That device certainly helped to unify the composition. The high base story elongates and distorts the proportions of the facade and makes the central motif of the pavilion appear underscaled. That motif, a shallow granite *distyle in antis* Doric element set above a rusticated arcuated base, displays carved wreaths in its entablature and resembles the Union Street entrance of the Bangor House. The panel of the pavilion pediment has a carved anthemion ornament very similar to that on Bryant's Nathaniel Hatch House of 1832 at 117 Court Street. This interestingly unconventional church, recently occupied by a Baptist congregation, is now empty. The stained glass windows added in 1883 have been removed, and the building, whose fate is uncertain, is boarded up. It is to be hoped that a viable use for the structure can be found.[10]

The former Universalist Church (now Emmanuel Baptist Church) in Belfast is another pavilion-fronted example with a high basement story. It was designed by Calvin A. Ryder and built in 1837–38. Here the pavilion is designed as a *distyle in antis* element with a low pediment and is set upon two paneled plinths flanking the front entrance. There are long, narrow windows between the Doric columns and the antae. The facade looks somehow as though it had been raised up for the insertion of a basement story, although probably that is not the case. The growth of the Sunday school movement during the 1830's may account for a demand for basement space in these and other two-storied

churches. The tower of this Belfast church is more appropriate in scale to the rest of the building than is the Bangor tower just discussed. Ryder placed an open Doric *distyle in antis* belfry above a tall square block and capped it with a smaller, anthemion-paneled block with a concave octagonal roof. The whole terminates in a fine weather vane representing a trumpeting angel. Except for the somewhat unsatisfactory solution of the problem presented by placing a classically proportioned front above a high basement, the Belfast Universalist Church ranks among the best of its type. Another church with a spireless tower, the Union Church (now the Town Hall) in Columbia Falls, was built in 1848. The facade is a standard Doric *distyle in antis* composition without any projecting pavilion. The base of the tower over the gable has elongated paired consoles, an unusual element, at its corners. Above the base is an enclosed belfry with clock faces. The belfry roof has acroteria and a tall baluster-shaped finial supporting a handsome weather vane. The entrance of this Columbia Falls church has suffered inept modern alteration.

From 1837 to 1859 a remarkable series of Greek Revival churches was built in Hancock County. Most in the group were the work of either Thomas Lord or Col. Benjamin S. Deane. No attribution, however, has yet been given the Methodist Church of 1839 in Bucksport. It has a projecting pedimented pavilion without columns. Paneled pilasters divide the bays. Here the problem of superposing an academically proportioned elevation on a basement story is successfully solved. Bryant's error in Bangor and Ryder's in Belfast had been to attempt a vertical linkage, the two-staged central motif in the first case, and the handling of the entrance and plinths in the second. In Bucksport the anonymous designer had the good sense to be perfectly straightforward; he simply divided the *entire* front right across into two stages by using a subsidiary cornice above the basement story. The Bucksport Methodist Church has a tower above the main gable composed of a square clock stage, a louvered belfry, and a tall spire. Sited on a hill, it makes a most handsome contribution to the townscape.

It has been argued that Thomas Lord's churches tend, on the whole, to be less sophisticated than those designed by Benjamin S. Deane, but the qualitative differences between the works of the two men are really not very great.[11] Both men produced masterly buildings, Lord at Ellsworth and Deane at Sedgwick, but both also designed quite run-of-the-mine churches as well. Lord's little Baptist Church at North Sedgwick has a three-bayed front of clapboards with paired pilasters at the corners and two entrances. It is only two bays long. The pediment bears an elaborately carved panel in the form of a tablet with the date 1845, and the rather squat belfry has a low double hipped roof ending in a tall obelisk finial. It must be granted that this small country church exhibits a certain naiveté.

On the other hand, Lord's Congregational Church at Ellsworth, built in 1846, is certainly one of the finest Greek Revival churches in New England, at least as far as the exterior is concerned. The interior is rather a dissappointment after the promise of the splendid front. This Ellsworth church is quite large, measuring forty-five by eighty-five feet. The facade is flush-sided, the other walls being clapboarded. The entrance pavilion projects beyond the main body of the church the distance of one shallow bay, and the church is four full bays long. The entrance is the only opening in the front. A beautifully proportioned, broad hexastyle Greek Ionic portico with a quite low pediment graces the facade and is, along with the graceful tower and spire, one of the two elements that make this church so very distinguished a composition. The tower has a square clock base above which is an octagonal plinth from which rises the open circular belfry. The belfry supports a louvered octagonal lantern from which ascends the step-based tall octagonal spire. This really splendid church corresponds quite precisely with the mental picture many people visualize when they think of a "typical New England church."

Around 1850 Thomas Lord built the church at West Brooksville. There he fell, if not from grace, certainly from gracefulness. The West Brooksville facade commits the solecism of having *three* pilasters, a cardinal sin against classical canons. With his attractive design for the Blue Hill Baptist Church, Lord made reparation for his sin against propriety at West Brooksville. The simple yet handsome church at Blue Hill, built in 1850, has a boldly projecting entrance pavilion supporting the tower. When viewed from the side, the tower appears to continue structurally from the ground upward instead, as in many examples, of appearing to be merely perched upon a roof. Here the tower has the familiar composition of tall square clock base, enclosed louvered belfry, and octagonal spire. The lintel of the tall entrance has carving characteristic of Lord's individual manner. The Baptist Church at Brooklin, built by Thomas Lord in 1853, is not as successful a composition as the Blue Hill church. There is no pavilion, and the placing of the windows so close to the middle pilasters of the front, instead of centering them in their bays, seems most awkward. The tower is very similiar to the tower of the Blue Hill Baptist Church, except that the base has no clock but has a low pediment below the belfry. It is apparent, from these examples, that Thomas Lord was a carpenter-architect without formal training who could, on occasion, rise to very respectable heights indeed.

Col. Benjamin S. Deane was responsible for one of the finest and most suavely designed wooden Greek Revival churches in New England, the Baptist Church at Sedgwick, built in 1837. While it is obvious that Deane used plates 51–56 in Asher Benjamin's *Practice of Architecture* (first published in 1833) in designing the church at Sedgwick, the significant point lies not in the similarities, but in the differences. Deane actually improved upon Benjamin and

FIGURE 48. *Hancock, Sedgwick Baptist Church, by Benjamin S. Deane (1837). Photo: Richard Cheek*

produced a better design than the one from which he drew his idea. Benjamin showed a tetrastyle Greek Doric portico without a pediment and crowned by rather fussy antefixes in his front elevation. Deane's use of a *pedimented* portico of the same order (Doric) constituted a vast improvement. Furthermore, Benjamin placed his cupola directly on his roof ridge, whereas Deane based his upon an attic podium extending the width of the portico but resting behind it on the main roof. He also placed his belfry, a more graceful one than Benjamin's cupola, on a taller base. The Sedgwick Baptist Church (Figure 48), now used as the town hall, is rightly regarded as one of the most beautiful Greek Revival churches ever built.

After the triumph of the Sedgwick church, the rest of Benjamin Deane's church-building seems somewhat anticlimactic. In 1838 he designed the Elm Street Congregational Church in Bucksport. It has an extremely shallow portico with four badly proportioned, much too slender, Doric columns that have bases, contrary to Greek precedent. The portico pediment, set so closely against the main pediment behind it, appears repetitious and fussy. The tower and spire above the roof ridge are heavy and rather ungraceful. The Congregational Church at Blue Hill, built in 1843 by Thomas Lord from Deane's designs, is a much better building than the previous one. It is, for one thing, much less fussy. The three-bayed front has paneled pilasters (paired at the corners) and a relatively low pediment with an elliptical window. The tall square tower base supports an enclosed (louvered) octagonal belfry and spire. The design is simple, direct, and well proportioned. The Methodist Church of 1859 at Orland has been attributed to Deane. It is a small church only two bays long and has an unfenestrated *distyle in antis* front with a transom-and-sidelighted entrance. Above the rather steeply pitched gable are an octagonal louvered belfry resting on a square base, and an octagonal spire. Except for its use of columns instead of pilasters, this little country church differs in no important way from a multitude of others.

Confusion still exists regarding the work of Lord and Deane. The Ellsworth Congregational Church and the North Sedgwick Baptist Church have been attributed to Deane as well as to Lord. Possibly Deane designed the latter, but as Lord billed the building committee at Ellsworth for plans he himself drew, it seems reasonably clear that he was the architect of that beautiful church. On at least one occasion, the building of the Blue Hill Congregational Church, it is certain that the two men worked together, Deane as architect and Lord as builder. There, for the present, the case must rest.

Among the various typological categories of building, the dwelling house, of course, continued to predominate numerically. Although the largest Greek Revival houses did not exceed the largest Federal houses in scale, the *average* house size increased to some extent. More significant than scale was the greater variety of house forms to be seen. Important improvements in domestic comfort also occured between around 1830 and the mid-1850's. Cast-iron stoves inset in fireplaces became common in the 1830's. These replaced the earlier brick-lined fireplaces and provided much more efficient heat. (They were sometimes called "chill chasers.") During the 1840's hot air central heating systems were introduced in some of the larger and best equipped houses. The furnaces were cast-iron ones set within brick castings and often heated only the first floor. While it was by no means common, inside plumbing also made its appearance in the most expensive houses during the 1840's. By 1850 or shortly thereafter, gas lighting was provided in the cities and in many towns. The increased availability of coal made the manufacture of illuminating gas practicable and also accounted for the widespread use of both fireplace stoves and the large cast-iron cooking stoves, or "ranges," that were replacing the older kitchen fireplaces and brick ovens by 1850. An expensive house in a city or town by around 1850 could have had most of the modern conveniences except those dependent upon electricity. Central heating, bathrooms, and fixed sources of lighting were, if not commonplace, at least available.

In Chapter 3 several instances where Greek Revival trim had been added to Colonial houses, particularly in the case of entrances, were noted. So great was the fashion for Greek forms that even quite new, i.e., Federal, houses were sometimes updated. The Johnson-Pratt House in Belfast, for example, was originally a large, square hip-roofed Federal house of central-hall plan. It dates from 1812, but its Federal appearance is now quite overshadowed, at least at first glance, by a Greek Ionic colossal order and heavy entablature added to the front and righthand side of the house during the 1830's. In Camden, the Captain Caleb Cushing House of 1799 (later owned by Edna St. Vincent Millay) had an Ionic *distyle in antis* entrance with a richly carved blind-anthemion transom added around 1845. Later, during the vogue for "good taste," when Colonial and Federal mannerisms were almost mandatory, amusing instances of backdating often occurred. A quite plain Greek Revival house, the Asa B. Palmer House of 1844 in Bath (now the Bath Marine Museum), for instance, was altered to a neo-Federal appearance as early as 1891!

The most characteristic Federal house form, the almost square hip-roofed house with central-hall plan, remained fairly popular during the heyday of the Greek Revival. Two Bangor houses by Charles G. Bryant, the Smith-Boutelle House at 157 Broadway and the Nicholas G. Norcross-John Huckins House at 80 Broadway, both built in 1834–35, have the well-established familiar form. The former has a fine Doric portico with wreathed entablature and formerly had a parapet of panels and balusters concealing its hipped roof. The doorway has a blind anthemion-carved transom like that of the Cushing House in Camden. The latter has a one-storied hexastyle Doric porch spanning its front. Originally, both hipped roof and porch had balustraded parapets now missing. The popularity of roof parapets during both the Federal and

Greek Revival periods must have derived solely from aesthetic considerations, as they could not have been very practical in so snow-ridden a climate as that of Maine.

The first known American design by the then newly-arrived English architect Richard Upjohn was his plan for the house of the Bangor lumber baron Isaac Farrar. Designed in 1833, the Isaac Farrar House was not actually built until ten or so years later and was completed in 1845. Very extensive alterations carried out in 1893–94 from plans by Wilfred E. Mansur (1855–1921) have almost totally changed the appearance of this square brick house. The three-bayed front originally had a recessed central bay with a very slightly projecting Doric *distyle in antis* portico, and the low hipped roof was almost entirely concealed by a paneled parapet. The cast-iron porches at the lefthand side and over the entrance portico that give Upjohn's elevation drawing so English Regency a look were evidently never built.[12] One room of the interior, the circular library, remains unchanged even to the folding shutters at the windows and the cast-iron coal grate of the fireplace. The broad, simple trim of this unusual round room is finished in beautifully grained West Indian crotch mahogany.

A "stripped classic" version of the Greek Revival style, wherein walls are articulated by broad pilaster strips with neither capitals nor bases, appears in both masonry and wooden buildings. The Isaac Farrar House has pilaster strips at the corners and a wide, shallowly projecting entablature below the eaves. Another brick house, the now-demolished Skinner House of around 1840 in Belfast, was a three-bayed example of the type with four pilaster strips supporting a deep entablature. The three bays thus appeared as long panels. The entrance of that handsome, severely plain house had a portico with paired Ionic columns. The hipped roof terminated in a low octagonal monitor.

Occasionally Greek Revival houses of the hipped-roof type have cupolas. The Henry Tall-man House, built in Bath about 1840, is one of those with a cupola. The front has flush siding on the first floor and clapboarding above the one-storied Doric porch that surrounds three sides of the house. Each floor has corner pilasters, and the first-floor windows are full length. The middle window of the second floor repeats the triad motif of the sidelighted entrance. The porch roof and cupola roof have ornamental parapets of open lattice work, and the main roof has a paneled parapet. The cupola fenestration repeats the design of the window above the entrance, and the porch columns, Roman Doric rather than Greek, have a pronounced entasis. This column type appears on a number of houses in Bath and seems to have been a purely local variant of the Doric order. In spite of its elaboration, the exterior of the Tallman House is neither confused nor overdone. One interior feature of this attractive house is so unusual as to merit mention: the doors of the three arches between the front lefthand room and the dining room are counterbalanced and rise upward into a second-floor partition instead of sliding to the side or folding in the customary way.

The house called "Riverside" in Newcastle dates from 1845 and is another example with a cupola atop its hipped roof. A tetrastyle colossal Doric portico fronts the house, and the entrance is at the side beyond the double parlors that look out onto the portico. "Riverside" is a particularly fine example of the plan type having the parlors across the front of the house.

If the word "cottage" may be defined as a house having only one *full* story, then it may be stretched to include some relatively large houses. It is in that flexible way that the term "cottage" will here be used. The most ubiquitous cottage type, the previously defined "cape," persisted in both brick and wooden examples as late as the 1850's. One well-known brick cape, the so-called "History House," a museum in Skowhegan, was built in 1839. It has the five bays that were standard for the type during the Greek Revival. Quite aside from its being built of brick, the fact that it has two chimneys instead of the central chimney almost invariably found in earlier capes marks it as belonging to the second quarter of the 19th century. The central hall has enclosed stairs ascending in a straight run. The front rooms have architraves with the corner blocks so typical of their period, but the hall has mitered trim. The ell extends behind the main block, as in most capes. "History House" has quarry-faced, or rough-dressed, granite basement, lintels, and sills. Similar brick capes with rough granite trim are to be seen on Route 202 in Windham and Gorham. A very handsome example, differing from those just mentioned in that it has smoothly dressed granite, floor-length windows, and a brick denticulated cornice, stands facing its long lawn at 48 Lower Beach Street in Saco. It appears to date from around 1840.

The Perkins Homestead near Newcastle (Figure 49) was built around 1850. It is not, by any definition, a cottage, as it has two and a half stories, but it is otherwise almost identical with the brick capes just mentioned when it is viewed from the front. In fact, however, it is a connected farm complex. In back of the rear ell containing the summer kitchen are joined to the house a large woodshed, a workshop, a carriage and wagon barn, and the large main barn. These wooden structures and the brick house form a connected group some 140 feet long. A connected house, shed, and barn group, all of frame construction in this instance, stands on Summer Street in Kennebunk. The Tripp House dates from around 1850 and is a true cape in type (Figure 50). The house is clapboarded and has paneled pilasters at the corners and flanking the front door. The main entablature and that of the entrance, together with the pilasters, give the house an air of great solidity. An ell is offset at the righthand side, and the sheds connecting it with the barn (which has its gable facing the road) are offset further back. A better example of a wooden Greek Revival Maine cape would be hard to find.

The General Alfred Marshall House in China dates from around 1844 and differs from most capes in having an Ionic porch spanning its front. The two front windows are floor-length. The porch gives this basically simple house an appearance of greater importance than most capes possess. The Hanson-Cramer House in Rockport was probably built in 1852. It was originally a central-chimnied cape before it was moved and remodeled extensively.[13] The dormers date from the remodeling of 1948. There are two offset wings, and the principal ornament of the exterior is a shallow distyle Ionic portico, a feature that appears locally on other capes. The Hanson-Cramer House has been attributed to John Pascal or his brother Alexander, but as both men arrived in Rockport only in 1852, it is possible that Tilson Gould was the designer and builder. If the house actually dates from as early as 1840, another local builder, Joseph Bowers, could have been the designer. The Dillingham House at 69 Pascals Avenue in Rockport is known to date at least before 1859 and resembles the original appearance of the Hanson-Cramer House very closely. The handsome entrance portico is identical in both houses. Since many builders continued to use the same details over a span of years, the dating of these cottages is, in the absence of clear documentation, often a matter of conjecture. While very few Greek Revival cottages had porticos, there was considerable variety in the design of their entrances. For example, on Route 1 in Searsport there are two attractive capes, one with a doorway flanked by Ionic pilasters and the other with a Doric *distyle in antis* entrance.

A Greek Revival cottage of the cape type on Route 88 in Falmouth Foreside appears to have been built around 1850. Unfortunately, two modern dormers break into the eaves line and rather spoil its appearance. In spite of that, it is worth notice for the five wreaths ornamenting its entablature. They may be of cast iron rather than carved wood. In any case, it seems probable that they once enclosed attic windows, now closed up. Circular entablature windows enframed by wreaths appear on several Greek Revival capes in Maine. There is one such cape on Route 1A in York, and another, with very "country" wreaths that look as if they had been cut out with a large cookie-cutter, stands in Riggs Cove at Robinhood. The Rhoda Partridge House at 1747 Congress Street in Portland was originally a conventional central-chimnied cape. It was built in 1805 and moved in 1839. Apparently around 1852 a half-story and the present Greek Revival trim were added. The taller proportions produced by the heightening of the house gave it a rather Italianate look, although all the details are still Greek. The most noticeable feature is the three wreathed entablature windows.

The cape was not the only form used for Greek Revival cottages. Story-and-a-half-high houses appeared in various forms, often, unlike the invariable placement of the capes, with their gable ends toward the road. The William R. Keith House (also known as the Howard Seymour House) in Thomaston claims a date of 1830, but it is based upon a design for a "Doric Cottage" first published in 1843 in Edward Shaw's *Rural Architecture*. The bays are articulated by rather heavy Doric pilasters supporting an entablature that does not carry across the gable end to form a pediment. An Ionic porch with balustraded roof runs across the front and down one side to the entrance. An offset rear ell connects with the barn at the lefthand side. The wide dormers at either side of the roof appear to be relatively modern additions. This house, designed by the builder-architect Keith for his own residence, is much more individual in its design than most Maine cottages. The William H. Burrill House at 13 Church Street in Belfast is even more unusual than the Keith House. It seems to have been built about 1840, and is extraordinary in that it has a cross-gabled roof, a rare form indeed for its time in Maine. The raking eaves of the gables spring from heavy entablature blocks above the corner pilasters. The house

has a side-hall plan, and an Ionic porch runs across the front and along the righthand side to a back door in the ell.

In Freeport several houses were built around 1849, among them two attractive cottages near each other. The Charles A. Litchfield House is a simple, two-bayed house with its gabled entrance end facing the road. The broad Greek Revival trim gives dignity and character to this unpretentious little cottage. The Isaac Sylvester House in Freeport is attributed to the local builder Edward H. Melcher. It is also a side-hall house with its entrance in the two-bayed gable end, but it stands with its four-bayed side toward the road and has a large ell extending beyond the front door at the other side of the main block. The trim is unusual in having blocks above the

FIGURE 49. *Newcastle, Parkins Homestead (c. 1850). Photo: Historic American Buildings Survey, by Cervin Robinson*

FIGURE 50. *Kennebunk, Tripp House (c. 1850). Photo: Richard Cheek*

windows along the street side, connecting their low triangular pedimental motifs with the soffit of the entablature. The white trim against the red walls of this house makes a striking effect. The second floor of the rear ell appears not to be original. On Route 1 on the western outskirts of Ellsworth there is a most unusual Greek Revival cottage built around 1850. The entablature carries across the front gable, but the gable is an equilateral triangle, much too steep for a classical pediment. Under the entablature, at either side of the two-bayed front block, Doric porticos are inserted. The plan is therefore T-shaped, as the porticos abut the wider rear portion of the main block. Except that there is no suggestion of a true temple-front, this cottage might be called pseudo-peripteral. On Route 8 in Norridgewock there is a true temple-fronted cottage of brick with a tetrastyle simplified Doric portico. The pediment has a paired window that may

be original. The dormers are obvious additions. As is the case in many other temple-fronted brick buildings, the portico entablature stops abruptly against the front wall of the main block. The Norridgewock cottage may date from around 1840.

Certainly one of the most fascinating and unusual cottages of the Greek Revival style in Maine is the Capt. Abraham Thing House, built in 1838 in Hallowell. The plan of the house is extraordinary: two twelve-sided parlors connected by sliding doors are fronted by a rectangular conservatory under an Ionic tetrastyle portico. The *cella* of the temple-fronted house swells outward at each side in pentagonal bays to accommodate the outer ends of the parlors. Behind the lefthand parlor are the entrance and stairhall. There is a room with an arched ceiling behind the righthand parlor. A dining room, kitchen, and back entrance are in the one-storied rear ell. The attic contains a front chamber lit by the gable window. The present rectangular window that now lights the chamber is a modern replacement of an earlier elliptical lunette. The three very large windows of the conservatory behind the columns give the facade so open an appearance that the Thing House is known locally as "The Birdcage." Some of the cast-iron work of the balconettes below the pediment window and at the angles where the bays project from the sides of the house replaces the original work. Inside, much of the original trim remains, but pseudo-Georgian overmantels have been, rather illogically, added in both parlors. The house was originally considerably larger. A rear wing beyond the present ell, and the lateral extension that joined the wing with the stable, have been demolished.[14] The Capt. Abraham Thing House, unquestionably one of the most creatively inventive Greek Revival cottages ever

FIGURE 51. *Kennebunk, Nathaniel Lord Thompson House, probably by the carpenter-builder Beniah Littlefield (1842). Photo: Richard Cheek*

planned, is not, however, quite unique. In East Vassalboro, the Thing House has a country cousin presumably built around 1840. The plan differs in that there is no conservatory, and a central hall entered from the Doric tetrastyle portico separates the two twelve-sided parlors. Pentagonal bays project at either side of the house just behind the portico, as in the Hallowell example. There is no cast-iron work on this simpler cottage in East Vassalboro, but the pediment still has a lunette window such as the Thing House had originally. Twelve-sided parlors, although extremely rare, may have had some slight vogue, as Oliver P. Smith, a Buffalo architect, published an Italianate design for a house with adjoining parlors of that shape as late as 1852 in his *Domestic Architect. . . .*

As almost all Greek Revival motifs, no matter how used or combined, were taken from ancient temples, the temple-fronted dwelling may be plausibly regarded as the most characteristically Greek Revival of all house forms built during the heyday of the style. For practical reasons, strict precedent obviously could not be followed. Greek temples, for example, had no windows, and their rectangular forms were certainly not suited to the demands of 19th-century domestic architecture. Ells, either at the side or in back of the temple-form main blocks, were appended to temple-form houses in almost every case. The house based closely on the Greek temple appeared in three slightly different types in Maine: amphiprostyle, pseudo-peripteral, and simple prostyle varieties. The amphiprostylar type, having a portico at each end, necessarily had its ell at one side. The other two types could have their ells either behind or beside their main block. Whatever the arrangement used, the order was invariably colossal, except in those rare instances where superposed orders occur.

The Nathaniel Hatch House at 117 Court Street in Bangor was built in 1832 from plans by Charles G. Bryant. In 1846 the extension at the lefthand side of the house was added by Isaiah

Rogers for Samuel Farrar, the owner at that time. The Hatch House has traditionally been called the Samuel Farrar House and has long been attributed erroneously to Richard Upjohn on the basis of unexecuted plans Upjohn noted having drawn for Samuel Farrar and, of course, his known work for Samuel's brother Isaac in Bangor. Recent research has clearly established the Bryant authorship of the so-called Samuel Farrar House, more accurately called the Nathaniel Hatch House.[15] Before a cinder-block rear wing was added to the house when it was radically altered for use as a Pentecostal church, the house was amphiprostyle with a rear portico overlooking the Kenduskeag Stream. The tetrastyle portico of fluted Doric columns facing the street remains unchanged. A Doric full entablature, complete with its triglyphs and metopes, encircles the house. The front entrance is in the center, with triple first-floor windows at either side, and there are brick pilaster responds behind the columns. The rear elevation was originally similar. The most immediately noticeable element of the facade is the beautifully carved anthemion motif of the triangular panel set within the pediment. The smaller-scaled similar pediment panel on Bryant's Pine Street Methodist Church has already been noted. The long clerestory-like low dormers are additions of 1846 by Rogers. Even in its sadly mutilated state, this formerly splendid brick house remains an ornament to its fine site. In its original condition, before the additions of 1846, not to mention later changes, the Nathaniel Hatch House was surely one of the most temple-like (as well as one of the earliest) Greek Revival houses in Maine.

The Nathaniel Lord Thompson House at 23 Summer Street in Kennebunk was built in 1842, probably from designs by the carpenter-builder Beniah Littlefield. It is sited with its roof ridge parallel to the street so that the front block conceals the large rear ell. The Doric tetrastyle porticos at either end have delicately railed second-floor galleries, and there are paired windows in each gable. The side-hall plan calls for entrances from each portico and double parlors facing the street. The front (street) wall of the house is divided into two main bays, each containing two windows per floor, by a central paneled pilaster corresponding with those at the corners. A paneled parapet at the side of the gabled roof completes the strong and handsome composition. A large stable adjoins the rear ell at the head of the driveway to the left of the house. A simple cast-iron fence of spear-headed palings supported by granite posts borders the front of the property (Figure 51). At 92 Main Street in Kennebunk an almost exact duplicate of the Nathaniel Lord Thompson House was built six years later in 1848. The Horace Porter House, now occupied by the local Water District offices, lacks the well-planted and secluded setting of its near twin, and it has lost its roof parapets. Otherwise, it is well preserved.

In the remote northeast area of Washington County at Robbinston, a remarkably fine amphiprostylar house faces Route 1. It appears to have been built around 1850. The order of the two tetrastyle porticos and the pilasters articulating the four-bayed flanks of the main block is Ionic. The gables have triangular attic windows with lozenge-shaped panes. The main block is entirely flush-sided, and the clapboarded side ell is offset one bay to block the end of the rear portico. The plan is a side-hall one, with double parlors at the front. The central bays at the portico ends of the house are blind. If this impressively handsome house need be faulted, it might be remarked that the gables are somewhat too steep and the columns and pilasters a bit too tall to suit strictly classical taste, but only a purist would quibble over that.

There are no peripteral Greek Revival houses, i.e., having columns on all four sides, in Maine or, for that matter, anywhere in America outside of the deep South. Maine has, however, pseudoperipteral houses with columns extending for two or three bays along the sides. The main blocks of these houses are T-shaped in plan. The earliest, and by far the finest, of Maine's houses

of this type is the Charles Q. Clapp House (Figure 52) built in Portland in 1832, probably from Clapp's own designs. Charles Quincy Clapp was an amateur of architecture and is known to have designed other Portland buildings. His brick rectangular house had no ell and therefore was as strictly geometrical in shape as is possible. Above a high brick basement (concealed by an embankment at the front) the house is T-shaped with three Ionic columns and an anta inserted below the entablature at either side of the block. The gabled front is treated as a temple-front motif, having the two free-standing columns at the outer corners and pilasters flanking the single front bay. The effect of a porticoed front is suggested without there actually being a portico. The long first-floor front window has nine-over-nine-light sash. The window above it is composed as a triad with richly carved side elements enframing oval lights. Originally, the roof carried three handsome acroteria in the form of urns on plinths, one above the gable apex and two above the eaves. Those roof enrichments and the handsomely paneled front door at the head of the lefthand colonnade have, unfortunately, disappeared. In 1914, when the house was altered to serve as the Portland School of Fine and Applied Art, the rear elevation was much altered. The front entrance appears to be based on figure 1 of plate 72 in Edward Shaw's *Civil Architecture*. Certain interior details reflect the influence of that book and of Asher Benjamin's *Practical House Carpenter*. Both were first published in 1830. The stem of the T contains one room. The stairhall is at the head of the lefthand colonnade, and there is a room in the corresponding position at the other side of the house. At the rear were, originally, two large rooms. Between the front room, the two rear rooms, the hall, and the room across from it is a windowless room in the middle of the house. Originally it was lighted through a circular railed opening in the floor above. That opening was below the skylighted coffered dome of a second-floor rotunda. The front first-floor room has a ceiling centerpiece with acanthus ornaments and a circular meander pattern. The door trim has carved corner blocks, and shell-carved center blocks. The once magnificent house is now in neglected condition. Portland, and indeed all Maine, cannot afford to lose the Charles Quincy Clapp House, one of the finest Greek Revival houses ever built in New England. A recent matching-grant offer by the Maine Historic Preservation Commission to the Portland Society of Art for the restoration of the Clapp House augurs well for its future.

In 1847 the William O'Brien House was built at 172 State Street in Portland. It somewhat resembles the Charles Q. Clapp House but has none of the enrichments that distinguished the older building. The O'Brien House has an Ionic tetrastyle portico, and the portico extends back for one bay behind the front wall plane at each side of the main block. The house has been altered for use as a funeral establishment. The Richard Means Nott House in Kennebunkport, built in 1851–53 is a curious example of this type. It might be termed *"pseudo*-pseudo-peripteral,"* as the colonnade extends across the front and down part of the righthand side only. The house itself is therefore actually off-center and has an L-shaped plan instead of a T-shaped one. The Doric colonnade is correctly proportioned and hence rather heavy, and there is a gallery at the second-floor level. The actual asymmetry of the house is therefore quite effectively disguised. The rather steep gable has paired arch-headed windows, and a pentagonal two-storied bay window projects beyond the portico at the right. The Nott House stands at the head of a street and, in spite of its odd plan, "reads" as a solidly handsome and perfectly symmetrical, quite monumental house. Another late example of the pseudo-peripteral type stands at 64 Middle Street in Saco. It probably dates from the mid-1850's. The order is Ionic, and there is no front portico. There are three columns at either side. In those respects, the house is like the Charles Q. Clapp House, but it has none of the refinement of the

Portland building. The walls under the porticos are flush-sheathed; the others are clapboarded. The cornice is denticulated in the Ionic manner, but the columns lack bases. The rear of the block has oval grille-fronted vents just under the entablature. This Saco house clearly shows that the Greek Revival was waning at the time when it was built.

Occasionally, although rarely, Greek Revival houses with superposed orders occur in Maine. A particularly attractive example stands at 63 South High Street in Bridgton. It appears to have been built about 1845 and stands with its gable end toward the street. The portico is Greek Doric on the first floor and Roman Doric on the second. The portico extends a bay beyond the house at each side on the first floor and is therefore octastyle at that level, as it continues in the form of a one-storied porch along the sides of the house. On the second floor, the portico spans only the width of the house itself and is therefore hexastyle. The entrance is centered on the five-bayed front wall. A long rear ell extends behind the main block of this quite large house. In Kittery there is a truly pseudo-peripteral house of about the same date with superposed Greek Doric orders. Now used as legal offices, the house stands with its gable end toward Route 103. The quite narrow three-bayed front has a central doorway, and there is a hexagonal cupola centered on the roof.

Many more simple prostyle houses with neither rear porticos nor lateral colonnades were built during the Greek Revival than houses of either amphiprostyle or pseudo-peripteral type. At 121 North Street in Saco the Stephen L. Goodale House stands with its flank toward the road and faces a broad lawn. The style is transitional between late Federal and full-fledged Greek Revival. The house is brick and has a wooden side ell that connects it with a barn. This especially handsome house appears to have been built around 1830, just at the time when the Greek Revival was replacing the Federal style in Maine. The prostyle form portends the future, but the details hark back to the past. The side-lighted entrance is placed under a louvered elliptical arch, and there are elliptical arches between the extremely slender Roman Doric columns of the tetrastyle portico. The rectangular gable window is set within a lunette-shaped panel that may originally have been entirely glazed. Although it is certainly not purely Greek Revival or typically Federal in appearance but a hybrid, the Goodale House is a beautifully proportioned and most elegant dwelling.

In 1832 the Zebulon Smith House at 55 Summer Street in Bangor was built. It is coeval with the Nathaniel Hatch House and just a year older than the Charles Q. Clapp House and therefore ranks as one of the very oldest temple-fronted houses in Maine. The flanks are brick above a granite basement, but the front and rear are wooden. The portico has four accurately proportioned Greek Ionic columns with pilaster responds against the flush-sided front. The entablature stops abruptly at the front wall, and the second-floor side windows rise above the entablature level. The gable lunette is relatively small and has the form of a Federal fanlight. The corner-block trim of the entrance and the triple windows at either side of it is still sufficiently delicate in proportion to be classed readily as late Federal rather than as Greek Revival in character. The Zebulon Smith House is important for its early date and as an example of a design that has not quite reached maturity.

On Route 201 in Vassalboro there is a large wooden prostyle house superbly sited on a rise in ample grounds. The entablature is carried completely around the main block, and, at first glance, that fine house appears to be a mature and academically "correct" example of the Greek Revival style. The gable has a fairly low pitch, the ell is all but hidden behind the main block, and the entrance is at the side, indicating that there are probably large double parlors across the front. A second glance, however, discloses a highly unclassical *five*-columned Greek Doric portico instead of the orthodox even-num-

FIGURE 52. *Portland, Charles Q. Clapp House, probably designed by Charles Q. Clapp (1832). Old photograph courtesy of Mrs. Barbara Matlock Warren, Mrs. Willard Clinton Warren II, and the Portland Museum of Art, copy by Mark C. Bisgrove*

bered set of columns. The house appears to date from around 1840 and is, in spite of the solecism of being a pentastyle building, a handsome example of the prostyle type. It clearly shows that builders of the period did not worry unduly about the academic principles but solved their design problems in often direct and practical ways.

The J. H. McLellan House of 1841 on Washington Street in Bath is certainly one of the finest prostyle brick houses in Maine. The main block of the house is placed with its Greek Ionic tetrastyle portico facing the yard, its flank along Washington Street, and its rear elevation on Garden Street. The entrance is at the lefthand side of the portico, and the offset ell extends to the side. The lintels and sills are granite, and the entablature runs around the main block. The gable contains a low, widespread elliptical window. A pair of large parlors occupies the Washington Street side of the main block, and the original neo-rococo brass and ormolu gasoliers (now electrified) are still in those rooms. This unusually handsome house is well-maintained and is now used as a funeral establishment. The so-called "Sophie May House," built in Norridgewock in 1845 for Cullen Sawtelle, is another brick prostyle example. The order of the tetrastyle portico is Doric, and the columns are placed on granite plinths, as the portico has no floor. The ell extends to the rear of the main block. The house is very impressive when viewed directly from the front, but the entablature ends at the front wall, thus giving the portico an applied look instead of an appearance of being integrated with the house itself, when viewed from an angle. The Cullen Sawtelle House is, nevertheless, an attractive building with a pleasant contrast between the white of its woodwork and the mellow pink of its brick. Its connection with the authoress Sophie May Clarke, a later owner, adds associative interest to the house.

The Governor Abner Coburn House was built in 1849 by the carpenter-builder and carver Jo-seph Bigelow for the lumber baron brothers Abner and Philander Coburn in Skowhegan. (Bigelow, a Skowhegan native, was also responsible for the carpentry and joinery of the Isaac Farrar House in Bangor.)[16] The house is an imposing, large-scaled building with an Ionic tetrastyle galleried portico spanning the flush-boarded front. A low, delicately patterned cast-iron railing edges the gallery. The entrance is at the side of the house and is centered on the three-bayed flank of the main block. It projects to form a one-storied vestibule with a *distyle in antis* front. The flat roof has a railing like that of the portico gallery. The paired doors are late-19th-century replacements. A rear ell extends for some distance and adjoins an offset barn with its gable end facing the driveway. The middle first-floor window under the portico is false, as the partition dividing the double parlors is at that point. The outer ends of these parlors have rectangular bay windows, apparently original, that project beyond the flanks of the main block. The strict geometry of the *cella* form is thus broken up, presaging the freer outlines so typical of the 1850's. The interior trim is surprisingly late, although very fine, as the house was extensively modernized shortly after Governor Coburn's death in 1885. Although of a later period than the Greek Revival, the dining room and the staircase are worth particular notice. The black marble Ionic mantelpieces and the plaster cornices and ceiling centerpieces of the two parlors are about all that remains of the original Greek Revival interior trim.

The town of Richmond has a number of rather naively designed prostyle houses of comparatively modest scale. Probably they were all the work of a local builder. The Capt. Theobald House in Richmond was built after 1847 but by 1855. It is unusual in having a tetrastyle portico of the seldom-used Corinthian order. The proportions of the Theobald House are good, and the pediment is not overly steep, but modern siding that is overscaled in width for the house has been applied to the walls and considerably mars the effect. Another Richmond house, that built for Capt. David Stearns between 1851 and 1855 at 3 Gardiner Street, has an offset rear ell and an entablature that projects beyond the wall plane of the main block and is supported by columns at the rear corners as well as by the tetrastyle front portico. The front gable window has latticed sash in the Gothic Revival manner. The house has a side-hall plan. The remarkable feature is the order used. It is *sui generis*. Octagonal shafts bear splayed octagonal capitals, each face having a carved conventionalized flower of tulip-like form, perhaps representing a lotus. The capitals terminate in egg and dart molding and octagonal abaci. Among the numerous prostyle houses of Richmond, the Stearns House has the most fetchingly "folk" details. A little further up the Kennebec River from Richmond, at the northwest corner of Middle and Chestnut Streets in Hallowell, the Cooper House of 1848 presents a more conventional Ionic tetrastyle portico to view. The scale of the Cooper House is hardly greater than that of its counterparts in Richmond, and the Gothic attic window betrays a similar naiveté.

At 72 Main Street in Orono there stands a somewhat larger and grander prostyle house, the Thomas Whitney House of around 1851, that combines Greek and Gothic elements. The four octagonal columns support a gallery with a low, cast-iron railing, and a rather steeply pitched pediment with a triad of traceried Gothic windows. The front second-floor windows are similar in design, but the triple first-floor windows have no traces of tracery. The front entrance has the standard Greek Revival transom and sidelights. While it does not bear analysis as serious architecture, the Thomas Whitney House has considerable charm. The efforts of builders lacking formal education often produced fresh and original results. From the academic point of view, nothing could be worse than a *three*-columned portico, yet the two-bayed prostyle house at 225 Main Street in Waterville, probably built about 1850, has an in-

nocence that is altogether refreshing. Its three columns are faceted and tapered to give the effect of fluting and entasis. Evidently the unsophisticated builder of that modest house enjoyed woodcarving, for he added fern-like enrichments of no traceable derivation to his entablature above each column and also over his front door. Modern siding has been applied to this house, and the interior is entirely altered. A short distance away on Main Street, another Waterville house shows the inventive variety of form created by mid-century carpenters from Greek precedents. The corner pilasters of that house have immense meander, or Greek key, elements serving as their capitals. In the nearby town of Fairfield, at the corner of Main and Summit Streets, there is another prostyle house with three columns. It may well have been built by the builder of 225 Main Street in Waterville. Unfortunately, the Fairfield example, which has a second-floor gallery, is in poor condition and is badly maintained.

Prior to the Greek Revival, only one double (semi-detached) house is known to have been built in Maine. The double house may be fairly considered to have been a new type, a form first appearing in the 1830's. It was confined almost exclusively to cities and towns, where land values were comparatively high. The Ward Houses at 97–99 State Street in Portland are about as early in date (1833) as any in Maine. Each of the three-bayed units is a mirror image of the other in plan. The entrances adjoin each other, and the side halls share a party wall. These three-storied brick houses are still rather Federal in appearance, as the recessed entrances are headed by elliptical arches. Four somewhat elongated Ionic pilasters carry an entablature and articulate the six-bayed facade into three principal bays. The third-floor windows are square, as are many third-floor windows in Federal houses. The righthand house of the pair, now occupied by American Red Cross offices, has undergone turn-of-the-century interior alterations. The parlors retain their Greek Revival black marble mantelpieces with Ionic colonettes, but the partition between the two parlors has been replaced by Colonial Revival columns. The doors and windows still have their original corner block trim, but the dining room trim is Colonial Revival, and the Greek Revival front stairs have been replaced by a much more elaborate Colonial Revival staircase. The handsome front of this double house is an excellent example of transitional late Federal–early Greek Revival style. Nearby, at 85–87 State Street, the Nathaniel O. Cram Block is a later, fully Greek Revival double house. This brick pair is raised upon a granite basement. Doric pilasters support an entablature with triglyphs and metopes, and all the front windows except those over the arch-headed paired entrances are triple, with narrow flanking sash. The semi-circular fanlights are large, as they span the doors and also their sidelights. The large continuous front dormer (slated) may be a later addition. The Cram Block was built in 1851. Although the righthand first-floor window lacks its cast-iron balconette and the bracket-supported balcony over the entrances has lost its railing, this well proportioned double house is by no means too far gone for restoration. A fine cast-iron and granite fence borders the property. The builders of this handsome double house were Moses and Ralph C. Russell. Mention should be made of a far less grand double house on a high granite basement on the east side of Park Street between Spring and Congress Streets in Portland. It is a four-bayed wooden house that probably dates from the 1840's. The double portico is supported on square piers, and there are paneled corner pilasters. The noteworthy feature of this (unfortunately) poorly maintained house, however, is the very richly worked ornamentation of the two first-floor window lintels. It is astonishing to find such elaborate work on so unpretentious a house, and it seems probable that those lintels are stock millwork with applied mastic ornament rather than carved work.

The granite paired fronts of the John Neal Houses at 173–175 State Street are, unlike the previously mentioned free-standing double houses, embedded in a row. The pair was built in 1836, probably from Neal's own designs. The facade is unusual on three counts; it is granite, it is four stories high, and it is designed with great subtlety. Very slight projections and recessions break up the planarity of this Yarmouth granite expanse of ashlar. One need only note the way in which the vertical monoliths flanking the central second-floor windows *recede* instead of projecting like the entrance pilasters below them to grasp the ingenuity of the mind behind this suavely sophisticated design. The entrances are at ground level, and meander-patterned iron balconettes front the second-floor windows. The two dormers may be later additions. The double parlors are on the second floor. The parlors of the lefthand house have eight-paneled mahogany doors with fielded centers in their panels. The wide doorway between the two parlors is flanked by Doric pilasters carrying a heavy entablature. The John Neal Houses, one of the most distinguished buildings in Portland, now serve as a cheap hotel for male transients.

The period under consideration also saw, for the first time in Maine, the appearance of that distinctly urban type, the rowhouse. In 1835 the largest group of rowhouses ever built in Maine was erected on Park Street between Spring and Gray Streets. The complex originally consisted of the fourteen four-and-a-half-story brick houses on Park Street and additional rows of three houses each on Spring and Gray Streets. The Gray Street row has been demolished. Each unit has three bays and a side-hall plan. Above the low granite basement the trim is brownstone. Like the John Neal Houses, the Part Street Row has (a rarity in Maine) a *piano nobile,* i.e., the parlors are on the second floor. Here the long parlor windows are fronted by a cast-iron balcony of anthemion pattern. The cornice is wooden. These fourteen houses fill an entire block with their simple and uniform fronts (except for the addition of later bay windows in places). As the site slopes, the row is stepped slightly about every three houses to accommodate the grade. Park Street Row, a truly major real estate undertaking for its day in Portland, closely resembles similar developments of the period in Boston. After long neglect, the row is now being thoroughly rehabilitated for use as apartments.

Wooden examples of the rowhouse type were also built during the Greek Revival. Usually these were quite modest dwellings erected as tenements, i.e., rental houses. The Gage Block, known as the Row House, was built in 1846 in Hallowell. There are five units in the row. The site slopes sharply to the rear, so, while there are two and a half stories on the street side, there are three full floors at the back. The entrances are not paired. Each three-bayed unit has a side-hall plan, and each has a single dormer. Aside from the general proportions, the corner pilasters and simple entablature, and the plain trim of the doorways, there is little to indicate Greek Revival "style" about this row. The Gage Block was recently the object of a preservation campaign and has now been well rehabilitated after years of neglect. Around 1840 a somewhat longer two-storied wooden row of similar character was built in Bath for Arthur C. Donnell.

In Bangor, where there are so many fine Greek Revival houses, it is not at all astonishing to find three of the best double houses in Maine. At 77–79 Broadway on the corner of Penobscot Street there stands the largest double house in Maine. It was built around 1835, probably for Dominicus Parker, and is now known as the Dwinel-McCrillis House after Rufus Dwinel and William McCrillis, two successive owners of one of the pair. This pair of brick mansions has, like the Park Street Block, a very Bostonian appearance. The broad elliptical bays at either end, seldom found in Maine, are exactly like the "bow fronts" so frequently seen on rowhouses of the period in Boston. The recessed entrances are similar to those called "northeasters" in Boston. Unlike the Neal Houses and the Park Street

Row in Portland, the Dwinel-McCrillis Houses have their long windows on the first floor, showing that the parlors are not placed on a *piano nobile*. These three-storied brick houses are unusual both for their size and for having, unlike almost all double houses, central hall plans. This thoroughly urban pair of houses is among the finest of its kind ever built in Maine.

Another Bangor pair of houses, the double cottage at 16–18 Division Street, is infinitely more modest in scale than the Broadway example but equally interesting in design. This double cottage was built in about 1836 from designs by Charles G. Bryant. It stands with its gable end toward the street and has fluted Doric corner pilasters. The entablature does not carry across the front to form a pediment. There is a small lunette just under the apex of the gable. At the sides of the main block there are low rectangular windows set *below* the entablature, an unusual arrangement. The most unusual feature, however, is the front portico. It is composed of four fluted Doric antae supporting a wreath-ornamented entablature and enclosing vestibules at either end. The front entrances face each other across the portico, and the vestibule windows face the street. The portico has a low hipped roof. It is rare to find so much care lavished upon the design of a cottage, let alone a double cottage (rare in itself), and it is even more unusual to find a cottage designed by an architect rather than by a journeyman carpenter. Bryant was one of the principal architects of Bangor in his day.

Charles G. Bryant was also the architect of what is incontestably the most creatively designed double house in Maine. It may also be justly asserted that the house (at 48–50 Penobscot Street on the corner of Pine Street and Penobscot) is one of the most handsomely designed houses single or double, ever built in Maine. Bryant planned the house for Governor Edward Kent and his law partner Jonas Cutting (Figure 53). It was commenced in 1836 and completed the following year. The house has a granite foundation and is flushed-sided except for the clapboarded rear ell. The main block has four front bays and is one bay deep. Five square piers support a wide entablature with iron grille-fronted attic windows above a continuous band of guttae. On the first floor, Doric columns and wreath-ornamented entablatures with denticulated cornices are set within the deep reveals of the piers. The upper surfaces of these minor entablatures form cast-iron-railed balconies before the second-floor windows. The paired entrances have sidelights and anthemion-carved blind transoms of elaborate pattern. The first-floor windows are triple and are elliptical in plan. Cast-iron railings in front of the Doric columns span the first-floor front window bays. At the sides of the main block there are elliptical first-floor bays with entablatures like the minor entablatures of the facade. Those bays are capped by railings of the same pattern as those in front of the second-floor front windows. Both upper and lower side windows are triple. The interiors of this extraordinary pair of houses are as unusual as the exterior. The parlors are circular (which explains the elliptical form of the front and side windows), and the circular front stairways are fitted partially within the reverse curves formed by the parlor walls. The parlor at 50 Penobscot Street still has its neo-rococo brass gasolier of around 1850 (now electrified) with its original ground and cut-glass shades. The imaginative freedom with which Bryant interpreted Greek Revival forms, and the fine sense of scale and proportion he manifested, place the Kent-Cutting House in the very first rank among Greek Revival dwellings anywhere.

Except for the cape type, the most commonly built house type in Maine seems to have been the two-storied central-hall house of either three or five bays placed with its roof ridge parallel to the road. This type occurs in both urban and rural settings and in both brick and wooden examples. An excellent brick house of this type stands at 33 Church Street in Belfast and bears a date of 1832. The entrance of the five-bayed front is recessed below a flat granite lintel. There is an arched entrance at the righthand side. The lintels, sills, and entablature of this pink brick house are painted white, providing an agreeable contrast with the dark green louvered shutters as well as with the masonry itself. The Nathaniel Treat House of 1835 or thereabout at 114 Main Street in Orono is similar in many respects to the Belfast house. The proportions are basically the same, but the Treat House has an arched entrance sheltered by a hybrid Doric portico capped by a balustrade. There is no side entrance in the main block, as at Belfast, but there is a subsidiary entrance in an offset ell at the end of a Doric side porch. The porch may be a later addition. The Treat House has a denticulated main cornice and wooden gables. The rear was altered around 1912. The front hall has elliptical stairs. The parlors have simple mantelpieces fitted with cast-iron inset stoves, or "chill-chasers," from the foundry of Jenness and March.

How much depends upon fine proportion in these brick houses may be seen by comparing either of the above-mentioned examples with the Martin Hawes House of 1835 in the Stroudwater section of Portland. As the latter is not as deep as the first two, it appears awkwardly tall and somewhat ungainly, although its five-bayed front is not materially different from others of its kind. The Daniel Melcher House in Freeport dates from around 1849, showing that brick and granite houses of this form retained their popularity for several decades. The Melcher House is an attractive example of its kind with an elliptical staircase and good, simple Greek Revival interior trim.

Occasionally, houses of this basic type have unusual features, such as the Ionic porch that spans the front of the wooden Ingalls House of 1837 at Mercer. One-story front porches are rare on Maine houses of this type. Aside from this example in Mercer, only the front porch of the General Alfred Marshall House (also Ionic) in China comes readily to mind. The fluted

FIGURE 53. *Bangor, Governor Edward Kent-Jonas Cutting Double House, by Charles G. Bryant (1836–37). Photo: Richard Cheek*

IV · The Greek Revival / *131*

columns of the Ingalls House were presumably stock millwork rather than the work of a local carpenter. Their capitals would tax the skill of any but the best carvers. The interior of the Ingalls House has stairs ascending in a straight run. The newel post has a columnar form that seems to be peculiar to Maine. There is a wide doorway with two-leaved hinged doors between the parlors. The trim has corner and (at the wide doorway) center blocks. There are no cornices or ceiling centerpieces.

A three-bayed house of the type, the Shaw-Chick House in Winterport may date from as early as 1838. It has a stripped classic front with very broad pilaster strips and an entablature dividing the flush-boarded facade into three panels penetrated by windows and the central side-lighted doorway. The dormer is a later addition. Except that it has a pitched roof instead of a hipped roof, the Shaw-Chick House resembles the Jared Sparks House in Cambridge, Massachusetts, designed by William Saunders and built in 1838. The ell extends to the rear, instead of to the side as in the Cambridge example. The Shaw-Chick House has an elliptical staircase and simple Greek Revival interior trim that differs slightly from room to room. At least three fireplaces have their original inset stoves with handsome cast-iron engaged Ionic half-colonettes. Near the First Parish Church in South Berwick there is a house that appears to date from about 1845. It has a very restrained five-bayed flush-boarded front with corner pilasters and an Ionic entrance portico. There is a large square cupola with paired arched windows on the roof. A long offset side wing connects the house with a stable, and it is the stripped classic front wall of that one-storied wing that is reminiscent of the Shaw-Chick House in treatment.

In Bangor two almost identical houses by Charles G. Bryant stand on High Street. The George W. Brown House at number 43 High Street was completed in 1836, a little before its next-door neighbor, the George W. Pickering House at number 39, finished in 1837. Both

houses were begun in 1835. These handsomely proportioned brick houses both have enclosed entrance vestibules with paired Ionic columns. The Brown House still has its vestibule roof railing of a delicate cast-iron pattern. Both houses have corner pilasters and full entablatures. The Thomas Lord House in Blue Hill was built about 1845. It is a good wooden example of the central-hall five-bayed type with roof ridge parallel with the front. It is a well proportioned house with corner pilasters and an entablature with modillioned cornice that does not carry across the gable ends. An offset stable with its broad side facing front connects with a rear ell. The most striking feature of the Lord House is its elegant little entrance portico of Ionic *distyle in antis* design with a pedimented roof. The Ionic columns, however, have no bases, showing Lord's lack of concern with strict precedent. The house is primarily of interest for its association with its noted builder-architect. A house on Route 1 at the corner of Pike Avenue in Searsport, another of the five-bayed wooden examples, merits notice for the subtle entasis given the Ionic pilasters flanking the entrance. The corner pilasters are ornamented with palmettes. This handsome house appears to date from around 1840. Like the three houses just mentioned, the Clark-Doane House in Wiscasset is a five-bayed clapboarded example of the type under consideration. It appears to date from about 1845 and is particularly noteworthy for its fine exterior ornamental carving. Paneled corner pilasters support a broad plain entablature pierced by oval windows with carved wreath surrounds. The distyle Doric portico is surmounted by carved cresting composed of a patera supported by horizontal scrolled console motifs. The triple window over the entrance is inset and flanked by paneled antae. This basically simple yet richly embellished house now has an incompatible addition at the lefthand side.

At the corner of French and Penobscot Streets in Bangor, Col. Benjamin S. Deane built a house for George K. Stetson in 1847. The house has three bays with paneled corner pilasters and wide pilasters flanking the middle bay. These resemble pilaster strips except that they have bases and naively unorthodox capitals that do not properly fit their shafts. The capitals are free interpretations of the Ionic form. A central pavilion is suggested by a low subsidiary gable over the middle bay, although that bay does not actually project beyond the wall plane. An octagonal cupola crowns the roof. The curved bay at the lefthand side of the house and the dormers are later additions. A large ell extends to the rear. Originally, the roof had a paneled parapet, and the main block had flush siding. Unfortunately, the house has now been covered with composition shingles that are disagreeable both in color and texture and that distort the scale of the building. The design of the George K. Stetson House was derived by Deane from a plate in Edward Shaw's *Rural Architecture,* published in 1843. In spite of its disfigured surface, the Stetson House is in basically sound condition. It is particularly significant as the only Greek Revival building still standing in Bangor that is known to be by the Bangor architect Benjamin S. Deane.

Three-bayed houses of the type under discussion exist in many places. An example at 14 High Street in Belfast appears to date from about 1845. It has a severely simple flush-boarded main block with the usual corner pilasters and full entablature. It is unusual because the entrance portico (capped by a delicate cast-iron railing) has paired columns of the rarely used Corinthian order. In this case the capitals are not at all standard. One must call these strangely hybrid capitals Corinthian for lack of a more accurate term, as they look more like that order than any other. Again, the freedom with which builders interpreted Greek precedents is demonstrated. Large and prosperous farms often had houses far grander than the cape type. In New Gloucester the Andrew Campbell Chandler House of around 1850 is a farmhouse of the two-storied, central-hall, gable-roofed type like those

just mentioned. It is like the house at 14 High Street in Belfast except that it is clapboarded and has no entrance portico. It has a large two-storied rear ell. The Chandler property is worth mention for its fine Greek Revival house, but it is truly noteworthy for its great barn. The Chandler Barn is placed well back of the road with its gable end facing the driveway. It is not connected with the house. The gable of this two-and-a-half-story barn has an octagonal window, and the octagonal form is repeated by the large middle cupola and two smaller cupolas athwart the roof ridge. Handsome as this barn is, its principal claim for notice is its immense size. It is said to be among the largest ever erected in Maine during the Greek Revival.

The William A. Farnsworth Homestead of about 1854 in Rockland has a main block with flush siding on the front and righthand, or garden, side. The opposite side faces a side street and is clapboarded. The corner pilasters and entablature are quite heavy, and the entrance is inset. The main block is around forty-two by thirty-one feet, roughly the scale of most houses of this type. An offset wing connects the rear ell with an attractive two-storied stable with a hipped roof and concave-roofed octagonal cupola. The house has been attributed to the W. H. Glover Lumber Company, a Rockland firm. Now a museum, the Farnsworth House has its original fittings: cast-iron hot air registers, gasoliers, and a cast-iron Walker kitchen range, as well as the carpets, draperies, and furniture of its period. The house and its contents illustrate perfectly the domestic arrangements of a prosperous Maine household of the 1850's. Unlike other fences previously mentioned, the fence bordering the Farnsworth property is wooden instead of cast-iron. Another Rockland house of this general type, the I. Snow House, is said to date from around 1861. If that is so, it must surely be the last house of the full-fledged Greek Revival style built in Maine. The main block is derived from Edward Shaw's *Rural Architecture* of 1843 with variations in detail. The facade is similar to that of the George K. Stetson House in Bangor. Here the pilaster order is Doric, the entrance has a portico with paired Doric columns, and there is a triple window over the entrance. The main block is flush-sided, and the subsidiary front gable has beautifully executed anthemion carving, the best feature of the exterior. A modern continuous front dormer and a side porch do not improve the appearance of this still handsome but poorly maintained house.

During the 1850's houses of the type being discussed were occasionally built with an admixture of Greek Revival and Italianate elements. The Connor-Bovie House at 22 Summit Street in Fairfield was built in 1856–58 and is a good example of this stylistically transitional variety. The clapboarded front has four paneled Doric pilasters, and the full entablature is carried around the main block. Italianate influence shows in the bracketed cornices of the windows and in the denticulated main cornice and the cornice of the entrance portico. The portico roof is supported on paired paneled piers instead of the more usual columns. The roof has a steep, forty-five-degree pitch. The ell extends to the rear, and there is a long one-storied stable at the lefthand side. The entrance sidelights have etched ruby glass. The stairs ascend in a straight run and have a turned newel post and balusters. The room to the left of the hall has trim with the original oak-colored graining throughout. There is an unusually wide opening between the double parlors at the right of the hall. It had folding, rather than sliding, doors (now stored in the stable). The windows have louvered inside shutters, the mantelpieces are marble, and there are simple circular plaster ceiling centerpieces but no cornices. There were, at one time, two kitchens in the ell, now opened into one. An early cast-iron inset stove has an oven door with a patent date of 1850. The later stove on the other side of the kitchen chimney is a Peerless range made by the Highland Foundry Company in Boston and patented in 1881. Not the least interesting fact concerning the Connor-Bovie House

is that it was the first Fairfield dwelling to be equipped with electric light. This remarkably unaltered house received its electricity in 1888.

Until the Greek Revival, houses sited with their gable ends toward the street were almost unknown. The popularity of the temple-fronted house accounts partially for the frequent occurence of houses so sited after 1835 or thereabout, and the division of city land into narrow lots was also a factor. The Charles H. Pond House at 175 State Street in Bangor, built in 1835, is a modest city house with its gable end facing the street and without a portico. It was formerly known as the Jonathan Young House, but recent research has shown that it was built by the Bangor architect and builder Charles H. Pond as his own residence.[17] The clapboarded three-bayed front has its entrance at the right, indicating the side-hall plan. The sidelighted doorway is framed by pilasters with palmette-headed panels supporting a heavy entablature ornamented with four wreaths. Above the cornice is a triangular parapet block motif with corner acroteria and anthemion carving. The low rectangular window in the gable pediment has a smaller-scaled ornament of similar design. The other windows have corner block trim of surprisingly slender proportions. The door and attic window trim is rather heavily overscaled and is based on designs by Asher Benjamin intended for a larger house. It is not known whether Pond executed the carvings himself. Perhaps he intended his rather conspicuous doorway as an advertisement of his skills.

The house on Washington Street in Bath now occupied by the Cosmopolitan Club appears to have been built around 1840. It has a four-bayed front with flush-sided first floor and gable and clapboarded second floor. The entrance is centered in the three-bayed left flank of the main block. This house has a feature common to a number of the front gable type—a one-storied porch running across the front and along one side. In this case the porch continues beyond the front and down the left, or entrance, side. The order is that form of Roman Doric peculiar to Bath and its vicinity and already observed on the Tallman House. The Bowker House at 165 Park Row in Brunswick, built at an undetermined date between 1846 and 1857, also has a one-storied porch along the front and one side of the main block. Yet another house with this L-shaped form of one-storied porch stands at the corner of Church and Grove Streets in Belfast. In that example the porch is Ionic and is capped by a low balustrade. The Belfast house seems to date from around 1845. Church Street in Belfast is virtually unspoiled and has as many good Greek Revival houses as any street in New England. At 5 Church Street there is a brick two-bayed two-storied house with its gable end facing front. The inset entrance has sidelights and an anthemion-carved blind transom similar to those already noted on the Captain Cushing House in Camden and the Smith-Boutelle and Kent-Cutting Houses in Bangor. This brick house has corner pilasters and entablatures at the sides but no entablature across the front. Instead of a pediment, there is just a gable. The most unusual feature of the house at 5 Church Street is the dog-toothed raking cornice composed of two rows of offset brick.

At 149 Main Street in Thomaston there stands a particularly handsome house with its gable toward the street. The flush-sided main block is articulated at both front and sides by strongly projecting broad Doric pilasters carrying a deep entablature. At the lefthand side there is a one-storied Ionic porch capped by a handsome balustrade. The entrance faces the street beyond the second bay of the porch, the line of which continues as an enclosed pair of bays and then jogs outward to the left to connect the house with the stable. The house was built in 1848 and is believed to have been designed by Capt. Charles Ranlett, its first occupant. The parlors extend across the four front bays of the house and are divided in the center by free-standing Corinthian columns. The Ranlett House double parlors have been described as "perhaps the finest draw-ing-room in the State of Maine."[18] Next door to the Capt. Charles Ranlett House, at 151 Main Street, is the Capt. William Henderson House, also built in 1848, probably from a design by Ranlett. Henderson was Mrs. Ranlett's brother-in-law, and the two houses are very similar. The Henderson House is somewhat simpler than its neighbor, as it has only corner pilasters. The roof is steeper, and the side porch has no balustrade, although there may once have been one. These two fine Thomaston houses were formerly attributed to Albert Morton or James Overlock.

A few Maine houses in the Greek Revival style do not fit any of the categories previously discussed. The Thomas A. Hill House at 159 Union Street at the corner of High Street in Bangor, for example, has a highly unusual shape. The brick main block is four bays deep on the first floor and only two bays deep on the second. Pent roofs spanning the front and rear elevations shelter the spaces beyond the second-floor wall planes. The main roof has a Gothic window in the pediment facing High Street. Small rectangular windows above the pent roofs light the second floor except at each end, where the two bays have full-sized windows. A flat-roofed porch with fluted Ionic columns surrounds three sides of the building. The porch floor is granite. Large triple-windowed dormers with stepped gables were added to the pent roof around the turn of the century, an addition was made to the wooden side ell around 1945, and the interior was extensively altered around 1952. The iron snow-stops above the main eaves may be original. This strangely composed house was built in 1836 and was, surprisingly, designed by Richard Upjohn. It is now used by the Bangor Historical Society.

In Orono, the Governor Israel Washburn House at 120 Main Street is unusual in that it has a side wing treated as a major element of the design. The house is also noteworthy for the excellent quality of its Greek Revival trim. It is a quite large house, measuring about thirty-two feet across the three-bayed front, plus the nine-

FIGURE 54. *Belfast, Joseph Williamson House, by Calvin A. Ryder (1842). Photo: Denys Peter Myers*

FIGURE 55. *Belfast, James P. White House, by Calvin A. Ryder (1840). Photo: Wayne Andrews*

teen-by-eighteen-foot side wing extending from the north wall, by eighty-five feet from front to rear. The pedimented front elevation and the wall of the north wing that faces the street are flush-sided; the rest of the house is clapboarded. The corner pilasters are paneled and have palmette ornaments. Their proportions are rather slender. A one-storied Roman Doric porch with both floor and roof balustrades spans the front. Another Doric porch, without balustrades, is placed against the south wall of the rear ell. The lintel of the sidelighted front entrance has a foliate-carved center block and meander-patterned corner blocks. The relatively delicate entablature has a ribbon-bracketed cornice and does not continue at the sides of the house. The pediment has a very small semicircular window. Aside from the porch and entrance, the other principal ornament of the exterior is the rectangular bay window fronting the north wing. It has palmette-ornamented piers and a balustraded roof. An offset barn is connected with the north side of the rear ell. The main block has a side-hall plan. The interior trim is quite plain, with uncarved corner blocks. The double parlors have black marble mantelpieces with cast-iron inner frames. All of the parlor windows, and the bay window of the north wing, are floor-length. The Governor Israel Washburn House, built in 1840, is transitional in its stylistic expression. Greek and Roman forms are intermixed, and the delicate scale of the exterior details is more Federal than Greek Revival.

The Elijah Kellogg House of 1849 in Harpswell is unusual in that it cannot be said to have an entrance front. The entrance is at the rear of the main block in an angle formed by the juncture of the main block with the rear ell. The elevated site of the house is secluded and overlooks Harpswell's Middle Bay. The four-bayed front of the main block faces the water and contains the double parlors with chambers above. The stair hall is behind the parlors and is flanked by a small room and a closet. The ell contains the kitchen. A small porch with a pier-supported roof shelters the entrance. There are corner pilasters, and the entablature surrounds the main block and continues on the flanks of the ell. The pediments have triangular windows with lattice panes. The interior trim is eared, or crosseted. There are folding doors between the parlors, and at least one fireplace still has a cast-iron fireplace stove with colonettes like those in the Shaw-Chick House at Winterport. The L-shaped stairs ascend in two runs and have newel posts of columnar form like that in the Ingalls House at Mercer. There is a cistern in the cellar. Both the exterior and the interior of the Elijah Kellogg House exhibit the chaste simplicity characteristic of rural Greek Revival houses at their best. After many years of neglect and damage by vandals, the house is now being restored to its former beauty by the present owner.

Full-scaled porticos with colossal orders were almost never applied to houses in Maine that had their fronts and roof ridges parallel. The Crooker House at Middle and South Streets in Bath, dating from around 1850, is an exceptional example of this rare type in that its tetrastyle colonnade uses the seldom seen Corinthian order. The five-bayed front is flush-sided, and the entrance has an iron-railed balcony above it. The dormer window overlooking the flat portico roof is a later addition. This dignified and impressive house was designed by the Bath builder Isaac D. Cole. Prostyle houses where the portico does not span the entire front are rare in Maine. The large house at 49 Pleasant Street in Gardiner has a main block whose two middle bays are sheltered by a pedimented portico with a colossal Ionic order—an anomaly in neo-classical architecture having *three* columns! The front is flush-sided, and the corner pilasters are fluted and have squat, unorthodox capitals composed of three acanthus leaves. The entablature frieze is paneled, the front pediment has a circular window, and the pediments of the main roof have windows with Gothic ogee arches. The house is capped by an octagonal cupola. There is a large rear ell. The entrance is at the right-hand side through a flat-roofed vestibule with a low cast-iron roof railing. The transom-and-sidelighted doorway faces the street and has etched glass of simple pattern. The double parlors are at the front of the block, and the dining room is behind the stair hall. The trim is simple, and the mantelpieces are of black marble. The parlors and stair hall have their original brass and ormolu gasoliers of neo-rococo design (now electrified). This curiously hybrid house is impressive in scale and is, in spite of its free-wheeling approach to classical canons, quite handsome. It was apparently built about 1850.

The Joseph Williamson House at 18 High

Street in Belfast is another example of the rare type wherein the portico does not span the entire front. The house was designed by Calvin A. Ryder and was built in 1842 (Figure 54). It is a very large wooden house for its time and place and differs from other prostyle examples in not being basically rectangular in plan. A very wide rear block projects one bay at either side beyond a front block that in turn projects one bay at each side beyond the three-bayed block immediately behind the tetrastyle Ionic portico. The columns rest upon granite plinths. The whole portico was moved forward to form a *porte cochère* in this century. Originally, the portico sheltered the three central bays of a five-bayed front block. The corner pilasters are very broad, and the deep entablature surrounds the house. The main roof is very low and is hipped. The pediment has a beautifully carved anthemion ornament and is particularly noteworthy for having the correctly low Greek pitch. The Joseph Williamson House is a superb example of its rare type.

If one were asked to select five houses as the best Greek Revival dwellings in Maine from the standpoint of design, houses equalling in caliber the Charles Q. Clapp House in Portland and the Kent-Cutting House in Bangor, the final two would be difficult indeed to determine from among many very good examples, but there is little doubt that the James P. White House in Belfast would be among the first three selected (Figure 55 and frontispiece). It does not precisely fit any of the types previously discussed. This strikingly handsome and beautifully detailed house was designed by Calvin A. Ryder and built in 1840. The subtle complexity of its variations on the Greek theme is unsurpassed by any other house in Maine. The rectangular two-storied main block is flush-sided, and the ell is clapboarded. The low base is granite. The rear block of the ell is as wide as the main block, giving the house an H-shape. The narrower two-storied ligature between front and rear blocks has inset one-storied Doric porches at either side.

The main block has a three-bayed front and is two bays deep. The facade composition comes to splendid climax in a boldly projecting central pavilion whose vertical thrust counters the horizontal expanse of the front and creates a dynamic tension dramatic in its effect. Both stages of the pavilion are Ionic *distyle in antis* elements, the second-floor one forming a one-bayed gallery over the deeply recessed front entrance. An elegant cast-iron railing fronts the upper half of the pavilion. The antae and columns of the upper portion are stilted, raising the pavilion entablature above the main entablature. The center pavilion is capped by a low pediment, and the pavilion entablature and roof extend across the hipped main roof to abut a large square podium with a balustrade behind which rises the tall octagonal cupola that completes the composition. All the carved enrichments of the exterior are concentrated within the central vertical axis of the house. The wreaths of the minor entablatures supported by the Ionic columns, the foliated scrolls and anthemion panel surrounding the windows above the entrance, the anthemion carving of the pavilion pediment, and the richly ornamental parapet of the cupola with its palmettes, scrolls, and acroterion blocks witness to the care lavished upon this splendid house. Within, there is a spiral staircase in the front hall. The hall trim has carved palmettes on its corner blocks, and palmettes also appear upon the eared architraves of the parlor.

This magnificently conceived and executed house, with its contrasts of plain surfaces and rich ornament and its marvelous balance of horizontal and vertical elements, is fortunate in having a worthy site. It stands within a large gore formed by the intersection of Church and High Streets. At the apex of the grounds is a charming latticed gazebo with ogee arches, lappeted eaves, an octagonal domical roof of ogee shape and a finial in the form of a birdhouse capped by a spirelet. Originally, the property was bordered by a handsome cast-iron fence of Greek Revival design set in a granite base. Fortunately, the section of fence along the High Street side of the grounds is still in place. It is to be hoped that the rest of the fence will eventually be restored. The James P. White House has, except for later four-over-four-light sash and the loss of a considerable portion of its fence, suffered almost no changes from its appearance in 1840. Both the house and its setting are irreplaceable assets not merely to Belfast or Maine but to the architectural heritage of the Nation.

The varied forms of the multitude of Greek Revival houses surviving in Maine give a characteristically 19th-century look to much of the state. It has been observed that among the great majority of the examples considered, proper architectural decorum prevailed. There were, however, occasional oddities, and none were odder than those built under the influence of the octagon craze. The vogue for octagonal houses was sparked by that eccentric figure, Orson Squire Fowler (see page 97 and note 3). It is unlikely that the fad would have had even minor success had not there been a widespread fondness for octagonal shapes at mid-century. The many instances where octagonal cupolas and even octagonal columns appeared will not have escaped notice. About a dozen or so octagonal houses were built in Maine, perhaps one or two more or less. Very few were Greek Revival. There is a Gothic example at 90 Hill Street in Biddeford, but most were in the Italianate mode so popular during the 1850's. One of the best of the Italianate examples is the Capt. George Scott House, a brick octagon on Federal Street in Wiscasset. On Route 11 in Oakland there is a wooden Greek Revival octagon probably dating from 1855. It is relatively small and simple, the only specifically Greek Revival element being the trim around the entrance. The interiors have been altered, but the original staircase with its newel post of volute plan remains. A large octagon, the Jesse Tucker House of 1856 in West Gardiner, has a Greek Revival entrance portico and trim in the same style. The Tucker House is very probably the best Greek Revival example of this peculiar house form in Maine.

4

PART 3

The Architecture of the Maine Shakers

Marius B. Péladeau

ONLY ONE RELIGIOUS SECT IN MAINE CAN BE credited with a characteristic development of architectural forms and of planning which has significantly contributed to the architectural heritage of the state. This sect is of course The United Society of Believers in Christ's Second Appearing, commonly known as the Shakers. Members of this celibate, communitarian religious society first came to Maine in 1780 and immediately succeeded in making converts

In the preparation of this contribution, the author wishes to thank Dr. Theodore E. Johnson, director of the Shaker Museum, Sabbathday Lake, Sister R. Mildred Barker, trustee of the Sabbathday Lake Community, and other members of the Village. David Serette has been very helpful in providing necessary photographs.

among various Protestant denominations, particularly in York and Cumberland Counties. By the 1790's they were sufficiently well established to found communities, or "Villages," at Alfred (1793), New Gloucester/Poland (1794) and Gorham (1807).

These three communities grew in population at the close of the 18th century and prospered in the early decades of the 19th. Gorham was merged with the Sabbathday Lake community in New Gloucester in 1819 to become the latter's Poland Hill Family; the latter finally was forced to close in 1887. Alfred and Sabbathday Lake continued strong into the third quarter of the century but both suffered a decline in numbers toward the end of the century. In 1931, the community at Alfred closed and the remaining members moved to Sabbathday Lake, New Gloucester. Sabbathday Lake remains a vital

Shaker Community to this day, the last in the world still incorporated as a religious entity.[1]

The Shakers, in Maine as elsewhere, exerted an influence on their contemporaries in far greater proportion than their numbers. Although they were never a large sect, their progressiveness in all aspects of rural and agricultural life was so highly regarded that their neighbors looked to them for leadership in nearly all aspects of farm life. The crops of Shaker orchards and gardens were closely watched to see which planting and harvesting methods gave the best results; the Shakers' development and use of labor-saving machinery were always in advance of such attempts by others; and their evolution of building styles and types, combined with their intelligent use of the natural topography of the land, sometimes was unconsciously imitated by the Maine farmer.[2]

The Shakers' life style revolved around worship and work for the common good of all, and was essentially a form of agrarian communism. The land was the source of their livelihood, and the siting of their Villages, the location of the buildings in relation to each other, and the specific construction details were all dictated by the intended use of the land and their associated trades and vocations. Both Alfred and Sabbathday Lake (Figure 56) were ideally located on gentle slopes of ridges overlooking bodies of water; these sites thus provided the advantages of waterpower from the brooks and streams flowing down to the lakes, and of slanting, well-drained orchards and fields, exposed to the rays of the sun and protected from winter winds.

Since nearly all the first Shaker believers were of Anglo-Saxon Protestant stock from the Commonwealth of Massachusetts and its District of Maine, it is logical that the roots of Shaker design derived from the work of 17th- and 18th-century New England master builders, carpenters, joiners and masons, the parents and grandparents of the first converts to the Shaker faith in Maine. In the same way, because the first buildings occupied by the Shakers were extant late 18th-century farm houses belonging to the original Believers at Alfred and Sabbathday Lake, it is clear why their later buildings consisted of pared-down late Georgian or early Federal structures, with the details of those architectural styles greatly simplified. Photographs survive of some of the original buildings at Alfred, which had been converted to the needs of Shaker celibate life. These illustrate the stages in the transition between the extant buildings they adapted, and the earliest buildings which they erected on their own; several of the latter still exist at Sabbathday Lake.

Insofar as the exteriors are concerned, no Maine Shaker buildings are unique, in the sense of being full-blown designs of the Shakers themselves. The interiors, however, incorporate features which they were forced to develop to meet the everyday needs of communal living. These needs required dual staircases and entrances to assure the separation of the sexes; large dining and kitchen areas to feed hundreds at one sitting; numerous work rooms for the many activities required to achieve self-sufficiency for each Village; separate quarters for children, adult Believers and religious leaders, (the Elders and Eldresses); and sufficient cupboards and storage space in these quarters (see Figure 57). All these and other demanding requirements were successfully met by the Shaker builder.

Shaker architecture, more so than the contemporary architecture of "the World," as the Shakers called the community around them, was "total architecture." By this is meant the special attention given to buildings in relation to the natural features of the land, and to one another, and the same attention to interior as well as exterior details; this concern with interiors resulted in the maximum use of floor and wall space. While it would be an insult to other good Yankee craftsmen to say that only the Shakers could design a simple, functional, building, one statement nevertheless holds true—the Shakers achieved complete functionalism more uniformly and more consistently than other Maine builders of the 19th century.

FIGURE 56. *Isometric view of Sabbathday Lake Village, New Gloucester, by Elder Joshua H. Bussell (1816–1900) of the Alfred Shaker Community; ink and watercolors, dated January 1, 1850.* *22 x 35 inches. Courtesy Shaker Library, Sabbathday Lake. Photo: Historic American Buildings Survey*

The Shakers brought to Maine architecture an outstanding quality, not only in the construction of individual structures, but also in the logistical planning that went into the overall plan of the Shaker Village so that farm-related trades could be carried out with maximum efficiency. This feature of their Villages is best illustrated by the series of isometric drawings of Alfred, Sabbathday Lake and Poland Hill done by Elder Joshua H. Bussell in the mid-19th century (see Figure 56). These charming bird's eye views of the Villages in ink and watercolors show the communities at the peak of their membership and prosperity. They give an excellent impression of the unified architectural expression a Shaker Village presented to its contemporaries.[3]

It is natural that among the buildings in a Shaker Village, the meetinghouses, centers of religious worship, constituted the focus of the communities. Almost as imposing were the large dwelling houses, where practically all community members lived and took meals, and the series of great barns around which farm life centered.

The meetinghouses at Alfred and Sabbathday Lake were the work of one of the greatest Shaker master builders. Brother Moses Johnson (1752–1842), a member of the Enfield, New Hampshire, Shaker Community, was a self-taught builder of rare excellence, and to him was assigned the task of traveling around the original eastern Shaker communities between 1785 and 1794 to design and supervise the construction of the ten meetinghouses in these villages.[4] He stayed long enough at each community to explain his concept of the structure to the local Shaker brothers and oversee the initial laying out and erection of the frame. Then he would move on to his next commission at another Shaker Village, leaving behind instructions as to the finishing of the interior.[5] The result was a remarkable uniformity from Maine to New York among the ten earliest Shaker churches.

Of the original meetinghouses in Maine, only the one at Sabbathday Lake, erected in 1794, survives today, but fortunately it is in such pristine condition that it has rightly gained the title of "the finest surviving Shaker meetinghouse" (see Figure 58).

The exterior illustrates the debt to the Anglo-Saxon New England past. The gambrel roof with pitches of nearly equal length, and with a steep first pitch, is closer to the English (or Connecticut) gambrel than to the Dutch (or Hudson River) gambrel, with its considerable overhang at the eaves, a very long first pitch, and a much shorter top pitch.[6] Since the first floor was used by the Shakers for their religious services and had to provide a seating and dancing area unencumbered by supports, Brother Moses supported the second floor by a series of ten massive boxed beams running the entire width of the building, each reinforced by strong boxed knee-braces (see Figure 59). These were painted a vivid, deep blue-green together with the rest of the woodwork. The contrast of these beams with the stark white plaster walls, chocolate-brown benches and yellow-ochre floors produced a striking effect.

This contrast between white walls and lightly stained or painted woodwork is almost universal in Shaker buildings except for barns and similar structures. The accent on specific tones contributes to the feeling of cleanliness and harmony of design, and emphasizes the perfect interior and exterior functionalism, which was the outstanding achievement of Shaker architecture. This effective use of coloration in both contrasting and complementary tones as part of an overall interior design specifically characterizes Shaker architecture.

Next to the Sabbathday Lake meetinghouse stands the Ministry Shop, to which the Ministry Elders and Eldresses moved when their quarters above the meetinghouse became inadequate for their numbers; in it they both lived and worked separately. Built in 1839, it is an interesting blend of out-of-date Georgian and current Greek Revival styles. Flawless storage cupboards and drawers on the third floor, built-in when the roof was raised in 1876, show that the mastery of de-

FIGURE 57. *Sabbathday Lake Village, Ministry Elders' Bedroom, second floor of the Meetinghouse; unchanged in color and arrangement since its completion in 1797, with the oldest built-in cupboard of its kind known. Photo: David Serette*

FIGURE 59. *Sabbathday Lake, Meetingroom on the second floor of the Meetinghouse; a large open area was required for Shaker worship. The Shakers sat on built-in benches at the edges of the room, and visitors on three-tiered seats in the corners. The room was heated by two Shaker stoves, of which one is shown at the right rear. Interior colors unchanged since 1797. Photo: David Serette*

sign remained with the Shakers long after they had enjoyed their most productive period. Now gone, but once completing the rank of buildings on the west side of the road, were the Schoolhouse (1880) to the north and the Seed House (c. 1820) to the south.[7]

Across the street from the meetinghouse and Ministry Shop stand two rows of parallel buildings, dominated by the massive Brick Dwelling, erected in 1883–84 to replace an earlier 1795 wooden Dwelling, which had become too small for the community's needs. Although the Shakers did not have the manpower to undertake the masonry work on this large structure, they did supervise and oversee the Dwelling's construction so that, in point of fact, it reflects the desires and needs of the Shakers at this particular time.[8] Another, perhaps the most important, Dwelling was found at the Poland Hill Family. This was an impressive granite Dwelling, four and one-half stories high, built totally of granite from the Shaker quarry. It was started in 1853 and completed in 1879 (see Figure 60).[9]

One Shaker of the 19th century, Brother Hewett Chandler, developed a reputation as a builder and designer in the mold of Moses Johnson.[10] It was he who drew the plans and erected the Shaker Schoolhouse in 1880. He also had a hand in remodeling and enlarging several buildings which are still standing at Sabbathday Lake. Brother Hewett Chandler was a surveyor as well and a craftsman in many other trades around the Village. It was an unfortunate stroke of luck that the Dwelling House which he designed in 1876 was never built. Instead, it was decided that workmen from "the World" would erect this Dwelling. Portions of Brother Hewett's architectural plans for the unbuilt version still survive in the Shaker Library. They reveal a talented man with excellent ideas about the efficient use of space, of proper ventilation and convenient egress, and with a good knowledge of the available building materials. Shaker architectural drawings are rare indeed. Considering that they came late in the 19th century, those of

Brother Hewett deserve special attention.[11]

If one turns again to the isometric drawing by Elder Bussell of Sabbathday Lake (Figure 56), one can see the effective total planning of the site and the functional placement of the different buildings in relation to each other. On both sides of the Dwelling were these buildings: the Girls' House (1796, remodeled 1901), where young girls were taken into the community, housed and educated; the Trustees' Office and Dwelling (1816), where Shakers entrusted with dealings with the "World" lived and had an office; the Hired Men's House (1796); and the Brethren's Shop, housing the rooms and machinery needed for the various trades carried on by the Brothers.

In a row behind these structures stood the buildings more closely allied with farm work. These included horse, ox and cow barns, all impressive in size; a poultry house; the greenhouse, ash house, Spin House, where the Sisters prepared flax and wool for looming; the Boys' Shop, where young men were taken into the community; the Herb House, Nursery, and the Sisters' Shop, containing work rooms for the Sisters.

On all sides were row upon row of orchards and plots devoted to hay, corn, herbs, and garden crops. Along the stream which ran north of the Village down to Sabbathday Lake once stood the great Shaker mill with its thirty-foot overshot wheel, and its ancillary buildings.

Alfred was planned and laid out in much the same manner, with minor exceptions. It still survives in part, but has been considerably altered by its later, non-Shaker owners. The great barn, however, is still relatively unchanged and exhibits the fine detail of Shaker construction (see Figure 61 of the comparable oxbarn at Sabbathday Lake). As at Sabbathday Lake, even today it is obvious that Alfred was planned as a village of model efficiency, designed to save steps and conserve energy.

The governing principles of intelligent site-selection and planning that characterized the

FIGURE 58. *Sabbathday Lake, Meetinghouse, framed in 1794 under the direction of Brother Moses Johnson of Enfield, New Hampshire, the* *first recorded Shaker master builder. Photo: Marius B. Péladeau*

FIGURE 61. *Sabbathday Lake Oxbarn (1847), built by the Shaker Brothers using modified Queen Post construction. Photo: David Serette*

Shaker communities of Maine have new relevance in the modern world. Wherever totally new and planned communities have been built, something of the kind of planning that was the special contribution of Shaker architecture is put into motion, although its roots are secular and do not originate in a religious vision. Thus, the unobtrusive but pleasing aesthetics of Shaker communities constitute a lesson in effective planning to modern architects, planners and landscape architects.

FIGURE 60. *Poland Hill Family, Stone Dwelling House (1853–79). The Poland Hill Family merged with Sabbathday Lake in 1887, and the property was sold in 1889; it was destroyed by fire in 1955. Old photograph by Brother Delmer C. Wilson, courtesy of the Shaker Library, Sabbathday Lake*

FIGURE 62. *Gardiner, Christ Church, by the Rev. Samuel Farmer Jarvis (1818). Photo: Historic American Buildings Survey, by Mark C. Bisgrove*

5

PART 1

Revival Styles of Maine Architecture:

from about 1840 to 1880

By William B. Miller

INTRODUCTION

BY THE 1840'S, THE STATE OF MAINE BEGAN TO assume a special character that set it apart from the rest of the United States. While its cities did begin to grow, Maine never achieved the impacted urbanization of the areas to its south and west. Likewise, although industry developed in Maine, it did not achieve the proportions which have elsewhere led to the problems of the present. This relatively slow development of the state is the reason that it still retains an admirable and somewhat rural quality. It is fair to say that Maine, as a province and young state, began the 19th century nearly on a par with the other states of the new republic, but by the end of the 19th century Maine was no longer abreast of developments elsewhere in America.

The Federal and Greek Revival styles in architecture are represented by outstanding examples in Maine; indeed, buildings continued to be built in these styles into the 1840's and 50's. There are some, moreover, to whom the modest and vernacular forms of Federal and Greek Revival have seemed to constitute Maine's only true building style; to such people, the changes in architectural style which began to appear in the late Federal and Greek Revival buildings of Maine may seem fortuitous, if not actually perverse (see Shipman below, pp. 84 and 93). The Gothic Revival signaled the first departure from these established styles.

The origin of the Gothic Revival style in architecture belongs to England of the 18th century. The style gradually affected town and country houses, church and state buildings. By 1834 when it was decided that the rebuilding of the Houses of Parliament in London should be done in a mediaeval style, the Gothic Revival movement had gained considerable status. Reformers in the Church of England sought inspiration from the Gothic past for new buildings. Polemic writing and archaeological research fostered commitment to the movement. In France, restoration had begun on the long neglected fabric of mediaeval cathedrals. In its trans-Atlantic crossing, the potency of the arguments for Gothic Revival were somewhat diminished; on the other hand, however, American Gothic Revival building soon became stylistically distinct from its origins.[1]

It is, of course, Romanticism which underlies this resuscitation of mediaeval architectural forms. Romantic naturalism, one phase of Romanticism, flourished and put out new growth in America. For Romantic painters and poets, Nature was to be studied and interpreted. The wonders of Nature, magnificently present in a pristine state in America, now provided an approved point of departure for the arts. Nature was seen, and cultivated as picturesque. In a development from this point of view, the irregularities, or the "naturalness," of mediaeval architecture were recognized as being in harmony with the Romantic interpretation of Nature.

CHURCHES AND HOUSES IN GOTHIC REVIVAL STYLE

In America early interest in Gothic Revival was evidenced by Benjamin Latrobe, who had been trained abroad and brought professional knowledge of all the styles of 18th-century England. However, his alternative, Gothic, plan for the Baltimore Cathedral (1805) was rejected in favor of a classical one.[2] Nearer at hand in Boston, Bulfinch's Federal Street Church (1809, no longer extant), has been described as a provincial reflection of 18th-century English "Gothick." This church became an influential model because "the meeting house arrangement was retained without significant change."[3] Bulfinch, of course, rarely worked in the Gothic idiom. His compromise, of "basically classical churches with pointed windows for the sake of a 'churchly' appearance,"[4] can still be spotted in many churches in Maine built and rebuilt in the first half of the 19th century. These churches are rectangular, symmetrical, structures with a single tower and spire at the front, built of wood, sheathed with clapboard, and almost universally painted white. The pointed arches above main windows and doors are usually "blind." Inside, the pointed arch is found as a decorative motif in the paneling and church furniture.

Examples of this rebuilding in Gothic style can be seen in the Phippsburg Congregational Church of 1802, with Gothic touches dating from 1847; the Oxford Congregational Church of 1826 and 1840; and the Baptist Meetinghouse in Yarmouth built in 1796, remodeled in 1825 by Samuel Melcher III, with Gothic additions made in 1837 by Anthony C. Raymond. Much the same combination of styles can be found in Dresden, Buckfield, New Sharon, Waterville, South Buxton, and in Harpswell (the last represented by the Elijah Kellogg Church of 1843).[5]

The Winterport Congregational Church, which is no longer used as such, is a good example of the traditional meetinghouse structure with Gothic detail. Calvin Ryder, who is cited as the contracting builder,[6] would have been a young man in 1834 when this church was dedicated. (Ryder later engaged in architectural practice in Massachusetts.) It is possible that Ryder was instructed to base the scheme of the Winterport church on the Orrington Corner Methodist Church because comparable Gothic detail occurs in both buildings.

In the Winterport church, the arches above the side windows are blind. Pointed arches on a

smaller scale grace the belfrey, in which a Paul Revere bell still rings. The main room of the church is now almost square in plan. Inspection reveals, however, that the original plaster continued up the front wall of the building into a space now used to contain the ladder to the belfrey; the coving of the original ceiling is clearly marked where the plaster stops. It is obvious that this main room was originally extended through the rectangular shape of the whole building, and that a vestibule built subsequently has caused its shortening to a square shape. One can also see that the shingles of the original building have been covered up, a clear indication of the secondary date of the latter structure. Although there is a record of a reshingling of the church in 1860, no record is known that mentions the change in the shape of the main room, or the addition of the belfrey.

In Gardiner are found two of the earliest and finest buildings in Maine in the Gothic Revival idiom: Oaklands, the mansion of the Gardiner family, and Christ Church (Figures 62 and 64). Both belong to the impulse to cast buildings totally in the mediaeval mode.

Christ Church, designed by the Rev. Samuel F. Jarvis and dating from 1819, chronologically belongs to the earlier period when classical prototypes inspired the architectural forms of American buildings (see Myers, Chapter 4, Part 2).[7] It is extraordinary that at this early date the design and appointments of the fabric make Christ Church more thoroughly Gothic Revival in style than a score of later meetinghouses embellished by a few "Gothic" details, but that remain essentially Federal or Greek Revival overall.

Christ Church is constructed of granite from

nearby quarries. The large scale of the building blocks, less than smoothly dressed, contrasts with the much smaller scale of the detail on the windows and doors. This combination imparts a sense of a rugged structure protecting its more delicate members. But the windows are generous in size and proportion, and fully glazed to the point of the arch. The tracery within each window progresses from the lower, larger, divisions to a flicker on the curving soffit of the arch. On the facade, the arches of the doorways seem bent to a load-sustaining stance. Windows and doors are emphasized with a dripstone or hood molding of stubborn granite members.

The square tower at the front is embedded in the main fabric of the church, but nevertheless projects forward. The bulk of the rising tower masks the ridge of the roof to the rear. An early lithograph shows smaller pinnacles which provided an additional detail of elegance, and echoed the shape of the spire.

The interior arrangement of vaults and pews marks off the nave, aisles and chancel in Christ Church. Recognizing this traditional division in Episcopal churches, one suddenly becomes aware that the whole interior space is quite uninterrupted by piers. The vaults are, of course, plaster, and their ribs descend into pendants; above them, an upper system of joined ribs terminates in rosettes. The cluster piers at the walls strike one as overscaled, but the color from stained glass windows and metallic appurtenances relieves any ponderousness the interior might engender.

In the adjacent church yard is a monument designed by Upjohn in 1864.[8] The Parish House of recent date shows how an imaginative contemporary architect can design an addition compatible with an older structure, which is also distinctive in its own right.[9]

The Boston architect Edward Shaw is credited with the design in 1836 of an early example of Gothic Revival architecture in wood.[10] In Machias, the Centre Street Congregational Church records reveal that an otherwise unidentifiable "Mr. Stephenson" submitted to the parish plans that were adopted.[11] Possibly Mr. Stephenson had seen Upjohn's St. John's in Bangor or the lithograph of it (see below, p. 155). Unlike St. John's, however, the Gothic idiom is here found on the exterior only. In addition, the five-sided mediaeval apse of the Machias example is different from St. John's, and unexpected in this context. The Centre Street Church makes use of buttresses and pointed arches, but clapboard and the extensive steps leading to the front doors and the rather broad facade mitigate against a full development of mediaeval church forms. In its own right, however, this church was considered ". . . the pride of the town," according to the local historian, "because of its size and beautiful architectural outlines," and further, it was ". . . recognized as the best framed church edifice in the state."[12]

Bath, fortunately, still has two largish wooden Gothic Revival church structures, the Central Congregational Church and the Winter Street Church. The latter—now part museum, part community center—was the earlier and was built in 1843 by the local builder, Anthony C. Raymond. It displays its Gothic character on the exterior only, and this is best seen in the variations in the pointed arches of the windows and doors, and set into the pilaster-like buttresses of the facade. Attention has been called to similarities of the Winter Street Church with the smaller Richmond-Dresden Methodist Church of 1848, and the Gardiner Universalist Church of 1842.[13] It should be observed also that all these churches seem to be variations in wood on the basic scheme in stone of Christ Church, Gardiner.

The Central Congregational Church in Bath (1846) has so many features in common with the First Parish Church in Brunswick that Richard Upjohn was credited with building it.[14] Both have board and batten on the exterior walls and wooden buttresses. The interior is quite thoroughly Gothic, unlike the Winter Street Church. The design for the Central Congregational Church, it has been asserted by the son of the local builder, was not Upjohn, but Arthur Gilman, a Boston architect and rival of Upjohn;[15] Gilman would have been in his twenties when he designed the Central Congregational Church.

Although Richard Upjohn first worked in Maine in an architectural style other than Gothic (see Myers, p. 116 above in reference to the Isaac Farrar House), his several commissions of the 1830's and 40's introduced a professional understanding of the Gothic idiom for churches and opened up some creative possibilities which were influential. A perspective drawing and the lithograph made therefrom of the exterior of St. John's Episcopal Church, Bangor, of 1836–39, clearly suggests masonry construction for Upjohn's first Gothic Revival church in Maine.[16] It has been asserted that this commission provided the prelude for Upjohn's major statement in Gothic Revival—Trinity Church, New York. Stone was the material proper to English and European Gothic with which Upjohn was familiar, and Trinity was built in stone; but at St. John's, Bangor, buttresses, crenelations, spires and pointed arches of varied curves, all in their correct mediaeval forms, were ultimately translated into wood. Inside, the working piers separating nave from aisles were described as having ". . . an organic feeling which is quite exceptional at this time." [17] This "organic feeling" was actually more consonant with the principles of true Gothic style than were contemporary meetinghouses with Gothic decorative details. Upjohn thus united historical accuracy and a theoretical understanding of Gothic in his design for St. John's Church, Bangor. The church did not survive the fire in Bangor of 1911, and was replaced by a church of late 19th-century Gothic Revival style designed by the architect's grandson Hobart B. Upjohn; (the latter should more properly be classed with the late Gothic churches discussed below, see pp. 166–67).

In the surviving Gothic Revival churches of the second quarter of the 19th century, the sig-nificant and inventive development takes place in the use and exploitation of wood. It is in this regard that the American Gothic Revival becomes a new thing, with no real counterpart in the English and European Neo-Gothic movement of the 19th century.[18] Upjohn himself led the way in this development. Two of his churches in Brunswick exploit the natural possibilities in wood. The First Parish Church of 1845 is a fairly large structure (see Figure 63).[19] Originally its spire soared high above the remaining tower which seemed sturdy and well reinforced by angled wooden buttresses. No doubt a gray or brown paint gave the exterior something of the substantial look of masonry. There can be no doubt about the material used for the walls, however, for board and batten walls can be nothing but vertically positioned wooden members. Although Alexander Jackson Davis is credited with the refinement of vertical siding which is known as board and batten, its use soon became widespread and particularly adapted to Gothic Revival.[20] The board and batten wall finish was a clear departure from the horizontal clapboarding of earlier Federal and Greek Revival styles; it harmonized, moreover, with the verticality of pointed arches and steeply pitched roofs. The double pitch of the roof of the First Parish Church notes the separation of nave and aisles, but the simple fold in the roof eliminates the possibility of clerestory lighting. On the other hand, the large roof area tends to bring the whole body of the church into one integral and simple form.

It is the interior of the First Parish church which provides a fanfare of wood exploited. The wooden piers expand into hammerbeam, truss, and rafter, in a treatment both structural and decorative. One can identify wooden members variously working in compression or in tension, balanced and extended, terminating in elaborate bosses, and making reverse curves in simply planed pieces. This elaboration of the interior makes the rest of the church fabric seem almost inert.

The intricacies of this structure in wood, deriving its Gothic forms from English mediaeval stonework, are indicative of the many challenges presented to builders in the Gothic Revival period. Architects, like Upjohn, proposed and designed; carpenter-builders, like Isaiah Coombs, the local man who supervised the construction of the First Parish Church, solved the problems. Perhaps, too, these ingenious carpenters suggested new paths for the architects to follow.

Gothic Revival architecture in wood seems to constitute a divergent stream from the pragmatic American inclination which produced clipper ships in this same period. Shipbuilders have been recorded as working on domestic carpentry. Thus the clipper ship, so functional in the eyes of Horatio Greenough,[21] and the intricate timber work at the First Parish, for example, may be seen as different responses to the challenges of working in wood. It is interesting to observe that in the shipbuilding town of Kennebunk stands the one Maine building most frequently illustrated in books on American architecture. That is, of course, the "Wedding Cake House," a Federal core with an exuberant and inventive Gothic overlay in wood on its exterior (Figure 121).

In St. Paul's, Brunswick (1845) Richard Upjohn develops a less pretentious but eventually more influential phase of Gothic revival architecture.[22] This is a small church with board and batten walls leading to a steeply pitched roof. Its lancet windows are deeply indented, and there is no bell tower or steeple. The interior space is covered by a pointed barrel vault executed in plaster and lath. Upjohn had many requests for such small parish churches, so he incorporated his experiences, such as at St. Paul's, into an architectural pattern book entitled *Upjohn's Rural Architecture* (1852).[23] This provided plans and details of what became known as "Carpenter's

FIGURE 63. *Brunswick, First Parish Church, by Richard Upjohn (1845). Photo: Richard Cheek*

157

Gothic," and as such is a distinctly American contribution to the Gothic Revival movement. Plans from this book were widely used. In Maine, St. Matthew's in Hallowell (1860) follows closely Upjohn's published indications. Variations in Carpenter's Gothic can be seen at St. Matthew's in Lisbon Falls (1860) and at St. Philip's in Wiscasset. Churches in board and batten Carpenter's Gothic can be found well into the middle western states. Another Maine variant, Grace Church, Bath, which is no longer extant in its board and batten Carpenter Gothic version, was designed by the son of Robert Hallowell Gardiner, the Rev. Frederic Gardiner; Francis H. Fassett, however, supervised the construction.[24]

Upjohn's third church in the town of Brunswick was the Bowdoin College Chapel.[25] This is a tall stone structure and an impressive architectural presence on the campus. Upjohn, first consulted about this commission in 1844, drew plans for the chapel in the following year, but a decade elapsed before the chapel had been completed. The simple round arches on windows and doors, the treatment of the twin towers on the facade, and the rather abrupt conjoining of the discrete architectural elements, have pointed to mediaeval German Romanesque style as the source of inspiration. Upjohn tended to reserve the Gothic style for Episcopal churches, but this is a case in which he explored a mediaeval style earlier than Gothic.

The interior of the chapel is based on the proportions and arrangement of English collegiate chapels. The pews run parallel to the sides of the chapel walls, with the open aisle in the middle. Lighted only by clerestory windows, the chapel is embedded in the fabric of the building so that classrooms, library, offices, art gallery all have been accommodated over the years in the peripheral parts of the plan. It comes as a surprise to discover a relatively small chapel in this large structure. Romanesque as a revival style did not become a dominant mode in architecture until the 1880's, when Henry Hobson Richardson de-

monstrated the possibilities of the style (see Shettleworth, p. 196 below).

In turning our attention now to houses, we again find an important example in Gardiner. The present Gothic Revival mansion of the Gardiner family is actually the second building at Oaklands (Figure 64). The first mansion house, as revealed in a sketch by Emma Jane Gardiner, shows a four-column portico fronting a two-story house which Robert Hallowell Gardiner built in 1810.[26] The original forty acres for this country seat of the family had been purchased because they were close to friends and their business in town; (the Gardiners had previously lived across the Kennebec River in Pittston and had found this inconvenient). The site for the mansion was selected by a Mr. John Richards, whom Mr. Gardiner characterized as "a gentleman of taste, familiar with the country residences of English gentlemen." Gardiner recalled that with "spy glass in hand, we climbed tree after tree to find the best view, and I do not think the location fixed upon, and on which the house is erected, could have been changed for the better."[27] Landscaped toward the southeast, the site provides a superb view of a downstream stretch of the Kennebec River.

Fire destroyed the Federal-style mansion at Oaklands on November 2, 1834. Since the fire started in the garret, there was time to save furniture, household effects and even the columns on the front.[28] After the fire it was apparently not difficult to persuade the Gardiners to rebuild in stone. As granite quarries were nearby in the town of Hallowell, it was even suggested to them that stone was cheaper than wood.

"A moderate ground plan was proposed, but one [member of the family] wanted an addition here, and another an enlargement there, till the plan greatly exceeded that first contemplated. Then to give it some architectural appearance, Upjohn was consulted."[29] In 1861 when Robert Hallowell Gardiner wrote his *Recollections,* Richard Upjohn, of course, was a famous architect and leading exponent of the Gothic Revival

Style, but in 1835 Upjohn had not yet executed in the Gothic manner a house with the pretentions of Oaklands. Gardiner, one suspects, was looking for a bargain; he contracted with an architect of great vision. Robert Hallowell Gardiner II, who edited the *Recollections,* adds a note that his father, upon crutches at the time and confined more than usual, occupied himself in planning the new home.[30] A model was made; the hall and stairs were entirely the design of Mrs. Gardiner. In Boston, Gardiner met Upjohn and presented him with the Gardiner family plans and the model, enjoining him not to change the general plan. But Upjohn's own plans and elevations for Oaklands make clear that he devoted full professional attention to this commission. He advised on the foundations, suggested a good formula for cement, and explained the plan and processes to the workmen on the job.

The account by Robert Hallowell Gardiner gives no indication that the family intended to rebuild Oaklands in the fashionable and romantic idiom of the Gothic Revival. Gardiner speaks only of the responsibilities he felt toward entertaining visiting clergymen and summer guests at his country residence. Oaklands has thirty rooms in all. Gardiner admits that "few country residences had so many attractions as our place had. . . ."[31] And in 1837 Nathaniel Hawthorne spoke of Oaklands in terms of a "castle or palace."[32] One can only infer that it was the architect who persuaded the Gardiner family to accept and build the present splendid palatial structure. On the other hand, the presence of Gothic Revival Christ Church in the town of Gardiner (see Figure 62), which was built in 1819 with the generous support of Robert Hallowell Gardiner, suggests that he was amenable to Gothic, parapets, drip moldings, and all. Perhaps the process of persuasion was not so difficult.

The Gardiners were committed to stone and apparently to a large and somewhat irregular plan. On the river facade the windows vary in size and proportion, yet the composition as a whole maintains a strict symmetry. The entrance facade shows a uniform size for twelve windows and one other slightly wider window occurs over the main entrance. Many windows have drip moldings but no other framing element cuts into the stone; some windows include portions of stained glass. The same Tudor arch at the entrance appears in interiors also. All these niceties point to a designing architect.

As an interior architectural composition, the entrance hall and staircase seem less felicitous than the splendid suite of rooms across the river facade. A feeling of spatial continuity is felt in these three rooms, which have Tudor arches between them. The bay of the middle room bows outward with generous fenestration.

The landscaping is still quite informal. The mansion is isolated, with utility and farm buildings placed at a remove from it.

Although Robert Hallowell Gardiner complained that Oaklands cost more than three times what he intended originally to spend, Upjohn produced for him a stately Gothic Revival composition that suited the social needs and station of the family. The stone masonry, the attention to its finished surfaces and crisp edges all bring an urbane sophistication to this country mansion. In this idiom and in its situation, Oaklands had few rivals. Oaklands today is a landmark in the history of the Gothic Revival style, yet curiously enough, it is an exception in the executed works of Richard Upjohn. The Italianate style ". . . proved to be almost standard in the more important examples of Upjohn's domestic work."[33]

While Oaklands, the manor house of the Gardiner family, is an exceptional example of Gothic Revival architecture, the Gothic Revival design of many modest dwellings built in the 1840's and 1850's popularized the taste for the picturesque and the romantic. Many of these houses survive in Maine. The John J. Brown House (1845) in Portland even survived the move from its original setting on Spring Street.

FIGURE 64. *Gardiner, "Oaklands," built for Robert Hallowell Gardiner by Richard Upjohn (1835–37). Photo: Richard Cheek*

This cottage derives its Gothic forms from the published drawings by A. J. Davis included in Andrew Jackson Downing's *Cottage Residences* (1845). Henry Rowe, the designer of the Brown House, and recently arrived in Portland, had been trained in England, but in this building he was influenced by the American fashion for Gothic Revival, rather than by English sources. Rowe subsequently built other Gothic Revival houses in Portland, few of which survive today.[34]

Cliff Cottage, the Godfrey-Kellog House in Bangor, presents all the aspects of the Gothic Revival one could wish to find in a modest example of domestic architecture in the style (see Figure 65). Although the exterior wood is painted gray, and apparently always was this color (as a recent examination of the many layers of paint affirms), the animation of all the other architectural forms and details brings about a comfortable balance with the sober color.[35] The house sits parallel to Kenduskeag Avenue and is approached down a curving driveway. The rather small story-and-one-half appearance from the front belies the extension of the house downhill. Moving to the southern, garden side of the property, one is introduced to the full elaborate extent of Cliff Cottage. It extends downhill at least four times the measure of the street facade. A wing ending in a bay window opens on to this garden side, and a cutback is provided with a porch. Up to this point the house is sheathed in clapboards, but its further extension turns to the vertical board and batten, so typical of Gothic Revival style.

The full extent of the sloping roof takes up half the elevation, but this plane is interrupted by large gabled dormers which provide light and space for the second floor. Bargeboards fastened to the underside of these gables provide a filigree in wood and contrast in scale with the larger surrounding forms.[36] These bargeboards and the railings above the porches are cut out in the wood and then chamfered. This beveling gives a slight three-dimensional treatment to the pattern; sunlight is reflected on these differing planes, and the decoration thus has a certain sparkle. In the same way the elaboration of the brickwork near the top enlivens the chimney stacks, and the red and blue panes of cut glass quicken the light in the main entrance-way.

The ample lawns and the view across the valley still sustain much of the original picturesque setting of Cliff Cottage. The nearby precipices at the Kenduskeag Stream of course provide the cottage with its name. Also nearby is the locally designated "Lovers' Leap." The romantic quality of this place would have been even more strongly felt in the late 19th century, because, as photographs show, the gardens were more elaborately laid out, with steps and terraces, walks, extensive plantings and a fountain. The gardener working for the Godfrey family at that time was John Jordan, a veteran of the American Civil War. More important is the fact that Jordan's native origin was the Azores where terraces have long been a frequent adjunct to gardening. Jordan's memory and experience would account for the terracing applied here to a Bangor garden.

From the same period, too, dates the Gothic Revival doghouse, now placed in the crescent of the driveway of Cliff Cottage. Both the batten and board siding and the bargeboards in the gables match the style of the main house. Evidently constructed for a large animal, this doghouse now accommodates itself to its role as a playhouse for children.

In 1947, a pamphlet was printed by the Godfrey family to memorialize Cliff Cottage on its one-hundredth birthday, and to recall the members of the family who had lived there.[37] John Edwards Godfrey bought the property in 1847 and built the core of what became a complex plan during the next half century. The pamphlet speaks more of the family than of the architecture as such. But changes and additions are credited to individual owners and thereby dated, roughly at least. The shed at the west became a kitchen; the dining room was enlarged in about 1868 when George Frederick Godfrey,

son of the first owner, brought his bride to live in Cliff Cottage. The frame of a new stable was raised, according to the pamphlet, in 1871, and the "workshop" building dates from the early 1880's.

In the house itself, additions were made to accommodate Judge Godfrey's desk off the library. A northern alcove was added to the dining room, probably originally for use as a cool room. Large panes of glass in the French windows replaced small panes, to help weatherproof the house. Light oak woodwork was installed in the dining room to match furniture designed for the room at this time (also see Isaacson below, p. 254). This account rehearses only some of the additions and changes which are cited in the pamphlet, and which can be observed in the structure of Cliff Cottage itself. By 1928, when Angela Godfrey Clifford bought the house, considerable deterioration had occurred. During the past twenty-five years its present owners have restored and repaired Cliff Cottage with loving care. In addition, the stable and work shop have been adapted to serve as an office for its physician-owner.

The front entrance opens into a hall which boasts a parquet floor, an early if not original feature in Cliff Cottage. This hall becomes the center of a ground plan in the irregular shape of a latin cross. A front parlor moves outward toward the street, ending in a bay window. At the left there is a music room, at the right a library and office. To the rear opens the larger space of the dining room, which leads into a china closet and the kitchen. The plan continues past a back door on to the porch, to the laundry in the rear. Upstairs, four bedrooms continue the plan of the ground floor, the master bedroom, with dormer windows on the south side, being located above the dining room. Addition-

FIGURE 65. *Bangor, Cliff Cottage (Godfrey-Kellogg House) (1847). Old photograph courtesy of Dr. and Mrs. Robert O. Kellogg*

al rooms, originally for servants, and the back stairs complete the plan.

Cliff Cottage seems to be a very small house at first glance from the street, but the foregoing account reveals how much is included. A feeling of intimacy and warmth is sustained throughout Cliff Cottage, however; the rooms are small, the ceilings are low, much of the woodwork remains unpainted. As can be well seen in Cliff Cottage, Gothic Revival in its domestic phase avoids the pretention of architectural formality and accommodates to a wide variety of domestic arrangements and decorative treatments.

A rather exuberant example of the Gothic Revival houses of around 1850 is found in South Robbinston. The complexity of the plan is matched by a comparable variety in the pitched planes of the roofs, the dormers and the porch. The bargeboards sport an inverted frond motif of heavy scale, yet the glass in the windows is divided into delicate segments of the pointed arch by curving muntins. Thus the picturesque effect is deliberately sustained throughout this particular house.[38]

The Linwood Cottage in Bucksport was sited to overlook the Penobscot River. Here the one-and-a-half-story wooden structure at the left terminates in a gable. A bay window projects on the first floor; above it, another smaller window repeats its angle. Shingles repeat the plan-shape of the projecting bay. Where the building turns at the right a square tower rises, and the shingles here create a diamond pattern. Next a dormer window grows out of a porch pillar. A generous overhang of the gable protects the pointed arch of the window, but this Gothic detail ultimately rests on a Greek pillar of the porch. The corner tower was described in 1855 as an Italian campanile.[39] Thus several distinct architectural styles contribute to a picturesqueness which may seem bizarre and un-historical to the purist, but which also is an indication of the inventive adaptations made by American builders.

A more modest example of Gothic Revival do-

mestic building is the Shurtleff-Jackson House of 1850 in Winslow. The rather simple plan is enlivened by bargeboards of bold pattern and the present contrast of red wall color with the white trim.

The house built for Henry Boody in Brunswick (now called the Johnson House) deserves special notice for several reasons (see Figure 66). It was designed in 1848 and built the following year. Its architect, Gervase Wheeler, was trained in England and had recently arrived in the United States. His drawing for this "Plain Timber Cottage Villa," as it was labeled, appeared in *The Architecture of Country Houses* published by Andrew Jackson Downing in 1850.[40] Through this publication, the house in Brunswick became the model for a residence built later in Worcester, Massachusetts. Thus, the design of the Boody–Johnson House influenced subsequent building, reversing the usual sequence in which building in Maine followed the lead of architectural fashion elsewhere.

Downing was the most influential propagandist for the directions architectural fashion was taking in the mid-century, and his several books went through many editions.[41] Downing generally continued to give examples of standard English forms, e.g. the small villa, the picturesque cottage. At first he advocated stone construction, but later he spoke favorably of wood, for this material had long been preferred in America. The Boody-Johnson House in fact reveals a transition between a design for stone construction to the exploitation of the possibilities of wood.[42] For example, the hood moldings over the windows derive from stone precedents; likewise, the water table or foundation "course" with its beveled top edge reads as an emphatic horizontal stabilizing member proper to a stone construction, but here of course, it was realized in wood. By the next generation, designers of wooden houses masked this foundation "course" with verandas or balustrades, or abandoned it altogether.

A neutral color, brown or grey, was certainly

intended to convey the appearance of stone on these Gothic Revival houses. The brownish tones of the Boody-Johnson House and the grey of Cliff Cottage in Bangor, which are both original, exemplify this choice of color in the style. Thus, the white paint or other bright colors seen today on Gothic Revival houses misinterpret the original intention of this style.

The treatment of wood was a conscious part of the design of the Boody-Johnson House on

FIGURE 66. *Brunswick, Boody-Johnson House, by Gervase Wheeler (1849). Photo: Richard Cheek*

Wheeler's part. He speaks of this house as ". . . framed in such a manner as that on the exterior the construction shows, and gives additional richness and character to the composition." [43] All this can be observed at the Boody-Johnson House in the corner posts, the board and batten sheathing, the half-timbered gables. This exposure of the construction and its treatment in a decorative way has marked this house as one of the early examples of the Stick Style. In this aspect, too, the Boody-Johnson House is an especially significant example of architecture in Maine, and in America.

One can point to other significant features of the Boody-Johnson House. The main body composes itself in a three-part manner, with two identical gables breaking forward from the center section. This three-part division is, of course, a venerable compositional device, but it was usually applied to much larger structures. Downing advocated efficient planning for the American private house; to the rear of the facade on the Boody-Johnson House absolute symmetry does not prevail, and this accommodates to flexibility in planning.

Picturesque form permits functional planning. The one-time Brunswick resident Harriet Beecher Stowe wrote a book with her sister in 1869.[44] In it they advocated and illustrated the plan of the whole house with function, convenience and hygiene in mind. This is clearly planning from the inside out, in anticipation of 20th-century practice, particularly in the planning of domestic architecture.

Other buildings as well as the Boody-Johnson House combined features of the Stick Style with Gothic details. A very prominent example of the Stick Style of construction is found in the bell tower of St. John Baptist Episcopal Church on the main street in Thomaston. The earlier, very simple, design of the facade in board and batten contrasts with the treatment of the tower, which stands as a separate unit at the right, and was added in 1872, with Francis H. Fassett of Portland as the architect.[45] Fassett made the support-

ing and bracing members in wood project from the sheathing of the tower, so that the "skeleton" construction is revealed. The facade and the tower of this church strike two distinct stylistic notes, but at the same time they demonstrate that differing treatments in wood can be aesthetically compatible, just as different Gothic styles in stone can work together in visual harmony. A later example of a church entirely in the Stick Style is the Unitarian Church in Augusta (1879), designed by Thomas Silloway and Albert Winslow Cobb of Boston.[46]

The success of Gothic Revival style clearly demonstrated that the long succession of architectural styles derived from classical sources had been broken. Greek Revival, Federal and Georgian all refer through the European Renaissance to sources in the architectural styles of classical antiquity, of about two thousand years earlier. Gothic Revival architecture recommended itself as a visible expression of Romantic sentiment, and for churches, it provided an aura of Christian venerability. The Gothic style presented new challenges and offered opportunities for new formulations in plan, and in a yet unexploited vocabulary of decorative detail.[47] As Henry-Russell Hitchcock has phrased it, the mediaeval revival style acted as a "solvent" on the classical mode.[48] It opened up the possibilities for change which led eventually to modern architecture in the 20th century.

Gothic Revival was only the first of several styles revived and then inventively exploited in America. At the same time, new building techniques, and the increasing availability of metal, brought even more dynamic changes to American architecture.

CHURCHES IN LATE GOTHIC REVIVAL STYLE

A mediaeval revival style of one sort or another continued to be employed for churches as a kind of "Sunday architecture," long after fashion and technology dictated other modes for "week day" buildings. Illustrations in *Portland and Vicinity* by Edward H. Elwell, published in

1876,[49] show eight churches variously described as "Gothic," "pointed," or "Norman." In Portland and other cities in the state the Roman Catholic churches by Patrick Charles Keely of New York present an urban and American adaptation of Gothic forms. St. John's Roman Catholic Church in Bangor of 1855, St. Joseph's in Lewiston of 1864, and in Portland the Cathedral of the Immaculate Conception of 1866, all by Keely, enclose so ample a volume that the red brick seems rather tenuous as a supporting and defining material.[50] Later in the century, as Oliver Larkin has observed, architects ". . . with less imagination and greater scholarship"[51] inherited and continued the Gothic Revival. In Lewiston, Trinity Episcopal church of 1877 by Charles Coolidge Haight of New York, exhibits many correct details in its stone structure, but the cramped and irregular plan fails as a whole to meet the architectural competition of the neighboring churches on the City Park. Haight was the first architect for St. Luke's, Portland.[52]

Architectural erudition can be seen in St. Andrew's Episcopal church in Newcastle which was designed in 1883 by the English architect, Henry Vaughan.[53] The church nestles into its hillside and displays exterior walls which carefully imitate the half-timber construction of English mediaeval building. The interior has many appointments of such a correct and appropriate nature that the whole church seems a sophisticated transplant to rural Maine. Vaughan is said to have painted the original stencil work on the ceiling in this, his second American commission. He did other work in Maine to the turn of the century, and he is best remembered for his contributions to the Episcopal cathedral in Washington, D.C.[54] At the turn of the century, several Episcopal chapels were built largely through the efforts of, and for, summer residents. The rather quaint, Gothic, fieldstone chapel of St. Peter's by the Sea, 1898, in Bald Cliff, York is typical. The chapel was given by a Philadelphia lady, Mrs. Nannie Dunlop Connaroe, and its architect, Charles M. Burns, was also a Philadelphian. In contrast to this late rehearsal of mediaeval style, the Kittery-Biddeford electric trolley car made a scheduled stop in front of the church.[55]

ITALIANATE STYLE

The architectural style which supplanted Gothic Revival in the decade before the Civil War is designated Italianate, Tuscan, or even Etruscan. Its distinctive decorative forms derive from Renaissance architecture which began in Italy in the 15th century. But by the 1850's when the Italianate manner reached the United States and Maine, it came for the most part by way of English example.[56] Italianate style and the later Victorian development of it could apply to a wide variety of building types—modest cottages, suburban houses, churches, and civic and commercial buildings. Italianate took for granted the freedom of planning permitted by picturesque mediaeval modes and was marked by variation in the treatment of details ranging from imitative and correct Renaissance forms to an exuberant inventiveness, which a later generation dismissed as a lapse in taste. Admittedly there is an almost separate awareness of the torso of the building in contrast to its architectural apparel, and the decoration does not always bear a functional relation to the structure. However, it is this very vigor and assertiveness of the man-made structure and the clamor of an individual statement which, if boisterous, nevertheless underlies most architectural statements. Total enjoyment of architecture ought to include a receptiveness for the ostentatious as well as for the reticent.

FIGURE 67. *Bangor, Pierce-Giddings House, by Benjamin S. Deane (1851). Photo: Bangor Daily News*

The Pierce-Giddings House in Bangor, now the Thomas School of Dance, was designed as a large frame residence in the Italianate manner (Figure 67). Although much of the lawn and garden have been lost on the State Street side, the house still dominates the corner at Forty-two Broadway and State. Dating from 1851 this house was designed by Benjamin Deane.[57] Much was built and much survives in the Italianate mode to confirm its challenge to styles of classical and Gothic inspiration. The Italianate speaks in terms of amplitude, of diverse building shapes, and decorative detail. There was freedom for the architect to experiment, for the client to select color and splendor, and for carpenters to elaborate in the brackets, moldings and balustrades.

The Pierce-Giddings House is close to the business center of Bangor. From the house there is a view toward the river, which is now partially blocked by the recent high-rise construction downtown. The gardens included a gazebo originally placed in the rose garden on the corner of the property which is now lost. (The gazebo itself still survives in a private garden elsewhere in Bangor.)

Surprisingly one discovers that this house has an approximate Greek-cross plan. This undoubtedly suggested itself to Deane to take best advantage of the orientation. Three principal rooms enjoy an exposure south, and the front parlor has windows on three walls. The entrance is gained through the north-east indentation and the north window in the original dining room

FIGURE 68. *Bangor, Low-McEvoy House, hall, by Harvey Graves (1857). Photo: Richard Cheek*

has an unusually large opening of three full double-sashed windows embraced by its own frame. This care in planning bespeaks the attentiveness of the architect and would seem to belie by fifty years Frank Lloyd Wright's boast of "exploding the box" in his use of the Greek-cross plan, for example in the Willitts House, in Highland Park, Illinois.

The entrance hall of the Pierce-Giddings house is lit by one window on the north side. The hall, as frequently in other architectural styles, is embedded in the plan and consequently receives little light directly from outdoors. Although the north window alleviates the situation somewhat in this case, the hall remains generally dark. At the left of the entrance one sees the stairs turn and descend from the second

floor and terminate in a newel post which supports a statue of a figure holding aloft a lantern whose illumination must have hovered centrally in the spaces of the hall and stairway; (this probably later fixture of "white metal" is comparable to the pair illustrated in Figure 69 of the Morse-Libby House hall). So the enclosed dark space is relieved by upward expansion, by this artificial illumination, and through the lighter areas seen through the doors to the rooms beyond.

Much of the interior of the Pierce-Giddings house has been adapted to its present use as a dance school, but the framing over doors and windows still remains and presents a satisfying relation between the low gable and generous architrave members at the top.

A notice in the *Whig and Courier* for April 7, 1857 announces that Mr. Joseph W. Low, Esq. intends to build a "fine mansion . . . on the most prominent point on Thomas's Hill" in Bangor.[57a] Six lots formed the original land holding. The notice speaks of plans including a cupola as "original with the architect . . . Mr. H. [Harvey] Graves of Boston." "Principally Roman" is the description of the style, which is today identified as Italianate. Since the details of the announcement accord with the present house to a considerable extent, the original effects intended by the architect can be felt today (see Figure 68). The gable roof slopes to the east, parallel to the front. "The roof is to project two feet over the walls, and to be handsomely finished with brackets. . . ." This generous overhang and the muscular brackets still provide a feeling of ample protection to this house on the hill. "The walls . . . to be finished in block-work . . ." refers, of course, to the wood sheathing of the exterior scored to simulate stone. A section of this "block-work" has been carefully imitated to replace a damaged corner of the house. A long piazza runs along the south side. The cupola, mentioned earlier, is a small glazed octagon which commands a fine view, now only partially blocked by the standpipe reservoir beside the house. The bird's eye view map of Bangor of 1875 shows this house as still quite isolated.

The notice in the *Whig and Courier* mentions not only the Boston architect, but also names the local contractors, Fogg and Benson, the painter, Marshall Dyer, and the mason, Ivory Small. The notice continues, Mr. Low "contemplates building [in] the present season." . . . "to be finished by one year from June next," i.e. 1858.

The original plan inside the house never pretended to innovation, and the arrangements have been modified somewhat during the more than a century of occupation. The original generous proportions of the twelve-foot ceilings in the front rooms and the ample spaces lend substantial dignity to the hall and the parlor at the north side. The stairs turn at the top and bottom of the flight. The bannister terminates in a mahogany newel post; the latter has a dish-like shape which is still useful for notes, if no longer for calling cards. In the hall the doors are framed with a flat member, but in the north parlor the windows are topped with a cavetto cornice, which projects more than those in the hall. Large and heavy curtains in the original furnishings would bring this feature into scale.

Some time after 1877 and before 1904 a sun parlor was opened to the south side. The sliding doors with leaded glass in this room, and in the dining room, are also to be dated from this period. The Low-McEvoy House, as it is now called, as a whole conveys the impression of having been lived in and enjoyed in a manner consonant with the original intention of its builder.

It is difficult to ignore the pretentiousness of the Morse-Libby House in Portland (Figure 69), and apparently just such an effect was intended by the client and the designer, who was possibly Henry Austin, in 1859.[58] The house, today known as the Victoria Mansion, is still sufficiently isolated in its street-scape so that the full architectural articulation can be unmistakably perceived. It sets back, it thrusts up, its architectural members seem flexed in every direction, in the most dramatic Italianate manner. Henry Austin built in this mode in New Haven, Connecticut. The style was hardy enough to endure, with modifications, into the last quarter of the century.

In the Morse-Libby House we are struck first by the bold asymmetrical arrangement of the large parts, and then by the ordering of each individual part into a symmetry of its own. This contradictory composition employs throughout the language of classical architecture—Ionic columns, triangular and segmental gables, consoles and balusters, quoins and cornices. A detail seen in one place reappears in a separate yet adjacent context, but the succession and application of details is never predictable. To experience such an exterior is to perceive abrupt jumps

FIGURE 69. *Portland, Morse-Libby House, 109 Danforth Street, by Henry Austin (1859–63). Colby Museum of Art architectural archives, photographer unknown*

and changes, but also to discover reassuring continuities.

In the Italianate mode here and elsewhere, a square tower rises above the neighboring elevations; this is a type of tower that continued to be used in Second Empire buildings. Its flattish roof, the generous cornice and grouped windows at the top level provide an outlook room in the tower, hence it is sometimes called by the Italian designation *belvedere*. The substantial stone fencing along the sidewalk repeats the baluster motif above the entrance and porch to the left.

The deliberate composing of architectural masses in irregular and non-symmetrical sequences arrived in America and Maine about mid-century, but this picturesque quality had long been practiced in England. The composition of the Morse-Libby House can be seen as an expression of an extreme position of the picturesque. Irregularity combined with classical detail is used to produce a sophisticated, highly fashionable result. Although the picturesque dominates the whole, a severity frequently invests the parts; the spectator may enjoy this elaborate play.

The Italianate mode commended itself as an efficient yet flexible planning procedure. The steep roofs of the Gothic Revival produce awkward attic spaces which only dormers can make usable. In the Italianate style, the retention of cubic shapes throughout means that interior space can be completely utilized. At the Morse-Libby House an artifice is employed to tuck a third story behind the entablature so that a bold two-story composition gives the intended effect.

The hall of the Morse-Libby House is dominated by a stairway which points toward the front door (Figure 70). The presence of this virtually sculptural intrusion brings the hall into balance. For everywhere else in several small scales the decoration extends or enframes; colors and textures contrast and continue from floor to ceiling in rich array; tiny mural paintings provide pictorial rewards after the visitor has made

his initial adjustment to the rich effects of the hall. It seems that wood, stone and metal are carved or cast in every way that can exploit the material. To the modern eye the appetite for such fare must needs be nearly gargantuan. But the modern eye has seen subsequent decades of architectural decoration which favored more continuous, if uniformly textured surfaces in the "Shingle Style" and in the "Arts and Crafts" decor. Of course Bauhaus modern must seem virtually sterile in comparison to the abundant and resplendant decoration in the Morse-Libby House, in covings and spandrels, escutcheons and rosettes. We need only be reminded that in a generation earlier than the period of the Morse-Libby House, flatness and considerably more reticent architectural forms were generally preferred. Federal and Greek Revival seem sober and restrained in comparison to this exuberance. It is apparent that the Morse-Libby House presents a fully extended statement of the Italianate style in the most magnificent form. Other examples will echo but faintly the splendor found in this Portland mansion.

A splendid Italianate house was built in Richmond for the local shipbuilder and entrepreneur Thomas Jefferson Southard in 1855 (see Figure 71).[59] It is a composition of discrete blocks in the structure of the building as a whole, to which is applied the intricacy of brackets, balustrades and arches. The cupola restates in miniature the basic geometry of the main body below, but to it has been applied the same brackets, paired and inverted, at the same scale as these members below. This implosive treatment brings an elaborate finale to the top of the building.

In Brunswick the residence of the college president, originally erected nearby in 1860 and moved to the present site in 1874, presents an Italianate statement less exuberant than the T. J. Southard House.[60] Flush siding and Corinthian columns at the entrance porch lend a reticence and dignity to the composition.

Italianate as a style has been identified in almost two hundred structures in the recent sur-

FIGURE 70. *Portland, Morse-Libby House, hall; wall and ceiling frescoes by Giovanni Guidirini. Colby Museum of Art architectural archives, photographer unknown*

172

FIGURE 71. *Richmond, Thomas Jefferson Southard House (1855). Photo: Kennebec Journal*

vey of Bangor.[61] Most of these are residences, but Italianate also applies to churches. The characteristic round arches, brackets and gables are found on Bangor's Unitarian Church, built in 1853 from plans supplied by John D. Towle of Boston. A similar but slightly less ornamented design of a year later came from Towle for the Hammond Street Congregational Church. The Chapel of the Bangor Theological Seminary (1859) also belongs to the Italianate mode.

Elsewhere in Maine one also finds Italianate style used for churches. Harvey Graves of Boston introduced elements of the English Baroque of Wren and Gibbs in the tower of the High

Street Congregational Church in Auburn (1859–1860). The Court Street Baptist Church of 1870 was designed by John Stevens of Boston, Mass. In Biddeford the McArthur Library was originally built as a church in 1863.[62]

Another mixture of styles can be observed in the First Congregational Church in Saco (1863).[63] Thomas Hill, the local architect-builder, drew upon sources reminiscent of the mediaeval Romanesque as well as the Italianate. In the belfrey, the consoles arch around the clock-faces, and above this the tall spire rises, producing a rather unusual composition for the whole tower. The First Congregational Church, Yarmouth, was designed in the Italianate mode in 1867 by George M. Harding of Portland.[64]

Institutional buildings of high architectural quality were added to the Maine scene in the Italianate style. Hathorn Hall (1857), one of the original buildings for the Maine State Seminary, Lewiston, which in 1864 became Bates College, still occupies a prominent position on the campus (Figure 72). It stands in the vicinity of buildings in other architectural styles with which the college has been visited. Hathorn Hall gives a clear and sober assertion of the Italianate manner, which was the architectural style in fashion at the time of the founding of the college. The original Building Committee, in appealing for building funds, seemed aware of its responsibility toward an architectural image. "We are founding an institution for coming time," the Committee statement reads, "and while we would avoid extravagance on the one hand, we would have some regard for public taste on the other." [65] Gridley J. F. Bryant, the architect, responded to the Committee's injunction with an Italianate design executed in a brick body with nicely appointed details in granite and white trim.

A portico in the Corinthian order announces the main entrance. A horizontal course marks the rather high ground story from the first. On each floor the windows are topped successively with a segmental arch, a round arch, and a flat entablature. A bracketed gable terminates the forward break on the facade. In the cupola a bell still rings the college hours. The interior once contained "chapel, recitation and society rooms, cabinet and library," and has been now adapted to office and classroom space.

Bryant, a Boston architect, worked elsewhere in Maine, designing jails and courthouses in Auburn, Augusta, Bangor and Machias;[66] (see Hansen, p. 258 below, in regard to his design of the Boys Training Center, South Portland).

EGYPTIAN REVIVAL STYLE

The search into the past for appropriate symbols to express contemporary feelings led to the design of monumental and architectural forms derived from the mortuary structures of ancient Egypt in American cemeteries. The obelisk was used for numerous memorials earlier in the century.

In Maine, a rather singular example of this impulse is seen in the tomb vault of F. O. J. Smith in Evergreen Cemetery, Portland (Figure 73). Its granite facade is based on the form of an Egyptian pylon; it has a slight batter in the elevation, and a cavetto cornice caps the central section. Flanking the entrance are diminutive pyramids. First constructed in 1860, the Egyptian design of this tomb may have been suggested by Smith himself. In 1876, the tomb was moved to Evergreen Cemetery from its earlier location.[67]

The W. A. Blake House, now the Prentiss and Carlisle Building, at 107 Court Street in Bangor still presents a stately architectural presence (Figure 74). During the second half of the 19th century this residence may not have appeared so white and isolated as it does today. Fencing, planting, ancillary buildings may well have provided a more picturesque ensemble, but then and today the inherent architectural forms of the house assert themselves and make the claims a wealthy owner would want appreciated. These features include a mansard roof above two full stories, a projecting entrance porch, and a central dormer window whose profile resembles the section of an immense church bell. These are the features that characterize the Second Empire of the Blake House, a style brought to Bangor in this example by the architectural firm of Ryder and Fuller of Boston, in 1857.[68]

FIGURE 72. *Lewiston, Bates College, Hathorn Hall, by Gridley J. F. Bryant (1857). Stereopticon photograph courtesy o fthe Maine Historical Society, copy by Wendell A. Ray*

FIGURE 73. *Portland, Evergreen Cemetery, F. O. J. Smith Tomb (1860). Photo: Maine Historic Preservation Commission, by Frank A. Beard*

At this date, mansard roofs were a very new fashion, and the Blake House may well represent their first appearance in Bangor. Calvin Ryder had earlier building experience in Maine as a young man in structures of a more vernacular character; (he built the Winterport church dis-

cussed earlier). Here, however, the latest in high fashion comes from the office of Ryder and Fuller, professional architects "up" in Boston. The drawings for the Blake House show cleanly inked lines and delicate washes to indicate to the builders of Maine the detail of high fashion. To be sure, extensive renovations at the turn of the century replaced many of the Second Empire specifications of the original architects, but the thrust of the original pretentiousness remains. It has been noted that the Blake House strongly resembles a house in Cambridge, Massachusetts,[69] a resemblance that can be explained in several ways. Perhaps the Bangor client admired Ryder's previous work; it is even possible that Ryder sold the same plans twice.

Although the exterior flush sheathing of wood has been scored to resemble stone construction, other elements on the facade, such as the brackets supporting the overhang and the coupled supports of the entrance porch, reveal sizes and strengths appropriate to the wood material and construction. Through American architecture this tendency recurs to shape both structure and decoration to the most limber and minimal form that the material will permit.[70] Thus many American architectural forms, particularly in rural interpretations, that have been dismissed as historically inaccurate do in fact follow this pragmatic law of functionalism. It may seem surprising to point to such an ornate example as the Blake House in substantiation of this law, but if the principle can be sensed here, one can see its relation afterwards to a wider range of American buildings.

The interior of this house, accessible today as the office of the land management firm of Prentiss and Carlisle, reveals a plan of amply sized rooms, with a majestic stairway of walnut descending the large hallway. A dining room of oval plan calls to mind the provision for a similarly shaped room in the Isaac Farrar House designed by Richard Upjohn; possibly the oval plan had been admired by the Blakes; (see Myers, p. 116).

The Blake House accommodates to its present adaptive use in a serendipitous way. The several managers of woodland holdings in Maine work in elegant offices appointed with mid-century and late-century moldings, paneling and carved passages of a refinement not immediately associated with the business concerns of the occupants. But the evident and happy concern of the present owners for their office building assures its continued preservation.

The mansard roof is characteristic of what is called French Second Empire style, which is associated with the architecture of the post-Civil War period. Among the buildings of the late sixties and seventies which have survived, many have long been neglected or altered to the detriment of their original stylistic character, and many have moved downward, as it were, in social function. Now, one hundred years later, critical attention has accorded a respectable place to the mansard in the heritage of American architecture.

A few notable examples of this widespread style in Maine are of interest. In about 1869, General Charles Roberts built his residence on State Street in Bangor with a mansard roof, but of cottage size. On this example, the mansard roof, like a helmet, invests the upper portion of the nearly cubic volume of the whole.[71]

In Kennebunk, generous spaces and discrete buildings preserve the character of a later 19th-century street-scape. Among the residences, the George L. Little House of 1875 is a splendid example of the mansard type; it incorporates a tower of complex design which adds much to the design of the house.[72]

The tower of the Governor Joseph R. Bodwell House in Hallowell of 1875 is central in the composition, its free upper roof sloping inward in its own mansardic repetition of the story below.[73] Built about 1880 in Auburn, the Charles A. Jordan House was the architect's own home, on which he lavished considerable attention;[74] this house incorporates a porch on its front. Another example, the Bangor Children's Home, designed by Henry W. Hartwell in 1868–1869, is a red brick structure with a *porte cochère* at its main entrance.[75]

In Portland, the James Phinney Baxter House, built in 1869–1870, was a notable example of the mansard style before its recent demise.[76]

PUBLIC BUILDINGS

In the parks of many cities and towns in the late 19th century the bandstand was a conspicuous ornament. Of the few surviving today the one in Lewiston City Park, dating from around 1881, is a splendid and well-maintained example.[77] The cast-iron parts, the decorated and painted dome, its polygonal shape, all lend a festive air to this less than serious public monument. Exotic architectural sources, such as Near Eastern domes, were frequently drawn upon for the designs of bandstands.

Government buildings designed by government architects brought distinguished architecture to several cities in Maine in the second half of the 19th century. Ammi B. Young's design of 1852 for the United States Custom House in Bath originally incorporated such a sober formality of academic correctness as to be considered more Renaissance Revival than Italianate. The building has been enlarged but still asserts itself as an important government symbol near the busy river front and the bridge traffic.

Young also designed the Custom House in Bangor and the Post Office in Portland, neither of which are extant. The Custom House in Waldoboro, also by Young, has now become the Public Library. The Custom House and Post Office of 1855 in Belfast continues to function as a government building and is located at an intersection of streets of nearly plaza proportions.[78]

During Young's tenure as Supervising Architect in the Treasury Department, the United States Marine Hospital at Martin's Point was constructed (1855–1859). Previously a summer hotel had occupied the site which affords a view of the city, the bay and the ocean beyond. The H-plan of this hospital permits many rooms to have outside windows. A three-story structure of

FIGURE 74. *William Augustus Blake House, 107 Court Street, by Calvin A. Ryder and Enoch Fuller (1857). Photo: Maine Historic Preservation Commission, by Frank A. Beard*

179

brick with quoins at the corners and a fairly heavy cornice, it has as its outstanding feature the five-bay, three-story porch defined and ornamented with cast-iron grill work, which is rather rare in Maine architecture.[79]

After the fire of 1866 two new federal buildings appeared in Portland. One of them, the United States Post Office and Courthouse of 1867–73 is no longer standing. It was considered one of the outstanding designs of its architect, Alfred B. Mullett.

The United States Custom House was designed by the same architect in a different and more contemporary style. The French Baroque of the 17th century was the inspiration for the Second Empire Style exemplified by many of Mullett's buildings. Here a rather strong sculptural articulation of the wall contrasts with the conservative classic components. Columns nearly in the round, pilasters and an arch with keystone frame a second arch within so that the window is deeply recessed. Emphatic entablatures separate the three stories on the downhill facade. The tower above each end and the forward break at the entrance provide a lift to counter the ponderous horizontal emphasis. The roofs of the towers present a convex surface in mansardic idiom similar to that of the 1850–57 additions known as the "Nouveau Louvre" in Paris, by Lefuel and Visconti. In 1876, the Portland Custom House was praised as a building "substantial, convenient, and elegant."[80]

Other federal buildings in Maine by Mullett include the former Custom House and Post Office at Wiscasset of 1868 and the Custom House at Machias of 1871. Another work by Mullett, the Custom House and Post Office for Rockland no longer exists.[81]

The building which once housed the Belfast National Bank (Figure 75) and the building for the Masonic Temple nearby in the business district of the city were both designed by George M. Harding of Boston. Israel Parker was the local master builder for both structures.[82] The bank was built on a triangular plot in 1879, and points

toward the open space of Custom House Square. In its present surroundings, the Bank seems a very elegant, somewhat diminutive Victorian presence in a neighborhood of stalwart architectural hulks of larger scale.

The bank facade on the square is nine feet wide. Ascending from the sidewalk at each end of the facade are stone buttresses, angled and decorated, which continue in brick, and then change to stone bulge-brackets supporting short columns of polished red stone; the latter support a segmental arch, dentilated in its soffit. Continuing upward there is a circular insert in the pediment which terminates in a gable. All of this elaborate formal development frames one window on the ground floor, and another window above the latter, capped with a pointed blind arch. At the main cornice, the line of the buttresses below is picked up and extended to stone pinnacles which intersect the steep gables. The termination is a combination of manipulated brickwork, a colonette, a carved keystone and a pinnacle which stops the march of the iron grillwork on the ridge. This extended description of the facade of the Belfast National Bank is intended to give a full impression of the decorative richness of this building; its richness is such that all the other buildings in the vicinity of this bank seem stark by comparison.

Francis H. Fassett, already noted as the architect of the tower of St. John Baptist Church, Thomaston, had been practising architecture in Portland for more than a dozen years when he designed a symmetrical double house (Figure 76) as a residence for himself and his son (and partner by that time, 1876).[83] Mansard roofs have been used here, but in the center the third story continues straight upward, although brackets in brick suggest this is a tower. The left and right gables of the third floor mask the mansard slant to the rear. The dominant effect is a play of slender vertical windows, grouped by twos and threes, rather deeply set in a ponderous fabric. Metal grillwork at a central balcony and at the very top, together with slender

FIGURE 75. *Belfast National Bank, by George M. Harding (1878–79). Photo: Historic American Buildings Survey, by Cervin Robinson*

columns at the entrance portico, help to relieve the heaviness; the original iron fence would have provided a welcome horizontal spread to the composition. Fassett followed fashionable styles during his long career. In this example the mansard seems suppressed, as if he were moving to another mode.

It is appropriate to end this discussion of Revival styles with another work by Francis H. Fassett. Fassett was first mentioned in connection with the board and batten Gothic Revival, and then as designing in the Stick Style. In the 1870's, his designs incorporate the mansard component of the Second Empire Style, as we have seen in discussing his own house (Figure 76). In many buildings he favored red brick and its coloristic treatment was characteristic of the Italian or Ruskinian Gothic style. This approach to brickwork can be seen for example, in the central part of the Maine General Hospital begun in 1874.

After the Portland fire of 1866 Fassett did much in the rebuilding of the city. But by 1880, Fassett was moving in his designs toward the more fashionable Queen Anne style, a change in his work that was undoubtedly due to the presence in his office of the young John Calvin Stevens.

FIGURE 76. *Portland, Francis H. Fassett Double House, by Francis H. Fassett (1876). Photo: Richard Cheek*

5

PART 2

Turn-of-the-Century Architecture:

from about 1880 to 1920

Earle G. Shettleworth, Jr.

THE DEVELOPMENT OF ORDERED COMPLEXITY:

JOHN CALVIN STEVENS AND HIS CONTEMPORARIES[1]

O N THE EVE OF MAINE'S CENTENNIAL IN 1920, the historian Louis C. Hatch observed:

During the last quarter, or possibly one should say the last half of the nineteenth century, Maine developed a new industry—she became a vacation state. At least one of three things is usually desired by the jaded city dweller after seeking relief from intolerable heat—the ocean, mountains, woods. Maine has them all.[2]

Responding to the unique natural setting of post-Civil War Maine, John Calvin Stevens of Portland played an important part in designing the homes and buildings which served visitors and residents alike. The overwhelming force of his creativity and production continued steadily from his first year as a professional in 1880 until his death in 1940.

Stevens' long career is of interest because his work reflects many of the major architectural trends from the Civil War to World War II. Moreover, he made a national contribution to the development of the Shingle Style during the 1880's. This pivotal decade witnessed the evolution of his architecture in several distinct phases, beginning with the Queen Anne, moving through the Shingle Style, and culminating in an Adamesque version of academic Colonial Revivalism, which became his preference for the remainder of his practice.

Despite the importance of John Calvin Stevens' career from both a national and statewide point of view, little is known about his work except for his *Examples of American Domestic Architecture,* a book which he co-authored with his partner Albert Winslow Cobb in 1889, and a commentary on three of his houses in Vincent Scully's brilliant pioneering study of the period, *The Shingle Style.*[3] In fact, much of the limited material that has been available contains erroneous information in regard to dates and the accreditation of design. For example, most of Stevens' production between 1886 and 1888 has been credited to the firm of Stevens and Cobb, but their partnership was not formed until 1888.

John Calvin Stevens was born in Boston on October 8, 1855, the second son of Leander Stevens, a grocer and hotel manager. His family settled in Portland in 1857, and he acquired his education in local public schools. At an early age he showed a talent for drawing, and he followed a special program of mathematics and surveying while at Portland High School. Upon his graduation in June of 1873, he had hoped to enroll in the Massachusetts Institute of Technology, which then offered the only course of formal architectural instruction in the United States. When this proved financially impossible, young Stevens chose the next best alternative by becoming Francis H. Fassett's office boy in September of that year.

At the age of fifty in 1873, Fassett was Maine's undisputed architect for all seasons, providing designs that ranged from suburban cottages and summer hotels to courthouses and hospitals. A quarter of a century of practice, combined with European travel and an extensive library, made Fassett unique in his ability to offer a solid preparation for the architectural profession in Maine.

As Stevens recalled in later years, "Mr. Fassett had an excellent library, and his boys had ample opportunity to make use of it, so that the office boy had only himself to blame if he did not profit by what was at his hand."[4]

John Calvin Stevens' talent and ambition did not allow him to remain long at sweeping floors and tending fires. He soon became a draftsman for Fassett and by 1880 had proven his worth to the extent that the elder architect offered him a partnership. The direct consequence of this promotion was the opening of a branch office of the firm on Pemberton Square in Boston, the center of architectural activity in New England. Stevens spent a total of eighteen months operating the Boston office. The only known work of importance completed there was the Hotel Pemberton, which was built at Hull on Boston Harbor in 1881.

Yet the young architect's stay in Boston was of far greater importance than this one commission would indicate. The former town house in which he was located at 5 Pemberton Square also housed the office of William Ralph Emerson, who had recently completed the design of the first fully developed example of the emerging Shingle Style, the C. J. Morrill House of 1879 at Bar Harbor. In his own words, John Calvin Stevens "became very friendly with W. R. Emerson and gained much inspiration from him."[5] In addition, Stevens became acquainted with Emerson's chief draftsman, Albert Winslow Cobb, who later joined him in Portland as a partner. Indeed, Emerson and his new architectural forms had a profound effect on Stevens and Cobb. In their book *Examples of American Domestic Architecture,* they spoke of their mentor in the most reverential terms:

There is an architect in this country, whose beautiful domestic work, scattered over a wide area from Mount Desert to Colorado Springs, is a delight to all who know it.[6]

John Calvin Stevens' Boston experience ended in 1882 when the pressure of work in Portland caused his return home. He continued to work with Fassett until April of 1884, when he started his own practice. This move was apparently endorsed by Fassett, who allowed his partner to become established independently while still in his office. Fassett even permitted Stevens to take at least one client, Walter G. Davis, with him when he left.

Stevens worked alone until 1888 when he invited Albert Winslow Cobb to join him in partnership. This association was dissolved in 1891. The firm has continued to the present with Stevens' son, John Howard Stevens, as a member from 1905 until his death in 1958, his grandson, John Calvin Stevens II, active from 1934 to his retirement in 1975, and his great-grandson Paul Stratton Stevens joining in 1966.

In order to understand John Calvin Stevens' architectural development, it is necessary to begin with the years which he spent under the tutelage of Francis H. Fassett. Throughout the decade of the 1870's Fassett ardently pursued his personal version of High Victorian Gothic architecture, a style characterized by its richly ornamental surface treatments which are comprised of a variety of competing details. His work was consistently of brick construction which was highlighted by such elements as sills and lintels of brown and cream colored stone, stringcourses of either stone, a few actual Gothic details, intricate ironwork cresting atop roofs and towers, a carved stone to identify the name and date of the structure, and touches of the Stick Style on wooden porches, doors and gable decorations.

Fassett applied this conscious synthesis of the period to virtually every project that he undertook. In these post-Civil War years, his assignments grew more challenging and complex. Not only were there the usual homes, churches, commercial blocks, and public schools, but also such divergent institutional structures as the Museum of Natural History, the Home for Aged Women, and the Maine General Hospital, all in Portland; an administration and classroom building for Gorham Normal School; and an addition to the State Hospital in Augusta. These last commissions reflect a society facing its needs in new ways and on a new scale.

The most notable example of Francis H. Fassett's work during this decade was his own home of 1876 at 117 and 119 Pine Street in Portland (Figure 76). Here he combined stone brackets and columns, wrought iron, and a French roof over the central unit, all within a vertical format of bays with tall, narrow windows. This imposing brick and stone mass was flanked on either side by a complex frame Stick Style porch; (see also Miller, p. 181 above).

As a draftsman, John Calvin Stevens first learned the use of architectural forms under the influence of the High Victorian Gothic Style. This is clearly reflected in his early sketchbooks which, in addition to conventional classical studies, contain pages of meticulously rendered Gothic details that are cited as having been copied from Pugin and such periodical sources as the *British Architect* and the *American Architect and Building News*.[7]

After Stevens was sent to Boston in 1880, he gained "a new outlook," as he noted in later years.[8] There he was active in the Associated Architects M.I.T. Sketching Club and became exposed to the current Queen Anne Style, as well as to the newly forming Shingle Style. From this point on, he appears to have functioned as the chief designer for the firm, while Fassett largely managed the business and attended to the clients.

As mentioned above, Stevens' most significant design in Boston and the only known work to have been constructed during his stay there was the Hotel Pemberton, a triple-decked resort hotel with wide porches around each level. The overall conception of the building is simple and straightforward. Yet as one looks to the roof, one sees the beginnings of Stevens' handling of Queen Anne features. The roof bristles with outcroppings of half-timbered gables, a cupola, and a French-roofed tower. The hotel was described in *King's Handbook of Boston Harbor* as being "in that quaint and somewhat outré form of architecture for which good Queen Anne has been held responsible, with towers, gables, balconies, and other picturesque adjuncts, and a coloring of olive and old gold which would delight even William Morris."[9]

Several important commissions in the Portland area brought John Calvin Stevens back from Boston in 1882. Among these was his first major commercial building, the J. B. Brown Memorial Block on Portland's downtown Congress Street. The vertical format of this five-story brick structure derives from Fassett's High Victorian Gothic work, but its overall conception reflects a simpler, more uniform mass. Gone are Fassett's embellished stone brackets and columns. In their place is an ornamental scheme which has been reduced to clean combinations of bricks and terra cotta panels. In both his preliminary and final designs for the Block, Stevens abandoned the symmetrical balance of Fassett's work in favor of the asymmetry of the Queen Anne style.

The year 1882 also brought three significant commissions from Samuel D. Warren, the progressive paper mill owner of Cumberland Mills in Westbrook. The first was the Warren Block, a multi-purpose community hall which exemplified S. D. Warren's benevolence at a time when concern for workers and the environment in which they lived was all too rare. A period newspaper account asserted that the building would "excell anything of the kind in the State if not in New England." [10]

Containing four stores, several offices, a public hall and a hall for the Odd Fellows and the Knights of Pythias, the Warren Block reflects the trend in late 19th-century American architecture which was concerned with interior function and allowed that consideration to dictate

exterior form. Thus, little traditional symmetry is present in Stevens' irregular and picturesque Queen Anne plan. An additional factor which governed the Block's design was its triangular site located at the intersection of two major thoroughfares.

The Warren Block has an elongated rectangular shape, stands three stories high, and possesses a somewhat irregular hipped roof with a small square domed tower. The building is of brick and frame construction and displays brownstone and terra cotta decoration. The first two stories are of brick, while the third is of wood sheathed in shingles.

Contemporaneous with the construction of the Warren Block were two additional S. D. Warren projects, ambitious Queen Anne Style homes for his mill agent William L. Longley (Figure 77) and for his son John E. Warren. The Longley House is handsomely sited on a hill adjacent to the mill and overlooks the mill pond. This dwelling represents Stevens' most articulate approach to Queen Anne design. The house itself is a simple cubical volume, from which gable-topped rectangular two-story units are projected forward at opposing corners. Within this context, Stevens added such distinctive elements as wooden scrollwork, fluted chimney brickwork, and terra cotta panels. The latter features, with their Eastlakian vases of flowers, were of sufficient quality to be published as designs in a Boston Terra Cotta Company catalogue of the period.[11]

In the nearby Warren House on Cumberland Street, Stevens began to move for the first time toward creating a house by using spatial order instead of the interplay of details and mass. The relationship of the volumes within the framework of the gabled main unit becomes the dominant theme, foreshadowing the Shingle Style, while spatial variation is achieved by employing undercut voids at the entrances. Here also Stevens exhibits his first significant work with the textures associated with the Shingle Style. Each story of the Warren House has a different skin;

the first, clapboards; the second, scalloped shingles; and the third, alternately long and short rectangular shingles. Queen Anne details are held to a minimum, pointing toward the architect's complete abandonment of them. This transformation from a features-oriented to a spatially-oriented approach is best witnessed in the "Sketch for Seaside House" of 1884, which reveals Stevens on the verge of totally integrating mass, spatial projection, spatial voids, and varied surface textures into one spatial program.[12]

In 1883, John Calvin Stevens designed a house which constituted a clear break from the complexities of the Queen Anne approach and can be considered his first Shingle Style work. The John H. Davis House at 62 Bowdoin Street in Portland is composed of volume-defining flat planes of shingles. While two types of shingles continue to be used, they are now employed to distinguish the major volumes of the house rather than to separate stories or spaces. Only one major decorative surface feature is present, a remarkably abstract panel of field stones set into the first-story brick wall of the facade.

The next year, 1884, saw Stevens' wholehearted adoption of the lessons he had learned from the Warren and Davis houses. At this time he was planning and building his own home at 52 Bowdoin Street. Here he first stated a design program which he frequently favored during his career: the ordering of the volume of a house through the use of an all-encompassing gambrel roof. Stevens' unifying solution for 52 Bowdoin Street immediately found its way into the *American Architect and Building News* and was subsequently published in the *British Architect* and the *Scientific American Building Monthly*.[13] Scully assessed its importance in the following terms:

As in the early Emerson houses of the late 70's, in which the roof became a plastic entity uniting the volumes of the house, so here the roof goes a step further toward drawing all subsidiary volumes under the dominance of one main volume. The house becomes one sculptural unit, three-dimensional but contained. The varied equilibriums of the cottage style are resolved into a single unity, and while there is still an indication of the movement of various spaces within the main volume, they are all eventually drawn in under one sheltering roof.[14]

Thus, Stevens achieved a spatial variety and continuity simultaneously, a quality characteristic of the best examples of the Shingle Style. His residence was followed by such gambrel-roofed commissions as the James Hopkins Smith House of 1884–85 on Falmouth Foreside (Figure 78), nine S. D. Warren Worker's Cottages of 1886 on Cottage Place in Cumberland Mills, Westbrook (Figure 79), and the Frederick Cony House of 1889 on Stone Street in Augusta.

Of these, the Smith House carried the gambrel roof to its strongest resolution. Here the proportions of the gambrel became broadened, because the architect was not confined to a city lot. With the Smith House, Stevens skillfully demonstrated his ability to use the gambrel as a plastic shape in order to execute his spatial intentions rather than a rigid Colonially-inspired format. The success of this design, achieved at a cost of $7,000, was noted by the contemporary critic George W. Sheldon, who wrote in his *Artistic County Seats* of 1887:

The architect of Mr. Smith's house, on the contrary, has struck out for himself, with due regard for the spirit and meaning of classic works, but without subservience to their forms and details. He desires, also, that the comparatively small cost of the building should be emphasized. One rarely sees so much breadth, so much roominess, and so much solidity obtained with so small an outlay of money. Effect has been sought by strength of mass and simplicity of form.[15]

The more ample proportions of the Smith House allowed for a freer plan than in the linear organization of 52 Bowdoin Street or a worker's

FIGURE 77. *Westbrook, Cumberland Mills, William L. Longley House, by Francis H. Fassett and John Calvin Stevens (1882). Photo: Richard Cheek*

FIGURE 78. *Falmouth Foreside, James Hopkins Smith House, by John Calvin Stevens (1884–85). Photograph courtesy of the Maine Historical Society, after George W. Sheldon,* Artistic Country Seats *(New York, 1887).*

FIGURE 79. *Westbrook, Cumberland Mills, S. D. Warren Workers' Cottages, Cottage Place, by John Calvin Stevens (1886). Photo: Richard Cheek*

cottage in Cumberland Mills. As Scully observed:

Here is open planning compactly organized, with the mass of the hall fireplace forming a plastic pivot around which the space swings, while the parlor fireplace pulls away from the main space to give meaning to its own special sitting area away from circulation. The feeling of extension to the outdoors is also very developed. In the unified mass of the exterior the gambrel roof is beautifully related to the deep void of the covered piazza. The porch penetrates the volume of the house itself, so that the interior and exterior are not merely closely related but actually interwoven in a serene extension of space which is continuous and clear.[16]

Another factor behind this form of planning was found in the simplified requirements of retreat living. Such informality allowed for the clustering of socially functional spaces along with the service spaces of the kitchen and the servants' piazza within the same volume.

John Calvin Stevens was in the first year of his private practice when he designed 52 Bowdoin Street and the Smith House. Of this productive year of 1884, he later wrote:

By that time I had become convinced that I had chosen the right vocation, for I was busy and happy in my work, as a man should be.

Progress meant plenty of study, and plenty of hard work, but I feel that it was well worthwhile, for it brought me the approval of men who represented to me the best in the profession.[17]

Stevens' desire to experiment with alternative solutions for a problem is reflected in two rejected proposals for the Smith House. One employs the gambrel roof within a symmetrical academic Colonial Revival framework. The other represents a dramatically different approach to the interweaving of form and space, using a major gable at one end of the house. This concept was further refined the next year in Stevens' project "A House By the Sea", which

was published in the *American Architect and Building News* for September 12, 1885.

The sketch for "A House By the Sea" of 1885 represented a major advance in John Calvin Stevens' architectural thinking. In this house, which regrettably was probably never built, Stevens projected an emphatic horizontal quality in both space and massing.[18] Here is found what was probably the architect's most masterful manipulation of the interior and exterior spaces of a house. The undercut void of the porch is assimilated into the structure even more solidly than in the Smith House. At the same time, elements of space which make up the whole are clearly articulated. Yet this is done within the context of a more complex articulation of volumes rather than the easier unification of a single dominating form.

The years of 1884 to 1888 were John Calvin Stevens' most successful in terms of his use of the Shingle Style. For Stevens and his contemporaries, this style functioned best when it combined the use of forthright architectural forms, local materials, and a natural setting. Thus, when Stevens once met a noted watercolorist, the artist exclaimed: "Oh! I know your work! You are the man who designs summer cottages that we can paint."[19] Indeed, between the 1880's and World War I, the Maine coast became dotted with shingled summer colonies such as York Harbor, Cape Arundel, Prout's Neck, Camden, Bar Harbor, and Grindstone Neck. John Calvin Stevens' Shingle Style work in its natural context reached its fullest expression at two of these summer colonies, Cushing's Island in Casco Bay and Delano Park on Cape Elizabeth.

Cushing's Island was first inhabited on a large scale by summer visitors to the Ottawa House, a resort hotel built in 1858. Twenty-five years later the hotel owners, the Cushing's Island Company, commissioned the eminent landscape architect Frederick Law Olmsted to create a plan for the future development of the island. Olmsted visited Cushing's Island in the spring of

1883 and was immediately impressed by the picturesque quality of the island's wild environment. In his report to the Company, he advised that:

The Island is not a good place for a neighborhood of smart and fine suburban residences such as many prefer to pass their summers in. Streets suitable to such an occupancy of it would be difficult of construction, costly and a blemish upon its natural scenery. Villas and cottages of the class in question would appear out of place, tawdry and vulgar upon it. Lawns and gardens appropriate to them are in large parts of the island out of the question. Notions of improving the island based on what has generally been attempted at many public favored places of summer resort should therefore be wholly abandoned. But to persons who wish to take as complete a vacation from urban conditions of life as is practicable without being obliged to dispense with good markets, shops and the occasional ready use of city conveniences; who have a taste for wildness of nature and who value favorable conditions for sea bathing, boating and fishing, the island offers attractions such as can be found, I believe, nowhere else on the Atlantic seaboard. To all such I recommend it unreservedly. The only danger of reasonable disappointment to such persons lies in the chance that others of incompatible tastes and ambitions will aim to make "improvements" of various sorts, and attempt a style of life incongruous with the natural circumstances and repugnant to tastes that the island is otherwise adapted to gratify.[20]

Olmsted went on to make additional recommendations for maintaining the rustic quality of the island. These included controlled lot sizes, building setbacks from the roads, a two-story height limitation, prohibiting the decoration of a house "in its upper or more exposed and conspicuous parts with jig-saw or other extrinsic and puerile ornament," and the planting of trees along paths.[21]

Of the approximately a dozen Shingle Style cottages which John Calvin Stevens designed for Cushing's Island between 1883 and 1909, one of the surviving examples is of particular interest. In the Sidney W. Thaxter Cottage of 1884–85, Stevens uses a unifying covering of shingles over the entire house, including a dramatic series of arched porch-roof supports. The porch void is fully integrated into the volume of the house, controlled by an emphatic double side-gable which the architect became increasingly fond of using. Internally, the Thaxter Cottage ranks with its contemporary, the Smith House, in the sophistication of its open first-story plan. In each dwelling the chimney and staircase are at the center, and the parlor, hall, and dining room flow freely from one to another with the kitchen being the only enclosed room. With its three-quarter circulation, such an arrangement points toward the completely open planning achieved within the next two decades by the cross-axiality of Frank Lloyd Wright.

Stevens' distinctive double gable reappeared on the C. A. Brown Cottage of 1886–87 in Cape Elizabeth's Delano Park (Figure 80). Sited on a bluff overlooking the ocean, the Brown Cottage seems to grow out of its rugged surroundings. As Scully observed, "There is a strong structural sense and a decisive visual impact. The house begins to take on that archetypal intensity toward which one feels the deepest yearnings of its period—however confused by semantic complexity to have been directed."[22] Here Stevens sensitively works with a combination of textures, natural materials and a volumetric control which includes a single projecting frontal gable and the double side gable.

In 1888 Albert Winslow Cobb joined John Calvin Stevens as his partner. By far the most important product of this three-year association was the publication of *Examples of American Domestic Architecture,* which appeared in 1889. With a text by Cobb and illustrations primarily by Stevens, this handsome volume represents Cobb's progressive social dogma attached to Stevens' engaging Shingle Style designs. The book was prepared with the purpose of influencing a change in the emphasis of architecture from the monumental to the domestic. As Cobb outlined in the preface:

The apparent need is that a reform in the prevalent style of American Architecture be instituted; that the art be released from the influence of an extravagant ideality, and directed instead by rational, righteous ideals; the aim of these ideals being to make architecture an instrument for general distribution of domestic comforts among our whole people.[23]

Cobb made clear that the authors' intention was to focus the attention of the architectural community on the living conditions of the general community. Characteristic of his text is the statement, "Indeed it is of far more importance that during our own day and generation we live wholesomely together in brotherly love and something like community of comforts, than that we build splendid, long-enduring monuments to catch the wonder of coming generations."[24]

Examples of American Domestic Architecture brought national and international recognition to the Maine firm of Stevens and Cobb. Shortly after its publication, Stevens became the first architect in the state's history to be made a Fellow of the American Institute of Architects. *The British Architect* featured a double page selection of plates from the book and remarked that such "American variety and originality" was "a better sign for the future than the easy acceptance of worn-out precedents which suffice for so large a bulk of English designers."[25]

The only sour note came in a review written for the *American Architect and Building News* by its editor, the Boston architect William Rotch Ware. While Ware praised Stevens' renderings, he charged that the volume was little more than an advertising trade catalogue for the firm and dismissed Cobb's essays as having "rather the rhetorical flavor with which young clergymen imbue their early discourses. . . ."[26] To these criticisms, Cobb responded in a private letter to the publisher William T. Comstock that "Five years experience in W. R. Emerson's office, and an incidental attendance at architectural sketch clubs, has taught me how the wind blows in the Boston neighborhood."[27]

As the decade of the 1880's ended, John Calvin Stevens faced a dilemma common to his profession at the time. The clarity and force of the Shingle and Romanesque Styles were being challenged by the revival of American Georgian and Federal forms as well as by the increasing popularity of academic English, French and Italian forms. While Stevens retained the Shingle Style in his vocabulary well into the 20th century and created a Romanesque design as late as 1916, the Colonial Revival came to dominate his work after 1890.[28] Thus, in the remaining fifty years of his career, he, like so many of his contemporaries, exchanged functionalism for formalism.

In relation to his earlier Shingle Style designs, John Calvin Stevens produced several important post-1890 buildings. One of his most successful is Bowdoin College's Psi Upsilon Fraternity of 1900–03, where he again displayed the encompassing gable roof, the uniformly shingled exterior, and the spatial interpenetration of his earlier work (Figure 81). In addition, the Fraternity House has a novel ground plan. Its two rear wings, neither visible from the street, project at angles from the rear of the main block to form the letter K, standing for the Kappa Chapter of the fraternity.

Perhaps the most intriguing later Stevens House in the Shingle Style is the Charles Hays Cottage of 1909–10 on Cushing's Island. This summer house embodies the tension of two separate approaches to design. Its ocean side shows a return to the unifying double gable of the Thaxter and Brown Cottages, while the facade is a perfectly symmetrical Colonial Revival composition. This symmetry is carried to the interior with a traditional central-hall plan. Yet the decor is not Colonial, but a skillfully articulated version of Mission Style arts and crafts motifs.

FIGURE 80. *Cape Elizabeth, C. A. Brown Cottage, by John Calvin Stevens (1886–87). Photo: Richard Cheek*

While John Calvin Stevens usually limited his use of the Shingle Style to domestic architecture, he developed a design solution for the shingled church which spread throughout Maine. Typical of Stevens' churches in this manner was the Freeport Baptist Church of 1897. The main body of the building was contained under the plastic envelope of a shingled roof. A dramatic angular tower stood in direct contrast to the softer roof lines. The general character and shape of this tower seem to have been derived from W. R. Emerson's Church of St. Sylvia of 1881 at Bar Harbor. In Emerson's church, however, the tower became a part of and flowed into the shingled mass of the roof instead of contrasting with it.

Reflecting the increasingly statewide nature of his practice, Stevens' shingled churches include the Union Church of 1899 on Vinalhaven Island, the Methodist Church of 1904 at West Southport, and the First Baptist Church of 1912 in Jay. The popularity of the form is further attested to by the fact that the Gardiner architect Edwin E. Lewis copied it in 1894 for the First Baptist Church of Houlton.

Far rarer either before or after 1890 is a Romanesque Revival building by John Calvin Stevens. The architect's most successful statement of this style is found in the Brown Memorial Library of 1899–1900 (Figure 82). Located in the rural community of Clinton, the library reflects as direct an inspiration from the work of Henry Hobson Richardson as any structure in Maine. During the 1870's and 80's, Richardson began to revolutionize American architectural design by the forceful unity with which he composed mediaeval Romanesque forms as well as by his facility in organizing space. Small community libraries were emerging at this time, and these became one of the building types frequently requested of Richardson and his contemporaries. Richardson solved the problem by creating one-and-a-half-story structures, such as the Crane Memorial Library in Quincy, Massachusetts of 1880–83, which were divided into three major

sections, an entrance hall flanked on either side by a reading room, and book stacks.

The Brown Memorial Library is one of several notable Maine examples of the Richardsonian library, which include Augusta's Lithgow Library of 1894–96 by Joseph L. Neal and Fairfield's Lawrence Library of 1900–01 by William R. Miller. But unlike these contemporary structures, Clinton's library is a purer example of the Richardsonian ideal. The exterior exhibits warm hues and contrasting colors in its stone walls and trim, as opposed to the monochromatic quality of the granite and slate used in the other two buildings. Moreover, the Brown Memorial Library is basically an asymmetrical composition, truer to Richardson's work than either the Lithgow or the Lawrence, which reflect a Beaux-Arts symmetry clothed in Richardson-derived exteriors.

Stevens' library at Clinton is a completely stone structure with a slate roof, reflecting the solidity of H. H. Richardson's architecture. It stands one story in height above a partially raised basement and is topped with a fairly steep hipped roof. The plan is basically rectangular in shape with a small rectangular projection on the rear and a slight bay projection on one side. The most emphatic variation from a rectangular plan is the five-bay projection on the right side of the facade. The principal entrance is enframed by a large arch. The exterior walls are constructed of roughly shaped pink granite from Conway, New Hampshire, which was laid in irregular coursing. The building is trimmed with red sandstone from Longmeadow, Massachusetts, a source favored by Richardson. The gray slate roof is a local product, having been quarried from the nearby banks of the Sebasticook River.

For all its subtlety and sophistication, the Romanesque architecture of the Brown Memorial Library was rarely repeated in turn-of-the-century Maine. Instead, the formal symmetry of the Colonial Revival captured both the private and public taste. As the *Industrial Journal* of Bangor observed in 1893:

Architects all over the country note with satisfaction the decadence of the bird-cage seaside-cottage style of town dwellings. . . . Now returns the old colonial mansion — plain, but big and airy — all level headed people rejoice at the resurrection of good sense.[29]

In addition to this rational aspect of the Colonial Revival, the style gained its appeal from a growing popular interest in colonial history, architecture and decorative arts. Such sentiment for the Colonial style is reflected in the comments of the novelist Sarah Orne Jewett of South Berwick regarding Maine's Queen Anne pavilion at the 1893 Chicago World's Fair. In a letter to the press she stated:

The Maine building may be a well-planned building, but it does not speak for Maine. It ought to have been a great, square house, with a hip roof and dormer windows, and a railing round the chimneys. The best houses in all our best old Maine towns were built so a hundred years ago, and nothing looks so well in our Maine landscape, or in the pleasant streets of our villages.[30]

For John Calvin Stevens, the use of the Colonial Revival actually predated Miss Jewett's comments by nearly a decade. Contemporaneous with his most advanced project in the Shingle Style, the House by the Sea of 1885, Stevens was also experimenting with Colonial forms. That year he designed the Cyrus F. Davis House at 175 Vaughn Street in Portland. This two-story hipped-roof frame dwelling is clearly a restatement of the chaste lines of an early 19th-century Federal-style home. While the size and placement of the windows vary, the symmetry of the facade is achieved through a centrally located doorway with a leaded-glass fan-light, fronted by an arched portico. Traditional planning continues on the interior with a central hallway flanked by two rooms on either side. In *Examples of American Domestic Architecture*, Albert Winslow Cobb characterized the Davis House as:

an extreme example of the applied unifying principle. Its form is the very simplest that can be devised for an architectural structure. Yet little touches of variety in the shape and disposition of the windows, and some telling detail at the front entrance, relieve the house from any offence of tameness.[31]

Neither John Calvin Stevens nor his clients remained satisfied with the simple Colonial Revival solution offered by the Davis House. Subsequent designs in the style became more elaborate and complex. Portland residences such as the E. H. Daveis House of 1890 at 6 Bowdoin Street and the Fred E. Richards House of 1893 at 150 Vaughn Street search a bit uneasily for an architectural identity. While their dominant theme may be Colonial, Romanesque elements introduce the lingering eclectic influence of the Queen Anne.

More purely Colonial is the John W. Deering House of 1893 at 89 West Street. This dignified home recreates the design program of the Davis House on a larger scale in brick, adding a broader portico at the doorway and a row of dormer windows across the front of the hip roof. In comparing the Deering with the Davis design, Cobb observed, "Here too the unifying principle has been applied; the breaks in the front wall-line being comprehended under one boldly overhanging roof" (see note 31). In fact, the Deering House is the very embodiment of Miss Jewett's "great square house, with a hip roof and dormer windows" (see note 30).

By the late 1890's John Calvin Stevens had embraced the Colonial Revival completely. Two turn-of-the-century examples, the Cape Cottage Casino of 1898 and the Governor John F. Hill Mansion of 1901 at 136 State Street in Augusta exhibit a scale and pretention unfamiliar in the architect's earlier work.

Constructed as part of a trolley park, the Casino was dramatically sited on a knoll overlooking Casco Bay. Clinging to its rugged surroundings with great arm-like verandas, this

FIGURE 83. *Portland, Richard Webb House, by John Calvin Stevens and John Howard Stevens (1906–07). Photo: Richard Cheek*

FIGURE 82. *Clinton, Brown Memorial Library, by John Calvin Stevens (1899–1900). Photo: Richard Cheek*

FIGURE 81. *Brunswick, Bowdoin College, Psi Upsilon Fraternity House, by John Calvin Stevens (1900–03). Photo: Richard Cheek*

ambitious frame building welcomed its guests through generous doorways fronted by monumental, columned porticos. The gable roof of the Casino and its oceanside portico were strongly reminiscent of Beacon Rock, the Newport summer residence which McKim, Mead and White of New York designed for Edwin D. Morgan in 1890–91.

Stevens also used the monumental portico as the dominant motif of Governor Hill's residence. This immense three-story brick Neo-Federal mansion displays a semi-circular portico on the facade and a rectangular one on the side. The latter doubles as a *porte cochère*. Both porticos are executed in granite with columns in the Grecian Ionic order. While the porticos as well as the facade doorway treatment are derived from the Greek Revival, the overall house form and such details as the granite window lintels

FIGURE 84. *Portland City Hall, by Carrere and Hastings and John Calvin Stevens and John Howard Stevens Associate Architects (1909–12). Photo: Richard Cheek*

are based upon the Federal style, reflecting a continuing eclecticism within the context of the Colonial Revival.

In fact, it was not usually the intention of John Calvin Stevens and his contemporaries to reproduce examples of 18th- and early 19th-century American architecture exactly, but rather to make their own interpretations of them. This becomes particularly evident in the distinguished series of red brick residences which Stevens designed for Portland's Western Promenade neighborhood between 1900 and World War I. Calmer in spirit and more restrained in detail than the Hill Mansion, these dignified homes represent a consistently skillful blending of the Georgian and Federal styles. Of them, Stevens' professed favorite was the Richard Webb House of 1906–07 at 29 Bowdoin Street (Figure 83). In 1915 the architect's son and partner, John Howard Stevens, wrote:

In modern work, the Richard Webb house on Bowdoin Street is considered one of the best examples of the Colonial style, being very satisfactory in its proportions and detail, and yet not an historical copy of an old house, but a new creation of the same style, and with the same feeling that is evident in the best old Colonial work.[32]

John Calvin Stevens' residential work in the Colonial Revival was not confined to the urban setting of Portland. Influential men such as the president of the Union Mutual Life Insurance Company, Fred E. Richards, considered him "head and shoulders above any other architect in the State of Maine."[33] As Stevens' reputation grew, he received commissions through the state as well as from beyond its boundaries. In response, he effectively adapted the Colonial Style for both the seaside and country house form. In 1912 he designed "Shorelands," the Camden summer home of Edward M. Hagar of Chicago. Titling it "A House by the Sea", he created the exact antithesis of his similarly named project of a quarter of a century before. "Shorelands"

is a symmetrically planned gable-roofed dwelling with either side of its second story faced in an elongated projecting dormer. While the house curves slightly to conform to the site, formal balance is its essential theme. On both its land and seaward elevations, the central focus is an elaborate arched doorway. Likewise, at either gable end stands a stone chimney which is flanked by a pillared porch.

The formalism of 18th-century Georgian architecture was accentuated in "Elmhurst," the great brick country house which John Calvin Stevens designed for the shipbuilding magnate John S. Hyde of Bath. Erected between 1913 and 1914, Hyde's mansion is situated in an extensive park-like setting on the outskirts of the city. The garden elevation is the most impressive, with its large second-story Palladian window framed between two massive chimneys. A network of staircases lead from the first-story level to a formal garden below, the work of the Portland landscape architect, Carl Rust Parker.

While a large proportion of Stevens' practice was devoted to residential work, he also made a significant contribution to the public architecture of early 20th-century Maine. Like thousands of his fellow Americans, the architect had visited the Great White City of the 1893 Chicago World's Fair and had come away an exponent of the City Beautiful movement. In 1929 he summarized his philosophy of civic improvement through architecture in the following terms:

A city is not only a place in which to do business, it is also a place in which people are obliged to live, and everyone desires to live pleasantly and happily. One way to bring about this very desirable condition is to have the city's institutions so built and cared for that they become points of interest and beauty.[34]

This philosphy was embodied in three of Stevens' major Portland buildings, the City Hall of 1909–12 on Congress Street (Figure 84), the Water District Shops of 1929 on Douglas Street and the Post Office of 1931–34 on Forest Avenue.

Portland's City Hall was actually designed by John M. Carrere of the fashionable New York firm of Carrere and Hastings. Of the associate role which the Stevens' firm played in the project, John Calvin Stevens observed, "I do believe that Carrere was influenced by the fact that we were his associates and worked out a design well fitting our community." [35] Carrere's primary design source was the New York City Hall of 1803–12. He viewed his Portland City Hall of a century later as the finest accomplishment of his career, excelling his House and Senate Office Buildings of 1905–06 in Washington, D.C. and his New York Public Library of 1911.

Indeed, the Portland City Hall ranks as the most impressive building of its kind in Maine. The central section is recessed, and the two flanking wings project forward to form a handsome entrance plaza. In this open courtyard, the paving stones are placed in a semi-circle leading to a broad staircase which rises above the basement story to three arched entrances. The simple detailing of the iron entrance gates is subtly repeated in the slender bell tower with its delicate metal sailing-ship weathervane. Likewise, classical pediments, columns, balustrades and urns are executed with a linear refinement characteristic of the academic taste. Yet for all of its graceful appearance, the City Hall is a large granite structure which accommodates numerous municipal offices and facilities as well as a 3000-seat auditorium with its famous Kotszchmar Organ. Thus, Carrere's calculated refinement successfully achieves the balance between handsomeness and solidity so necessary for a public building. [36]

While Carrere and Hastings' Portland City Hall shared the French Renaissance overtones of its New York parent, John Calvin Stevens felt more at ease with the Colonial Revival in designing his civic buildings. In using the latter style for the Portland Water District Shops, it was the architect's stated purpose "to make a utilitarian building attractive to the eye" (see note 34). He chose the central portion of the brick complex to house the tools and appurtenances for serving mains and meters, a blacksmith and carpentry shop, and a tower for drying hose. The hose tower was enclosed by a Georgian spire which forms the focal point of the building. The middle section is flanked on the east by a two-story wing which contains Water District Offices and a large assembly hall for employees. The west wing serves as the meter department's garage.

Each of the three parts of this symmetrically composed complex has a gabled Colonial roofline as well as pronounced Federal doorway and window details executed in both granite and wood. Apart from the hose tower, the most notable architectural feature of the Shops is the facade of the meter department garage. Here the Palladian motif is evoked by a large central doorway which is capped by an arched window and flanked on either side by a grouping of three windows.

The last important public building of John Calvin Stevens' career was the Portland Post Office. Planned in 1931 and erected between 1932 and 1934, this stately two-story brick structure enjoys a prominent site on Forest Avenue overlooking Deering Oaks park. Its 232-foot long facade is an essay in formal Georgian symmetry. The central section is divided into thirteen recessed bays and is flanked on either side by a projecting three-bay pavilion. Over each of the central arched doorways is a carved granite shield displaying either the national, state or city seal. Similarly, each of the thirteen second-story windows in the central section has a granite lintel bearing a star to represent one of the original colonies. Perched atop the central bay is a watchful granite eagle with the postal seal in front of his talons.

Regrettably, the Post Office's imposing statement of Colonial Revival architecture was marred during the 1960's by a poorly scaled addition to the north wall. Further damage occurred in 1975 when an insensitive interior remodelling destroyed the richly appointed first-story marble lobby which ran the entire length of the building. The only survivors of this desecration were two of Henry E. Mattson's forceful Works Progress Administration murals of coastal Maine scenes.

As construction was underway on the Portland Post Office in 1932, the magazine *Architecture* published a feature article on John Calvin Stevens. Its author, Ellis F. Lawrence, noted of the seventy-seven-year-old architect that "he is something of a romanticist when it comes to Colonial work, for he lives in the midst of fine old examples which he has been called upon to remodel and restore" (see note 19).

Nowhere does this statement become apparent than in Wiscasset's First Congregational Church of 1908 and the Waterford Church of 1928 (Figure 85). Both churches were designed to reproduce on their original sites 19th-century meetinghouses which had been destroyed by

fire. In the case of the Wiscasset church, originally planned in 1840 by Samuel Melcher III of Brunswick, Stevens took the liberty of substituting a federal fan for a Gothic pointed arch over the door and windows. Likewise, at Waterford he added a simple Greek Revival portico to what had been a predominantly Federal-style building. Yet in both instances, he so masterfully recreated the essence of the church that the visitor must look carefully before discovering he stands in front of a copy rather than the original. Through restoration projects in communities such as Wiscasset and Waterford, Stevens contributed immeasurably to preserving the visual charm of coastal and inland Maine villages.

FIGURE 85. *Waterford, Waterford Church, by John Calvin Stevens and John Howard Stevens (1928). Photograph courtesy of John Calvin Stevens II, Cape Elizabeth*

FIGURE 86. *Bar Harbor, "The Turrets," John J.
Emery House, by Bruce Price (1893–95). Photograph courtesy of the College of the Atlantic*

While John Calvin Stevens favored the Shingle Style and the Colonial Revival as architectural expressions in harmony with the Maine landscape, other members of his profession, both in and outside of the state, preferred the more elaborate European-inspired styles of the period. This was especially evident in the summer houses and resort hotels which dotted the coastal and lake regions. As the distinguished New York architect Bruce Price noted in 1886, "The cliffs of Newport, the rocks of Mt. Desert, the shores of Shrewsbury and the beaches of Westchester, Connecticut and Long Island have cottages that would be mansions in England, villas in Italy, or chateaux in France." [37]

Like many of his contemporaries, Price considered Mount Desert second only to Newport in its importance as a summer resort. The architect was probably familiar with the development of the island's principal community, Bar Harbor, for he designed three of its major landmarks, the West End Hotel of 1878–1879, the Craigs of 1879–80, and the Turrets of 1893–95 (Figure 86).

The first summer visitors, or "rusticators," began coming to Bar Harbor in the late 1850's, drawn by the spectacular scenery and the salubrious sea breezes. These early arrivals stayed first in primitive boarding houses and later in large frame hotels such as the Stick Style West End. By the late 1870's a few substantial cottages, including the Craigs in Queen Anne Style, began to appear, built for the most part by Bostonians. As the century drew to a close, the stamp of social distinction was placed on Bar Harbor with the arrival of prominent families not only from Boston but also New York, Philadelphia and other centers of new industrial wealth. President Eliot of Harvard, J. P. Morgan

and George Vanderbilt of New York, and the noted publisher Joseph Pulitzer were among many of the socially elite who solidified Bar Harbor's position as a watering place of the rich and famous. There now arose numerous stately "cottages" on beautiful grounds, of which the $100,000 granite Turrets ranked as one of the most ambitious.

Its builder, J. J. Emery of Cincinnati and later New York City, was a typical late-19th-century financier with diverse business involvements. Taking over his father's lard and candle making business, he and his brothers developed it into the largest such industry in the country. Emery also invested extensively in real estate in major cities across the country and had nearly 2,000 tenants in apartments he had constructed in Cincinnati alone. In addition, he was a major force in promoting the Cincinnati Southern Railroad.

When Russell Sturgis wrote his *Architectural Record* critique of Bruce Price's work in 1899, he stated that "There is a large class of buildings erected by Mr. Price in which the French architecture of the early part of the XVI century has been used with great freedom and intelligence." [38] Among the examples of Price's Chateauesque style which Sturgis illustrated was J. J. Emery's immense Bar Harbor summer "cottage," the Turrets.

The West End Hotel, the Craigs and much of 19th-century Bar Harbor perished as a result either of changing economic and social conditions or the disastrous 1947 fire which leveled nearly a third of Mount Desert Island. Yet the Turrets remains, its architectural drama undimmed by recent years of disuse. Sited on a rise by the shore, the house is essentially rectangular, stands three to four stories high and has a highly picturesque roofline of hipped and conical forms with dormers projecting from them. Although these varied elements give the design the appearance of romantic asymmetry, there is actually a basic balance in the composition of both the facade and ocean elevations.

The once splendidly furnished interior of the Turrets is now empty. However, its elegant spaces survive unaltered. The first floor features a living hall with a grand staircase. A richly paneled dining room is located to the left of the hall. At its right is a large drawing room. The second floor contains suites of family bedrooms, while the third and fourth stories have servants' quarters and storage rooms.

The Turrets stands today as a haunting reminder of a vanished way of life. Yet the "great freedom and intelligence" of Bruce Price's design remains intact. When the Turrets' present owner, the College of the Atlantic, completes its adaption for educational purposes, this monumental French chateau on the Maine coast will find new purpose for the future.

The remarkable scale and display achieved in Bar Harbor's mansions was surpassed in other parts of Maine only by such great summer hotels as the Poland Spring House (Figure 87), the Mount Kineo House on Moosehead Lake, and the Samoset Hotel in Rockland. Of this triumvirate, at one time entirely owned by the enterprising Ricker family, the acknowledged leader was the Poland Spring House.

The development of Poland Spring as a resort has a long history. Jabez Ricker settled in the area in 1794 with his wife and ten children. One of his sons, Wentworth Ricker, opened an inn on the road to Portland in 1797. He ran the hostelry until 1834 when he turned it over to his son Hiram.

Through the years the Ricker family had been cured of various illnesses by drinking the water of a nearby spring. In 1859 Hiram Ricker asked Dr. Eliphalet Clark of Portland to try prescribing Poland Spring water to patients with kidney trouble. Dr. Clark agreed and soon reported

great success. This convinced Ricker that it could be sold commercially for medicinal purposes. Marketing operations began in 1859 and soon required a Boston office with a resident sales agent.

Business at the inn improved as people arrived to take the waters. Accommodations became so crowded during the season of 1869–70 that a major addition was built. Yet this did not solve the space problem for long. Thus, in 1876, the Poland Spring House was erected on Ricker Hill above the inn. When this stark frame structure with its large mansard tower opened for the first season, it had 120 rooms and a total frontage of 262 feet.

The increasing success of Poland Spring as a resort necessitated a constant enlargement of the hotel into the early 20th century. While minor additions were made to the building virtually on an annual basis, major remodellings occurred in 1884, 1889, 1893, 1898 and 1903. Queen Anne and Colonial Revival motifs predominated in the 1889 renovation by John Calvin Stevens and Albert Winslow Cobb. The firm also added a ten-by-sixteen-foot dining room window which required the largest piece of glass in the state. The stylistic theme initiated by Stevens and Cobb continued to be employed in 1893 by George M. Coombs of Lewiston and again in 1898 by Coombs in conjunction with his partners Eugene J. Gibbs and Harry C. Wilkinson. In 1903 Wilkinson received the commission to place the final touches on the immense facade. By then practicing in Washington, D.C., he provided the designs for great Baroque corner and entrance towers which ranked as the building's most prominent features. The 1903 remodelling brought the size of the Poland Spring House to more than 400 rooms, with a frontage of approximately 325 feet on either side.

By the turn of the century, Poland Spring was known as one of the most fashionable resorts in America, and the distribution of its water was world-wide. Besides creating the Poland Spring House, the Ricker Family expanded their original inn and called it the Mansion House. Finding that this was not sufficient, they erected a third hotel, the Riccar Inn of 1913. For the enjoyment of their guests, they brought the Maine pavilion back from the 1893 Chicago World's Fair and converted it into a library, art gallery, and museum. They constructed a huge stable, laid out America's first resort golf course, and provided a fine boat house at an adjacent lake. They even built a non-denominational stone chapel in about 1910 from designs by G. Henri Desmond of Boston. Over the spring itself was placed a spring house and a bottling plant in which guests could watch the bottling process through large plate glass windows. Erected in 1905, these elegant Beaux-Arts temples to the waters were the work of Harry C. Wilkinson.

Endowed with its famed water, its extensive recreational facilities, and its striking natural setting, Poland Spring continued to flourish into the 1920's. Change came with the Great Depression of the 1930's, which dealt a severe blow to the way of life which had supported Poland Spring. The Ricker family sold the entire complex in 1940. Another three decades passed before the Poland Spring House finally closed its doors in 1969, having spent the last three years of operation as a National Job Corps Training Center. On the eve of July 4, 1975, the hotel met its inevitable fate by fire, leaving an unfillable void on the Maine landscape.

Vanished also are the other two hotels of the Rickers' summer resort empire, the Samoset on Rockland Breakwater and the Mount Kineo House at the head of Moosehead Lake. Originally constructed in 1888 as the Bay Point Club, the Samoset was purchased in 1902 by the Rickers and substantially enlarged under the supervision of the architect Forest Walker. Walker's bold Queen Anne and Colonial Revival forms were partially modified during a 1916–17 remodelling by John Calvin Stevens and John Howard Stevens. Likewise, in 1915 the Stevens firm added a Colonial tower ornament and porches to the Mount Kineo House, a

Queen Anne style hotel of 1884 by the Boston architect Arthur H. Vinal. This structure was the last of a series of hotels which had occupied the location since 1844.

Stevens himself initially favored the Shingle Style for summer hotels. He applied it with facility in designing such examples as the Bay of Naples Inn of 1898–99 and the Belgrade of 1899. In both cases, he skillfully massed a picturesque assortment of towers, turrets, gables, dormers and verandas into a unified architectural statement. His later Colonial Revival work is reflected in the Marshall House of 1916 at York Harbor. Built of red brick, this large cube shaped structure was surrounded by columned piazzas. In the center of the flat roof was a stylized pavilion which resembled a widow's walk.

Like the resorts of the Ricker empire, those at Naples, Belgrade, and York have disappeared. Along with them have gone such equally notable hotels as the Rangeley Lake House, which featured a three-story hipped-roof central pavilion flanked on either side by a four-story one. Only in a few coastal enclaves like the Kennebunks does there still linger any flavor of the summer hotel era. Here remain two important early 20th-century survivors, the Shingle Style Narragansett on Kennebunk Beach and the Colonial Revival Breakwater Court, now the Colony, at Cape Arundel in Kennebunkport.

At the turn of the century, two architectural trends dominated the Maine scene, the restrained classicism of the Neo-Renaissance and Colonial styles and the exuberant romanticism of the last phase of such revival styles as the Romanesque and the Gothic. Nowhere is this contrast more evident than in the Walker Art Building of 1892–94 on the Bowdoin College Campus in Brunswick (Figure 88) and a series of major landmarks in the industrial city of Lewiston.

The Walker Art Building ranks as one of the finest smaller works of the eminent American academic architect, Charles Follen McKim, senior partner of the New York firm of McKim,

FIGURE 87. *Poland Spring House, by George M. Coombs, with additions and changes by Coombs, Eugene J. Gibbs, Harry C. Wilkinson, John Calvin Stevens, Albert Winslow Cobb, and John Calvin Stevens (1875–1930). Old hand-colored photograph by Brother Delmer C. Wilson, courtesy of the Camden-Rockport Historical Society, copy by Wendell A. Ray*

Mead and White. In his design for Bowdoin's art gallery, he created a self-contained jewel box which embodies the virtues of the academic tradition, simplicity, dignity, serenity, and a concern for proportion and detail.

Architectural historian Denys Peter Myers has skillfully described the Walker Art Gallery in the following terms:

The rectangular red brick structure is trimmed with limestone and is set on a broad podium of granite. The three-bayed facade has as its central and principal element a limestone Palladian motif fronting a deep barrel-vaulted loggia. A parapet conceals the flat roof. Above the central bay is the other primary exterior feature, a dome of Pantheon type on a low drum. The open loggia leads into the central sculpture gallery, a rotunda lit by an oculus in the dome. The four tympana in the rotunda are painted by four of the leading American artists ot the period, John LaFarge, Elihu Vedder, Abbott Thayer, and Kenyon Cox, whose respective allegories of Athens, Rome, Florence, and Venice suggest the veneration in which European culture was held by educated

Americans in the age of late Victorian gentility. The employment of painters and sculptors by architects to bring together all three of the fine arts in a single project was not at all infrequent in major American buildings of the 1890's and was particularly appropriate for an art museum such as the Walker Art Building. The building went well beyond the merely practical needs of functionalism to achieve the status of monumental symbolism.[39]

A striving for monumental symbolism of a different nature is apparent in the bold architectural statements which appeared in Lewiston. Over the park looms the Baroque tower of Boston architect John C. Spofford's City Hall of 1890–92. The emphatic Romanesque arches of the Great Department Store still dominate Lis-

FIGURE 89. *Monmouth, Cumston Hall, by Harry Hayman Cochrane (1899–1900). Photo: Douglas Armsden*

FIGURE 88. *Brunswick, Bowdoin College, Walker Art Gallery, by McKim, Mead and White (1892–94). Photo: Richard Cheek*

bon and Main Streets as a remnant of one of Coombs, Gibbs and Wilkinson's most successful commercial designs. This Sullivanesque block of 1898 was planned for Bradford Peck, who two years later wrote the utopian novel *The World A Department Store,* with illustrations of an imaginary Beaux-Arts city by Harry C. Wilkinson. The Coombs firm also left its mark in the exotic pair of Eastern domes atop the Kora Shrine Temple of 1908. Another Lewiston architect, William R. Miller, shared Coombs' love of dramatic architectural effect. This is reflected in Miller's octagonal Gothic tower on the Sisters of Charity Hospital of 1900 and in his square Romanesque tower on the First Universalist Church of 1903. A huge Romanesque tower also became the dominant feature of Cumston Hall of 1899–1900 in the nearby town of Monmouth (Figure 89). This extraordinary multi-purpose community building was both designed and decorated by the versatile local artist Harry Hayman Cochrane.

The period extending from 1880 to 1920 was one of great change in Maine architecture. In this regard, Denys Peter Myers has noted, "As the century drew to a close, the dynamic thrust of the shingle style toward astylar architecture waned and a new interest in historicism waxed."[40] Whether Shingle or Revival in nature, the forms of turn-of-the-century Maine architecture embody a vitality and integrity that bespeak a new confidence. The American industrial society had matured, had lost its earlier timid conformity, and viewed its future as secure and bright. Within a decade and a half, this golden vision was shattered by the guns of August.

FIGURE 90. *Kennebunkport, Perkins Grist Mill (1749). Photo: Richard Cheek*

5

PART 3

Industrial and Commercial Architecture

Marius B. Peladeau

Every person wants to live in an attractive home to satisfy his pride and need for confidence and security. Industry and commerce likewise attempt to locate in structures of pleasing design so that clients and customers may conduct their business in attractive surroundings. Thus, industrial and commercial architecture plays an important, though often overlooked role in our lives.

In Maine, the urban architecture of industry and commerce mirrored the current styles of residential structures, but in rural areas it was often ill defined. Potato barns, ice houses, lumbering camps and lime kilns followed no school or style of architecture. Yet they were designed to serve a need and played important parts in their individual communities.

Commercial architecture in Maine com-

menced with the first settlers. In addition to houses, they erected mills and comparable structures connected with their trades (see Candee, pp. 21–26). Because these were usually framed in wood and were susceptible to replacement as new technologies developed, few early 18th-century industrial structures survive today. There are two notable exceptions, the Old Grist Mill, or Perkins Tidal Mill in Kennebunkport (Figure 90), and the John Hancock Warehouse in York. The former was built in 1749 and is one of the last remaining examples of an 18th-century tidewater grist mill in the country. Now in use as a restaurant, most of the old mill equipment is there and the original structure remains basically unchanged. Architecturally, Perkins Grist Mill is distinguished by exposed framing, knee braces, mill machinery and early hardware.

The John Hancock Warehouse, built in the mid-1700's, is the only commercial building of its era in Maine. Owned by the famous Massachusetts patriot and Joseph Tucker in the latter part of the 18th century, it served as an outlet for Hancock's business ventures in the District of Maine. It has been restored in recent years and is open as a museum. Again, the framing and form is indicative of the 18th century.[1]

Two other exceptional early mills survive in Maine, the Grist Mill on the Little River Road in East Lebanon,[2] built in 1774, and the Dinsmore Mill at Palermo, erected in 1817 on a site which saw mill activity before 1800. The architectural integrity of the East Lebanon Mill has been preserved over the years, and much of its original equipment still survives. It is currently undergoing restoration. The Dinsmore Mill has been in the Dinsmore family since 1817. It is one of the few all-purpose mills in Maine still intact, with dam, water wheel and its original mill equipment.

With the settlement of inland Maine after the Revolution, one-man businesses expanded into small factories, still owned by enterprising individuals, but employing increasing numbers of workers. The now demolished Mayhall Woolen Mill of the 1790's in Gray is thought to have been the first of its kind in the nation. The North Wayne Axe Company grew from a blacksmith shop into a sizeable local industry. This firm erected a small but dignified factory building along the brook in North Wayne; it stands empty today awaiting adaptive reuse.

The second and third quarters of the 19th century saw the accelerated growth of industry in Maine, due mostly to the abundance of water power. Small Greek Revival mills, such as the North Berwick Woolen Company, sprang up in communities throughout Maine, including Harmony, Warren, Guilford, Oxford and Oakland. The post-Civil War era brought the Italianate and French Second Empire styles, well suited to the larger mills then under construction in the state; (also see in regard to the Italianate and Second Empire styles, Miller, pp. 167ff. and 177ff. above). The Italianate towers of the Worumbo Mill have dominated the Lisbon skyline since 1864. The Pejepscot Paper Mill in Topsham, started in 1868, also in Italianate mode, is the earliest surviving example of Maine's 19th-century wood pulp mills, and ranks as one of the most handsome and well preserved industrial sites in the state.

All this building activity in smaller communities was, however, overshadowed by the greater development simultaneously under way at Biddeford and Lewiston, the two giants of 19th-century industrial Maine. Lewiston's water power potential began to be systematically utilized after 1850 by the Lewiston Water Power Company and its successor, the Franklin Company.[3] These corporations planned a model industrial city, imitating the successes already achieved at Manchester, New Hampshire, and Lawrence, Massachusetts. Streets were laid out in a grid system, and the progression of development from the river was a well ordered one. First came the mills and the canals which provided the necessary water power; then blocks of housing for the mill operatives, with a band of landscaping to separate them from the mills. Next came the downtown business district, with portions set aside for city government and a park for recreational purposes. Around the park were clustered a hotel and churches. Finally, the land furthest from the river was apportioned for residential and farm use. This plan was followed to a great degree at Biddeford and other mill towns, with variations dictated by local topography.

The earliest surviving mill buildings in Lewiston are the Lewiston Falls Manufacturing Company mills of 1846 in the Greek Revival style; because of its boldness, strength and simplicity this style was well suited to industrial adaptation. Greek Revival architecture was to dominate Lewiston in its first period of development in the late 1840's and 50's, thanks largely to Albert H. Kelsey. A Massachusetts architect and

FIGURE 91. *Lewiston, Androscoggin Mills, by Amos D. Lockwood and Albert H. Kelsey (1860–61; 1867;* *1872). Photograph courtesy of the Maine Historical Society, copy by Wendell A. Ray.*

builder, Kelsey came to Lewiston in 1850 and was given charge by the Franklin Company of overseeing the development of the mills and city. He was instrumental in locating and building the canals, planning the streets, placing the Common, and building the Bates, Hill, Androscoggin, Lewiston and Continental Mills during the 1850's, 60's and early 70's. The Bates Mill was erected in 1852, the Hill in 1854 and the Androscoggin in 1860. Employee housing was erected at the same period.

The first example of employee housing was the Hill Company boarding house on Canal Street. This brick structure combined the Federal style with its double chimneys at the gable ends, and the Greek Revival with its strong horizontal granite window lintels and sills. Although by mid-century, the Italianate and Second Empire style were making their impact felt in Lewiston and Biddeford, the mills, the workers' housing and individual residences continued to combine features of earlier styles with these current styles. The Continental Mill housing complex of 1865–66 reflects the simplicity of the Greek Revival in its main structure and the more elaborate ornamentation of the Italianate style in its cornice.

The Androscoggin Mill of 1860 was, at the time of its erection, the finest mansard-roofed mill in Maine (Figure 91). Its immense size is well proportioned, and taken in context with its landscaped grounds, was considered by one English gentleman who visited it to be worthy of housing a grand public museum. Today its towers have been reduced, and the row of striking dormers in the mansard roof have been removed, a sad commentary on modern expediency. The Continental Mill, also in Lewiston, marks the high point of Victorian industrial architecture during the third decade of factory construction in Maine. Fortunately it survives intact. An enlargement in 1872 of the earlier Porter Mill of the 1850's, the Continental Mill combines the French mansardic roof with a magnificent polygonal Second Empire tower crowned by another decorative mansard roof.

Biddeford was developed in much the same manner as Lewiston, under the direction of Samuel Batchelder.[4] Another Massachusetts native, Batchelder came to the community in 1831 and recognized the great potential of the Saco Falls. By 1839 he had erected four mills under the aegis of the Saco Water Power Company, which he formed to oversee development of the industrial complex, and the City of Biddeford itself. By 1848 Batchelder had constructed two massive mills on speculation. They were occupied in 1850 by the new Pepperell Manufacturing Company and marked the start of Biddeford's great economic growth. Batchelder directed the city of Biddeford in nearly all aspects of this growth, financing hotels, banks, the post office, the railroad depot, machine shops, tenements and dams.

The great complexes of Lewiston and Biddeford, in which the controlling companies exercised a paternalistic authority over nearly all aspects of city life, were imitated in smaller mill communities throughout Maine, including Augusta, Winslow-Waterville, Vassalboro, Bruns-

wick, Dexter, Topsham and Pejepscot. Even cities such as Auburn and Gardiner were dominated by their great expanse of shoe factories.

Although nearly all mill companies provided housing for their operatives, none were so beneficent as the S. D. Warren Paper Company in Westbrook and the Oxford Paper Company at Rumford (also see Shettleworth, p. 188). Over a three-decade period, S. D. Warren built streets of frame structures from the cottage designs of A. J. Downing and in the Queen Anne and Shingle styles of John Calvin Stevens (Figure 79).

The concept of Hugh Chisholm, founder of the Oxford Paper Company, was a more unified one. Between 1901 and 1902 he erected Strathglass Park (Figure 92), which consisted of fifty-one substantial brick duplexes in a park-

FIGURE 92. *Rumford, view of Strathglass Park, by Cass Gilbert (1902–04). Photo: Maine Historic Preservation Commission, by Frank A. Beard*

like setting. The housing was the work of the eminent New York architect, Cass Gilbert, while the landscaping was planned by the Boston landscape architect, W. W. Gay. To enhance the attractiveness of the Park and to avoid the sterile sameness found in much 19th- and early 20th-century industrial housing, Gilbert designed seven different exterior variations of the same commodious interior accommodations. Of the fifty surviving duplexes, thirteen feature the bold geometry of the Shingle Style translated into brick, eleven have a double turreted roof line, nine a single Dutch gable, eight a double Dutch gable, four a gable, three a combination of gable and Dutch gable, and two a double gable. The duplexes were rented to mill workers at a nominal sum, and maintenance was performed by the company. Strathglass Park is a remarkable example of enlightened industrial paternalism and remains today a monument to the foresight of Hugh Chisholm.

As the first half of the 19th century witnessed the stimulation of Maine industry, it also saw the growth of Maine business, especially at ocean and river port communities. Today many of these survive in a nearly intact state, a testimony to the good taste of those who constructed commercial structures, especially during the Greek Revival period. There are several towns with excellent Greek Revival commercial blocks: Newcastle, Damariscotta, Hallowell, Portland, Searsport, Belfast and Wiscasset (see Myers, Figure 45 and pp. 103, 106 above). They all show the traditional relationship between the two important functions of a town—business and residential. Hallowell was a good example of this interplay of functions in a well ordered urban scheme. The back of Water Street, the main commercial avenue, opened out onto the wharfs and docks of the river port. The shop fronts of these Water Street commercial blocks made them accessible to pedestrian shoppers. Rising on a series of terraces above the commercial and port area, in parallel steps, was the residential district, highlighted by a number of fine

Federal, Greek Revival and later 19th-century buildings.

It is Bangor and Portland, however, which best illustrate the great commercial vitality of 19th-century Maine. The Wheelwright Block at Hammond Street and Broad Street in Bangor is Maine's first Second Empire commercial building. Erected in 1859 from designs by Col. Benjamin S. Deane, and Edwin Lee Brown, it has survived the great Bangor fire of 1911 and more recent urban renewal. Although the first and fifth stories have been somewhat altered, it is still an imposing structure with its curved mansard roof, ornamental wooden cornice, and Italianate window treatment. Also in Bangor is another grand mansard-roofed business structure, the Adams-Pickering Block at Main and Middle Streets. Designed by the local architect George W. Orff, it was erected in 1871. With its first-story cast-iron front and facade of Hallowell granite, it was among the most sophisticated Victorian commercial buildings in eastern Maine. Its fine wooden and slate details and Italianate window treatment make it a distinguished element of downtown Bangor.

Portland is likewise fortunate to have retained many of the fine commercial structures erected after the Fire of 1866. The entire Portland Waterfront, now a National Register Historic District, retains a homogeneous post-Civil War appearance, interspersed by a few earlier structures. Three of the most important buildings, however, are sited slightly away from the waterfront on Middle Street, between Pearl and Franklin Streets. The Woodman, Rackleff and Thompson Blocks, taken together, are generally considered the most high-style Victorian commercial buildings ever erected in Maine (Figure 93). This magnificent trio stand today practically unaltered and serve as a textbook example of the best of mid-century commercial design. They are the work of George M. Harding, a Portland architect who did much to rebuild the commercial district of the city after the fire.

The Woodman Block of 1867 was built in the

FIGURE 93. *Portland, Woodman, Rackleff and Thompson Blocks, corner of Middle and Pearl Streets, by George M. Harding (1867–68). Photograph courtesy of the Maine Historical Society, copy by Wendell A. Ray*

French Second Empire style for George W. Woodman, a dry goods dealer and manufacturer. It is distinguished by cast-iron pilasters and arches on the first story and highly decorative carved stone arches over second- and third-story windows. This elaborate composition is capped by a mansard roof with pronounced mansard dormers at all four corners. Next to it stands the Rackleff Block, also built in 1867 from Harding's designs. Features such as the first-story cast-iron arcade and the second- and third-story window trim are identical to those of the Woodman Block. However, the Rackleff Block was designed to be an individual unit with a horizontal Italianate roof line rather than a mansard one. The Thompson Block is the last of the trio. Constructed in 1867–68, it is four stories high, with a mansard roof. The facade of the Thompson Block is more complicated than the other two, being an interesting interplay of horizontal and vertical elements. The first floor again employs cast iron. The other floors make great use of freestone arches in the fenestration and string courses.

Modified versions of the great mid-century Second Empire commercial blocks at Bangor and Portland can be found in nearly every Maine community. Although the work of local builders rather than known architects, they retain the good proportions and attention to detail which marked the urban high-style buildings which were their prototypes. Among the smaller town blocks in the Second Empire Style are the distinguished T. J. Southard Block of 1882 in Richmond, the attractive small bank on Route 1 in Searsport now occupied by the Merrill Trust Company, and the mansard-roofed block in Abbott Village, which houses a general and hardware store on the street level and the meeting hall of a fraternal organization on the second.

In the 19th century, the railroads epitomized the perfect application of technology to the needs of modern civilization. The railroads stood for engineering expertise, ease of communication and facility in moving raw and finished products to and from markets. The railroads meant much to Maine, and although their halcyon days are now past, vestiges of the architectural contribution they made still survive.

To the farmer, businessman and industrialist, the railroads meant the movement of freight, but to the average person, they meant passenger service; service which linked their towns—and their lives—to the outside world. Portland was the end of the Boston and Maine and the beginning of the Maine Central radiating inland as well as along the coast. It was, therefore, the hub of Maine's railroads. Lewiston provided the starting point for several important branch lines spreading north and northwest. From Bangor, the Bangor and Aroostook ventured northward into the great expanses of Piscataquis, Penobscot and Aroostook counties, while the Maine Central went down the coast to Hancock and Washington counties.

Each of these points had extensive rail facilities. The great Portland passenger terminal, demolished in 1961, is now the site of the newest symbol of modern technological civilization—the shopping center, geared to the needs of people in automobiles. It was erected in 1888 in the French Chateau style from designs by the Boston architectural firm of Bradlee, Winslow and Witherell. Equally impressive was the Grand Trunk Railway station in Portland, also razed in the 1960's. It was built in 1903 in the late Richardsonian Romanesque style. The architects were Spier and Rohns of Detroit, Michigan.

Both the Grand Trunk and the Maine Central were able to standardize their respective designs of depots to a great extent. A good example of a surviving Grand Trunk station is the one at Yarmouth (1906), preserved and maintained by a local civic organization (Figure 94). Typical of the early Maine Central stations is the one at Bucksport, now receiving adaptive use by the local historical society as a museum of regional memorabilia. It was erected in 1874 with Italianate features and remained in use until the end of passenger service over a decade ago. Atypical was the station on the Rumford branch of the Maine Central at Bemis, built in the "log cabin" style around the turn of the century as a reminder to debarking passengers that they had truly arrived in the "north woods."

Besides the great stations at Portland, there were impressive terminals at Lewiston, Skowhegan, Waterville, Bangor, Rumford Falls and Sebago Lake. The stations at Sebago Lake and the original Lewiston depot were quite similar, with twin towers, one Queen Anne, the other in French Chateau style, and long covered platforms extending out from both ends of the station proper. The station at Lewiston, as well as the first one at Rumford Falls, were replaced by nearly identical Colonial Revival structures, with large arched Georgian windows. They were designed by the Boston firm of Shepley, Rutan and Coolidge before 1918. Both survive today, although altered for commercial uses.

The most modern station in Maine was the one built at Augusta after World War I; it was the only example in the Art Deco style, both on the exterior and interior. This station represented the last attempt by the railroads to retain passenger service before the onslaught of the automobile. It, too, was demolished recently.

Spanning streams and rivers has always been a challenge to man, with results ranging from temporary, make-shift structures to bridges of great beauty and strength. The oldest known bridge in Maine is Sewall's Draw Bridge at York, built of wooden pilings in 1761 and reconstructed early in this century. It is probably typical of many spans which once existed over narrow, shallow bodies of water.

One hundred and twenty covered bridges once existed throughout the state.[5] Unfortunately, only eight original and a reconstructed one survive today; they are found from York County in the south to Aroostook County in the north, and date from 1857 (the Hemlock Bridge at Fryeburg and Low's Bridge between Guilford and Sangerville) to 1911 (the Watson Settlement Bridge near Littleton). Two utilize a Long truss, three employ the popular Howe's truss and five are of Paddleford construction, a modified Long truss. In addition, two of the latter are strengthened with laminated wooden arches.

Maine's two longest covered bridges are now gone, the 792-foot structure across the Penobscot between Bangor and Brewer, and the 600-foot bridge at Norridgewock. Other equally impressive spans were at Bethel and Old Town.

The most interesting of Maine's bridges were the three wire and chain suspension bridges at Kingfield, Strong and New Portland. Only the last survives today, but it is lovingly maintained and is one of Somerset County's prime tourist attractions. Spanning the Carrabasset River, the New Portland Wire Bridge, or Col. F. B. Morse's "Fool Bridge" as it was called by the skeptical townsfolk who voted $2,000 for its construction in 1840, is 188 feet long and 12 feet wide. Its four-inch steel cables were ordered from Sheffield, England, hauled overland by oxen from the port of Hallowell, and strung into place from two heavily braced, 25-foot high sheathed wooden towers in 1841. The roadway was suspended from the cables the following year and the bridge was opened to traffic on June 20, 1842. The suspension bridges of neighboring Kingfield (1852–1916) and Strong were erected at about the same time and were nearly identical in design. As far as can be determined, the New Portland Wire Bridge is the only one of its type left in the country.

Another bridge, unique to Maine, is the graceful Two-Penny toll footbridge spanning the Kennebec River between Waterville and Winslow. It is the only private toll footbridge in the United States today. Constructed in 1901 (and reconstructed after the flood of 1903), the 700-foot long steel suspension pedestrian span was intended for the passage of millworkers between the two communities. Inflation has caused the toll to rise to five cents in recent years.

Maine also seems to have the monopoly on Cobwork bridges, the only one in the country being located over Will's Gut between Bailey's and Orr's islands in Casco Bay south of Brunswick. It was erected in 1926–28 as a unique solution to a difficult engineering problem. The swiftness of the tides in Will's Gut, and the battering of floating ice in winter, created unusual challenges in determining the design. Granite slabs were laid in cellular or open construction, first lengthwise, then crosswise in a crib-style manner. No mortar or cement was used. The open cribbing construction permits the tidal currents to flow freely and allows the structure to withstand the buffeting of waves and ice floes.

Of more modern appearance are the suspension and cast concrete bridges of recent decades. Two extremely graceful suspension bridges exist in Maine, the one connecting Deer Isle and Stonington with the mainland over Eggemoggin Reach (1939), and the handsome Waldo-Hancock suspension bridge of 1931 over the Penobscot River at Verona, near Bucksport. The cast concrete bridge at Norridgewock, erected in

1928, is probably the most attractive of this type in Maine, while the Million Dollar Bridge of 1914, connecting Portland and South Portland over a portion of Portland Harbor, was the longest and most costly of its time.

Two railroad bridges deserve special note. The steel Gulf Stream Trestle on the old Somerset Railroad, near Bingham, was an engineering marvel, especially considering the remoteness of the site and the difficulty of moving men, machinery and steel to the location. Built in 1904–05 by the Boston Bridge Company, it was 700 feet long and 125 feet high. The railroad was abandoned in 1933; it is sad to report that at the time of writing, this outstanding piece of railroad engineering is in the process of demolition, because it has been judged a hazard and could not be restored.[6] The other large steel trestle was constructed by Canadian Pacific Railways at Onawa, east of Greenville, on its main line to the Maritime Provinces.

During the first half of the 19th century, after the completion of the famous Erie Canal in 1825, a rage for canal building swept the nation. Two major ones were constructed in Maine. The oldest is the Georges River Canal, extending from Warren at tidewater, twenty-eight miles inland to the town of Liberty. It was started in 1793 and came into the hands of Gen. Henry Knox, George Washington's former Secretary of War, in 1794. He expanded and improved it, but it fell into disuse at his death in 1806. It was rebuilt in 1846 and continued to serve the surrounding region until better roads and the advent of the railroad spelled its demise in 1850. Portions of the canal and its lock system have been preserved and restored in the Warren area. The thirty-eight-mile Cumberland and Oxford Canal, Maine's only other such waterway, was completed in 1830 and remained in use until 1872. It extended from the Sebago Lake basin on the north through Standish, Windham, Gorham and Westbrook to the Fore River at Stroudwater, and was designed to give the interior of southern Maine an outlet to the sea. Most of the canal bed is visible today and over seventy percent of it can be followed on foot. It is now a Historic District on the National Register of Historic Places.

The different kinds of Maine industry, trades and crafts required structures suited to their specialized needs. It is possible here to mention only some of these, leaving it to the curiosity of the reader to visit and examine them in more detail. In nearly all cases, the buildings are utilitarian and are hardly distinguished in an architectural sense. Yet the ability of their Maine builders to construct buildings suited to specialized trades in harmony with the landscape attests to the common good taste of our forebears.

The numerous woolen mills fostered ancillary trades. A requisite step in preparing wool for the looms was the carding mill. The best known example is South Waterford's Hapgood Carding Mill (c. 1830), now reconstructed and in operating condition at Old Sturbridge Village, Massachusetts. The Acadians of the St. John Valley in northern Aroostook County were also growers of sheep and processors of wool. In addition they raised large crops of buckwheat, which they preferred to other grain. Still intact today and serving local farmers is the Gédéon Corriveau Buckwheat and Carding Mill on Route 1 in Frenchville. The unusually complete carding machinery in the Corriveau Mill dates from the 19th century. Old Sturbridge Village also possesses another significant Maine structure, the Nash Cooper Shop, built about 1840, and originally located at Waldoboro. The lime industry in neighboring Rockland and Camden required a large annual production of wooden casks and barrels to ship the lime to markets and the Nash Cooper Shop is typical of the many which dotted the region fulfilling this need.

The lime industry itself spawned a unique form of building.[7] The first lime kiln in Knox County was opened in the mid-18th century and as early as 1817, casks of Camden lime were shipped to Washington, D.C., for use in the construction of the new United States Capitol.

Throughout the remainder of the century, lime from Thomaston, Camden and Rockland was highly esteemed for its quality and purity. Increased competition from other states and the advent of new building materials caused the demise of the industry in the early 20th century. Most of the lime kilns fell into disrepair or were demolished. Those that survive are of field stone and brick construction, in which wood was burned to produce lime from the quarried stone. Today the old kilns of the Rockland-Rockport Lime Company and the Merriam and Shepherd Lime Companies, along the Rockport waterfront, are in a poor state of preservation. A movement is currently under way to restore at least one of them.

In 1901, Maine led the Union in the production of granite. This industry required the construction of elaborate stone-cutting, carving and polishing sheds adjacent to the granite quarries. Some of these barn-like structures survive at Hallowell and Frankfort. The massive gable-roofed wooden granite shed at Frankfort, once part of the Mount Waldo Granite works, and a part of the entire quarry area are on the National Register of Historic Places. This shed is the largest building from the granite industry left in Maine.

Shipyards played an important role in Maine's 19th-century economic prosperity. Large and small, they dotted the coastline, numbering in the hundreds. Today rotting piles and impressions in the mud flats are all that remain of most of them. The Percy and Small Shipyard, started in 1894 at Bath, is the last surviving yard in the country where large wooden merchant vessels were built. The four remaining structures of what was once a large, active complex, are being restored by the Maine Maritime Museum at Bath.

Ice harvesting was another of Maine's late-19th-century economic mainstays, at least along the numerous tidal rivers. Large and commodious ice houses, insulated with sawdust or wood shavings, lined the Kennebec and other rivers.

The ice was harvested in mid-winter and throughout the spring and summer, coastal schooners came to the ice-house wharves to load ice for distant points, often as far away as South America and the Orient. One of the last surviving ice houses in Maine, typical of the many family-sized businesses which flourished on inland ponds and lakes, is located at South Bristol. The Thompson Ice House is the last commercial natural ice business in Maine. The location was also one of the earliest to produce ice for shipment outside the state, the first ice being cut there in 1826. It is owned and operated by Herbert Thompson, a direct descendent of the original proprietor, Melvin Thompson.

Maine attempted to develop its iron ore potential in the 19th century. In 1843, Moses Greenleaf, the famous mapmaker and surveyor, discovered iron ore in Piscataquis County, and in 1845 the Katahdin Iron Works, north of Brownville Junction, was incorporated. It operated until 1890, when a shortage of lumber to fire the charcoal kilns, and increased transportation costs to major markets, caused it to bank its fires for good. At its peak, 2,350 tons of raw iron per year were produced in fourteen bee-hive kilns, a blast furnace and a casting room. Today, only one of the bee hives and the blast furnace tower survive, rebuilt in 1966 under state supervision. The site is now a state park.

Several urban areas saw the development of iron foundries by the first half of the 19th century. There were early foundries at Bangor and Augusta, among other locations. The largest and most famous, however, is the Portland Stove Foundry, still operating on Kennebec Street in Portland. The company has been located at its present site since 1880. Its five major interconnecting wooden buildings are all intact, and are utilized for their original purpose. As such, the Portland Stove Foundry provides a rare glimpse of the industrial past, a view of a unique manufacturing operation carried on at the same location, using virtually the same tools and methods through nearly a hundred years. Rarely in in-

FIGURE 95. *Bangor Standpipe, by Ashley B. Tower (1898). Photo: Richard Cheek*

dustrial history has such continuity been maintained.

Lumbering was the keystone of Maine's prosperity in the past century. A legacy of this past is the Ambajejus Boom House,[8] in Township T1, R9, on the West Branch of the Penobscot River on Ambajejus Lake. The state's waterways served as avenues on which the great log harvests were floated to the mills downstream; the famous log drives were a feature of the spring season. The logs were collected on the various lakes and held for the start of the drive behind booms, anchored on the shores across bodies of water. There has been a Boom House at Ambajejus since 1835; (Thoreau visited there in 1846). The present building was used continuously from 1907 until the West Branch drive finally ended in 1971. Beside the Boom House the booms still stretch across the mouth of the West Branch as a monument to the log drives of the past.

Even further north in Piscataquis County is Chesuncook,[9] an outstanding example of a Maine woods frontier town which housed the diverse population of men and women who served the logging industry in the past century. It was lumbering in the "hell roaring days" which made Chesuncook a wilderness outpost. The architecture of the lumbering village is simple and straightforward, but it illustrates a way of life and a mode of working that has now largely changed.

Public and governmental architecture is beyond the scope of this section (see Miller and Shettleworth, pp. 178ss and 201ss), but mention should be made of the Bangor Standpipe (Figure 95), erected in 1898 according to plans drawn by the aptly named Ashley B. Tower of Wallace, New York and Holyoke, Massachusetts.[10] Besides its primary function of providing water for the City of Bangor, it was designed as an observatory from which the citizens of the town could admire their metropolis and the surrounding area. It was built to be a landmark in its own time, dominating the skyline of the city. It is an outstanding survival of an era in which people believed that even so functional a structure as a standpipe should be aesthetically pleasing as well. The use of the Shingle Style for the exterior made it an oddity even at the time of construction, and it remains today one of the few public structures in Maine erected in this architectural style.

Related to standpipes are the gas works, once a familiar sight in many urban areas. Unfortunately the finest of these, at Lewiston, was demolished in 1975. A magnificent cast-iron internal structure dating from about 1853 in the shape of a six-sided polygon, it was highlighted by a series of six triple-tiered columns in a perfect application of the Greek Revival style to a utilitarian structure.

All of Maine's early wharves, such as the great Union Wharf of the 1790's in Portland, are now gone. Several custom houses still survive; these are also discussed above by Miller.

Maine's agricultural heritage left an architectural legacy, as did the various industries mentioned above, but space does not permit an intensive treatment of the subject here. In passing it can be noted that the corn canning factories, which dotted the 19th-century rural landscape, potato barns and storage sheds in Aroostook County, Grange halls, barns, siloes and other farm-related structures, were all built with specific needs in mind, and nearly always in a style which was sympathetic to the landscape.

The commercial and industrial architecture of Maine deserves a close examination, especially since it has been less valued and appreciated than residential architecture and is more easily threatened by modern technologies. Architects and owners lavished almost as much skill on the design of business structures as they did on private homes. Recognition of this fact will perhaps increasingly encourage the attractive and profitable adaptive use of many notable commercial and industrial buildings that now stand empty or under-utilized in many Maine towns.

6

The Development of Modern Styles of Architecture:

Roughly from 1920 to the Present

Philip Isaacson

However much our buildings may once have referred to specific qualities of climate or social history that are unique to Maine, almost nothing about the forms they have assumed since 1920 stems from local imperatives. To the extent that regional architecture exists at all in this country, Maine has largely reflected the formal developments of the other Northeastern states.

The last twenty-five years may prove to have been the golden opportunity, if not the golden age, of building in Maine. For the first time in a century, Maine offered architects a dependable flow of commissions, some so substantial that they lured talents from beyond our borders. The results have been less uniform than in earlier and perhaps less sophisticated times. A few of those commissions have placed superlative build-

ings in our midst. More have set down useful if not innovative structures. Too many, however, are of unrelieved vulgarity. The last category will not be discussed here although examples of it have intruded upon much of our landscape.

The extent of the opportunities lost in the last twenty-five years of the period covered in this chapter can best be judged by comparing it with the output of preceding periods. The 1920's were the prelude to the Great Depression. The decade began with the still vital Colonial Revival style. Its forms, once a reaction to the over-complexities of late Victorianism, were particularly hardy in the state. While progressive European designers were developing a vocabulary of forms expressive of the technological and aesthetic realities of modern life, an architectural hypothesis later called "modern architecture," Maine represented a community of attitudes congenial to the survival of the Colonial Revival style.

The state was not unique in this regard, but it was particularly stubborn in support of the point. Homes, post offices, and school buildings bore the stamp of the style throughout the decade and for several more to come. So resolute was the Revival that it reached its most expanded moment in the 1940's to 50's in Colby College's Mayflower Hill campus by Jens Frederick Larson. Built after European modernism had won the battle for responsible architectural expression, this new campus was the most elaborate nongovernmental architectural program in the state's history. Its bland towers and halls, wrapped around the diverse contemporary functions they concealed, rose even as buildings whose designs were grounded in modern realities took shape elsewhere in New England and the world. It is unfortunate that the plans for this project, which were drawn up before World War II, were not redrawn in a more contemporary spirit when circumstances again permitted the continuation of the entirely new Colby campus.[1]

The example of the Colby buildings, which are inevitably out-of-scale in comparison with genuinely 18th-century buildings, and which lack the delicate coloration created by the natural ageing process, led to further projects in the same style. At a time when Neo-Colonialism had a purely political connotation in other parts of the world, Bates College followed Colby into a dated architectural excursion marked by classical columns, porticos and multi-paned windows. The incongruity of this architecture of the 1950's and 60's is pointed up by the balance of the Bates campus.

Presided over by Gridley J. F. Bryant's elegant Italianate Hathorn Hall (1857), the original Bates campus illustrates the organic growth of a small New England college (also see Miller, p. 175 above). The vernacular traditions of the region, mansard Victorianism, "Collegiate Gothic," reflections of Henry Hobson Richard-

son, and even a kind of decorative *moderne,* combined with other styles to grace a well-treed urban campus. Keeping pace with architectural attitudes current from time to time elsewhere in New England, the Bates campus was a tranquil interlude along the edge of a New England textile community.

The school's growth in the 1950's opened up an area of land separated by a private road from the original campus. The visual division provided by the road and the general architectural temper of the times should have encouraged the use of current aesthetic forms to maintain the College's architectural traditions. Instead, Bates embarked on a Neo-Georgian episode that did not run its course until six such new buildings found their places and three older ones, a boiler house and the *moderne* dormitory among them, had been thoroughly Colonialized. Bowdoin College in Brunswick and the University of Maine at Orono fared somewhat better, but neither entirely escaped from the hands of revivalists of 18th-century style.

Both Colby and Bates, however, have subsequently built structures of outstanding architectural design (see pp. 245, 247), a sign of the almost universal change of taste that has resulted from the development of modern architectural forms.

Against this early uncreative background, it is not surprising that more ambitious goals were not achieved. If the colleges, seats of enlightenment, did not require their buildings to acknowledge the world in which they were sited technologically and stylistically, who would do so? Some answers to the question will be given in the following pages.

The persistence of the Georgian style is, of course, far from a full account of the architectural story in Maine from the 1920's through the 1960's. The Depression absorbed the 1930's. It was a period of minimal construction, one in which architects had both the time and incentive to give even small commissions careful study. Clients motivated to venture into a reconciliation of European *avant garde* design with the aesthetic images comfortable to Maine were, however, all but non-existent. It is difficult to fault anyone, designer or client, for their circumspection during such dark times.

Even as the rationale for a modern architecture to internationalize all forms and attitudes was being refined in Europe, Americans were becoming geographically polarized. During the Depression domestic problems were the order of business and while Americans went about the process of solving them, they stayed at home. If there was a cohesive national aesthetic in the architectural and plastic arts prior to the 1930's it began to fragment during the Depression decade. The same regionalization of style which can be perceived in American art became apparent in architecture. "Styles" developed that were reflections of local attitudes. Radical architecture, to the extent it was practiced at all, for example in California, had a parochial quality that would not be congenial in the Mid-West or New England. Modern architecture came to mean one set of formal values to the *avant garde* of Boston, another to their brothers in Chicago, and still a third in San Francisco. Derived in

each case from the ferment of European thinking, their values were tempered by the exigencies of local architectural traditions.

Walter Gropius, a chief theoretician of European modernism, or the International Style[2] as it came to be called, and his more pragmatic associate, Marcel Breuer, fled Nazi Germany and settled at the Harvard Graduate School of Design. Their impact on Maine will become apparent in later portions of this chapter, as will New England's impact upon them. Their influence in their own backyards was modest during the Depression years, and it is not an understatement to say that they had virtually no effect on architecture in Maine at that time. But while architects conscientiously undertook the few traditional commissions offered during the 1930's, architectural theory was developing in Cambridge and elsewhere, that would contribute to radical changes in their formal concepts. World War II had the effect of *homogenizing* the American people. Its end and the ensuing prosperity liberated them to the formal satisfactions of contemporary design. The extent to which such satisfactions have succeeded is the main concern of the paragraphs that follow.

COMMERCIAL BUILDINGS IN BEAUX-ARTS AND ART DECO STYLES, AND CHICAGO-STYLE SKYSCRAPERS

It would seem that a survey of the development of modern architecture in Maine should follow historical lines for the sake of clarity. Successive examples should be cited to illustrate each of the classical stages in the development process. Unfortunately the architecture of Maine during the last half century does not fit neatly into the usual chronological molds. Examples of certain germinal styles are lacking; others arrived and then withered; and still others came, but out of historical sequence. Nevertheless, our commercial buildings provide us with a body of physical facts from which we can deduce a local response to the stream of progressive events out-

side of our community; and these are facts that chart the demise of Beaux-Arts eclecticism and its handmaiden, the Colonial Revival.

The ultimate American commercial building is the skyscraper. Our national invention, it is a tangible embodiment of our energies and technological resourcefulness. Its symbolic importance has, in some cases, stationed it in our midst without regard to the economic considerations that inspired its form initially. Maine has no skyscrapers. With laudable Yankee shrewdness we have avoided buildings, no matter how symbolic, that don't pay the rent. Nevertheless, we have not been insensitive to the lure of tall buildings or, in one case, to low buildings with a tall-building point of view.

Skyscrapers first arose in Chicago. In the last two decades of the 19th century, Chicagoans embellished their Loop with buildings of exceptional height. Having developed the elevator, fireproofing and the self-supporting metal frame, which provide the basic technology of skyscrapers, they set about defining a system of aesthetics applicable to these extraordinary structures. The cultural ambitions of their city attracted men—Daniel Burnham, John W. Root and Louis Sullivan among them—who developed a mode of vertical expression to enhance the buildings; this is a mode whose fundamentals are still in use.

Portland's first tall buildings (and they are not very tall) followed Chicago's by thirty years. Herbert Rhodes' Chapman Building (1924) was built to dominate Monument Square and still towers over the area. It has been joined by latter-day neighbors of considerable height but it maintains its position in the skyline through an uneasy and ill-considered two-story addition. Obscuring the line of the original cornice, the new stories deprive the building of a logical terminus and of any distinction that its designer conferred upon it.

The stone-clad walls of the original Chapman Building rise in rigid order from a classically adorned two-story base. The latter is a reasonable Beaux-Arts excursion, but the actual shaft of the structure is entirely ambiguous. In its lack of clarity, it fails to proclaim itself either as a massive block or a vertical form. Its windows mark the floor levels of the building, and thus the horizontality of its contents, but the eye is never urged up the facade in order to create tension between the horizontal and vertical elements. Although the walls exhibit considerable texture and appreciable scale, these qualities are insufficient to endow the building with much visual energy. The Chapman Building is an early attempt to bring a cosmopolitan view of the American city to Maine and its distinction

lies in this effort and not in its actual fabric. Its immediate neighbor to the north, the Fidelity Trust Building, fared much better in its actual plan.

Built in 1910 from the designs of G. Henry Desmond, the Fidelity Trust Building expresses itself in a series of piers revealing a progression of steel columns across its facade (see Figure 96). The effect is to suppress the spandrels and windows that fill in the spaces between the rising piers, which beckon the eye upward and endow the structure with a loftiness that belies its eleven stories. Here the skeletal frame is exploited in the cause of visual dynamics, and the architect acknowledges that his building's covering is only a skin of masonry. No attempt is made to suggest that the Fidelity Trust is a grand cut-stone pile but it is allowed instead to acknowledge its debt to modern technology. The assertive steel skeleton advises the viewer that he is looking at a tall building, one that has had to be made of a heavy network of beams, girders and columns to stand so tall. The columns of its face give sheerness to its rise, and the absence of an emphatic cornice continues the illusion.

The Fidelity Trust Building was built during the heyday of Beaux-Arts formalism, in which Gothic as well as Renaissance buildings were sources of inspiration. It was considered quite appropriate to apply a Gothic veneer to tall buildings. As the New York architect Cass Gilbert demonstrated in his epochal Woolworth Building (1910–13), a soaring effect could be imparted to a building through the use of unbroken piers in the Gothic mode. This effect was heightened through the elimination of the cornice, an element as unnecessary to the Gothic as it was necessary to the Renaissance. The attitudes expressed in the Woolworth Building were enormously influential and had an evident effect on Desmond, the architect of the Fidelity Trust Building in Portland. The simplicity of his building, and, probably, a restricted budget, did not permit the Gothic stylization of the important piers, but he was able to treat the terminus of the walls in the manner of a Gothic crown, through the use of classical motifs. In this effect he was influenced not only by Cass Gilbert, but by the New York firm of Howells and Hood, whose handsome Chicago Tribune Building (1922–1924) is the most celebrated of the Gothic genre. Desmond's discard of the cornice was part of a prophetic movement, for as incongruous as a Gothic skyscraper may sound, this form dominated the aesthetics of American skyscraper design until its displacement by the logical modernism of the International Style. Thus, while the later Chapman Building gives the impression that its stone walls are part of its supporting structure, the design of the Fidelity Trust Building was able to express the essential innovation of skyscraper architecture of the period.

While the history of the tall building in Maine, as elsewhere, is virtually the history of the building of banks, that is not invariably the case. The American Telephone and Telegraph Company, through its various subsidiaries, also commissioned tall commercial buildings. After undergoing rapid expansion in the late 1920's and early 1930's, the Company searched for an architectural style that would express the burgeoning technology of its activities. Its functions, supported by increasingly complex machinery, were more industrial than commercial, but the Telephone Company chose to keep its business headquarters downtown. Its decision dictated the use of multi-storied buildings. A style that would admirably symbolize these functions was conveniently at hand. That style, Art Deco, was as "officially" the style of tall American commercial buildings in the late 1920's as the Beaux-Arts style had been for our earlier governmental buildings.

Art Deco took its name from the 1925 Paris Exposition Internationale des Arts Décoratifs et Industriels Modernes and is synonymous with the terms "moderne" and "modernistic." While its forms ultimately provided the Main Streets of our state with decoratively-fronted furniture

FIGURE 96. *Portland, Fidelity Trust Company, by G. Henry Desmond (1910). Photo: Richard Cheek*

stores and movie houses, they were originally intended as coverings for high-rise steel-framed buildings. Art Deco was to give the tall buildings of America a warm and sensuous appearance. It was a theatrical style (indeed the theater was a prime source for its design), optimistic, laced together with rich colors and an almost infinite complexity of surface forms. The other influences upon it were as various as its forms. Louis Sullivan, that quintessential American Frank Lloyd Wright, French, German, and Dutch formal attitudes, futuristic imagery, the waning Arts and Crafts movement, the Beaux-Arts itself, and even a New York City Zoning Ordinance of 1916, went into the amalgam. Out of it came a timely and inviting style that managed to be both stage-like and a proclamation of America's technological strength.

In 1931, Densmore, Leclair and Robbins designed a six-story building for the New England Telephone and Telegraph Company in Portland. Rising from a low, black granite base, the finely finished limestone-faced building is in the Art Deco style. It is not in the sensuous style of New York Art Deco, but is rather a sedate, cooled down version of the style, one that the company deemed appropriate to Maine. The first story is marked off by a firmly raised limestone band accentuated by simple dentils. The squat shaft rises unbroken above the band, accepting shallowly indented bronze-framed windows. The building terminates in an inscribed banding composed of circles and thin verticals and has no cornice. The central portion of the shaft between the bandings is severe. In contrast with earlier tall commercial buildings in Portland, the facade is a single clean plane accentuated at its sides with vertical strips of windows. The latter are separated from one another by stone panels richly carved with stylized flowers and are set off from the balance of the face by indentations running their entire length. Between the first-story windows and the initial horizontal banding is an inset of five stone plaques, each decorated with the Company's

bell symbol or with geometric flowers. A somewhat less elaborate five-story building was designed for the Telephone Company by the Densmore firm and erected in Bangor in 1929–31. Using buff-colored brick instead of limestone, the architects achieved a textured, tapestry-like surface which was quite conventional to Art Deco.

More classically appointed early Art Deco buildings in larger communities had a richness not found in the Maine versions. The bases and termini were elaborated by the application of fields of curvilinear and geometric ornament. The ornament, usually terra-cotta or metal panels, could be brightly glazed and intricately patterned by forms derived from nature, but in streamlined versions, or from a vocabulary of geometric shapes; typical among the latter were expressionistic zig-zags and lightning bolts. The application of such decorative motifs may be seen in the panels integrated into the facade of the Singer Building on Main Street in Lewiston, designed by Pulsifer and Eye in 1934.

Coinciding with the Depression years, Art Deco found its broadest local application in small commercial structures such as the Singer Building and in store-front remodeling. Giving older buildings a "modernistic" look was a venture merchants could undertake at a time when major new construction was not possible. In such remodeling, Art Deco in Maine achieved its most flamboyant form. Colored glass panels were applied to existing facades, and show windows were turned into a new geometry. Old angles were smoothed into curves, the circle was introduced, streamlined lettering appeared on signs and aluminum was first used as a decorative metal. The excitement and glitter conjured up by all of this was a happy antidote to the general gloom of the times.

The Veterans Administration Hospital, Togus, by Coombs and Harriman (1930) is Art Deco's most substantial local expression but not its most arresting. That title is reserved for the Lamey-Wellehan Building (1936), a small gem

110 LISBON STREET · LEWISTON MAINE · 1934

FIGURE 97. *Lewiston, Lamey-Wellehan Building, by Coombs and Harriman (1936). Drawing by Gridley Barrows, A.I.A.*

by the same firm (see Figure 97). On Lewiston's Lisbon Street, the Lamey-Wellehan Building substituted black glass sheathing for the rich masonry found in more elaborate structures. The sleekness of the glass, accentuated by polished aluminum trim, gave the building considerable sophistication. Although limiting themselves to only two materials, the designers created a high degree of visual interest through the banking of the windows. By inserting a mezzanine into the two-story structure, they were able to arrange the windows in stacks and thus achieve a pier-and-spandrel effect much like that found in taller buildings. The lower casement in each

stack was topped by an aluminum panel embossed with a simple rectilinear design. The latter was, in turn, the visual support for a more elaborate set of casements and transoms which were finally surmounted by a second aluminum panel, embossed, in this case, by a succession of chevrons. The peak of the top row of chevrons protruded above the roof line giving the whole a vitality far out of proportion to the size of the structure. The first floor harbored another hallmark of the Style, the curving horizontal. In this case, show windows curving from the sidewalk to the front doors, led the eye into the deep interior. From the sign to the hardware on the doors, the appointments were all of a piece, and gave the structure a perfect consistency. This building remained in nearly pristine condition until recently, when its upper stories were resurfaced with an unfortunate granular material. The original front door has been replaced, but a secondary door serving the upper floor is intact as a handsome artifact of the period.

1932 is conventionally given by architectural historians as the demise of Art Deco, but as in all things, dates are more helpful to the historian than to the practitioner. Art Deco continued to find its way into the signs, theaters, store fronts and even into the homes of Maine through the years of World War II. Its forms, often much altered, are still to be seen in our downtowns and in one instance, the Manufacturers National Bank Building in Lewiston, were employed as late as 1953. The Depression, World War II, and a shift in taste, are given as the reasons for the abandonment of Art Deco. The last is the most probable, for as rich as the style was, and as omnipresent in large cities, Art Deco was doomed to a relatively brief life from the beginning. An attempt to disguise the essentials of Beaux-Arts architecture through physical showmanship, it could not resist the influential development of the International Style; this new and important style embodied a system of design principles which was intended to have universal application.

The International Style, like its immediate predecessor, was a European import, this time from Germany, Holland and France. The work of Gropius, Mies van der Rohe and Le Corbusier (Charles-Edouard Jeanneret) following World War I exhibited certain principles in common. These principles included regular and pure proportions, consistent simplicity and a clear expression of function. Under the pressures of Cubism, the intellectual rationalizations of the great Bauhaus School (first at Weimar and then at Dessau), and the propaganda of Le Corbusier, this initial communality grew into a new aesthetic. And this aesthetic has been so influential that its goals modify our architecture, even today. Those goals, of precision, lightness, and elegance of effect, reflected certain visual yearnings that have rarely been gratified in architecture. They were achieved by diminishing the role of mass, by encouraging order through regularity rather than symmetry, and by avoiding applied decoration.

Architecture was conceived as an exposition of volume; that is, instead of proclaiming a building as a great static mass, it permitted the inner volume of the building to express itself. Otherwise stated, interior space was given pre-eminence over its enclosure. The walls of a building held the interior in a tight embrace; they were drawn around the area like a stretched membrane, a thin impermeable restraint. Glass was the perfect architectural material and where a less ephemeral skin was indicated, the plane of the windows was brought into line with the outer surface of the wall, thus denying the latter's thickness.

The International Style pursued asymmetry as an aesthetic virtue. It achieved order through consistency, through a rhythmic arrangement of standardized units. Finally, as already suggested, the Style was opposed to ornament. Moldings were eliminated, roofs were flat and left capless to deny the line between structure and sky and increase the illusion of intangibility. It was not an architecture of light and shadow but rather an architecture of insubstantiality. It used a vocabulary of forms to express the technological realities of the times, one that made constant allusion to the machine. The attraction of the values of austere beauty, objectivity and visual cleanliness espoused by the Style was undeniable, although these values of-

FIGURE 98. *Augusta, One and Two Central Plaza, by Scott Teas Associates (1974). Photo: R. Bruce Huntingdon*

ten had little relation to actual social realities.

The aesthetic of the International Style, as expressed in primary shapes, large fields of glass and decorative restraint made its way to Maine during the years following World War II. But a nearly classic statement of the Style did not appear here until 1974, long after the classic phase had given way to other adventures both in Maine and abroad. That exercise in classicism, One and Two Central Plaza in Augusta by Scott Teas Associates (see Figure 98), coming so many years after the fact, has a wry and almost satiric quality. It is as though its designers sought to mock the vagaries of recent modern design by thrusting a rigid point of reference into our midst. Whatever their intentions, they have supplied us with a flat-roofed, capless piece of rigid geometry. Its enclosing walls alternate between three broad passages of reflecting glass and a tight veneer of colored, glazed masonry. The tiled walls are relieved by ribbon-windows at the exact plane of the face of the tiles. A protruding tower and a row of stilts along its northwest side area are clear expressions of the Bauhaus idiom as developed by Walter Gropius in his Harvard Graduate School dormitory complex in Cambridge, Massachusetts (1950). The designers' intentions may perhaps be gauged by their choice of material for the mullions in the reflecting glass curtain walls, and in the horizontal strip window trim. Departing from the bronzed aluminum so usual to this time, they selected a specially milled teak. If the building is intended to challenge much of the local design of the 1950's and 1960's by reverting to pure Bauhaus tenets, the teak appears to challenge one of the most important of these tenets. The International Style achieved its effects through a fine arrangement of mass-produced and standardized parts. In Central Plaza, although such parts were commonly available, the architects chose to detail their windows with custom-milled wood, using an ancient technology found in hand-built boats. If the International School was grounded in the need to express modern technology, Central Plaza defies that need by calling for hand-fashioned and installed fittings; the windows thus constitute almost a Pop Art touch in an unyielding body. This is a building of uncommon sophistication, which is handsome by any standard.

One and Two Central Plaza is not a tall office building although its horizontally paned curtain walls suggest a much taller structure if their relationship to the portal is ignored. Like it, the Unionmutual Life Insurance Company Home Office (1971) in Portland (see Figure 99), does not fit neatly into a succession of tall commercial buildings. Designed by Hugh Stubbins and Associates, Inc., it is only 112 feet high but its length, 420 feet, gives it great scale and importance. Two of its four levels are contained within a meticulously articulated concrete cradle. The remaining levels, sheathed in pinky-gold reflective glass, rest lightly upon that cradle. The building, a great glass tower laid on its side, exemplifies the Americanization of the International Style, or more accurately, the fruition of that style in this country. The concept of a glass tower was an obvious goal of the Style. As the skyscraper was the perfect emblem of the new technology, so a glass skyscraper would be the consummate expression of the new aesthetic. Its airiness and luminosity would become the symbol of a new metropolis which would express the same lightness in all its architecture. For political and probably also technological reasons, no glass tower was to rise in Europe before 1939. The realization of that ideal was left to the America of the 1950's. Within the first few years of that decade, great crystal shafts poked their way into the skies over New York and Chicago. Once the first distinguished glass towers had been built, however, glass towers of derivational International Style became standard features of the American urban scene,[3] even of communities without congested centers. The Unionmutual Building, in its twenty-eight acre site, suggests something of this impulse.

It is not difficult to justify the glass tower as an

FIGURE 99. *Portland, Unionmutual Life Insurance Company Home Office, by Hugh Stubbins and Associates, Inc. (1971). Photo: Samuel Robbins*

urban form. If it could bring a new purity of spirit to the city and relieve the pressures of urban life, then it was welcome. The use of massive quantities of energy to light its sealed interior, heat it in winter and cool it in summer were not wasteful if the mass of the city could be converted into contained volumes. It is more difficult to relate that rationale to a Maine pasture. By definition the site is light and airy and in bad weather, its openness makes it quite vulnerable. The site requires both response and respect; the architects of the Unionmutual Building met the first test handily. They acknowledged the site by making strong references to the broad field. The two-step horizontally layered structure, a low concrete frame topped by a flat glass box, has a pleasing hierarchic quality revealing itself from solid to open in logical order. Whether the design respects the site is a more difficult question. A building is a made ob-

ject and under no obligation to mimic nature. It is in fact in opposition to nature, but it is possible for a building to complement nature and thus enhance its surroundings. If this is a fair test of respect in site planning, then the Unionmutual Building does not adequately meet it. A vast glass box, at once both unyielding and visually vulnerable, placed in the middle of a Maine field, is an uncomfortable solution. Although it draws its glass skin tightly around itself, it is nevertheless threatened by a climate that has never encouraged the profligate use of glass. If there *are* Maine attitudes in architecture, one would be a becoming sense of thrift in glazing.

An aggressive climate in all seasons and a rough, unmanicured landscape call for the emphasis of mass, for an isolation from natural forces. The Unionmutual Building embodies an image drawn from a purely urban vocabulary, and achieves a cosmopolitan, if locally irrelevant, result.

Apart from the irrelevance of Unionmutual's style to its site, however, it exhibits an almost

234

flawless application of later International Style. The building is a huge shimmering plane of light, a great hall without exterior shadow or substance; it is conceived as a textile made up of reflections and of a thin linear grid to hold them in place against the sky. It is as though a passage of space has been enclosed in a membrane and cradled lightly within the broad field. The thinness of the retaining grid is designed to restrain the visual energies present in a more conventional building. The sequence of mullions moving in modulated regularity down its face is as unobtrusive as possible. Rather than to zone the structure into defined areas and to set up a tension between them, the mullions serve as an incised decorative pattern secondary to the great reflective plane of the wall itself. The wall has a discernible scale but, because it is without texture, it is without apparent density. Being thus weightless, the mass disappearing into the reflected sky, it does not tie into the earth but rests upon its concrete base as a great cubic object.

The elegant and aloof Unionmutual Building is Maine's pre-eminent glassed "tower." Its simple, dematerialized shape, reminiscent of Gropius' Bauhaus School Workshop at Dessau (1926), compares favorably with the best structure of its type in our largest cities, for example with Lever House in New York (see note 3).

In a reaction against the sequence of derivational International Style towers of glass in the Avenue of the Americas, Eero Saarinen designed the Columbia Broadcasting System Building (1965), in the same avenue, in a new and massive idiom. Built of reinforced concrete with exterior bearing walls, the CBS Building has a shaft which rises directly from a flat plaza instead of from the terminus of the first level, as had become standard in New York. The walls are composed of the structural columns, sheathed in black granite, and strips of grey glass. Angled from the plane of the wall to form V-shaped fins, the sheathing gives the impression, when one approaches the wall from an oblique angle, that the building is made of heavily ridged stone.

As the angle of approach changes, the vertical ribbons of glass separating the piers emerge, and then disappear again when the original angle is resumed.

Portland has a diminutive version of the CBS Building in its Casco Bank and Trust Company Building (1970) at Monument Square. Designed by Walker O. Cain and Associates it rises ten stories from the brick pavement. Substituting a tan Roman brick for Saarinen's vertical sheets of Canadian granite, its designers achieved an unbecoming squatness that adds little to the quality of the city. The Casco Building, like the CBS Building in New York, can be comprehended as a whole; that is to say, as in the CBS Building, the straight shaft works its way up in one unbroken line from the sidewalk to the roof. But whereas Saarinen provided a perfectly flat depressed plaza from which the sheer rise commences, the Portland site slopes toward its easterly end, revealing a sharp stretch of foundation. This inauspicious beginning, the truncation of the shaft and the layers of tan brick deprive the structure of the somber dignity of its prototype. The cold and unyielding severity of Saarinen's concept did not lend itself to a warming up and a diminution in size. Compounding the problem of truncation, the addition of a penthouse to the top of the Casco Building emphasizes the low terminus of its walls. While it is unlikely that any large urban building in Maine, for economic reasons, could achieve the authority of its prototype, Casco does represent an opportunity lost. An independent structure at the junction of two important streets and a fine square, it had a unique chance to make a forceful statement. It missed that chance.

Another Portland bank, with a less advantageous site, made better use of its opportunities. If the Casco Bank Building suggests a return from the gossamer-enclosed volume to a proclamation of mass, the Maine Savings Bank Building (1972–74, see Figure 100) confirms the trend. The work of Pietro Belluschi and Jung/ Brannen Associates, the building is a great elemental block recessed from the street by a paved plaza. The latter, in turn, is bounded on one side by a serrated line of single-story shops and by a two-level bank on the other. The shops and the banking offices are clean, assertive bronze-trimmed structures, but the ten-story bank building is of singular architectural quality. It has the size, force and visual energies of an important architectural conception.

The block, of a distinctive brown-purple brick to compensate for the interruption in the long wall of Congress Street, plays off horizontals against verticals with consummate skill. So subtly is the process organized that the viewer becomes involved in a continuing series of visual decisions. The six banks of windows, utilizing more of the wall surface than the surrounding brick, raise the issue of the building's physical nature. Is it a glass wall supported by brick or a brick wall punctured by glass? The issue is further complicated by the carrying of glass and brick at different vertical levels and finally, by allowing the glass to project beyond the face of the brick. A brick face with inset windows would have decided the issue but in permitting the windows to pop out from the face the problem is compounded. Likewise, the architects ask us to decide whether we are dealing with horizontal windows in vertical stacks or horizontal windows in horizontal strips layered one upon the other.

The decisions depend on the vantage point. Firm lines of brick separating the third from the fourth levels and banding the top of the structure intensify a feeling of horizontality when it is viewed from the facade. This is supported by heavier brick facing on the beams that separate the windows vertically from that on the columns which divide the windows into a system of stacks. When viewed from the side where the banks are reduced from six to three, the horizontals bow to the insistency of the verticals. Here all ten levels are exposed, the bottom three being unencumbered by the various low structures that bound the plaza, and the building is per-

mitted a modest soar.

It is not difficult, under such conditions, to conceive of the structure as a punctured slab rather than a horizontal block. Whichever view is adopted, the designers have organized the field of the wall in such a way that visual energies of one sort oppose those of another in tense equilibrium. As the eye moves upwards over the stacks it is arrested by the horizontal sweep of the two wide bands of demarcation and the narrower banding within the stacking; thus the forces which organize the block vertically contend with others that organize it horizontally. Zones oppose zones and a convincing sequence of one form is confronted by a sequence of another which is equally successful. This is a splendid building, full of coherency and visual intelligence. In it, Maine's tall commercial buildings reach their first maturity.

The Unionmutual and Maine Savings Bank buildings represent logical extensions of the work of Gropius, but the Merchants National Bank Building in Bangor (1974) by Eaton W. Tarbell and Associates approaches the aesthetic proposed by Le Corbusier. The latter, although an originator of the International Style, was one of the first to modify its principles. His earliest structures, the Stein House (1928) near St. Cloud and Savoye House (1930) at Poissy-sur-Seine, both in France, are as uncompromising in their purity as any conceived in the Style. By 1931, however, Le Corbusier had introduced plastic forms into his *oeuvre* and following World War II his work contained highly sculptural passages. Abandoning the thin skins necessary to the *prisme pur* of the classical International Style, the architect utilized site-poured concrete, a material that lends itself to expressionistic use. The Merchants Building is hardly an emotional departure from International Style, but in its variation from the basic glass box it permits the accentuation of form for purely sculptural effect. Piers are broken, elevator shafts protrude from the body of the building and are fluted for good measure, and other formal pas-

FIGURE 100. *Portland, Maine Savings Bank Build-ing, by Pietro Belluschi and Jung-Brannen Associ-ates, Inc. (1972–74). Photo: Mason Philip Smith*

FIGURE 101. *Bangor, Merchants National Bank Building, by Eaton W. Tarbell and Associates (1974). Photo: R. Bruce Huntingdon*

sages move in and out across its face. All of these details, to be sure, are functional appliances, but they have been nevertheless manipulated for effect. While still a building of strong linear forms, Merchants Bank lacks the former sense of mission, the urge to purify form into a membrane containing inner space. In its place is a massive skeleton which dominates the sequence of dark glazing that it contains, and in which the positive effects of light and shadow are exploited. The smooth textile has been replaced by a calculated monumentality and considerable aesthetic drama. It is an assertive, almost brutal, attempt visually to monopolize an area, and in the approach to it from the north, this attempt is admirably successful. Of all this state's tall commercial buildings, the Merchants Building is the most adventurous and while it may not have reached its goals consistently, they were the ones most difficult to attain.

The early intellectualizations of the Interna-

tional School had certain pragmatic American roots. When Gropius, Le Corbusier, and other theoreticians cited the rationalistic advantages of precision and rectilineal adherence, they illustrated their theories by referring to the new industrial buildings that had developed around our Great Lakes. Indeed, from 1906 through the 1940's, American heavy industry rehoused itself in structures whose beauty exceeded the utilitarian demands they were designed to fulfill. The European modernists saw in them a symbolic interpretation of a new technological spirit.

Their American designers, however, in most cases understood them as outgrowths of that technology, without any special philosophic connotations. With few exceptions, those designers were men who were willing to put aside the aesthetic considerations normal to an architectural practice, in order to concentrate on the practical demands of their clients. Whether, as a consequence, they ought properly to be called building engineers instead of architects is beyond the scope of this chapter; but it is clear that in their work they did develop a powerful statement that seems inherently American.

Traditional American mill construction is multi-storied with heavy interior timber supports. Maine, particularly at Lewiston and Biddeford, is rich in fine old bearing-wall structures of the type. When it was introduced the steel frame had serious limitations for industrial use. Steel is not fireproof; it fails to dampen vibrations when one floor is superimposed on another; and it is vulnerable to corrosion. By the turn of the 20th century, however, buildings could be framed in concrete reinforced with bars of steel, a technique that, while laborious, did away with the major disadvantages of steel. Reinforced concrete, following Ernest Ransome's United Shoe Machinery Building in Beverly, Massachusetts (1903–05), became a standard method of framing multi-storied factories. The system was typically rendered with an exterior structural frame exposed to form a series of bays. As the bay filling was non-bearing, it could be easily adapted to a client's needs. The bay is usually seen with its lower area filled with brick topped by a concrete sill; the sill, in turn, supports a curtain of glass.

The automotive industry, generally, and the Detroit, Michigan, architect Albert Kahn, in particular, were early proponents of reinforced concrete and pragmatic industrial design. The manufacture of automobiles revolutionized the requirements of American factories and Kahn met those requirements between 1903 and 1942, seeing Ford from its first Model T's through its World War II days at Willow Run. His clientele included Chevrolet, DeSoto, Chrysler, Glenn Martin, Curtiss-Wright and others. Caught up in the initial enthusiasm for the motor car, Kahn was able to satisfy the tough-minded needs of American industry without apparent relation to the great movements or styles (among them Wright and the Internationalists) that swirled around him. In 1906, Kahn, in an act of major architectural significance, produced plans for the George N. Pierce Plant in Buffalo, New York, to be used for the manufacture of the Pierce-Arrow sedan. In providing a one-story roof-lit scheme, this plant permitted the organization and logical flow of processes

that would become the hallmark of American mass production. The Pierce lesson was not lost on Henry Ford, who by 1915 was planning that mammoth industrial complex, his Ford Rouge Plant. By the same token, it was not lost on the Directors of the Bates Manufacturing Company, who were planning a new weave shed for one of their Lewiston textile plants. The Pierce philosophy was reexpressed at Ford Rouge but the Pierce form, as well as its philosophy, was reexpressed by Kahn at Bates.

Unlike its prototype, the great Bates weave shed (1919, see Figure 102) has two levels, the lower being almost entirely below the surface of the flat site. The exposed concrete frame displays a long march of bays, each divided horizontally by a concrete sill at the level of the upper floor and then subdivided vertically by a heavy brick mullion. The resulting areas are then filled first with brick, topped by a second concrete sill and then by glass. As was the case with similar construction for Ford at Highland Park, Michigan (1909), Kahn prescribed steel sash of substantial size uninterrupted by large mullions for Bates. This was replaced in later years by conventional glass brick, which does not seriously detract from the building's initial effect. Like the momentous Pierce plant, the grid formed by the concrete frame is emphatically expressed, but, unlike Pierce, its pragmatic severity is re-

FIGURE 102. *Lewiston, Bates Manufacturing Company Weave Shed, by Albert Kahn (1920). Photo: R. Bruce Huntingdon*

FIGURE 103. *Portland, American Can Company Boiler Plant, probably by Albert Kahn (c. 1940).* Photo: *R. Bruce Huntingdon*

lieved somewhat by a strongly dentiled cornice. The weave shed's most prominent feature is a great central monitor, or sawtooth roof with windows, flowing continuously over its interior bays. The sawtoothed skylight and long supporting beams provide a relatively unobstructed floor area with natural lighting. By bringing natural illumination to the entire plant, its 322-by-637-foot area is opened up horizontally to organized manufacturing processes. The building illustrates Kahn's early principle that plan-dimensions need not be limited by the penetration of light from windows placed in the walls, for the monitor permitted a building designed for a process rather than a process fitted into a building.

Kahn's Highland Park Plant, a multi-storied structure, less adventurous than the earlier Pierce Plant, served as an influential prototype for early 20th-century industrial construction. The influence of that citadel of the immortal Model T can still be felt in Portland's Burnham and Morrill and American Can Company Plants, among others, but Kahn's continuing contributions to innovative industrial design had further impact.

When the powered assembly line forced Ford into one-story activities, Kahn abandoned reinforced concrete for steel. Vibration is not a problem in single-story structures and steel, for all its shortcomings, goes up quickly and occupies less space in plan dimension than reinforced concrete. As we have seen, steel-framed buildings can be thinly clad, and from the first building at Rouge through a vast series of World War II industrial projects, Kahn used great passages of glass. Brick masonry formed the usual base. Next came a concrete sill, which, in turn, was followed by a steel sash and glazing. The glazing fell outside the line of the most exterior columns, and thus permitted the simple prismatic envelope so admired by the International School. The difference is that this envelope resulted from considerations of function and economy, while at Dessau and Poissy-sur-Seine it was primarily symbolic.

A perfect illustration of Kahn's mature style can be found in the boiler plant of the American Can Company complex in Portland (see Figure 103). While its designer has not been identified,[4] its elevations virtually duplicate the north elevation of Kahn's Chrysler Corporation Tank Arsenal (1941) in Detroit. The low masonry base, the sill and the thin steel sash restate one another almost exactly. In the American Can example, we are left with a gridded glass cube, defined in its extremities and sited on a masonry podium. In it, function and economy combine to produce unselfconscious elegance. Its combination of engineering expression and pragmatism achieves an organic result that the International School, and particularly Mies van der Rohe, reached only through the greatest intellectual exertions.

While the boiler house is a remarkable piece of architecture, the work of Albert Kahn is not the sum total of modern industrial design in Maine. Today's metal factory buildings are generally delivered to the site by truck without the apparent intervention of an architect. A number of interesting corrugated steel buildings were designed by Alonzo J. Harriman, however, for the New England Shipbuilding Corporation at South Portland. The complex, including docks, power plant, roads, railroads, fabrication plants and building basins, like Kahn's projects of the 1920's and 1940's, was vast, and demanded completion in a brief period. Time being of the essence, the Harriman design was governed by the practical imperatives that regularly influenced Kahn. The fabrication building (1941), for example, a splayed corrugated metal structure, has a becoming matter-of-factness, and might appropriately be called a vernacular structure. The needs of the moment, and the demands of the things contained, appear to have dictated an essential form.

The Dragon Cement Plant of Martin Marietta Cement, Eastern Division, at Thomaston is one of Maine's few heavy industrial developments and its most formidable. A complex of buildings aggregated over a period of time (1927–1971), its capacity to overpower the viewer comes from both the specific functions of the structures and from their material. Light industrial buildings have a generality of form that reveals little about the processes going on within them. The Dragon Plant with its great silos and other specialized structures, on the other hand, asserts itself as the agent of a complex technology. The buildings, formed of great technological shapes to accommodate their purposes, have been cast of concrete, the very material they were designed to produce. This wedding of purpose and fabric gives the Plant a remarkable, if brutal, homogeneity.

FIGURE 104. *Lewiston-Auburn Water Pollution Control Authority Administration Building and Treatment Plant, by Camp Dresser and McKee (1971–74). Photo: R. Bruce Huntingdon*

Concrete, an ordinarily impassive substance, does lend itself to less forbidding uses, as we have seen in the Merchants National Bank Building. In light industry, when treated with an equally light hand, it can be a grand material. The Lewiston-Auburn Water Pollution Control Authority's administration building and treatment plant (1971–1974, see Figure 104), designed by Camp Dresser and McKee, is a fine example of the art. In their various shapes, the Pollution Control buildings actually suggest the processes of sewage treatment they serve, and are a highly sophisticated response to the need. The raw appeal of form marks and the other abrasions of poured concrete embellish the solidity of wide horizontal banding and firmly structured bays. Both the administration building and the two-level plant are conceived as great blocks, milled at their edges and then punctured with a progression of voids. Their relation to function and their visual consistency give them a highly persuasive quality.

The New England Telephone and Telegraph Company's ESSTSPS (Electronic Switching System and Traffic Service Position System) Building in Portland, by Alonzo J. Harriman Associates, Inc. (1975), carries the use of concrete to one of its final conclusions. If the Water Pollution Control buildings *suggest* elemental blocks, the Telephone Company's ESSTSPS Building *is* an elemental block. Clothed in concrete panels, the building is a great elongated cube relieved only by banks of horizontal ribbing and an occasional window. A row of vertical windows deeply indented into the westerly wall emphasizes the mass of the structure. Gone is the International Style's original tenet about enclosing volume. This Telephone Company building teaches that the proclamation of mass can be as rewarding visually as its denial. If the International Style began with the emulation by theorists of industry's glass walls, it has ended by absorbing industry's massive solidity. It is a turnabout to widen the aesthetic spectrum.

The ESSTSPS building is a difficult exercise. In limiting itself to a basic form without ornament, the choice of materials, the proportions and the precision of execution become critical. There is little to divert the eye from an erroneous judgment. The statement of density and weight must be flawless for even the nominal equilibrium generated when the void of windows challenges the authority of the mass is absent. The considerable force of this austere conception is the measure of its success.

The vocabulary of industry, or better stated,

the vocabulary of technology, is not limited to industrial buildings. It has adopted itself to other requirements, such as the Casco Bank and Trust Company Branch Bank (1970) bridging Fore and Commercial Streets in Portland, and the Portland International Jetport Fire Station (1973) in South Portland. In the former, the work of Wilbur R. Ingalls, and in the latter, by Group Design, the aesthetics of heavy concrete are adapted to small commercial and institutional buildings. The Bank, a bridge in fact as well as in metaphor, is as much a practical piece of engineering as it is a building. The Fire Station commands attention even in the company of such authoritative objects as jet planes and control towers.

In the same way, our educational buildings have not escaped the language of the engineer. The Clifton Daggett Gray Field House at Bates College (1926, see Figure 105) illustrates the integration of industrial conventions with the then-popular Collegiate Gothic. In the period before the Colonial Revival, Maine campuses, like others in New England, acquired little Gothic citadels as libraries, dormitories and for other purposes. When Bates College needed a complex of athletic buildings in the 1920's, Gothic style was chosen to resolve that need. The firm of Coolidge and Carlson developed designs for a great field house (or cage) flanked by men's and women's gymnasia. The field house was to be eighty feet high with a 180-by 180-foot plan. Since it was to span a great space without the use of interior columns, the architects of the field house turned to the great girders and trusses of heavy industrial construction. Over this frank expression of the technological, they fitted a three-tiered cascade of skylights and roof, and then anchored the latter to a wall in Gothic style of local waterstruck brick. The unfolding of the building—from brick wall, to slate roof, to industrial glass—follows a logical sequence of closed through transparent spaces with consummate artistry. In combining conventional institutional with industrial shapes, the architects of

FIGURE 105. *Lewiston, Bates College, Clifton Dag-gett Gray Field House, by Coolidge and Carlson (1926). Photo: R. Bruce Huntingdon*

FIGURE 106. *Auburn, Washburn School, by Alonzo J. Harriman Associates (1951). Photo: R. Bruce Huntingdon*

the Field House produced a most felicitous solution. The necessary great volume of the interior, modified by the exterior Collegiate Gothic, gives it the respectability demanded by the academic community. Nearly a half century passed before Bates again adopted so progressive an architectural attitude.

In 1951 the Harriman firm delivered designs for a new Washburn School to the City of Auburn (see Figure 106). The relevance of Washburn School to this inquiry is again found in the adaptation of an industrial aesthetic to another purpose. The clarity of the brick walls, the curtain windows over a brick base, the smoke stack, and the exposed steel joists, all speak of the forms of light industry. The harmonious translation of those forms into an environment suitable for elementary education confirms one of the initial tenets of the International Style; that is, there are rational lessons in that most practical of buildings, the factory, for many areas of human activity. More importantly, perhaps, the Washburn School confirms that there is a valid aesthetic which draws its expression from structure. It is not an attempt to bring technology into art, as was the case with the International Style, but rather an acknowledgment that the mechanical or technological aesthetic is a major aesthetic in its own right.

RECENT ACADEMIC AND INSTITUTIONAL BUILDINGS

While the influence of the factory on our academic buildings is interesting to reflect upon, the true importance of the latter lies in their impact upon one another and in their extension into the non-academic community. The first major buildings to rise above a chance mix of imported modernisms were built on our campuses. Their appearance, late as it was, represents the initial local commitment to significant modern design.

Bowdoin, whose campus evolved over the centuries without the awkward choices of Colby and later-day Bates, led the way with its Senior Center (1964, see Figure 107). The first contemporary project to achieve great quality, the three-building Center houses the college's seniors. A sixteen-story tower contains student residences, conference rooms, accommodations for lecturers and administrative offices. The tower is linked to a two-story building, which has a lounge, a dining commons and kitchen. A third building provides apartments for the administrators of the Senior Center Program. Constructed of local brick, the tower is articulated by great vertical voids cut deeply into its surface to harbor the window-stacks. With its walls curving inward from ground level to the base of the third story and a system of indenting the four corners that suggests chamfering, the building recalls features of Burnham and Roots' Monadnock Building (1885) in Chicago. While the lack of a curving cornice distinguishes it from the Monadnock's Egyptoid shape, the top story is capped with a huge parasol that may be regarded as its visual equivalent. Voids alternate with solid brick, straight rises alternate with curves, and the slight vertical bulge of the shaft opposes the sharp horizontality of the two outlying buildings. Historical allusions aside, Bowdoin's Senior Center is a powerfully sculptured vertical block of monolithic proportions.

The lower structures, though absolute in their rectilinearity, show the same vertical movement. The solidity of their walls is modified at regular intervals by window voids and at times, is horizontally subdivided, all in the rhythmical asymmetry prescribed by the International Style. The Senior Center was conceived out of a concern for quality and permanence. While much of the architecture of the state was moving toward standardization, this group of buildings preserves the sense of discovery, and gives the user many of the visual pleasures, afforded by important architecture.

Colby moved decisively away from the strictures of Neo-Colonialism in 1967 when Benjamin Thompson and Associates, Inc. designed a complex for dormitory, fraternity and sorority houses on a wooded site above the original Mayflower Hill Campus. Working with massive forms not unlike those in the Lewiston's Water Pollution Control Buildings, Thompson put together an almost brutal masonry environment. The unyielding materials, brick, concrete, and steel, and the strict discipline of the architecture create a demanding and dramatic set of physical circumstances. In one elevation a system of brick piers, interrupted by continuous concrete spandrels, is used to build a regular cellular structure, up to four stories in height, topped with a heavy concrete horizontal. Other elevations present painted brick walls pierced occasionally with deeply cut windows. In these other elevations, the massive horizontal above limits the structure vertically, much as it does on the cellular side. The floor-level concrete spandrels are repeated in short passages above and below the occasional windows to provide visual continuity. Like all recent masonry buildings, this is a proclamation of the mass and the antithesis of earlier substanceless planes. The Colby buildings are complemented by landscaping, which slightly modifies the original circumstances of the site. While

FIGURE 107. *Brunswick, Bowdoin College Senior Center, by Hugh Stubbins and Associates (1964). Photo: Ezra Stoller ESTO*

FIGURE 108. *Lewiston, Bates College Library, by The Architects Collaborative (1972–73). Photo: R. Bruce Huntingdon*

FIGURE 109. *Waterville, Colby Museum of Art, by Johnson-Hotvedt Associates (1973). Photo: Steve Rosenthal*

Thompson's complex has an insistent visual uniformity, it informs the resident that he or she is living in a building of consequence. These residence halls are emphatic, and perhaps even somewhat arrogant.

Bates College made its break with the past in 1972–73 with its library, designed by The Architects Collaborative (see Figure 108). Occupying the central position in its campus, the building is designed to draw student traffic to and *through* it. Its relationship to existing facilities required a main entrance and lobby area on the second level and, accordingly, it is difficult to take the visual measure of the structure. Its appearance varies considerably from various vantage points and the resolution of the second-story entrance required certain uneasy pragmatic concessions, but these are minor considerations in a building of such importance.

A waterstruck brick with colored grouting gives it a uniformly textured surface. Composed of an arrangement of lead-clad shed-roofs and virtually windowless side walls, the Library fronts on a raised plaza while its rear elevation is supported by a long arcade. The pitch of the roof suggests a height greater than the four stories it shelters and a small dependency, likewise shed-roofed, is an arresting complement. This, even more than Colby's dormitories, is a presiding monolith, designed to dominate the old and provide the College with a new symbol. In comparison with the other college buildings, the Bates College Library dominates the buildings around it, but some limitation is maintained over this dominance by the careful articulation of the windows in the elevation over the arcade. This bold building, whose incidental mission is to express the character of the school, stems from the same source as the new Bowdoin and Colby structures, since these two were designed by Cambridge architects. The Bates Library is less resourceful than the former, and less forbidding than the latter, but like both of the other buildings it is a major contribution to the architecture of Maine.

The formidable style of Colby's fraternity-dormitory complex was modified in the 1973 addition to its Art Museum (see Figure 109). By Johnson-Hotvedt Associates and in the same vein as the Bates Library, it has the outward appearance of five independent shed-roofed structures, joined by a common umbilicus into one great sawtoothed monitor. The serene interior is the first really human space in the new breed of academic structures. The great areas and demanding materials of the first buildings are replaced by comprehensible scale, white plaster and warm carpeting. Space is revealed to the viewer as a series of subtle experiences, one following the other in clear sequence. Of a rare breed, a structure designed to enhance rather than dominate its contents, the Colby addition establishes a dialogue between itself and its Neo-Georgian predecessor rather than attempting to harmonize with it through superficial cosmetic devices.

The first of the new art museums in Maine was the Museum of Art of Ogunquit. Built in 1951, it accommodates itself unostentatiously to its seaside site. Approached along a long gravel walkway, the low concrete building slowly emerges from the naturalized plantings of the area. A shallow gabled roof, concrete block interiors, and tile or slate floors, define its finish and design. Its definition in terms of its responsibility to the site is more complex. The building is entered at a low-ceilinged mezzanine. As one reaches the main floor, a panoramic view of the entrance to Perkins Cove appears through a glassed rear wall. Whatever effect that prospect of ocean may have on the art on display, it shows a notable willingness on the architect's part to efface his art to a spectacular locale.

Philip C. Johnson was equally self-effacing in his private gallery for Nelson Rockefeller. Built at Seal Harbor in about 1957, it occupies the interior of an old coal wharf. The gallery consists of a single room about twenty by sixty-eight feet, the area being laid out on 40-inch module. The modular scheme is expressed in a rug-textured rose granite floor and a channeled white ceiling. The walls are made up of fabric-covered panels whose joints are aligned with those of the floor and the channels in the ceiling. A baronial fireplace oversees the space, an elegant, highly sophisticated bit of rectilinear architecture. This gallery is a precursor of certain of the attitudes incorporated by the architect into his redesign of the interior of the Museum of Modern Art in New York (1964).

Edward Larrabee Barnes' new Art Building for Bowdoin (1975–76) is the most perilous undertaking of all our recent buildings. Devoid of ornamentation, it relies principally upon the exactness of its proportions, materials and workmanship. Without personal idiosyncrasy or decorative devices to distract the eye, the building's initial severity seems almost to disdain beauty. Although the building requires a certain effort to understand it, it is an effort that is amply rewarded. A complement in mass to McKim, Mead and White's adjacent Walker Art Building (1892–94), Barnes' Art Building is formidable in the demands it makes upon itself. Supporting a multiplicity of underground exhibition spaces it provides classroom and studio space for the College's art department. The unyielding mass of the exterior, pierced in summer to permit through passage, is modified by its flawlessly appointed interior. In this work, the architect displays an evident affinity for the early buildings of Le Corbusier. More than elsewhere in Maine, the *prisme pur* can be found intact at Bowdoin.

Consisting of chapel, offices and various residence facilities, the Newman Student Center at the University of Maine, Orono, by Willoughby M. Marshall, represents a diminution in scale of the International Style. The tightly-drawn skin is broken from time to time, and the shed roofs are interpreted in indigenous materials. With its rough-sawn vertical siding and its roofs of split cedar shakes, it may be seen as an expression of the International Style modified by local design traditions. It can be argued that the white-painted vertical boards, and the cedar roofs with their steep inclines are derived from the sheds and small outbuildings of Maine; that they temper the austerity of the International Style in accordance with prevailing local attitudes. But while the white wood and pitched roofs do, in fact, represent a domestication of the style, they exemplify a nationwide process that began in the 1950's; the fact that they harmonize with the Maine environment adds distinction to this modification of the International Style. (This subject will be treated in more detail under "Residential Buildings" and "Innovative Developments" below.)

Further, it is fair to say that the Newman Center by Marshall and the new Bates Library by The Architects Collaborative, both Cambridge architects, are more than passingly related; many of Marshall's conclusions also have their equivalents in the work of Edward Deihl Associates, Inc. for the Dead River Company at Jerusalem (now Carrabasset Valley). In the Reddington North and Valley Crossing developments (1969) Deihl dealt masterfully with the aesthetics of rough-sawn boards and shingle roofs.

The new synagogue center for Congregation Am Echad in Auburn, presently under construction, further explores the issues raised by Barnes at Bowdoin and, among others, Marshall at Orono. In an essentially binuclear concept, its architect, Howard Barnstone Associates, joins a gable-roofed sanctuary with a less severely angled shed-roofed area by means of a great glass gallery. The forms, modifications of the barns and attached sheds of the region, represent a conscious attempt to evoke a traditional formal vocabulary and more than a little effort is made to restate the verities of old meetinghouses. The appurtenances of contemporary design puncture and extend the tight membranes of the eaveless structures establishing tense irregular fluctuations in their stretched planes. Like the Bowdoin Art Building, Barnstone's work brings a highly cosmopolitan view of design to Maine, but unlike Barnes, who was required to respond only to a Beaux-Arts neighbor, Barnstone has elected to review the traditions of a region.

The YWCA Pool Building in Lewiston (1971) by the Harriman firm and the Central Fire Station in Auburn (1971) by Deane M. Woodward also reflect similar concerns. Woodward, like Barnes, has taken the primal block in tight masonry form as a point of departure, but unlike Barnes, his accretions mold and extend the block to emphasize its mass. The building, an austere expression of purpose, is an architectural conception of a very high order. The YWCA Pool shares its tight cladding with the buildings by Woodward, The Architects Collaborative, Barnes, *et alia,* but in its great battened copper roof, the designer has added a form that, by comparison with the prevailing rigidity of line, is almost expressionistic. Because of the building's situation, the roof, neither floating nor securely anchored to the continuous brick base, appears as an upper or second facade. The counterpoint between the rectilinear precision of the walls and the sweep of the broad-eaved roof modifies the mass and gives this recreational structure a warm approachable quality.

RESIDENTIAL BUILDINGS

The private homes of Maine do not provide a continuum of forms by which to chart the development of contemporary architecture. The major periods may be represented by one example or another but such examples usually exist in cultural isolation; they do not significantly affect the way Maine people think about architecture. The Otis Ward Hinckley House (1916, see Figure 110) at Blue Hill illustrates the point. With it stuccoed walls, exaggerated wood trim, and broadly overhung hipped roof, it exemplifies the precedents laid down by Frank Lloyd Wright in the suburbs of Chicago at the turn of the century. Wright drew upon the waning Shingle Style, Ruskin, the Arts and Crafts movement of William Morris, Japanese art, the architecture of H. H. Richardson and Louis Sullivan, and the vernacular American aesthetic of the picturesque, among other sources, to develop his own great personal style. The dark wooden strips implanted in the stucco planes that emphasize the rectangularity of his forms came from Japanese prototypes, as did the hipped roof with its floating eaves. Drawing these together, Wright imposed order on a suburban aesthetic that had turned irregular and restless, but which remained a suburban aesthetic. It was meant for the flat treeless plats on Oak Park and Kenilworth Avenues in Oak Park, Illinois, for an upper middle class neighborhood that had lately been a prairie, and not for the coastal woodlands of Maine.

When Wallace Hinckley prepared the design for his cousin, Otis Ward Hinckley, his apparent impulse was to bring Wright and Wright's Oak Park followers, Drummond, Van Bergen and Maher, to Hancock County, without regard to the effect of placing the kind of house suited to genteel Kenilworth Avenue among rock ledges and pine trees. Wright's intention was to promote the deep-rooted, natural qualities of a site and a neighborhood, but his turn-of-the-century designs had little relevance to Maine. The Otis Ward Hinckley house is a handsome residence but it did not point toward Maine's future. Wright's views are obliquely acknowledged in the Abbot Graves House in Kennebunkport, and his later, more natural work, is apparent in passages of Eaton W. Tarbell's house for Russell Peters in Bangor (1959).

The modern home did not come to Maine from the drawing board of Frank Lloyd Wright. It made its tentative debut in 1936 from designs prepared by George Howe for Clara Fargo Thomas.[5] The resulting low house of native materials is cantilevered over the waters of Seal Harbor, a choice its architect (who designed Philadelphia's epochal Philadelphia Saving Fund Society Building) shared with Wright.

Another essay into the genre was Alonzo Harriman's 1939 home for Professor Raymond L. Kendall in Lewiston. The Kendall House, a low hip-roofed, tight-skinned hybrid of modernisms and vestigial Colonialism does not acknowledge the New England advent of Gropius and Breuer. Their appearance at the Harvard Graduate School of Design in 1937 set the stage for the introduction of the International Style in these parts, and it seems probable that the 1944 Harold Tandy House at Hampden Highlands represents the first example of the style in Maine. Designed by Tarbell, it is bisected laterally by a great fieldstone core. The siding of wide natural cedar clapboards that are now, alas, painted, and its fir-panelled interiors and fieldstone, relate the structure materially to its sloping meadowland site. The angled roof, the combined living-dining room, "picture" windows and masonry interior walls are features of Americanized International Style. Although in much debased form, they are also the hallmarks of the omnipresent ranch house, in this early home they represent a striking radicalism. While the Tandy House sports industrial railings and an exterior steel spiral stairway in the manner of Gropius' own home in Lincoln, Massachusetts, its approach to the International Style is nevertheless much tempered by local attitudes. Tarbell's views became more firmly fixed in his 1946 Guest House in South Brewer for Eastern Fine Paper Inc. with its proto-butterfly roof, its firm gravel stop, horizontal siding and strip windows. Like the Tandy predecessor, it draws inspiration from the teachings of

FIGURE 110. *Blue Hill, Otis Ward Hinckley House, by Wallace Hinckley (1916). Photo: R. Bruce Huntingdon*

Breuer. In 1949, Breuer himself designed a Maine building, a home for Arnold Potter in Cape Elizabeth.

The Potter House is the first Maine structure to be designed in the International Style without qualification of any kind. It preceded any local commercial essay in the Style and, speaking broadly, represents its domestication. In it, Breuer reveals what he had learned during the first years of his American experience. Instead of turning to the great industrial images of Detroit, as one might expect, he looked about him and saw the directness and formal clarity of New England wood construction. The local stone was persuasive as was the balloon frame and white walls. These permitted the abstractions that the Internationalists delighted in but called for the modification of *avant garde* style into structures that could easily and comfortably be recognized as "homes." In the Potter House, as in all of his houses of the period, Breuer used broad abstractions—window walls, a butterfly roof, and passages of glass—to contrast with nature. The earthiness of his materials, stone, slate and raw cypress do not signify a conscious allegiance to the natural, but rather point to the end of the dematerialized in the International Style. In its textures and recessed windows, the Potter House, though still planar and full of loft, constitutes an assault on the thin membrane. The early elegance of the Style has given way to palpable materiality.

A courtyard house by F. Frederick Bruck in Lewiston (1961) represents a fusion in formal attitudes. The thin skin of the International Style as enunciated by Breuer is wedded to a symmetrical planar quality that would satisfy a confirmed Miesian, while certain courtyard details are wooden counterparts of Le Corbusier's later efforts in concrete.

The International Style was somewhat tempered by Edward Larrabee Barnes in his Haystack Mountain School of Crafts at Deer Isle (1961, see Figure 111). At Haystack, a tiered complex descending a ledged site, the white cedar shingle indigenous to our coastal buildings is woven into a textured surface and then stretched around simple bold shapes. Here the architect, like Breuer, has sought out a local material, in this case the unpainted shingle, to express his surfaces; but he was not prepared to pierce the cube. More of a traditionalist than Breuer, Barnes maintained the tautness of the cube by eliminating eaves and pulling the shingled coating over the roofs, as well as the walls. The shed roof is one of the few concessions to liberalized attitudes, but in his general design, Barnes in 1961 is more insistent on the original virtues of the International Style than Breuer was in 1949. The weathered skin of the buildings and the steep inclination of their roofs bring them into accord with local idioms and in spite of their strict discipline they are a great complement to a magnificent site.

In his Mount Desert Island residence for August Heckscher (1974), Barnes reiterates his insistence on the tautly-drawn cube. Actually four small buildings, the Heckscher project makes a playful gesture towards the shape of fishermen's shacks; but, in the end, like Barnes' other local work, it is a tense, serious business. Three of the buildings have gabled roofs, without eaves or other overhang, roofs that are angular extensions of their walls. The continuous shingle coverings unify the structures, four modified cubes elegantly sited on a wooden platform. Although the architect puts on a modest face, it is not without considerable effort. The size and locations of the windows, the relationship between openings and shingle levels, the snugness of the decking, are all calculated with infinite care. The Heckscher House is a model of visual simplicity, but it is a simplicity born of impressive creative exertion, and has no more in common with a lobster shack than does the Petit Trianon with a milk shed.

FIGURE 111. *Deer Isle, Haystack Mountain School of Crafts, by Edward Larrabee Barnes (1961). Photo: Joseph W. Molitor*

The verities of the International Style are not without their challengers. A bold new proto-aesthetic has worked its way into Maine—an approach to design that is congenial to our rough rural landscape. Without a name, the new style is an eclectic reaction to the strictures of Internationalism. More to the point, the new style purports to celebrate American, as opposed to international, attitudes. Drawn from Shingle-Style mansions, the California wood tradition as found in the work of Greene and Greene, the intellectual pluralism exemplified by the late Louis Kahn, and certain existing vernacular attitudes, the new style maintains a lively mix. Shingle-style porches, gables and bays join unexpectedly and at unexpected places with simple utilitarian forms. Local shapes and local details synthesize with tense International passages. In its most extreme form, the new style is a mix of complexity and contradiction. It finds wit and more than a little irony in its conflicting elements. Finally, in its variety it seeks to develop a new American vernacular, one of common forms, but of uncommon symbolic power.

The work of Adams Associates in the Deer Isle environs exemplifies the progression toward the new aesthetic. A 1965 project, the Klaver/Adams Partnership, consists of two small separate cabins on a wooden deck, connected by a pathway (Figure 112); in it Adams uses broad-eaved broken parabolic roofs to express the plastic qualities inherent in cedar shingles. The Klaver/Adams project, after an evident bow to Barnes' Haystack School, is the first abstraction drawn from the old Shingle Style in over a half century. Later designs by this firm show a gradual withdrawal from the stern International prescription. The Gordon McClure House (1972), rectilinear but full of angular variety,

substitutes shiplapped pine for cedar-shingled walls. In it, as in other work of the period, the vertical board of native woods becomes a hallmark of the new style. Rough-sawn boards, hitherto used as siding for barns, are the skins and interior coatings of the buildings. Against this almost overwhelming embrace of natural texture, the designers insert occasional industrial forms and then freely add whimsical touches.

Steven Moore/John Weinrich's Gilpatrick House (1975) at Locke Mills carries whimsy to its most developed local state. In a Pop Art outburst, eyebrow-shaped windows join windows in square, rectangular and right-triangle shapes. That quintessential Americanism, the porch, is punched into the block of the building, rather than allowed to lean against it like its Shingle Style ancestor. Topped with the ribbed metal roof ubiquitous to interior Maine, the Gilpatrick House is intended to suggest a conglomeration of picturesque elements.

The Arthur Blatt House in Auburn (1973) by Stephen Blatt, the Robert W. Adams House on Deer Isle (1971–72) by Adams Associates and the Henry Woodbridge House on Vinalhaven (1973–74) by John B. Scholz are all, in fact, picturesque conglomerations. Designed in separate sections and then joined, the components are intended to remain visually separate. Gazebos abut hipped roofs, Bauhausian stair towers connect with broken plane surfaces, and shed-roofed cubes tumble against one another. It is not certain that this work actually refers back to earlier American idioms, but it certainly signals a return to romanticism. In the work of these young men we find the first pictorial architecture in this century. Their buildings become figural landscapes. Krumbhaar and Holt's spectacular home for Charles Foote in Rockport (1973) and

FIGURE 112. *Deer Isle, The Klaver/Adams Partnership, by Adams Associates (1965). Photo: Nancy Werth Woodward*

their 1971 home for Beverly Cunningham in Trenton are less passionate examples of the new style. While acknowledging the virtues of the picturesque, they nevertheless, defer to the taut, sharp shapes of the International Style. In them the contrast between influences is marked.

The odd relationship between forms, the whimsy, the references to the past and to the vernacular recommend themselves to residential architecture, although they are also seen, much modified, in Scholz's Riley Country Day School in Glen Cove (1975), in Moore/Weinrich's Our Lady of Ransom Church in Mechanic Falls (1973–74), and, obliquely, in Woodward's Multi-Purpose Center for the City of Lewiston (1974).

The residential work of Cooper Milliken is singularly poetic. Disregarding conventional forms, Milliken brings a light spirituality to his houses that is the antithesis of the raw pine work of architects such as Adams Associates and Scholz. He expresses himself lyrically in his 1961 Trenton home for John J. Nolde. In contrast with the rough finish espoused by the new style, every detail in the Nolde House is given all of the designer's attention. Consistency and restraint give his work a fine harmony.

Remarkable houses have not been the exclusive province of the architect. In 1966, the painter Willard Cummings designed a small home for the artist Ben Shahn on the grounds of the Skowhegan School of Painting and Sculpture. Like Barnes and Adams, Cummings divided the program among more than one building; in this case he used two, siting them on a wooden deck. The resulting shed-roofed structures reflect local formal attitudes with an insight seldom found in trained designers.

A number of radical structures, both architect- and non-architect designed, have appeared in re-cent years. John N. Cole's post-industrial home in Brunswick, constructed substantially of salvage, acknowledges its environmental obligations with particular sensitivity. The Brian Kent-Janet Kence home in the Augusta area (1974) also acknowledges post-industrial ethics with its attention to alternative energy systems and environmental concerns. The Mark A. Willis House in Raymond, a series of shed roofs and related berms, is a rare example of the tight-skinned International Style structure modified in accord with ecological realities. This list could be extended substantially and could include solar energy prototypes but these few examples are given as indications of the breadth and vitality of innovative architecture in Maine.

This brief survey necessarily omits unrealized projects such as Buckminster Fuller's designs for the University of Maine at Machias, as well as the proto-Prairie-style dining room in the Godfrey-Kellogg House in Bangor, and other worthwhile structures. It also omits certain practical pieces of engineering, among them the Waldo-Hancock Bridge at Bucksport (1937), the great radome at the Andover Earth Station, the array of twenty-six antenna towers at the U.S. Naval Radio Station, Cutler (1961), which through concept, materials and quality achieve the quality of works of art. Finally, it omits new efforts in multi-unit housing that, in a brief time, will deserve their own chapter.

It has been suggested that regionalism has played a minor role in the recent architecture of this state although certain forms seem particularly congenial to our land and people. Our review of the accomplishments of modern architects may also serve to support the proposition that superior design is becoming an important criterion by which Maine buildings are judged.

7

The Architecture of Maine's Schools

Janet Hansen

THE EARLY SETTLERS OF MAINE WERE OBLIGED to comply with the educational decrees of the Massachusetts Bay Colony. One of these educational acts, the Law of 1647, was quite compelling in this respect, as it required "yt where any towne shall increase to ye numbr of 100 families or householdrs, they shall set up a gramer schoole. . . ."[1] Records show that this law was well enforced, because the towns of Kittery and York were penalized for non-obedience in the year 1673. The fine at this time was £20, quite a severe punishment by current standards to urge compliance.[2]

Throughout this early period, the tendency in local districts was to avoid the construction of a permanent educational building. The result of this approach was the so-called "traveling school," which was conducted in private homes on a seasonal basis. In all probability, the curriculum of these "traveling schools" was similar to that of the "reading schools," which were also held in family residences. The curriculum generally consisted of fundamental reading and writing. These schools prepared students for the

grammar schools, where in turn they were prepared for the university. By the year 1800, only seven such grammar schools existed in the state.[3]

Upon occasion, public buildings such as town halls or meeting houses served as schoolrooms. One of the earliest recorded instances in Maine of a separate building being specifically built for educational purposes is that of York in 1724.[4] An amusing later account of such an early schoolhouse in Kennebunk relates:

It was built of large round logs notched at the ends so as to let into each other. . . . The walls were about six feet high, with a roof over the top, though the gable ends were entirely open. There were no windows. . . . The only way of entering for masters and scholars was by climbing up on a stile at the end and jumping down into the house. . . .[5]

This description suggests that the school was still in an incomplete stage; perhaps a door, windows and a fireplace would have been added later.

The town of York possesses a restored schoolhouse with a history that parallels the conjec-

FIGURE 113. *Alna District School, by Moses Carlton or Samuel Averill, carpenters (1795). Photo: Historic Preservation Commission, by Earle G. Shettleworth, Jr.*

tured development of the Kennebunk school. One of the oldest surviving schoolhouses in New England, it was erected in 1746 and later improved by the residents of York Corner in 1755. Narrow clapboards sheath the exterior of this one-room schoolhouse, while two small windows, originally of oiled brown paper, provide the interior with a meager amount of light.[6]

Towards the end of the 18th century in Maine, the humble one-room schoolhouse began to acquire architectural embellishments. These new schools were the first to be built in the Federal style, a style that represents the conscious formation of a new and specifically American idiom. A good example of a school which displays such Federal touches is the District School at Alna (Figure 113). Built in 1795 as a frame structure with a hipped roof, the schoolhouse received further embellishment one year later in the form of an open, octagonal, domed and spired cupola. Clapboards still cover the exterior, but the addition of a simple, molded cornice and the

delicate cupola contribute to a new effect of refinement. Sash windows may have become less expensive during this period, for the Alna school now possesses eight large windows.[7] It is difficult, however, to prove that these windows were part of the original structure.

A comparable school of this period is found at Day's Ferry, Woolwich. The doorway and windows of this example exhibit the influence of Federal style. Due to the existence of local brickyards, this schoolhouse was built of brick.[8]

A new form of educational institution, the academy, became popular in Maine at the turn of the 19th century. The incorporation of an academy was a difficult step for a town. Before the townspeople could apply for a charter, they had to produce proof of sufficient capital to cover the cost of construction. The usual method for procuring these funds involved the circulation of a subscription sheet. Often, individuals would contribute a plot of land for the site of the academy. Until 1820, application for a charter had to be made to the General Court of Massachusetts. As it happened, the academies in the District of Maine benefited from the Massachusetts Law of 1797, in which academies with a permanent endowment of $3,000 could receive a grant of a half-township of land.[9]

Three academies typical of those built in the early 19th century are located in Gorham, Wiscasset, and East Machias. The oldest of these, Gorham Academy, received its charter in 1803. Most boards of trustees of such institutions consisted of local figures, such as judges, lawyers, and ministers, but sometimes a carpenter's name would appear among the others. This was the case of Samuel Elder, "a house joiner by trade," who "contracted to build the [Gorham] academy"[10] (see Figure 114). The board had made certain specifications concerning the construction of the academy; it "was to be made of wood, fifty feet long and forty feet wide, two stories high, and with a cupola for a bell."[11] Mr. Elder built the academy accordingly, but he also vitalized the wooden structure with Adamesque detail. It seems possible that he consulted a copy of Asher Benjamin's *The Country Builder's Assistant* which helped transmit information about the Adamesque style across the ocean to the United States. A Roman Doric portico with a pavilion above and steps on three sides constitutes the entrance into the academy. On the corners, Mr. Elder placed quoins to contrast with the plain, flush siding. All of the windows are simple rectangular openings, except the round arched windows over the main door. In compliance with the specifications for the building, a square belfry with open arches and a spire adorns the hipped roof.[12]

About a year later, the Wiscasset Academical Association was built. This brick structure was used as a school until 1923; (it now serves as a museum). The Old Academy at Wiscasset differs most from its contemporary at Gorham in the amount of exterior ornamentation. Little

FIGURE 114. *Gorham Academy (1806). Photo: National Register of Historic Places, by Donald E. Johnson*

FIGURE 115. *Blue Hill Academy (c. 1845). Photo: Denys Peter Myers*

traces of Adamesque influence are seen in the plain brick facade of the Wiscasset academy. Only the wooden cupola and the segmented arches over the windows lessen the severity of its design.[13]

Further north along the rocky coast of Maine, an excellent example of Federal style architecture is to be found in Washington Academy, East Machias. The projecting central bay and bell tower of this two-story academy are the lone recipients of decorative elements. In this central portion Doric pilasters rise one and a half stories to support a round-headed arch. As at Gorham, rounded windows are employed exclusively in the projecting central bay, while simple rectangular ones are used elsewhere. Wooden cornices divide the square bell tower into two sections. Above this bell tower, a balustrade masks the transition to an open octagonal cupola. The Federal style achieved a balanced perfection in the Washington Academy building of 1823.

The vogue for revival styles of architecture began in the 19th century, slightly overlapping with buildings still designed in Federal style. Revivals of Greek, Romanesque, Gothic and Baroque architecture reflected the prevailing mood of Romanticism during this period. Many books containing architectural plans and details were available for purchase by the layman architect, even in the most remote areas of rural Maine.

The first Greek Revival buildings in America were probably private homes and official buildings such as banks. Two early, quite similar Greek Revival buildings can be viewed in Ellsworth. Built in the 1830's, one served as a town house, while the Hancock County offices, recently moved from Castine, occupied the other.[14] In the 1890's, the two buildings became public schools, housing the upper and lower grades separately.

The Greek temple style soon caught the attention of the designers of Maine's academies. In the years between 1840 and 1850, the construc-

tion of academies reached its peak in Maine and eight academies constructed along Greek Revival lines remain from this fruitful decade. The town of Skowhegan offers Bloomfield Academy, built by a local builder, Joseph Bigelow, in 1840.[15] Only six years later, a simplification of Bigelow's brick Bloomfield Academy appeared in nearby Athens.[16] The Athens academy exemplifies clearly the way in which a rural builder took liberties in applying Greek classical elements. A long wooden plank, painted white and attached to the brick facade of the academy bears only a minimal resemblance to the pilasters which adorn more sophisticated Greek Revival structures.

Another fine example of a Greek Revival academy building was built at Blue Hill in 1845 (Figure 115). This is the example immortalized by Mary Ellen Chase in *A Goodly Heritage*. Mary Ellen Chase attended the academy at Blue Hill during the 1890's. About it, she commented, "there lingered about her brick walls and white portico something of the Reverend Jonathan Fisher."[17] Fisher was one of the ardent promoters behind the academy when it opened in 1803. The strict classical curriculum which he initiated in the early years of the academy remained the foundation for the education of the 1890's. Appropriately enough, the curriculum of the Blue Hill Academy reflected its Greek Revival architecture.

In the middle of the century, public taste began to turn from the relatively austere Greek Revival style towards the more elaborate Gothic, Italianate and Romanesque Revival styles. Because of the more complicated nature of structure and decoration in these Gothic and Renaissance Revival styles, architectural training was needed for their construction. One such building, the Maine State Reform School (now the Boys' Training Center), a massive brick, octagonal structure which was erected in 1853, displays a combination of Gothic and Italian styles. This example was designed by Gridley J. F. Bryant of Boston, who was responsible for several other important buildings in the state (see also Miller, p. 175 above). Bryant was the designer of the Charles Street Jail in Boston, and the Boys' Training Center is reputed to be one of his earliest designs for a reform school.[18]

Shortly after 1853, several architects opened practices in the state of Maine. It was in this period that the State Board of Education contracted for the construction of several new Normal Schools for the state. Normal Schools were training institutions for teachers of grammar school children. Francis H. Fassett of Portland designed the main building of the Western Normal School in Gorham, Corthell Hall. He chose to build the hall using Ruskinian Gothic motifs.[19] At Hebron Academy, John Calvin Stevens, another Portland architect, employed the Romanesque Revival style in Sturdivant Hall;[20] (see Figure 116, and further in regard to Stevens, Shettleworth, Chapter 5, Part 2). Unlike the buildings of H. H. Richardson in the Romanseque Revival style, which combined many textures and colors of stone, Maine schools constructed in the Romanesque style generally display a simpler combination of brick with brownstone or terra cotta trim.

In the 1890's, the Queen Anne style made its appearance in Maine, somewhat later than in the rest of New England. This style which is essentially a variant of Neo-Colonial style, involved the revival of decorative features of mediaeval cottages, such as casement windows, mullions, and half-timbering. George M. Coombs, a Lewiston architect, picked the picturesque late Queen Anne style for the Farmington State Normal School of 1895.[21]

Throughout the period of Romantic Revival architecture, the one-room schoolhouse was still prominent in Maine. People today often reminisce about "the days of the little red schoolhouse" in complete disregard for buildings contemporary with one-room schools built in elaborate revival styles.

One example of such simple 19th-century local schools is the "Little Red Schoolhouse" in

FIGURE 116. *Hebron, Sturdivant Hall, by John Calvin Stevens (1890). Photogravure courtesy of Earle G. Shettleworth, Jr., copy by Wendell A. Ray*

Farmington (Figure 117). A group of local citizens recently contributed to a successful preservation effort to save this school, which now serves as an example of this type to students of the present generation. The Farmington schoolhouse, which is like many rural schools of the 19th century, offered some improvements over earlier models. A higher ceiling insured better ventilation for the wood-burning stove, and desks and seats for the children were in proportioned sizes to accommodate different ages.[22]

These and other improvements in the construction of schoolhouses can be attributed to the work of Henry Barnard, State Commissioner of Education in Rhode Island. In the introduction to his manual entitled *School Architecture*, Henry Barnard stated: "The attention of parents and local school officers was early and earnestly called to the close connection between a good school-house and a good school."[23] The Maine State Board of Education, formed in 1846, asked the Maine legislature to set aside funds to buy copies of Barnard's book for each township. Unfortunately, as so often happens in

FIGURE 117. *Farmington, Little Red Schoolhouse, by the carpenter Zephaniah Vaughan (1854); now a county information center run by the Wilton and Farmington Historical Societies. Photo: D. Richard Sturges*

FIGURE 118. *Millinocket, George W. Stearns High School, by Harry S. Coombs (1923). Photo: Great Northern Paper Company*

such cases, the money was not appropriated. Not to be thwarted in their efforts for this worthwhile project, the Board devoted the last fifty pages of their 1851 and 1852 annual reports to plans and ideas for the construction of better schoolhouses.[24]

Concern for the welfare of students has not diminished from the mid-19th century until the present day. Interior improvements, such as better lighting and heating, the installation of interior plumbing, and the addition of libraries, gymnasiums, laboratories, and manual training facilities, occupied the builders of the first quarter of the 20th century. Such luxuries were often obtained at the expense of exterior adornment. Builders of schools began to adopt an economical rectangular frame structure which is sometimes ornamented with a few Colonial Revival motifs. The New Gloucester High School, built in 1902–1903 is illustrative of this type.[25]

Frame buildings, however, proved to be extreme fire hazards and non-flammable materials such as brick and stone became more popular. The financial problems of the period of the two World Wars and the intervening Depression forced architects to keep economies in mind. Today the results can be seen in all states of the Union in the form of drab and unimaginative public edifices.

In Maine, the advent of this early 20th-century institutional architecture coincided with an attempt to centralize the public school system. Small rural schools were eliminated, while towns built larger schools to accommodate students from outlying areas. The gradual process of consolidation began in 1897, when the state passed a law allowing several towns to unite and control the schools within their combined boundaries. During this period, the state also initiated a stronger compulsory school law and set up a fund to finance the transportation of students to and from rural areas.[26] The conformity in design of schools of this period can be attributed to a new duty of the state superintendent of schools, "to procure architects' plans and specifications for school buildings of not exceeding four rooms each and full detail working plan thereof."[27] He would then furnish these plans to towns wishing to build new schools. In sparsely populated northern Penobscot County, a new high school was erected to replace one which had burned. Millinocket's Stearns High School of 1923, resembles many schools of this era (Figure 118). The year 1928 saw the building of a new Catholic high school in Bangor. Underneath the lavish Ionic decoration of John Bapst High School can be seen the same basic interior plan as that of Stearns High School in Millinocket.

Little construction took place during the depression and wartime of the 1930's and 40's, but the 1950's brought a surge in the building industry. At this time, the United States passed into a new "age," characterized by the experimentation with nuclear power and the race to the moon.

FIGURE 119. *Topsham, John A. Cone Elementary School, by Krumbhaar and Holt Associated Architects (1968), view of the interior showing the octagonal shape of the building. Photo: William Searle*

These technological developments soon began to affect the educational world. A new emphasis was placed on the study of science in schools.

Schools built during the 1950's are among some of the first schools to exhibit the use of modern building materials such as steel, reinforced concrete and more extensive areas of glass (see Figure 106, the Washburn School, Auburn). Architectural design varied from school to school, as it does today, depending upon the taste and economic fortune of the individual towns.

Two schools of the 1960's demonstrate that schools need not be dreary prisons for students. At Kent's Hill School in Readfield, a team of designers remodeled Bearce Hall, a traditional classroom building, into a Learning Center. Walls were removed, and carpeting laid to create a warm atmosphere for individual and group learning.[28] An Ellsworth architectural firm devised an exciting plan for the John A. Cone Elementary School in Topsham. The structure, built in 1968, utilizes the geometric shape of an octagon for its basic exterior plan (see Figure 119). Another feature of the plan is the idea of a ramp leading to the entrance, a solution conditioned in part by the site chosen.[29]

What takes place inside the school tends to affect the organization of interior spaces. A widespread experimentation with open education has occurred within recent years on the elementary level. The Houlton Elementary School has found that moveable partitions work well in an open education situation. In an open classroom, space is divided into "flexible interest areas" which students "are free to explore." A teacher lecturing to a large class is a rare sight in an open classroom. For the most part, a teacher practicing open education works with individuals or small groups. In some cases open education is accompanied by the dissolution of grade barriers.[30] This form of education has some familiar qualities. The personalized education which our forefathers experienced in numerous one-room schoolhouses now seems to be enjoying a successful revival under the name of open education.

8

Maine Landscapes:

Design and Planning

Harriet Pattison

PART ONE: EARLY LANDSCAPES

THE RECORD OF LANDSCAPE ARCHITECTURAL practice in Maine opens with the arrival at Orono in 1866, of Frederick Law Olmsted, Sr. to consult with trustees of the proposed Maine Agricultural College. But the creation of landscape within this region has an older history, one that has not been compiled because documents are few. Yet there is evidence, to be traced with the eye and the mind's eye.

EDEN: LOST AND FOUND

Maine ought to have been a primitive Paradise. Allowing for cold winters and poor soils, the land was richly endowed with renewable resources, geographic advantages and scenic beauty. Had it been remote, with formidable frontiers, the Abnaki would have kept it "forever wild." But deep harbors and many rivers made the territory inviting, its prize timber, fish and game were highly desirable and the Indians, overwhelmed by numbers and stratagems of European invaders, were finally driven from Eden.[1]

Wilderness was the Indian's inheritance. It was also his creation, as only the aborigine has ever successfully perpetuated that state. If humanized landscapes represent so many fusions of nature's order with the order of ideas, then the relative paucity of Indian remains may suggest a mind in which nature and idea were joined. In any case, the land, so fiercely contested, was the same for Indian and colonist;

though each produced modest settlements on well chosen sites,[2] their landscapes proved to be remarkably different. The Indians insured a stable environment by adapting themselves to its changes, whereas the settlers, prompted by a secular view of nature and by agricultural traditions stronger than sea-roving ones, sought the permanence of rigid boundaries and structures and thereby became agents of incalculable change. Sophisticated tools enabled them to clear and plant strips of waterside land and to put down roots: fences, piers, foundations, thresholds and memorials, all of stone. Houses in these early villages had small dooryards and, though randomly spaced according to site features, invariably faced the waterfront, like boats into the wind (Figure 120). Moreover, common circumstances and building traditions, together with persistent family ownership, made them look alike. Land was occasionally set aside for a common but street systems were rare; individ-

FIGURE 120. *Matinicus, showing the traditional orientation of vernacular buildings in fishing villages. Photo: Down East Magazine, by Robert Hylander*

ual paths led to the docksides and few, besides the farmer, kept horses. This early pattern and unity survived only in remote fishing villages and wilderness mill towns. Yet beneath some crooked routes of modern city streets, may lie traces of these old foot paths.

TOWN AND COUNTRY

With the establishment of peace, farms occupied the hinterlands by way of the rivers and scarce roads, their outbuildings strung out behind in rambling, connected series. Houses in town faced new streets from large, often handsomely fenced, lots (Figure 121). Structures were diversified and districts evolved. A new

264

expansiveness seemed to animate builders of the young republic. Whereas early homesteaders tended lilacs and old world flowers, and named villages in memory of their origins, town fathers now invariably planted roadsides with the native elm,[3] cultivated wild grapes on their arbors and invented descriptive place names (or appropriated Indian ones) in a new alliance with the land. Decked in shop signs, commercial streets accommodated horses and vehicles with hitching posts, watering troughs, and rarely, carriage sheds (elegant forerunners of our parking garage), such as those at Kennebunkport.[4] Simple houses were embellished with the amenities of entry porch, rear garden and gazebo. The country house reappeared in a park setting reminiscent of England, but with rustic overtones; the Black House at Ellsworth is a surviving example of this form. On farms and coastal outposts early building methods and styles persisted, but groups of structures, such as the Riggs Family-Wharf Buildings at Robinhood Cove,[5] sported new alignments that foreshadowed the best designs for government light stations. Weather and tides, rather than custom, must have dictated terms for survival here, just as climate eventually triumphed over style in the vernacular of steep roofs and "continuous architecture."

Maine towns recovered from the 1807 Embargo by developing land routes and industries; as new fortunes were made, tall, elegant brick houses with trim setbacks and stable yards joined ranks with the white, frame dwellings built by the sea trade. Into the narrow lots crowded buildings with gables to the street, adding to the congenial variety of facade and roofscape within the envelope of stately trees. A fair index to the prevailing level of urbanity in those years was the commissioning, in 1801, of Boston's Charles Bulfinch by three prominent merchants to draw up a city plan for Bangor. Introducing the grid system (soon to replace old, responsive street patterns everywhere) the proposal centered upon a point of the Penobscot River which was intended to be the locus of a

FIGURE 121. *Kennebunk, "The Wedding Cake House" (George W. Bourne House), c. 1826. Gothic Revival details and fence (the latter now demolished) added c. 1855. Colby Museum of Art, by Walker Evans*

commercial venture. Lamentably, the main thrust of the town's growth occurred elsewhere and the plan never materialized. The possibilities of this dramatic riverfront were apparently not exploited subsequently either by landscape architect, Warren Manning[6] in 1911 (whose Beaux-Arts scheme transported Venice to the banks of the Kenduskeag Stream (Figure 122), or by the Bangor Planning Department in its recent, comprehensive city plan.

Prosperity in the towns unfortunately encouraged the desertion of farms by families struggling against hardships; that later led to the "Ohio fever" (the depopulation of New England through mass westward migrations). It also brought more forests under the ax. Initially, English shipmasts had consumed the mightiest of the pines and then, nearly a third of the land had been cleared for cultivation. But it was the demand for lumber and paper that felled the remainder of Maine's original forests, both the mixed hardwoods and the northern spruce. Much of the game followed that retreat. Fish life was depleted with the damming of rivers for power and log transport and by waste accumulations, creating conditions which also hastened the decline of the picturesque riverside farm. The railroad accelerated these changes; gradually supplanting schooner and steamer in freight and passenger transport, it redistributed population and placed remote and vulnerable areas in sudden jeopardy by linking them to markets.

PARK BEGINNINGS

As the edges of the wilderness were thrust aside, it appeared to be less threatening and became the subject of poetry, painting and naturalists' investigations: Audubon, Thoreau, Longfellow, Cole, Church (Figure 123), Agassiz—each cast new light upon the Maine landscape, holding it forth for an appreciative view. Preservation of its remnants within the growing cities began to seem important, though the creation in 1836 of promenades on Portland's rocky Bramhall and Munjoy Hills provoked the *Eastern Argus* to protest that only the rich, with horse and carriage, would benefit (tramcars were uncommon before the 70's).[7] The presence of the sea and open land on these hills must have mitigated effects of crowding, for it was not until 1866 that Portland had its first park: Lincoln Park arose from the ashes of the great fire in the city's core, conceived as a fire break on the site of an old tenement.

Bangor, at the frontier's edge, was more enterprising. With fortunes and population multiplied by lumbering, it launched ambitious programs of civic and residential improvements, the first of which was a garden cemetery, closely patterned after Mount Auburn in Cambridge. The Bangor Horticultural Society was organized to advance the purchase and design of its fifty-acre tract close to the Penobscot River. Charles G. Bryant, a local architect, presented a plan for "Mt. Hope," which consisted of two areas: one for burial, the other, for an horticultural garden.[8] Despite loss of Society backing, it was completed as designed, in 1836, joining the vanguard of a movement that would create America's parks. With its handsome cast-iron fences, Greek Revival monuments, ponds and hillocks, it continues in operation and maintains a useful plant collection.

Bold as this idea was, its realization was accompanied by an even more daring enterprise on the part of three Bangor entrepreneurs anxious to promote rowhouse development similar to that on Boston's Beacon Hill. One project, designed in 1834 by the versatile Bryant, was to have eighty-eight brick houses, enclosing a nine-acre common (Chapin Park) donated to the city on the condition that it be surrounded by "double rows of trees, fenced in, with gravel walks between."[9] Bangor entered into this arrangement and another, involving a twenty-two acre tract (Broadway Park). These, together with Thomas Hill (delayed by the Panic of 1837 into the mid-Victorian era) furnished isolated but imaginative models for neighborhood development and public financing of open-space.

THE GARDENESQUE STYLE

By the mid-19th century, expanded industry, populations and civic pride were effecting changes more profound than a mere application of granite and brick to facades and pavements;[10] the latter enrichments have been unfortunately obliterated in modern times by bland macadam and concrete. Architects and landscape gardeners were increasingly consulted, bringing imagination to designs for institutions, mansions and parks. This period ushered in the idealized "English" landscape popularized in the 40's by Andrew J. Downing, of which "Oaklands" is an

FIGURE 122. *Kenduskeag Basin, Bangor, view from Kenduskeag Bridge towards the south, by Warren Manning (1911). Proposal (unbuilt) for the development of downtown Bangor after the 1911 fire. Courtesy of the Bangor Daily News*

FIGURE 123. *Mount Katahdin, by Frederic Edwin Church (1826–1900). Courtesy Yale University Art Gallery*

early example (Figure 64). Despite polarities in architecture, the gardenesque spirit dominated landscape design into the 20th century, with parks and estates becoming virtual paradigms of the style. Thus, houses were provided with broad set-backs and sweeping drives, their high foundations clothed with flowering shrubs and vines. All were adrift in lawns that flowed even over steep terraces and were accented with specimen trees; many of the latter were non-native, such as the gingko and copper beech, reflecting the Victorian passion for plant collecting. Garden ornaments were also conspicuous, from gazebos to urns and iron deer. The restraints of the promenade were balanced by the informalities of naturalistic paths, herbaceous beds and water-courses. "Norumbega" in Camden, built in the 1870's, reveals the rawness of this style before Olmsted's genius refined it. Ultimately, the neo-classic disciplines, so primly mobilized against the excessive and non-urban, were jettisoned in zealous pursuit of the romantic image.

Frederick Law Olmsted, Sr.'s brief excursions to Maine (including one, last, unhappy sojourn at Deer Isle), together with visits of his most gifted associate, Charles Eliot—whose youthful sketches of Mt. Desert reveal an intimate knowledge of the island—have led to speculations about their activities in the state. Though the Olmsted firm has commanded Maine's choice commissions—accounting for one hundred and thirty works in its files—only a few, such as the Orono campus plan, the Vanderbilt estate on Mount Desert Island, the Fogg Memorial Square at South Berwick,[11] and a residential development on Cushing's Island in collaboration with John Calvin Stevens, were indisputably designed by its founder (also see Shettleworth, p. 192–93). Olmsted's Orono plan (Figure 124) was largely rejected, owing perhaps, to its peculiar combination of military and domestic accommodations, a theme which preoccupied him just after the Civil War. The firm's early plans and reports for Portland's parks (1895–96) bear Eliot's mark and, certainly, his informal proposals for public reservation of Maine's scenic lands inspired his father and other founders of Acadia National Park.[12] But for these influences and some vestiges of the Orono plan, there are disappointingly few remains of either artist's work though their achievements elsewhere long inspired the profession.

The Summer Colony

One movement during this period was destined to eclipse all others in its significance for landscape. Sometimes called the second colonial invasion of Maine, it was heralded by an increased mobility among city-dwellers, such as the residents of Portland. In search of recreation they took day-trips on steamboats in Casco Bay or went on inter-urban trolleys to rural amusement parks and "watering places." Underwood Park (Figure 125) and Old Orchard Beach were among the more popular destinations they visited. There they found casinos, open-air theaters, small zoos, and handsomely landscaped gardens, and could practice archery, go canoeing, play tennis and croquet, or walk among woods and along beaches. (The automobile effectively dispersed these activities so that now, only a few, *fin de siècle* pleasure parks, on the order of Copenhagen's Tivoli Gardens, remain, all of them abroad.) It is likely these local excursions were impelled by the same wanderlust that, in the summer of 1847, carried a boatload of vacationers to Maine's first coastal resort hotel at Appledore Island.

Preceding these harbingers of the touring public, were, as mentioned, artists and naturalists—"rusticators" in search of the primitive. Undaunted by their discoveries (which sometimes proved raw and terrifying)[13] they returned from the wilderness with a bounty of paintings, essays and collections which were devoured by a public hungering for new diversions. Americans have always been ambivalent about wild lands, alternately fascinated and challenged by them.[14] Even now, conservationists must crusade against

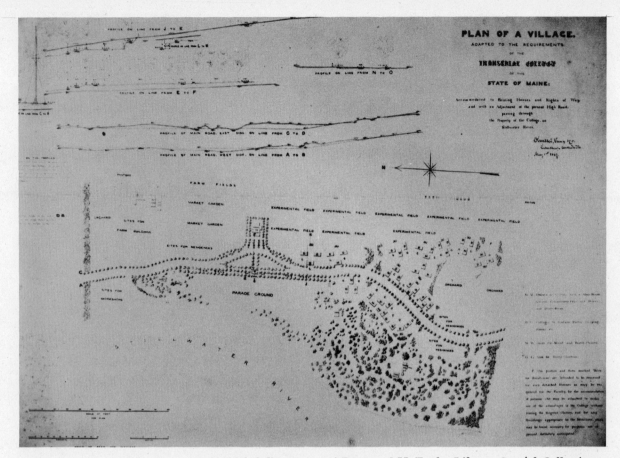

FIGURE 124. *Orono, Plan for an Industrial College, by Frederic Law Olmsted (May, 1867). Courtesy* *of Raymond H. Fogler Library, Special Collections, University of Maine at Orono, copy by Jack Walas*

the popular belief that these areas should be put to "economic" use. Nonetheless, there were venturesome and romantic individuals who did set off, down east and into the north woods, to find enlightenment in solitude and the simple life. At first, local campsites and boarding houses provided for the visitors, but as demand increased, summer hotels—those immense, wooden warrens surrounded by manicured recreation grounds, golf courses, cottages and piazzas [15]—appeared on ocean promontory and lake front from the Isles of Shoals to Frenchman Bay and the White Mountains (see Figure 87 and Shettleworth, pp. 205–08). The immense piazza of Appledore, on which the rich and famous strolled, symbolized this era. Bridge to the natural world, it was a forerunner of the indispensable Maine veranda which has replaced the

polite entry porch and utilitarian dooryard of earlier days. (Appledore's own banished front yard was charmingly portrayed by Childe Hassam in his sketches of "Celia's Garden"; the garden itself is now being restored by Cornell University.) This vast structure was long since destroyed by fire, a common fate suffered by sister hotels after their spectacular but brief heyday.

The so-called "summer colony" had evolved, by 1900, from these beginnings into permanent enclaves of "cottagers." Members of this group did, in fact, *colonize* Maine to the extent of expropriating coastal property and transferring land control and financial decisions out of the state. Also in the course of provisioning the colonists, "catering to the summer trade" became an occupation of many local people whose in-

FIGURE 125. *Peaks Island, Underwood Park, owned by the Yarmouth and Portland Street Railway, at the turn of the century. Photo: Down East Magazine, by J. Harry Lamson*

FIGURE 126. *Planting plan for East Garden, Mr. G. H. Milliken—"The Haven"—Northeast Harbor, Maine, by Beatrix J. Farrand. Courtesy of the Documents Collection, College of Environmental Design, Department of Architecture, University of California, Berkeley*

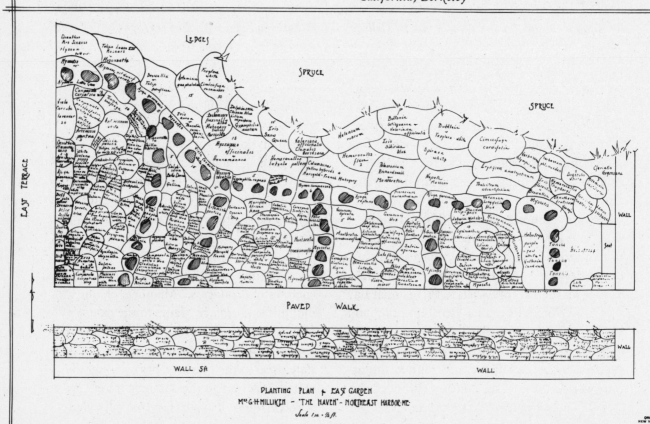

herited attitudes frequently gave way to the newcomers' priorities; thus the substitution of aesthetic criteria for productivity in land evaluation, as well as the construction of high-speed roads. But if the region forfeited a measure of autonomy or risks enviromental damage by furthering tourism, its legacy from the resorts has been substantial, chiefly from the assembly of scenic lands (promoted today by the Nature Conservancy and The Maine Coast Heritage Trust) and the generous outlay of private funds for improvement of buildings and landscape. In turn, Maine has enriched the national spirit with symbols and circumstances of rustic life in vital contrast to a preoccupation with technology. Its "genius of the place" has been sufficiently strong to evoke a native imagery. Even in the ultimate fantasy that was Bar Harbor, the villas and gardens of its shores affected a modesty and naturalism unlike those of Newport or Palm Beach, enlivening, rather than subjugating, their surroundings with the fanciful play of shingled silhouettes and joyously colorful flowers.[16] It is no wonder that bitter battles to ban the motor car were staged by summer residents who treasured these retreats. Perhaps, as one observer suggests, the end results would have been more desirable had they won.[17]

PART TWO: GARDENS AND LANDSCAPE ARTISTS

For a brief time, the presence of that wealthy and sophisticated society made the art of landscape architecture come brilliantly to life and, though the landscapes themselves have mostly vanished, documents and personal recollections survive to enlighten us concerning them and their creators.

BEATRIX FARRAND

Distinguished among designers of the period for unerring taste, imagination and horticultural knowledge, fortified by a commanding presence and astonishing energy, was Beatrix Jones Farrand (1872–1959), Maine's foremost gardener.[18] Though a New Yorker by birth, Mount Desert was her summer home and the location of at least forty of her works. A cherished project, the development of "Reef Point," her family's six-acre estate at Bar Harbor, would have preserved the finest horticultural collection north of Boston had it survived a quixotic decision of her old age to have it destroyed. Impeccably trained by the Arnold Arboretum's Charles Sargent, she introduced a wide variety of plants at "Reef Point," many of them from comparable zones in China. But, devoted to native flora, she used exotic material sparingly, as accents to natural scenes which she controlled formally to achieve successions of impressive vistas and intimate "rooms." Equipped with a painter's eye, she would conduct the planting of a garden *in situ*. Her superb, architectural details were tried out as full-scale "dummies" and her continued surveillance (even to managing a client's payroll) and adjustment of original designs, led one familiar to remark that "the plants all trembled whenever she paid a visit for fear they would be moved!" Her clients (for whom a Farrand garden was a supreme accolade) included Yale and Princeton Universities, the White House and Robert Woods Bliss of Dumbarton Oaks, Washington, D.C. Many of them had houses on Mount Desert but few traces of her labors there remain. Of those estates which escaped the great fire, only three of four subsequently preserved their original outlines or plantings, but the succession of clearings and heather drifts in the Gerrish Milliken garden remain to reward the visitor (Figure 126).

FIGURE 127. *Seal Harbor, John D. Rockefeller garden, "The Ayrie" (1928–33) by Beatrix J. Farrand. View of the "Spirit Path." Photo: Ezra Stoller ESTO*

The Abby A. Rockefeller garden at Seal Harbor is the only Farrand design in its original splendid condition. Representing a close collaboration of Mrs. Rockefeller and the artist, it is a masterful blend of native plants with ancient far eastern sculptures and architectural motifs and is renowned for its central, sunken flower garden, a composition of brilliant hues, produced by Maine's cool nights and sea fogs, which evokes the spirit of England's Gertrude Jekyll (whose sketches are in the Farrand library). Yearly plans are made for these herbaceous borders, which never fail to draw astonished pleasure. Most haunting, is the long "Spirit

Path" with its flanking procession of Korean stone figures spaced upon a billowing carpet of native groundcovers (Figure 127). These form a ceremonial reception for the gardens beyond. All is surrounded by an imposing Chinese wall which here, as in the orient, keeps the wilderness at bay. That this masterpiece must suffice to represent Beatrix Farrand is grievous, but that her valued professional library of twenty-seven hundred volumes, files of design drawings and herbarium of two thousand plants gathered at "Reef Point," long intended as gifts to Maine, were finally left to the University of California (notwithstanding purchase offers from the Rockefellers) comes as a bitter, if intended, blow to the artists and gardeners of Maine, whose appropriate and rewarding heritage it might have been.

CHARLES SAVAGE

One who keenly felt that loss but succeeded in rescuing some rare specimens from "Reef Point," was another artist, Charles Savage of Northeast Harbor. He was a trustee for Mt. Desert of a twenty-acre preserve left by Joseph H. Curtis, an early "rusticator" and landscape architect for Boston's Public Garden. Entrusted with a modest endowment and the concepts of its founder, Savage devoted his own labor, funds and ideas to building a worthy memorial. His first project, begun in 1928, involved the development of the wooded uplands and shore area of "Asticou Terraces" along with its shelters and Thuja Lodge (a cabin retreat, housing Curtis' memorabilia and the nucleus of a horticultural library). Later gifts, primarily from John D. Rockefeller, Jr., enabled Savage to establish a 140-acre wild park and to create the beautiful "Asticou" and "Thuja" gardens. Their designs, inspired by Japanese tradition, bear indisputable evidence of an original artist from his conception for monumental, carved cedar gates to the mingling of the humblest representatives of local flora with exotic annuals and imports from "Reef Point." Savage daily supervised the construction and maintenance of these gardens and trails among the spruce and cedar (thuja) woods. He devoted hours to the library and herbarium (which he had hoped to merge with those of "Reef Point") even painting exquisite watercolors for the manuscript *Catalogue of the Botanical Library, Thuja Collection*. When he resigned his duties in 1965 to attend to business affairs, Savage could proudly deliver a gift greatly multiplied and enhanced for the benefit of the public in which he, like Olmsted before him, vigorously believes. Speaking of his optimism regarding the advance in popular taste, he recalled Mrs. Farrand's remark: "Yes, but it is so slow!" His own, unorthodox albeit urbane, appreciation of old and new combines an admiration for Capability Brown and the modern automobile; at least, he applauds its capability for releasing every man from his birthplace to go forth and "do" Bar Harbor, if not more remote scenes.[19] The yearly crowds of unsolicited visitors to his gardens seem to justify his faith.

ERIC SODERHOLTZ

Within the "Thuja Gardens" is a large, hand-turned concrete vase holding itself erect with a grace and importance that only splendid proportions can support. It is the work of another artist, Eric Soderholtz, who lived and worked in nearby Gouldsboro. His designs for garden ornaments found favor with architects and patrons of the great houses across the bay. A Swedish immigrant to Boston and a professional photographer, he studied European ceramics while on an assignment abroad. Having admired concrete pots there, he resolved to experiment in making some for himself. The results were so promising that he built a workshop, hired helpers and produced a quantity of concrete pieces from wood molds he devised, shipping urns, fountains, pots and sundials all over

the country. His designs were in competition with the most skilled European craftsmen and earned him national recogntion.

HANS HEISTAD

Hans Heistad (1871–1945) was another immigrant who embraced the opportunity and spirit of the new world.[20] Educated as a landscape designer in Germany and his native Norway (whose royal order he bore) he was first employed in Maine at Bar Harbor by the Olmsted office and, later, as supervisor for the many projects of Cyrus Curtis in Rockport, where he eventually settled. Heistad's skill in transplanting native material was proverbial and his work, according to one associate, is instantly recognized years later for its unfailing grasp of aesthetic and horticultural suitabilities. Variously described as a wood sprite and a Norseman who sang beautifully, it would appear that he was an endearing person who retained a child's sense of wonder. Unluckily, few of his works survived a generation of neglect: the extensive rose gardens of the Osborne tract north of Camden have all

FIGURE 128. *Camden Hills State Park, stone and wood shelter, by Hans O. Heistad (c. 1938). Photo: George Pohl*

but disappeared into a leaping tangle of briers and the Curtis-Bok estates have undergone drastic cut-backs. Drawings in the possession of his daughter show that he designed the trails and footbridges at Camden Hills State Park (c.1938), as well as the beautiful stone and wood shelter (Figure 128). Its elemental form, superb jointing and fluid masonry work suggest parallels with Japanese temple construction and a kinship with the nearby stone cottage Heistad built on the summit of Beech Hill for the Gribbell family (1916). This earlier cottage, called "Beechnut," patterned after a Norwegian mountain house, is near collapse, but its unique sod roof still bears an annual crop of wild flowers to rival the surrounding meadows. Old photographs depict its massive beams and rugged masonry as well as its delicately crafted furniture and impressive entrance gates. Reverence for materials is inherent in the design and execution of these details and supports the undeniable integrity of the whole.[21] Fortunately, Heistad's penchant for stonework lengthened the life of some projects. At "Weatherend," the Gribbell property on Beauchamp Point, to which he devoted many years and the full range of his design talents, the stalwart seawalls and outlines of planting beds and walks (even a balanced "meteor") on the sea ledges among giant mugho pines and rampant ground covers, have defied time, enduring from the day every tree and stone was hauled by horse and placed by hand.

RECENT GARDENS

Also on Beauchamp Point are the "Spite House" gardens, celebrated since the 1930's for their beauty and horticultural variety. The gracious setting of this noble house (see Shipman p. 82 above) moved by barge to its present location, was designed by Wheelwright and Stevenson of Philadelphia who reserved a spacious forecourt (a stylistic liberty carried out with éclat!) accented by specimen elms and lilacs,

with a delicately wrought fence, assembled from pickets discovered in a local barn. The garden side of the house opens onto box-edged brick terraces, brilliantly awash with perennial blooms, and surrounded by lawns carpeted with groundcovers under sheltering spruce that part for a flower-bordered walk leading to an overlook above the sea. Nearby, an octagonal gazebo with elegantly arched openings marks the transition between formal gardens and the forest with its meandering paths and incomparable collection of woodland plants. The creator and owner of this exquisite scene was Donald Dodge.

One intensively cultivated, small property in Northeast Harbor, belonging to Thomas Hall, takes advantage of level changes, rock outcrops and abandoned foundations to fashion a variety of spaces, furnished with specimen and trained plants. The Halls, with Howard Kneedler as consultant, have also carried the oriental themes of their contemporary house into the garden, creating a circle of "steles" in the forest at path's end and nesting a Japanese pavilion on a wooded promontory below the house. This recent work is exceptional, for, though many of Maine's newer buildings are well sited, most of them fail to engage the land, much less to be committed to the ephemeral aesthetic of a garden. Yet, wherever plants are cultivated for pleasure and enhancement of exterior spaces, forms of garden art will emerge from these practices, as the creation of a garden (which offers both a poetic analogue for the creation of the world and a way to participate in its *élan vital*) is a recurrent theme in our culture.[22]

FIGURE 129, B. *(Detail) Rockport Harbor lime kilns, of historic significance, have been preserved in harborside landscaping. From Frank Claes photo.*

Projects of a public nature proved more durable than private work as the Great Depression and World War II halted estate construction and hastened the break-up of existing properties. Having demonstrated their services, landscape architects were summoned to plan resort hotel grounds, garden cemeteries, campuses, town developments, parks and golf courses.[23] Thus, on the Olmsted drawing boards at various times, were designs for the capitol grounds; parks in Pittsfield, Auburn, Brewer and Portland; town plans for Waterville and Northeast Harbor; and campus development for Bates, Bowdoin, Colby and the University of Maine. The last three institutions have consulted other out-of-state firms at later dates, namely Vincent Cerasi, Carol Johnson, and Innocenti and Webel, respectively. Also during this time, the University of Maine at Orono had the benefit of Dr. Roger Clapp's advice for campus planting and development of its arboretum. The latter is virtually the only collection in the state since the potential of Coburn Park in Skowhegan, with its hundred species of trees,[24] and design by Joseph Curtis, failed to be realized. Portions of the large campus at Orono have hundred-year-old groves of elm and Norway spruce planted by the faculty; from them Dr. Clapp drew the theme, and expanded the role, of plants, until they have become the unifying element in this diverse complex.[25] Some other professional designers of institutional and commercial projects in the state have been Clarke and Rapuano, Sasaki and Associates, The Architects Collaborative, and Maine-based Myron Lamb, Wolcott Andrews, and Moriece and Gary.[26]

In the last forty years, landscape architects have devoted major efforts to the design of parks and open-space planning; these are projects which have involved many people, making it difficult to distinguish individual contributors.

But the achievements of this period are significant, whether or not their authors can be named. Some parks have developed in response to the nation-wide movement initiated by Olmsted, Eliot and Horace Cleveland. In this category belong Portland's parks, Acadia and Baxter Parks, state park and highway projects and the present constellation of government agencies, professional planning services and voluntary organizations concerned with management of natural and scenic lands for public benefit. Others, of modest scale and community-oriented, stem from New England's tradition of the town green, such as Bangor's residential squares and various town centers—now losing their elms and endangered by traffic encirclement. These parks, commonly furnished with bandstands, memorials, benches, flagpoles and flower beds, occasionally have fountains but because Maine has no water scarcity, they are unconvincing as a rule. (Some recent designs incorporating sculpture, such as that in Bath by William Zorach and Westbrook Mall by Moriece and Gary, are exceptions.) Two splendid examples of this genre were created some years ago in a harborside park at Rockport and the Bok Amphitheater of Camden.

TOWN PARKS

It is difficult to imagine Rockport's waterfront as it was before the fire of 1907—bristling with masts, wharves piled with limerock and firewood, massive chimneys pouring smoke—and before its subsequent transformation into a park by Mary Curtis Bok, who hoped to beautify the town and provide employment during the depression.[27] Seven kilns and some nearby abandoned quarries in this limestone belt were all that survived of a vanished industrial landscape. But restoration of the kilns, construction of ex-

FIGURE 129, A and B. *Rockport Harbor in the late
19th century, and after transformation into a park*

*by Mary Curtis Bok in the late 1930's. Photo:
Frank Claes*

tensive seawalls and landscaping of the site (and of adjoining properties) proceeded, under Olmsted supervision, to create a lovely park (see Figures 129, A and B showing the harbor before and after these changes). For a score of years it was enjoyed by the community until some local enterprises began to encroach upon it. When these finally moved out, leaving a wrecked site, the town built marina and parking facilities there. Now, forty years after their initial recovery, the kilns have collapsed from neglect and there is a drive underway to rescue *one* of them, along with some quarries. Were it not for this effort and the presence in Rockport of Walker and Mary-Lea Memorial parks, town improvement might seem a lost cause.

Camden also benefited from the generosity of the Boks, specifically in planting of the town green and harbor's edge, and in the creation of an exquisite work of art, the Bok Amphitheater, adjoining the library and overlooking the harbor. It was designed by Fletcher Steele of Boston,[28] in 1929 (Figure 130). Every effect, proportion and detail of this singular space seems elegantly calibrated, from the placing of boulders among the low, dressed-stone walls and the encircling tiers of broad steps to the classic, bronze, standing urn lamps and two brick pavilions graced with Camperdown elms. The same control is apparent in the massing of cedars to define the enclosure; the positioning of elm, birch, yew, euonymous and the climbing hydrangea flung over the higher walls; and in the dramatic ascending vista of the library lantern and doorway above a flight of steps that curves about a garden sculpture below. It is the vision of *A Midsummer Night's Dream*. This, too, presents a sorry tale of neglect, of insufficient funds and vandalism resulting in the miserable intrusion of a floodlighting pole, inappropriate plant replacements or none, failure to restore damaged lamps and to build an adjoining children's garden as planned. Perhaps most jarring is the addition of "memorial" planting in disregard of the existing design and the dedication of this ground to

FIGURE 130. *Camden, Bok Amphitheater, by Fletcher Steele (1929). Photo: George Pohl*

all, as a "demonstration of beauty and possibility that lie close at hand in every Maine town."[29] If support and respectful restoration are not forthcoming, this unique creation, more admired than any other by landscape artists and visitors, will not endure.

Fortunately, care of Vesper Hill Children's Chapel and garden, another of Camden's exceptional landscapes, and sprung from the delightful imagination of the late Helena Bok, continues under the guidance of Elmer Crockett, designer, plantsman and for many years, member of the Olmsted staff in Maine. Most planting in this small park within a wood, including a Biblical herb garden, is grouped about the monolithic stone base of this open-air chapel. Its post-and-beam structure is approached by a roofed stairway, draped with massive hydrangea vines which leads to a surprise view of sea islands from beneath the high, peaked roof of the chapel bay.

THE PORTLAND PARK SYSTEM

As with community parks, the establishment of large municipal and regional preserves was frequently the work of individuals. The father of Portland's park system was the forceful and dedicated James Phinney Baxter, founder of a business empire, of cultural institutions, historian, and mayor of Portland at the turn of the century. He sought to unify the city with parkland *as the catalyst*, and began by acquiring tracts to complete the Promenades and Deering Oaks Park (given in 1879). As Mayor, Baxter commissioned Olmsted, Olmsted and Eliot to study Back Cove, to the northwest of the city, and sought approval of their plan which advocated an ingenious solution to the foul conditions there. This involved the construction of sewers, a simple dyke to flood the flats, thus creating a salt-water pond, and a hundred-foot-wide, landscaped, circuit drive, with costs partially defrayed by enhanced property values. Ultimately, the only part of this proposal to be realized was the (Baxter) boulevard. The condition of the Cove continued to deteriorate from further contamination and landfill operations. It was the subject of several unrealistic and costly engineering studies, and remains a serious problem today. Both the City Planning Department and an Audubon volunteer group have recently submitted suggestions which share the reasonableness of the 1896 proposal and provide hope for intelligent efforts to eliminate this long-standing blight.

Baxter did succeed in promoting a portion of the Olmsted Brothers' master park plan of 1905 (Figure 131). In the creation of neighborhood parks (now more than forty) and major land acquisitions, he pioneered the "greening" of his city where "Nature has gradually furnished magnificent coherence in trees and other plantings."[30] Since 1937, the Parks and Recreation Department has revived neighborhood park and playground construction, improved existing park facilities, introduced pedestrian plazas and renovated historic quarters. This program has mitigated the destruction of historic and aesthetically significant buildings that, with highway construction, had weakened the city fabric. The peninsula still retains an unusually inviting residential scale and abundance of open space which may forestall suburban growth.[31]

BAXTER PARK

At the same time that cities were acquiring a cultural veneer, the major land areas of Maine saw little change. With almost half its population concentrated along the littoral and a mere fourteen per cent of land under cultivation, over ten million acres, or half of the state, remained in "wild lands" (sparsely populated, unincorporated, forested wilderness) largely under the sway of the giant paper companies which—through purchase and leasing of government and private lands—had accumulated vast, contiguous territories. Though potato and poultry farms, blueberry harvesting, lime and granite quarrying, shipbuilding and small manufacturing, each with its characteristic landscape, have variously contributed to the economy, paper production has dominated Maine's market and territory. Until recently, these areas remained relatively undisturbed though managed for production, and represented a haven for sportsman and naturalist. However, there are moves afoot to "develop" the wild lands (witness the promotion of Moosehead and Sugarloaf for "second homes"[32]), and whether speculation can be controlled is in doubt.

Percival Proctor Baxter, son of Portland's mayor, must have sensed that these lands would soon be endangered. The urgency with which he pressed for the establishment of a forest park in the Katahdin region, when he was governor of Maine, characterized all of his subsequent endeavors in its behalf. He had been captive since his youth to Katahdin's spell (see Figure 123) and, when his proposals were defeated, he resolved to overcome public apathy and the powerful opposition of pulp and paper interests by purchasing and assembling the park as a private citizen. This task, beginning in 1930, took all of thirty years and a substantial fortune as well as the acumen of a seasoned politician.

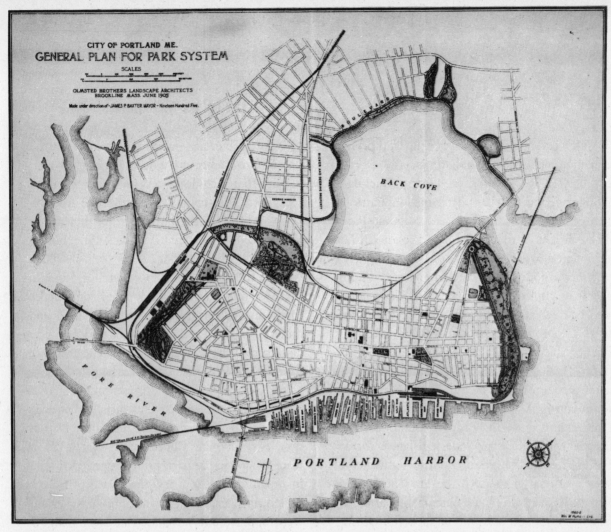

FIGURE 131. *Portland, General Plan for Park System, by Olmsted Brothers Landscape Architects (June, 1905). Courtesy of the Parks and Recreation Department, City of Portland, copy by Del Cargill*

Baxter's first purchase was a 5,960-acre tract which included most of Katahdin with its rare tundra vegetation. He deeded it to the state in trust, with explicit restrictions as to its use and administration, creating and endowing a politically independent commission to maintain the land and his policies of preserving it "forever wild" for the people of Maine. He continued to persuade adjacent landowners to sell him scenic parcels until, at his death, he had put together some 200,000 acres, one of the largest preserves in the nation, encompassing forty-six mountain peaks and ridges and 140 miles of trails through dramatic wilderness.

As reported to the legislature following his death, the Baxter Park Authority proposed to inventory the lands and produce a master plan in keeping with the spirit of the trust which insisted that nature be experienced on its own terms. The Commissioners interpreted their duties to encompass the curtailment of automobiles and restriction of visitor levels according to natural tolerances. Moreover, their concessions to snowmobilers and,[33] most deplorably, to timber-cutting interests (Baxter's nemeses), despite public outcry, lead one to the cynical conclusion that even the astute Baxter could not devise a political-proof agency to administer his gift. However, long before wilderness preservation became a popular cause with its appropriate national heroes, Baxter set for himself, and achieved, a monumental, idealistic task which remains to be acknowledged by the nation.

ACADIA NATIONAL PARK

Maine had another pioneer of the land preservation movement. Though financially assisted by John D. Rockefeller, Jr., George Bucknam Dorr waged as long and determined a battle as Baxter in the making of Acadia National Park. The summer of 1901, Harvard's President Eliot summoned a dozen leaders of Mount Desert's summer colony, the Bostonian, Dorr, among them, to consider preservation of the island's perishable beauty. The Hancock County Trustees of Public Reservations were promptly formed and succeeded by 1908 in assembling for park development five thousand contiguous acres through gifts which included the highest mountain peak (Cadillac), forests and streams. Dorr assumed an increasingly important role and in 1913, when the state legislature threatened to revoke the group's tax-free status he began a campaign to have the land declared a national park, which became reality after six years of legal and political manoeuvres. During his term as its first custodian, Dorr also mediated the bitter dispute over the automobile's presence on the island and when his compromise was accepted, he became even more deeply engaged in controversy by sponsoring a Rockefeller proposal to build carriage roads in the park. It was approved and construction began on fifty miles of road reserved for equestrians, cyclists and hikers and on a peripheral service (motor) road. The design of these roads and their sixteen handsome, arched stone bridges remain today (Figure 132), the outstanding features of the park. The path system was also created at this time, by Waldron Bates. But Dorr's mission was not yet accomplished. In 1928, he sought to extend the park limits beyond the island by ingenious strategies, including substitution of the name "Acadia" for "Lafayette" and relocation of a naval radio station from Otter Cliffs; Dorr

thereby succeeded in acquiring the dramatic coastlines of both the cliffs and the Schoodic peninsula. The Olmsted office assisted in planning roads and visitor accommodations for these areas—as they had earlier for Ocean Drive and Newport Mountain—areas which are host to a unique ericaceous and salt-tolerant plant community that includes a very southerly group of Jack Pine. This colony of picturesque trees has been so distorted by the wind that they are no longer readily identifiable as Jack Pine, but are here called Schoodic Pine.

As in the past, John D. Rockefeller, Jr.'s support was unwavering. He donated construction funds and eleven thousand acres of land and, much later, when one-third of the park had been damaged by fire, he provided for the costly removal of debris and purchased lands adjoining scenic roads to insure the preservation of their natural character—important gifts, to be recognized only by their absence. During the Depression, two Civilian Conservation Corps camps were located in the park providing needed labor for maintenance and new projects; in the same period, another five thousand acres of wild lands were opportunely purchased at Dorr's suggestion. Finally, in 1942 a major portion of Isle au Haut was deeded to the park by the children of Boston landscape architect William Bowditch.

The erect and craggy Dorr, with drooping mustaches, was described by one acquaintance as "looking like a forest."[34] At ninety, he strode along Acadia's paths in pith helmet and debated the merits of Homer translations. By then, the park had grown to almost thirty-five thousand acres and had become the second most visited one in the country. For the last fifty years, it has operated without a master plan, an acknowledged deficiency. When a draft plan was circulated in 1972, it provoked criticism because it failed to consider local impact or participation in administrative decisions, to adequately confront the need for restricting visitor numbers, and to set realistic goals. At present, the park is staffed with seasoned park personnel whose ac-

FIGURE 132. *Acadia National Park bridge; carriage path, Stanley Brook Road (1931). Photo: National Park Service, by P. Rothe*

tivities focus entirely upon maintenance and interpretive aspects of the grounds.

STATE PARKS

Efforts to establish a state park system gained momentum from the success of Acadia and Baxter and in 1938 the new State Park Commission directed construction, by Works Progress Administration crews, of Aroostook Park. Soon, four other areas were in operation and acquisition policies were under study. During the war, several historic sites and scenic Reid Park on the ocean were added. Active in the design of the latter was Myron Lamb, Harvard-trained landscape architect from Limerick (who said of his years with the Olmsted office in Brookline that it was "like belonging to a very fine, private club"). In this period, Camden Hills Park with five thousand acres of forested hills and shorelands, passed from federal jurisdiction to the state and, by 1970, the Commission had added a

score of other new sites. Since 1973, the (renamed) Bureau of Parks and Recreation has maintained more than twenty-three parks (including several designed by landscape architects such as Moriece and Gary's Lower Range State Park at Poland Spring), numerous memorials, boat-launching facilities, and the Allagash Wilderness Waterway. The last is a trail-blazing park, in that along its eighty-five mile river associated lands are to be maintained in their natural state. Much of this parkland was donated by individuals, such as the late L. M. S. Smith, whose gift of Wolfe's Neck Park at Freeport was characteristic of the support he gave to conservation causes. (His advocacy of cattle farming as a practical, open-space tactic "far better than industrial parks and shopping centers" remains unheeded.)[35]

Today, the Bureau faces problems of mounting use—some tourist projections for the year 2000 conjure up a nightmare for planners. While there are encouraging signs among campers that desire for more rugged experience is increasing, park policy tends to structure recreation more in terms of facilities rather than natural assets. Land acquisition would seem to be its first priority, in the face of rising speculation, followed by a re-evaluation of the supposed benefits from out-of-state tourist promotion. Pursuit of Mayor Baxter's connected open-space strategy, to effect a matrix configuration of parkland, could also rationalize site selection. Opportunities for purchasing such extended tracts still exist in northern and western Maine (though the alienation there of 400,000 acres of public lands to private control remains a bitter irony). Moreover, the imminent reversion of unclaimed islands to the state may transform the park concept altogether.

HIGHWAYS

Greater than the effect of these constructive forces is the power of transportation systems to shape our environment and economic destinies. Movement by water, rail, and road has often determined the existence of towns and the exploitation of resources. It is not coincidental that Maine's wild lands remained trackless *and* were inaccessible to early water transport, that coastal resorts ended at Frenchman Bay *with* the Bar Harbor Express, or that the viscera of an old town, like Ellsworth, have been strung out for miles on an "improved" highway. There is some humor in the fact that modern highways have had to follow horse-and-buggy routes, parallel to the north-south orientation of Maine's floodplains. But this temporary setback for technology, created problems more serious than the classic phrase, "Come to think of it, you can't get there from here!" as old routes, which once coursed leisurely through towns, have become mad rivers of traffic, dealing death to these communities. So long as roads are not distinguished from streets, towns will continue to sacrifice their leafy promenades and war memorials to the highway minotaur and no "beautification" projects such as Wiscasset's gallant efforts can restore the flow of business and social life to their centers. Activities of the Department of Transportation—until recent protests by citizens caused it to alter course—have often been inimical to those aspects of Maine landscape which are of value. Bridge construction, highway widening and new throughways only hasten the destruction of the Maine scene so ardently sought by the traveler at the end of the road. To reverse this condition would require investment in alternative means of tourist transport (to rival the private car in pleasure, novelty and economy), and in revived systems of public transport between towns.[36] It should be remembered that in the 19th century, there were at least thirty different rail, steamboat and stage services in the state and that, only today, has our choice of travel means narrowed to one.

Particular stretches of the Maine Turnpike have been commended for superior design, notably the area between Waterville and Bangor (a part of which was planted after designs by W. Gordon Hunter of Kittery). In route determination, restriction of commercial rights and vegetation management, such praise seems earned but in design response to the local scene, the results seem to be less successful. Thus, rivers are passed over uneventfully, straight alignments predominate and planting schemes seem alien and mechanically repeated (such as weeping willows at underpasses). But the effects the north-south extensions of this highway produce, in terms of generating new landscapes, should ultimately determine the verdict of its success.

PART FOUR: PROSPECTS

The land has been host to many uses and patterns of settlement representing the broad capabilities of human culture. But the burden of these accommodations has become unwieldy as technology multiplies the power—and growing population, the need—to exploit land. Ingenious formulas and machines seem to undermine not only environmental stability but our self-reliance as well, and resources, expended for a world arsenal, are wanting for humanitarian purposes. These conditions disturb thoughtful individuals. Many of them are drawn into activities which promise to reverse destructive processes and attitudes in our society. Land planning has become one focus of this spirited crusade and has evoked enthusiastic support in Maine where, since 1970, land-use programs have anticipated those of most other states and of federal legislation. Furthermore, Maine has been spared the worst ravages of industrial pollution and urban sprawl due to a lag in growth. Its unencumbered lands and physiographic advantages, joined to the appeal of spartan traditions, invite those who are testing emergent techniques and values—those in quest of new landscapes.

Maine legislators have created special agencies to deal with the land crisis. They have forged legal tools and comprehensive plans to effect reforms.[37] So armed, the role of advocate for citizen groups becomes a challenging one, as the key to action is in their hands. The achievement of the Saco River Corridor Association is an example of such efforts: under the leadership of a landscape architect, it brought about the prohibition of destructive riverside development in a region threatened with sub-divisions; in another instance, the Isle au Haut community supported James Haskell, Jr.'s study of alternatives to the unresponsive projections of the National Parks Administration. Similarly, the Townsend Plan for the Kennebec Valley sought to forestall land speculation on the river, in the wake of its scheduled clean-up.

Traditional Maine ways can continue to inspire methods and goals for land-based reform. Private property has been a cornerstone of Yankee tradition, but an improvisational theme frequently runs counter to it (i.e. the cooperative association of Monhegan islanders; user-rights of hunter and fisherman, etc.). Insularity, fostered by primitive conditions in parts of the state, has bred habits of independent thinking, skilled workmanship, ingenuity and thrift, as well as a sense of personal responsibility for the fate of the land. If convinced of the necessity, Maine people can adopt radical rules and launch fledgling institutions, as demonstrated in their support of

land and pollution controls and of numerous organizations devoted to understanding and protecting the environment.

Currently, there is a resurgence of these once popular, voluntary associations. Some venerable organizations have survived from earlier times, only to flounder because of the changed interests of modern life. One of several associations that failed in this transition was the scholarly Portland Society for Natural History (1850–1970). The Josselyn Society (of botanists) proved to be a healthy exception. By the 1920's, new directions were visible in the village improvement societies, garden and sportsmen's clubs and in the pioneering Maine Audubon Society; the last now has five thousand members and supports a wide spectrum of educational and conservation activities. Organizations patterned after these early groups multiplied in the ensuing decades. Today, there are over one hundred of them affiliated with the prestigious Natural Resources Council which has led joint campaigns for conservation legislation, monitored the performance of public agencies, and promoted ecological studies. Not only have these groups been constituted, but there has been widespread private support of environmentally oriented institutions as unique and innovative as the College of the Atlantic at Bar Harbor (opened in 1972); likewise, public funds have been made available for natural science research, technical assistance programs and policy studies of the University of Maine and for consultants such as the Center for Natural Areas, which is expertly staffed and affiliated with the Smithsonian Institution. These organizations and activities are a valuable resource for the people of Maine from which they may draw a wealth of information, ideas and leadership when they face choices involving their lands and their future.

What are the prospects for Maine's landscape? Many present crises and opportunities involve land and its use in relation to energy, industry, transport, tourism, housing, forests, fisheries, farming and revenues. Maine's 4000 miles of extended coastline should continue to draw tourists, though tolerance of their random invasions may end. But it may also support wind and tidal power development, intensive aquaculture or, with unfathomed risk, nuclear and off-shore drilling projects. Its wild lands—source of a vital industry, of sportsmen's quarry and of other, as yet unknown, potentials—present a rare opportunity for composing landscape on a broad scale and resolving the differences between ecological, economic and aesthetic values with responsive land-use design. As long as the natural processes which sustain these lands are not disrupted, Maine can continue to benefit from having this unusual frontier. Efforts to link other corners of the state and to preserve their natural assets could be furthered by superposing a permanent landscape matrix on this half of Maine, within which evolving communities could flourish. If its citizens determine to preserve and manage large natural areas, there already are agencies and statutes to implement such plans, notably those governing transport, "developments," and shorelands. On the other hand, if laisser-faire attitudes toward land changes persist, few opportunities for landscape improvement will be realized.

Human concerns hinge upon the resolution of these wider issues; one that reflects upon the quality of the environment is the plight of the native builder. Every prefabricated ranch house, every mobile home, diminishes his craft and adds to the blight of indifferent, hastily assembled structures that characterize most recent town and "strip" development. It will be an incalculable loss if the tradition that produced the admirable cape, the sturdy vernacular of boat sheds, the cabinetwork of "cottages" and present-day, exported millwork,[38] disappears through failure to teach the secrets and appreciation of the builder's skill to a new generation, or of local markets to supply native materials and simple tools to those with modest means and plans.[39]

The trials of patience that attend the building of a house and, even more, the daily round of traps, or the long wait for crops or trees to mature, forge attachments with a particular locale. If childhood memories are interwoven with these ties, they become all the more binding. Without them there is little motivation to build a superior environment. Given these loyalties, if Maine's people choose to develop the best of their native capabilities, the landscape architect will face a renewed challenge of creating forms to express these desires. Few professionals are on the scene and it would seem that they are, for the most part, following the senior Olmsted's dictum about developing President Eliot's "place": "For heaven's sake, Charles, leave it alone!" Ultimately, though, art will be needed to celebrate new themes and to fashion a further transformation of Maine's remarkable land.

Notes

INTRODUCTION

1. Chapter 7, "The Architecture of Maine's Schools," originated as a senior research paper by Janet Hansen, Colby '75, under the direction of Professor William B. Miller. Another author, Earle G. Shettleworth, Jr., Colby '70, devoted his research as a Senior Scholar to the subject of Portland architecture.

2. The authors of the various chapters in this work were: Louisa Dresser, Nina Fletcher Little, James Thomas Flexner, Donelson F. Hoopes, Lloyd Goodrich, John I. H. Baur and James M. Carpenter; in addition to a foreword by Colby President Robert E. L. Strider, the book has an opening chapter by Mary Ellen Chase.

3. Among the other exhibitions at the Colby Museum devoted to Maine subjects were: *Maine: 100 Artists of the 20th Century* (June 25–September 30, 1964); *The Land and Sea of Five Maine Artists* (May 5–June 20, 1965); *Maine: A Photographic Essay* (August 9–September 4, 1966); *Jeremiah Pearson Hardy: Maine Portraitist* (September 30–October 30, 1966).

   James M. Carpenter was the founder and Director of the Colby Museum of Art from 1959–1966, and Hugh J. Gourley III has been its Director since 1966.

CHAPTER I
THE EARLIEST SETTLEMENTS

1. The 16th century A.D. is taken as the beginning of effective European contact, meaning those European-Indian relationships which created any impact of significance on the native peoples, or which were recorded in acceptable historical form. There is no currently acceptable archaeological evidence in Maine for earlier contacts by Norse, Irish, or other European groups.

2. Samuel de Champlain first remarked on agriculture when he reached the mouth of the Saco River on his voyage of 1605; see H. P. Biggar, ed., *The Voyages of the Sieur de Champlain, Book I; Acadia and New England,* vol. 1 (Toronto, The Champlain Society, 1922).

3. Recent discoveries in northern Canada have revealed 30,000-year-old tools, and other sites in the New World show a comparable antiquity. Not all of these sites, however, are universally accepted by archaeologists.

4. The evidence for tundra environment comes from the study of palynology, the science of studying plant pollen deposited in bogs and lake bottoms. Radiocarbon dates of the deposits allow palynologists to reconstruct the past vegetation at particular times in the past. For a detailed account of Maine's past floral history consult, R. B. Davis, Theodore E. Bradstreet, Robert Stuckenrath, Jr., and Harold W. Borns, Jr.: "Vegetation and Associated Environments During the Past 14,000 Years Near Moulton Pond, Maine," *Quaternary Research,* 5 (1975), pp. 435–465.

5. George F. MacDonald, "Debert: A Palaeo-Indian Site in Central Nova Scotia," *Anthropology Papers,* No. 16 (Ottawa, National Museums of Canada, 1968).

6. David Sanger and Robert G. MacKay, "The Hirundo Archaeological Project: Preliminary Report," *Man in the Northeast,* No. 6 (1973), pp. 21–29.

7. Bruce Bourque, "Comments on the Late Archaic Population of Central Maine," *Arctic Anthropology,* XII, No. 2 (1976), 35–45.

8. Since the melting of the past glacial advance, sea levels around the world have been rising. In the Gulf of Maine the rate of rise has been very rapid, with profound effects on the configuration of the Gulf and the animals it supports; see David Sanger, "Culture Change as an Adaptive Process in the Maine-Maritimes Region," *Arctic Anthropology,* XII, No. 2 (1976), 60–75.

9. William A. Ritchie, *The Archaeology of New York State* (New York: Natural History Press, 1965).

10. Swordfish are no longer plentiful along the central Maine coast. They are basically restricted to warmer waters and present summer surface temperatures are too cool. For further details see note 8.

11. This burial practice, once distributed from Maine to Labrador, is known as the Moorehead burial tradition; see David Sanger, "Cow Point: An Archaic Cemetery in New Brunswick," *Mercury Series*, No. 12 (Ottawa, National Museums of Canada, 1973).

12. Isaac Kingsbury and Wendell S. Hadlock, "An Early Occupation Site, Eastport, Maine," *Massachusetts Archaeological Society Bulletin*, XII, No. 2 (1951), 22–26.

13. Elsewhere in the Northeast archaeologists call this time period the Woodland and define it in terms of the appearance of pottery, burial mounds, and agriculture. The apparent absence in most of Maine of true, man-made burial mounds, and well established agriculture, suggests that it is meaningless to adopt the Woodland terminology and its substages for this area.

14. David Sanger, "Prehistory of Passamaquoddy Bay: A Summary," *Bulletin of the Maine Archaeological Society,* 11, No. 2 (1971), pp. 14–19.

15. Studies of animal bones, especially of migratory and seasonally present birds, confirm the coastal winter occupation pattern from Passamaquoddy Bay to Penobscot Bay. Other indicators of winter occupation include deer with naturally shed antlers and the absence of young animals of species which give birth during the spring.

16. R. Thwaites, ed., "Lettre du P. Biard," in *Travels and Explorations of the Jesuit Missionaries in New France,* vol. II (Cleveland, 1896), p. 41.

17. It is very difficult to find agreement by scholars as to what to call the Indians of Maine during the 17th century. Depopulation and other pressures resulted in severe dislocations of people. One approach is to refer to the Maine Indians as the Abnaki, a term which would also include their close cultural and linguistic neighbors in the Canadian Maritime provinces.

18. T. J. C. Brasser, "Group Identification Along a Moving Frontier," in *Proceedings of the 38th International Congress of Americanists* (Stuttgart–München), 2 (1968), p. 262.

1. Wendell S. Hadlock, "Recent Excavations at DeMont's Colony, St. Croix Island, Maine," *OTNE,* XLIV, No. 4 (Spring, 1954), p. 93 (hereafter cited as Hadlock, "DeMont").

2. Edward M. Riley, "Brief History of Saint Croix Island," typescript copy, National Park Service, North East Regional Offices, Philadelphia, p. 4.

3. *Ibid.,* p. 5.

4. Hadlock, "DeMont," pp. 94–99; J. C. Harrington, "Preliminary Archaeological Explorations on St. Croix Island, Maine," typescript report and evaluation, July 30, 1951, National Park Service, North East Region, Philadelphia, pp. 5–8.

5. Charles E. Banks, "New Documents Relating to the Popham Expedition, 1607," *Proceedings of the American Antiquarian Society,* N.S. 30, Part I (1929), pp. 309–315 (hereafter cited as Banks, "New Documents"); Henry O. Thayer, ed., *The Sagadahoc Colony, Comprising the Relation of a Voyage to New England* . . . (Portland, Maine, 1892), pp. 1–85 (hereafter cited as Thayer, *Sagadahoc*).

6. Banks, "New Documents," p. 311; Thayer, *Sagadahoc,* p. 66.

7. Banks, "New Documents," p. 312.

8. Thayer, *Sagadahoc,* pp. 167–187, "Location of the Colony" with insert map opposite p. 177 showing the 1607 plan superimposed upon Point Popham in 1891; Gardiner Lane, "An Archaeological Report on Excavations Carried Out at Sabino Head in Popham Beach, Maine—The Site of Fort St. George 1607–1608 A.D.," Unpublished Report for the Maine State Parks and Recreation Department, 1966, p. 4; George Carey, "Fort St. George Historical Research," Unpublished Report for the Maine State Parks and Recreation Department, 1966, pp. 31–45.

9. William Strachey, *History of Travaile into Virginia* . . . (London, 1618), reprinted in Thayer, *Sagadahoc,* p. 85.

10. *Ibid,* p. 86.

11. James Phinney Baxter, ed., *The Trelawney Papers,* Documentary History of the State of Maine, III (Portland, 1884), pp. 31–32 (hereafter cited as Baxter, *Trelawney*).

12. Richard Candee, "A Documentary History of Plymouth Colony Architecture; Part III," *OTNE,* LX, No. 2 (Fall, 1969), p. 50.

13. York *Deeds*, 10 vols. (Portland, 1887–1894), vol. I, p. 10 (hereafter cited as York *Deeds*); Everett S. Stackpole, *Old Kittery and Her Families* (Lewiston, Maine, 1903), pp. 51–53.

14. Baxter, *Trelawney*, p. 32.

15. *Ibid.*, pp. 48, 113, 119, 165.

16. *Ibid.*, p. 142.

17. *Ibid.*, p. 201.

18. *Provincial Papers of New Hampshire*, 9 vols. (Concord, 1867–76), vol. I, p. 83 (hereafter cited as *NHPP*).

19. *NHPP*, I, pp. 76–77.

20. Charles E. Banks, *History of York, Maine*, vol. I, p. 42 (hereafter cited as Banks, *York*).

21. MS letter, Thomas Gorges to his father, July 19, 1640, from a typescript of the original MSS notebooks in the Exeter City Library, Devonshire, transcribed by Robert E. Moody. Professor Moody was kind enough to call these manuscripts to my attention and allow me to take notes from his complete transcription prior to his publication of the complete set of Gorges notebooks (hereafter cited as Gorges, *Notebooks*). For a brief study of these manuscripts and their author, see Robert E. Moody, "Thomas Gorges, Proprietary Governor of Maine, 1640–1643," *Proceedings of the Massachusetts Historical Society*, 75 (1963), pp. 10–26.

22. York *Deeds,* II, pp. 11–12.

23. Massachusetts Historical Society, *Collections*, 5th Ser., vol. I, p. 37 quoted in Harold Shurtleff, *The Log Cabin Myth*, (reprint, Gloucester, Mass., 1967), p. 77.

24. *NHPP,* I, p. 61; the original MS is lost, but was first published by Jeremy Belknap in *The History of New Hampshire*, vol. I, appendix II (Dover, N.H., 1812).

25. *Massachusetts Archives*, vol. III, p. 437.

26. *Massachusetts Archives*, vol. III, p. 444; Mason's letter to Gibbons, May 5, 1634 begins "These people and provisions, which I have now sent wᵗʰ Mr. Jocelyne, are to sett upp two mills upon my owne division of land . . .," *NHPP*, I, p. 89. Gibbons' reply indicates that the ship was unloaded July 18 and "the 22d day the carpenters began about the mill . . .", *NHPP*, I, p. 92.

27. Ferdinando Gorges, *Briefe Narration* . . . (London, 1658), quoted in J. P. Baxter, *Sir Ferdinando Gorges and His Province of Maine* (Boston, 1890), vol. II, p. 58.

28. John Winthrop, *Journal* (Savage ed.) vol. I, (Boston, 1825), p. 129. The sawmills to be erected were, presumably, the iron components to be installed once the carpenters built the frame (see n. 26 above).

29. Gorges, *Notebooks,* [np]. See note 21, above, for a description of Robert E. Moody's forthcoming publication of these MS letters.

30. *Ibid.,* [np].

31. *Ibid.,* [np].

32. *Ibid.,* [np].

33. *Ibid.,* [np].

34. Winthrop Papers, MSS Massachusetts Historical Society, vol. II, p. 39.

35. *Province and Court Records of Maine* (4 vols.; Portland, 1932–64), vol. 1, p. 161 (hereafter cited as *MPCR*).

36. *Records and Files of the Quarterly Courts of Essex County, Massachusetts* (Salem, 1911), vol. I, p. 251.

37. York *Deeds*, II, p. 69.

38. "Pascatway [sic] River in New England by I. S.," MS map c. 1655, British Museum, Crown Collection, Topography vol. 120, p. 27.

39. William Hubbard, *A Narrative of the Indian Wars in New England* . . . (Worcester, Mass., 1801), pp. 283–4.

40. Massachusetts Historical Society, misc. bound MSS, vol. 2, p. 5.

41. Benno M. Forman, "Mill Sawing in Seventeenth Century Massachusetts," *OTNE*, LX: 4 (Spring 1970), p. 111 from the Rhys Jenkins MSS, Science Museum Library, London, folder "Sawmills and Sawing," item 27, No. 8, folio 1, recto (hereafter cited as Forman, "Mill Sawing"); and Ellen B. Wood, ed., *Rowland Vaugh, his Booke* (London, 1897), p. 157.

42. K. G. Farries and M. T. Mason, *The Windmills of Surrey and Inner London* (London, 1966), p 234; Forman, "Mill Sawing," p. 111.

43. York *Deeds*, I, p. 17.

44. *Ibid.*, II, p. 164.

45. *Ibid.*, II, pp. 129–130; for a fuller exploration of sawmilling along the Piscataqua also see Richard Candee, "Merchant and Millwright," *OTNE*, LX: 4 (Spring, 1970), pp. 131–149, which was the basis for part of the above text.

46. Banks, *York*, vol. II, pp. 101–103.

47. Edward Emerson Bourne, "The Garrison Houses of York County," *Collections of the Maine Historical Society*, VII (Bath, Maine, 1876), pp. 111–113.

48. *Ibid.*, p. 113.

49. *Documentary History of the State of Maine*, vol. V, p. 91; Henry E. Dunnack, *Maine Forts* (Augusta, Maine, 1924), p. 168.

50. Kittery *Town Records*, I, p. 131; *Documentary History of the State of Maine*, vol. V, p. 429.

51. Kittery *Town Records*, I, p. 175, II, p. 12; York *Probates*, no. 20549.

52. York *Deeds*, II, p. 34.

53. *Ibid.*, III, p. 30; Banks, *York*, vol. II, pp. 245–248.

54. *MPCR*, vol. II, pp. 292–294.

55. "The Diary of Samuel Sewall, 1674–1700," in *Collections of the Massachusetts Historical Society*, 5th Series, vol. V (Boston 1866), p. 37.

56. York *Deeds*, VII, pp. 129–30. The same relationship between a sawmill and a new log house may be seen in a lease of a sawmill erected in 1728 by the heirs of Gov. John Leveret along the Saco River in Biddeford. Having built the mill, they contracted with John Stackpole to "build a Log house one Story high with a roof boarded and shingled thirty feet long & eighteen feet wide, a stack of Chimneys in the middle fitted for two fire places to be done Strong & workmanlike. . . ." Benjamin Haley, who leased the mill for four years, agreed to hire a number of men who would "reside at the mill or Dwelling house," as the log building was invariably known, "& tend the mill. . . ." I am indebted to Professor Robert E. Moody of Boston University for a typescript of this contract of Oct. 27, 1729, which he plans to publish among the Saltonstall Papers.

57. W. D. Williamson, *History of the State of Maine* (Hallowell, Me., 1832), vol. II, p. 77n.

58. Banks, *York*, vol. II, pp. 223–25 provides the only clear argument that the McIntire house was the Maxwell garrison and cites all evidence of Maxwell's house

being the only Scotland Parish garrison; see York *Probates*, no. 12712, will of Alexander Maxwell, 1707, also York *Deeds*, VII, p. 87.

59. MS building contract of May 7, 1754 between Plymouth Company and Gersham Flagg; photocopy at the Society for the Preservation of New England Antiquities, Boston.

60. York *Deeds*, V, Part I, p. 16 (1682).

61. York *Probates*, II, pp. 10–11 (1707); York *Deeds*, III, p. 126 (1683), IV, p. 24 (1684), and IV, p. 52 (1685).

62. York *Probates*, II, pp. 10–11; York *Deeds*, V, Part I, p. 16.

63. York *Probates*, nos. 6104 and 8277.

64. MS of building contract between Francis Moore, John Watts, and Edward Hutchinson, dated March 23, 1714/15, in Joseph Downs Library, Winterthur, Maryland.

65. *MPCR*, vol. II, pp. 292–294; York *Probates*, nos. 9648 and 9649; York *Deeds*, II, p. 155, V, p. 54; Kittery *Town Records*, II, p. 133.

66. Mrs. Ida F. Twinbly, compiler, "Typescript of the Early Town Records of Biddeford from 1653 to 1733," Augusta, Maine, 1906, microfilm in Maine State Archives, pp. 127, 133, 135.

67. York *Deeds*, V, Part I, p. 47.

68. York *Probates*, no. 4412; York *Deeds*, V, Part I, p. 65.

69. *MPCR*, vol. I, p. 332.

70. *Ibid.*, vol. IV, p. 31.

71. *Ibid.*, vol. I, pp. 227–28, 301; Banks, *York*, vol. II, p. 158.

72. York *Deeds*, V, Part I, p. 13.

73. York *Probates*, no. 9535 (vol. II, p. 163).

74. *MPCR*, vol. IV, p. 115.

75. York *Deeds*, IV, pp. 102–04.

76. *Ibid.*, IV, p. 64.

77. *MPCR*, vol. VI, p. 27.

78. I wish to thank Professor Neal Allen who has compiled the court records for this decade for the statistical evidence of imprisonments at York.

79. Records of the Court of General Sessions of the Peace, York County Court House, Alfred, Maine, vol. VII, 7 October 1729.

80. MSS Daybook and Ledger of William Pepperrell Sr. and Jr., 1717–1721, collection of Joseph W. P. Frost, Eliot, Maine, pp. 298, 354. Students of later 18th century additions to the house should consult the Pepperrell MSS at the New England Historic Genealogical Society in Boston, notably the 1735–1736 carpentry bills of Edmund Moody.

81. "A coppy [*sic*] from Mr. Jn. Drew for work done to Capt Archibald Macphaedies [*sic*] Brick House at Piscataqua," Macpheadris MSS collection, Warner House Association, Portsmouth, New Hampshire; William G. Wendell, "The Macpheadris-Warner House in Portsmouth, New Hampshire," *Antiques,* LXXXVII, No. 6 (June, 1965), pp. 712–715; Arthur C. Haskell, "Early Interior Door-Ways in New England," *The Monograph Series*, XVIII, No. 5 (October. 1932), p. 238.

CHAPTER 3

COLONIAL ARCHITECTURE

1. Dr. Neal W. Allen, Professor of History at Union College, Schenectady, first discovered the documentation cited above by Candee; (letter from Allen to Myers dated February 12, 1969 in HABS files.)

2. Abbott Lowell Cummings, *Architecture in Early New England* (Sturbridge, 1974) gives an admirably clear account of this structural system.

3. Richard M. Candee concluded that nothing remains of the 17th-century house except a reused summer beam in the cellar; (letter from Candee to Myers dated October 16, 1968 in HABS files); also see p. 43 above. Mr. Joseph W. P. Frost, a Pepperrell descendant who owned the house until August, 1975, believes the house was merely remodeled; (letter from Frost to Myers dated December 8, 1969 in HABS files).

4. Data on Bellamy's work were supplied by Joseph W. P. Frost; (letter from Frost to Myers dated December 8, 1969).

5. Ernest Allen Connally, "The Cape Cod House: an Introductory Study," *Journal of the Society of Architectural Historians,* XIX, 2 (May, 1960) traces the origin

and development of the type. The terms "Cape Cod house," and "Cape Cod cottage," or just "cape" do not seem to have gained really wide currency until the 1920's and 1930's, when developers popularized modern adaptations of the type. Architects like Royal Barry Wills designed innumerable "Cape Cod cottages" during the 1930's. During many summers spent in Maine and New Hampshire during the late 1920's and the 1930's this author *never* heard the type called anything but "farmhouse."

6. Mrs. Ambrose C. Cramer, founder of the Mary Meeker Cramer Museum in Camden, was primarily responsible for this restoration. The Conway House is open to the public in the summer, and is adjacent to the museum.

7. Russell V. Keune and James Replogle, "Two Maine Farmhouses," *Journal of the Society of Architectural Historians*, XX, 1 (March, 1961).

8. Mr. and Mrs. Frederick M. Haggett, owners of the house have the original receipt. It reads as follows: "Georgetown August 19, 1775/then Rec'd: of James McCobb one hundred an twenty/Pounds Lawful money in full for Building his house/and in full for all amounts between him and me/Rec'd by me Issac Packard."

9. John Mead Howells, *The Architectural Heritage of the Piscataqua* (New York, 1937), p. opp. fig. 97. Howells says, "This is interesting as proving once more that the universal habit of painting Colonial interior woodwork white was not a Colonial habit at all. The 'Colonial' builders left their woodwork unpainted, or painted it in gayer and warmer tones."

CHAPTER 4

THE FEDERAL STYLE

1. The "traditional" emphasis in Federal architecture, and the regional diversity among early neo-classical styles, are developed by William H. Pierson, Jr., in his *American Buildings and Their Architects,* vol. I: The Colonial and Neoclassical Styles (New York: Doubleday, 1970), Chs. 6 and 7 (hereafter cited as Pierson, *American Buildings*).

2. See Edward H. Elwell, *Portland and Vicinity* (Portland: W.S. Jones and Loring, Short and Harmon, 1876; reprint edition by Greater Portland Landmarks, Inc., 1975), pp. 14–15, 54–62. Cf. also Works Project Administration, *Portland City Guide* (Portland: Forest City Printing Co., 1940), pp. 37–41.

3. The Hugh McClellan House has been extensively studied, and the Historic American Buildings Survey has produced photographs, drawings, and data de-

tailing its structure and history. There is also a recent, detailed survey of the house (1975) by the Society for the Preservation of New England Antiquities.

4. The precise connection between Parris and Bulfinch is not entirely clear. The David Sears House in Boston (1816) is definitely the work of Parris. But he apparently worked for Bulfinch on the Massachusetts General Hospital a few years later; see Pierson, *American Buildings,* p. 419, and *Dictionary of American Biography* (New York: Chas. Scribner's Sons, 1928), vol. XIV, p. 255.

5. See Harold Kirker, *The Architecture of Charles Bulfinch* (Cambridge: Harvard University Press, 1969), pp 89–91 and 152–155 (hereafter cited as Kirker, *The Architecture of Charles Bulfinch*).

6. See entry under descendents of Isaac Cobb in *Genealogy of the Cobb Family of New England,* vol. I (copy in Maine Historical Society).

7. The history of the Ingraham House, with several pictures showing the stages of architectural dilution, can be found in *Portland,* a publication of Greater Portland Landmarks, Inc. (Portland, 1972), pp. 116–117.

8. Plans and elevations for the Hunnewell House are preserved in the Boston Athenaeum. They are illustrated and discussed in Fiske Kimball, *Domestic Architecture of the American Colonies and of the Early Republic* (New York: Charles Scribner's Sons, 1922; reprinted by Dover Publications, 1966), pp. 150, 217. Further discussion may be found in Denys Peter Myers' *Maine Catalog,* Historic American Buildings Survey (Augusta: Maine State Museum, 1974), pp. 42–43 (hereafter cited as Myers, *Maine Catalog*).

9. Kirker, *The Architecture of Charles Bulfinch,* pp. 93–100.

10. The builders' manuals, particularly those of William and James Pain and Asher Benjamin, seem to have circulated widely in Maine during this period. Consequently, it is frequently impossible to say whether a specific Maine "housewright" depended more on them or on his personal observation of other buildings, such as those in Portland, Portsmouth, or Salem.

11. The account books of Samuel Melcher, III, which, though incomplete, are invaluable in tracing the histories of certain buildings in the area, are located in the archives section of the Bowdoin College Library.

12. For a summary of the McCobb family feud and for interesting pictures of the house being moved, see the article "Spite House" by Mary Cramer and Isabel Currier in *Down East Magazine* (September 1969).

13. Aaron Sherman's extraordinary craftsmanship in the Ruggles House is well known. What is less appreciated is the very high quality of several other resi-

dences, both in Columbia Falls and in neighboring towns, which probably can be attributed to his influence if they were not his actual work.

14. While the wide fan and side lights were used as early as 1800 in Portland, they did not become common further north (east) until after the war. Thus, the typical entrance c. 1800–1810 was apt to have a narrow fan, either elliptical or semi-circular, matching in width the door itself. Wooden fans also were in common use by 1815 or thereabouts.

15. Melcher's church in Brunswick was superseded in 1845 by the present Gothic structure designed by Richard Upjohn. The single extant drawing of the old building shows it to have been a very plain, yet handsome edifice. Melcher, French, and Anthony Raymond of Bath were among the more prolific church builders along the central coast during these and the following several decades. Cf., for example, Melcher's church on High Street in Wiscasset (1840) and Raymond's Winter Street Church in Bath (1843), (see further below).

16. For a more detailed discussion of this church, together with a front elevation and longitudinal section, see Myers, *Maine Catalog*, pp. 55–58.

17. *Ibid.*, pp. 65–66.

18. The early Bowdoin buildings are described in William D. Shipman, *The Early Architecture of Bowdoin College and Brunswick, Maine* (Brunswick: Brunswick Publishing Co., 1973).

CHAPTER 4, PART 2
THE GREEK REVIVAL

1. The statistics included in these historical data are drawn from Dorris A. Isaacson, ed., *Maine—A Guide 'Down East'* (Rockland, Me., 1970), *passim*; John H. Morrison, *History of American Steam Navigation* (New York, 1958); and Slason Thompson, *Short History of American Railways* (Chicago, 1925).

2. Henry-Russell Hitchcock lists ninety-four authors of pattern books published before 1895 in his *American Architectural Books*. Among those popular in Maine were Asher Benjamin's *Practical House Carpenter* and *Builder's Guide,* Edward Shaw's *Civil Architecture* and *Rural Architecture,* and Chester Hills's *Builder's Guide.* Curiously, Minard Lafever's *Modern Builder's Guide* and *Beauties of Modern Architecture,* two Greek Revival books very influential elsewhere, seem to have had slight impact in Maine. In the 1835 edition of his *Practical House Carpenter,* Asher Benjamin said, "Since my last publication the Roman School of Architecture has been entirely changed for the Grecian."

3. Orson Squire Fowler, *A Home for All; or, The Gravel Wall and Octagonal Mode of Building* (New York, 1848) was the book that spread the gospel of octagonal houses from Maine to California. No gravel wall (concrete) examples are known to have been built in Maine.

4. The 1855 *Maine Register and Business Directory* carried an advertisement by Washburn and Brown, Architects, with both a Portland address and a "principal office" in Boston.

5. Earle G. Shettleworth, Jr., "A Mark Upon the Land—The Life and Work of Charles D. Lawrence, A Mid-Nineteenth-Century Fairfield, Maine, Builder," *OTNE*, 58 (1967), pp. 31–48.

6. Bulfinch's original drawings are preserved in the Maine State Library, Augusta.

7. The *Portland Advertiser* for January 10, 1854 described the fire. On June 13, 1854 the *Portland Advertiser* reported the discovery of a copper plate within the cornerstone that read as follows: "Hic lapis/ urbis Portlandiae impensis/ Martin Van Buren/ Praeside/ Reipublicae Americanae/ Edvardo Kent/ Gubernatore/ Reipublicae Mainensis/ a Levi Cutter/ summo urbis magistri/ Calendis Septembrino/ Anno Christi MDCCCXXXVIII/ Ricardus Bond Architectus."

8. William Havard Eliot, *A Description of Tremont House* (Boston, 1830).

9. Philip Chadwick Foster Smith, "The Metamorphosis of East India Marine Hall," *Historic Preservation,* 27, No. 4 (1975), pp. 10–13.

10. James B. Vickery, *An Illustrated History of the City of Bangor, Maine 1769–1969* (Bangor, 1969) reproduces an old photograph showing the church before the loss of the upper stage of the tower.

11. Samuel M. Green, "Thomas Lord, Joiner and Housewright," *Magazine of Art,* 40 (1947), pp. 230–235. Green's contention is that Deane was *much* more sophisticated than Lord.

12. Everard M. Upjohn, *Richard Upjohn, Architect and Churchman* (New York, 1939) illustrates two original drawings and an old photograph of the Isaac Farrar House.

13. The architect of the alterations was the owner, Ambrose C. Cramer, A.I.A. In a letter dated August 21, 1975, Mrs. Ambrose C. Cramer kindly supplied data regarding possible attributions.

14. The map of Hallowell published by E. M. Woodford in 1855 clearly shows the original outline of the Thing House.

15. Earle G. Shettleworth, Jr., *Bangor Historic Resources Inventory* (Augusta, 1975), p. 27. Penobscot County Deeds Registry documents confirm the sequence of ownership, and Bryant's contracts for another building refer to the Hatch House as his work. The source of this information is Mr. Shettleworth.

16. Charles H. Ashton in NRHP Nomination, Governor Abner Coburn House, Skowhegan, January, 1974, includes data on Joseph Bigelow, including the quotation from the *Bangor Weekly Courier* of July 1, 1845 referring to the Isaac Farrar House. "The carpenter work has been executed by Mr. Joseph Bigelow of Skowhegan, an old acquaintance of Mr. Farrar, and been completed so in a manner to command high plaudits for its accuracy, thoroughness, and beauty—indeed few men can equal it while probably none can excel it."

17. Earle G. Shettleworth, Jr., "Pond designs in 1830s left mark on Bangor," *Bangor Daily News*, November 24, 1975, p. 19.

18. Samuel M. Green, "The Architecture of Thomaston, Maine," *Journal of the Society of Architectural Historians*, 10, No. 4 (1951), pp. 24–31.

CHAPTER 4, PART 3

THE ARCHITECTURE OF
THE MAINE SHAKERS

1. Besides the Community at Sabbathday Lake, there are a few Shaker Sisters living at the Canterbury Community in New Hampshire, but the direction of the land and buildings has been transferred to a non-profit museum corporation called "Shaker Village, Inc." See "A Note from the Shaker Parent Ministry," *The World of Shaker*, IV, No. 2 (Summer, 1974), p. 3.

2. The imitation of the Shakers by "the World" in the areas of husbandry and labor-saving devices is well documented by the authors cited below. The direct debt of Maine landowners to Shaker architecture, on the other hand, is a conjecture on the part of this author. It is felt, however, that the close attention they focused on Shaker life in all its aspects, and the obvious borrowing in other areas of endeavor, make it extremely probable that Maine people imitated the environmental and architectural strengths of the Shaker villages themselves. For a concise discussion of specific borrowing of Shaker crafts and industries, see Theodore E. Johnson, *Hands to Work and Hearts to God: The Shaker Tradition in Maine* (Brunswick: Bowdoin College Museum of Art, 1969), [n.p. 4–5]. For a broader view, see Edward Deming Andrews, *The People Called Shakers,* rev. ed. (New York: Dover Press, 1963), pp. 113–15; 116–35.

3. Elder Joshua (1816–1900), long-time member of the Alfred Community, made several versions of these isometric views. One each of Alfred, Sabbathday Lake

and Poland Hill survive in the Sabbathday Lake Shaker Library today. The Library of Congress has another one of Alfred; the Henry Francis du Pont Winterthur Museum, Winterthur, Delaware, has one each of Sabbathday Lake and Poland Hill, as well as one of Canterbury, New Hampshire; and Dr. J. J. G. McCue of Lexington, Massachusetts, has two of Alfred and one of Poland Hill. One of his Alfred views is on loan to the Museum of Fine Arts, Boston, Massachusetts, and may be seen in its Shaker display. We thank Dr. Theodore E. Johnson, director of The Shaker Museum, Sabbathday Lake, Maine, for this information.

4. For a fuller discussion of Brother Moses' work, see Marius B. Péladeau, "The Shaker Meetinghouses of Moses Johnson," *Antiques*, XCVIII, No. 4 (October, 1970), pp. 594–99 (hereafter cited as Péladeau, "Meetinghouses").

5. There is no written record or oral tradition which indicates that Brother Moses carried architectural plans with him from village to village. Rather, in the tradition of 18th-century housewrights, buildings were designed and framed from memory. Likewise, his records of travel make it obvious he did not stay long after the frame was erected, but rather left it to local Shaker brothers to carry out his instructions regarding the interior finish work.

6. For photographs of the other Shaker meetinghouses, all with the same roof line, see Péladeau, "Meetinghouses."

7. As dictated by Shaker custom, buildings which had outlived their usefulness were either torn down or removed from the community. They were not allowed to stand empty and idle. This explains why views of Maine Shaker Villages, from those of Elder Joshua in the mid-19th century to the present, show buildings either moved or removed at different periods.

8. The Shaker brothers did, however, quarry all the massive granite blocks used in the foundation of the Dwelling from a rich vein of granite on Shaker land and hauled it overland to the building site.

9. Following the closing of the Poland Hill Family in 1887, the property was sold in 1899 to private interests. After remaining vacant for many years, the Dwelling was intentionally burnt to the ground in 1955 by the Hiram Ricker Company of Poland Spring House fame to prevent its use as a competitive summer-resort hotel.

10. Details of Brother Hewett's construction of the schoolhouse, his designing of the Dwelling and his other work around the Village are found in the Sabbathday Lake *Church Journals*, now in the Shaker Library at the Village.

11. In general, published discussions of Shaker architecture focus on the styles and construction details of individual buildings, with particular emphasis on the uni-

versal built-in cupboards and peg rails. Although these are attractive features of Shaker design, a discussion of this nature does not consider the wider vision of all Shaker builders, which took in buildings in relation to each other and to the land on which they were sited. For a narrow investigation of functionalism in relation to Shaker interior design see Eugene M. Dodd, "Functionalism in Shaker Crafts," *Antiques,* XCVIII, No. 4 (October, 1970), pp. 588–93.

Most articles on Shaker architecture have concentrated on the villages of the sect at New Lebanon and Watervliet, New York, and Hancock, Massachusetts; for example, see D. M. C. Hopping and Gerald R. Watland, "The Architecture of the Shakers," *Antiques,* LXXII, No. 4 (October, 1957), pp. 335–39. For one of the few discussions of Maine Shakers, see Marius B. Péladeau, "The Shakers of Maine," *Antiques,* CVII, No. 6 (June, 1975), pp. 1144–53.

CHAPTER 5, PART 1

REVIVAL STYLES OF MAINE ARCHITECTURE

1. For general discussions of the Gothic Revival, see Kenneth Clark, *The Gothic Revival* (London, 1928) and Henry-Russell Hitchcock, *Architecture of the Nineteenth and Twentieth Centuries* (Baltimore, 1958), (hereafter cited as Hitchcock, *Nineteenth and Twentieth Centuries*).

2. Talbot Hamlin, *Benjamin Henry Latrobe* (New York, 1955), p. 237.

3. See Everard M. Upjohn, *Richard Upjohn, Architect and Churchman* (New York: Columbia University Press, 1939 and Da Capo Press, 1968), p. 11 (hereafter cited as Upjohn, *Upjohn*).

4. Denys Peter Myers, *Maine Catalog,* Historic American Buildings Survey (Augusta, Maine State Museum, 1974), p. 106 (hereafter cited as Myers, *Maine Catalog*).

5. Earle G. Shettleworth, Jr., *Maine Historic Resources Inventory* (Augusta: Maine Historic Preservation Commission, 1974), p. 31 (hereafter cited as Shettleworth, *Maine Inventory*).

6. Ada Douglas Littlefield, *An Old River Town . . . History of Winterport* (New York, 1907), p. 217.

7. Myers, *Maine Catalog,* pp. 106 and 185, note 51. Earle G. Shettleworth, Jr. is credited with the discovery of Jarvis as the designer.

8. Upjohn, *Upjohn,* p. 221.

9. Myers, *Maine Catalog*, p. 106; this addition was designed by Deane Woodward in 1965.

10. *Ibid.*, p. 107.

11. Earle G. Shettleworth, Jr. and Frank A. Beard in NRHP Nomination, Centre Street Congregational Church, Machias, April 4, 1975.

12. George W. Drisko, *History of Machias* (Machias, 1904), p. 200.

13. Myers, *Maine Catalog*, p. 107.

14. Upjohn, *Upjohn*, p. 207.

15. Myers, *Maine Catalog*, p. 111.

16. Upjohn, *Upjohn*, pp. 44–46, fig. 10.

17. *Ibid.*, p. 45, fig. 9.

18. This distinctiveness was recognized by Kenneth Conant as ". . . our quaint American Folk Gothic," see Upjohn, *Upjohn*, p. vi.

19. *Ibid.*, p. 73.

20. See Vincent J. Scully, Jr., *The Shingle Style and the Stick Style*, rev. ed. (New Haven, 1971), p. xxxviii and note 44 (hereafter cited as Scully, *Shingle Style*).

21. Horatio Greenough, *Form and Function*, Harold A. Small, ed. (Berkeley, California, 1947), *passim*.

22. Upjohn, *Upjohn*, p. 91.

23. *Ibid.*, pp. 90–91.

24. Myers, *Maine Catalog*, pp. 111, 112, and 185–86, notes 59 and 60.

25. Upjohn, *Upjohn*, pp. 80–81.

26. Robert Hallowell Gardiner, *Early Recollections of Robert Hallowell Gardiner, 1782–1864*, Robert Hallowell Gardiner, II, ed. (Hallowell, 1936), ill. facing p. 140 (hereafter cited as Gardiner, *Early Recollections*).

27. Gardiner, *Early Recollections*, p. 141.

28. *Ibid.*, p. 213, note.

29. *Ibid.*, p. 215.

30. *Ibid.*, p. 215, note.

31. *Ibid.*, p. 214.

32. Nathaniel Hawthorne, *The American Notebooks*, Claude M. Simpson, ed. (Columbus, Ohio, 1972), pp. 41–43.

33. Upjohn, *Upjohn*, p. 93.

34. Earle G. Shettleworth, Jr., "Henry Rowe's Structures Were Outstanding," *Evening Express* (Portland), September 4, 1965, p. 16.

35. Dr. and Mrs. Robert O. Kellogg have been most helpful in supplying information about Cliff Cottage.

36. Bargeboards from the Capt. Henry Stewart House, Farmington, (now destroyed) are included in the Colby Museum of Art exhibition, *Maine Forms of American Architecture*, through the courtesy of the Farmington Historical Society.

37. Angela Godfrey Clifford, *Cliff Cottage, 1847–1947* (Bangor, 1947).

38. Edmund V. Gillon, Jr. and Clay Lancaster, *Victorian Houses, A Treasury of Lesser-Known Examples* (New York: Dover Publications, Inc., 1973), pl. 26.

39. Notice and illustration in *Drew's Rural Intelligencer* of May 5, 1855, cited by Earle G. Shettleworth, Jr., in NRHP Nomination, Linwood Cottage, Bucksport, December, 1973.

40. Scully, *Shingle Style*, p. xlvii and note 68; also see Polly Greason (Mrs. A. L.), "The Johnson House," unpublished paper, University of Maine at Portland–Gorham (1974); copy on file at Historic Preservation Commission, Augusta.

41. Henry-Russell Hitchcock, *American Architectural Books* (Minneapolis, 1946 and 1962).

42. Scully, *Shingle Style*, pp. xxx–xxxvi.

43. Quoted in *ibid.*, p. xlviii.

44. James Marston Fitch, *American Building, the Historical Forces that Shaped It*, 2nd ed. (Boston, 1966), p. 118.

45. Myers, *Maine Catalog*, p. 112.

46. Shettleworth, *Maine Inventory*, p. 5.

47. Oliver W. Larkin, *Art and Life in America,* revised ed. (New York, 1960), p. 168 (hereafter cited as Larkin, *Art and Life*).

48. Hitchcock, *Nineteenth and Twentieth Centuries*, p. 112.

49. Edward H. Elwell, *Portland and Vicinity* (Portland, 1876), pp. 42–49 (hereafter cited as Elwell, *Portland*).

50. Myers, *Maine Catalog,* p. 143 .

51. Larkin, *Art and Life*, p. 172.

52. Myers, *Maine Catalog*, p. 143.

53. *Ibid.*, p. 147.

54. *Ibid.*, pp. 147 and 190, note 9.

55. Anon., "Summer Chapels in Maine," *The Northeast* (a publication of the Episcopal Diocese of Maine), 8, No. 6 (July, 1961), pp. 4–20.

56. Myers, *Maine Catalog*, p. 71.

57. Earle G. Shettleworth, Jr., "Benjamin Deane," *Bangor Daily News*, September 15, 1975, p. 15. Mr. and Mrs. Arthur Thomas have been most helpful in supplying information about the Pierce-Giddings House.

57a. Mrs. Charles D. McEvoy, Jr. kindly brought my attention to the notice in the *Bangor Daily Whig and Courier*, and was helpful in supplying other information about the house.

58. Myers, *Maine Catalog*, p. 133–37.

59. *Ibid.*, p. 131.

60. *Ibid.*, p. 129.

61. Earle G. Shettleworth, Jr., *Bangor Historic Resources Inventory* (Augusta: Maine Historic Preservation Commission, 1975), *passim* (hereafter cited as Shettleworth, *Bangor Inventory*).

62. Shettleworth, *Maine Inventory*, pp. 4, 3, 12–13 respectively.

63. Myers, *Maine Catalog*, p. 114.

64. Shettleworth, *Maine Inventory*, p. 73.

65. Alfred Williams Anthony, *Bates College and Its Background* (Philadelphia, 1936), p. 140.

66. · Myers, *Maine Catalog*, p. 181, note 10, calls attention to an unpublished paper on Bryant by Earle G. Shettleworth, Jr.: see Shettleworth, *Maine Inventory*, pp. 3, 5, 7 and 42 respectively.

67. Earle G. Shettleworth, Jr. and Frank A. Beard in NRHP Nomination, F. O. J. Smith Tomb, Portland, October 24, 1974.

68. Myers, *Maine Catalog*, p. 138.

69. *Ibid.*, p. 138.

70. This is the thesis of John A. Kouvenhoven, *Made in America* (New York, 1948).

71. Shettleworth, *Bangor Inventory*, p. 83.

72. Myers, *Maine Catalog*, pp. 155–157.

73. *Ibid.*, p. 155.

74. Richard D. Kelly and Earle G. Shettleworth, Jr. in NRHP Nomination, Charles A. Jordan House, Auburn, October, 1973.

75. Shettleworth, *Bangor Inventory*, p. 90.

76. *Portland, A Publication of Greater Portland Landmarks Incorporated*, Martin Dibner, ed., architectural text by Patricia McGraw Pancoast (Portland, 1972), p. 181 (hereafter cited as Dibner/Pancoast, *Portland*).

77. Shettleworth, *Maine Inventory*, p. 38.

78. Myers, *Maine Catalog*, pp. 123–25.

79. Earle G. Shettleworth, Jr., "U.S. Seamen Had to Pay 20¢ a Month to Get Hospital Care," *Evening Express* (Portland), August 2, 1967, p. 32.

80. Myers, *Maine Catalog*, pp. 147–150, and Elwell, *Portland*, p. 84.

81. Myers, *Maine Catalog*, p. 150.

82. *Ibid.*, pp. 145–46.

83. *Ibid.*, pp. 165–68; Myers calls attention to the pioneering work on Fassett done by Earle G. Shettleworth, Jr. See also Dibner/Pancoast, *Portland*, pp. 190–92.

TURN-OF-THE-CENTURY ARCHITECTURE

1. In preparing the following discussion of the Queen Anne and Shingle Styles, the author is indebted to Mark M. Wilcox of Portland for the use of his 1975 Brown University undergraduate study, "John Calvin Stevens, the Development of Ordered Complexity Within the Shingle Style."

2. Louis C. Hatch, *Maine: A History*, 3 vols. (New York: The American Historical Society, 1919), vol. II, p. 903.

3. John Calvin Stevens and Albert Winslow Cobb, *Examples of American Domestic Architecture* (New York: William T. Comstock, 1889, hereafter cited as Stevens and Cobb, *Examples*); Vincent J. Scully, Jr., *The Shingle Style* (New Haven: Yale University Press, 1955), pp. 113–120 (hereafter cited as Scully, *Shingle Style*).

4. John Calvin Stevens, unpublished autobiographical sketch, collection of John Calvin Stevens II, Cape Elizabeth, Maine (hereafter cited as Stevens, autobiographical sketch).

5. *Ibid.*

6. Stevens and Cobb, *Examples,* p. 29.

7. John Calvin Stevens, manuscript sketchbooks, Maine Historical Society, Portland, Maine.

8. Stevens, autobiographical sketch.

9. M. F. Sweetsir, *King's Handbook of Boston Harbor* (Cambridge, Mass.: Moses King, 1882), p. 30.

10. *Westbrook Chronicle*, April 27, 1883.

11. Boston Terra Cotta Company, *Catalogue-Part V* (Boston, 1884), p. 66.

12. John Calvin Stevens, "Sketch for Seaside House," *American Architect and Building News* (Boston, May 3, 1884), pl. 436.

13. *Idem*, "House at Portland, Me.," *American Architect and Building News* (December 20, 1884), pl. 469; and, in *The British Architect* (London, March 19, 1886); and, "A Colonial House," *Scientific American, Architects and Builders Edition* (New York, January, 1892).

14. Scully, *Shingle Style*, p. 118.

15. George W. Sheldon, *Artistic Country Seats,* (New York: D. Appleton, 1887), p. 179.

16. Scully, *Shingle Style*, p. 119.

17. Stevens, autobiographical sketch.

18. On June 3, 1886, the *Portland Daily Press* made the following statement concerning "A House by the Sea":

    Last September the American Architect published an illustration of the "House by the Sea," by John Calvin Stevens of this city, the same drawing exhibited in the New York Art Exhibition. Mr. Stevens has just received an order from San Francisco to make a full set of plans for a house of the same description, the structure to cost about $12,000.

    When Stevens and Cobb republished the "House by the Sea" drawing in their *Examples of American Domestic Architecture* of 1889, they titled it, "A-House-by-the-Sea in California. Exterior. Cost $8,000." John Calvin Stevens II of Cape Elizabeth owns a set of six undated plans by his grandfather for "House Near San Francisco, California" in which the "House by the Sea" rendering is translated into working drawings. However, no record has been found as to the identity of the California client and whether he actually built the house.

19. Ellis F. Lawrence, "John Calvin Stevens," *Architecture* (New York), July, 1932, p. 2.

20. Frederick Law Olmsted, *Report and Advice of the Development and Improvement of Cushing's Island, Maine,* privately printed (Portland?, 1883), pp. 1–2.

21. *Ibid.,* p. 4.

22. Scully, *Shingle Style*, p. 120.

23. Stevens and Cobb, *Examples*, preface.

24. *Ibid.*, p. 25.

25. "American Domestic Architecture," *The British Architect* (January 24, 1890), p. 60.

26. William Rotch Ware, "Books and Papers," *American Architect and Building News* (December 14, 1889).

27. Letter, A. W. Cobb to W. T. Comstock, January 14, 1890, collection of John Calvin Stevens II, Cape Elizabeth, Maine.

28. Stevens' Romanesque design of 1916 was the Bailey Public Library in Winthrop, which is similar in appearance to the Brown Memorial Library in Clinton.

29. *Industrial Journal* (Bangor, August 11, 1893), p. 8.

30. *Ibid.* (May 19, 1893), p. 2.

31. Stevens and Cobb, *Examples,* p. facing pl. XXXII.

32. Letter, J. H. Stevens to Lucien Libby, March 15, 1915, pp. 2–3, Maine Historical Society, Portland.

33. Letter, F. E. Richards to Arthur Sewall, May 28, 1895, p. 1, collection of John Calvin Stevens II, Cape Elizabeth, Maine.

34. John Calvin Stevens, "Beauty As a Water Works Investment," *Water Works Engineering* (New York, October 23, 1929), p. 1547.

35. Letter, J. C. Stevens to E. F. Lawrence, December 11, 1931, p. 1, collection of John Calvin Stevens II, Cape Elizabeth, Maine.

36. In his discussion of the Portland City Hall, the author wishes to acknowledge his debt to the perceptive description of the building which appears in *Portland, A Publication of Greater Portland Landmarks Incorporated*, Martin Dibner, ed., architectural text by Patricia McGraw Pancoast (Portland, 1972), pp. 212–16.

37. Bruce Price, *A Large Country House* (New York: William T. Comstock, 1886).

38. Russell Sturgis, *The Works of Bruce Price* (New York: The Architectural Record Company, 1889), p. 27.

39. Denys Peter Myers, *Maine Catalog*, Historic American Building Survey (Augusta: The Maine State Museum, 1974), pp. 172–173.

40. *Ibid.*, p. 173.

CHAPTER 5, PART 3

INDUSTRIAL AND
COMMERCIAL ARCHITECTURE

1. See Denys Peter Myers, *Maine Catalog*, Historic American Buildings Survey (Augusta, Me.: Maine State Museum, 1974), pp. 27–28 for the Perkins Grist Mill and John Hancock Warehouse.

2. Frank A. Beard and Earle G. Shettleworth, Jr., in NRHP Nomination, Old Grist Mill, East Lebanon, April 4, 1975.

3. Information concerning Lewiston's development is derived from Richard M. Candee, "The Design of the Mills, the Plan for the City" (typescript of lecture, Lewiston Public Library, 1973); Joseph G. Elder, *History of Lewiston* (Lewiston, Maine, 1882); Eva M. Leitman, "An Historic Perspective of the Franklin Company's Role in the Development of Early Lewiston, Maine" (typescript, Lewiston Public Library, undated); Earle G. Shettleworth, Jr., "Nineteenth Century Lewiston, An Architectural View" (typescript of lecture, Lewiston Public Library, 1973); and Augustus R. Turner, *Souvenir Program of the One Hundredth Anniversary of the City of Lewiston* (Auburn, Maine, 1895).

4. Roger R. Johnson, "Samuel Batchelder, 1784–1879" and "Economic History of Biddeford, Maine" (both typescripts, Biddeford Economic Improvement Commission, 1971).

5. Data on Maine bridges is from the files of the Maine Department of Transportation, Augusta.

6. Tony Paolini, in *Bangor Daily News,* March 23, 1976, p. 17.

7. For a thorough treatment of this subject, see Roger L. Grindle, *Quarry and Kiln: The Story of Maine's Lime Industry* (Rockland: Courier-Gazette, Inc., 1971).

8. Earle G. Shettleworth, Jr., *Maine Historic Resources Inventory* (Augusta, Me.: 1974), p. 117.

9. *Ibid.*, p. 118.

10. *Ibid.*, p. 6.

CHAPTER 6

THE DEVELOPMENT OF MODERN STYLES OF ARCHITECTURE

1. For a description of the genesis in 1931 of the master plan for the Mayflower Hill campus, its actual firm conception in drawings in 1937, and the stages in which the various structures were built (beginning in 1938 and ending in the latter part of the 1950's), see Jens Frederick Larson, "A Thrilling Challenge," *Colby Alumnus* (January, 1954), pp. 6–8.

2. The term "International Style" is a product of the Museum of Modern Art's first architectural exhibition, in which this new style was introduced to the American public; see Henry-Russell Hitchcock and Philip Johnson, *The International Style: Architecture Since 1922* (New York: W. W. Norton & Co., Inc., 1932). The authors referred to the style in lower case letters, but the director of the museum, Alfred H. Barr, Jr., gave European modernism its formal name when he capitalized the term International Style in the preface.

3. As is well known, a depressing sequence of skyscrapers was built along the Avenue of the Americas in the blocks between 50th and 55th Streets, in imitation of the first great New York towers such as Lever House by Skidmore, Owings and Merrill (1951–52) and the United Nations Secretariat by Wallace Harrison and others (1947–50), as well as of the 860 Lake Shore Drive Apartments in Chicago by Mies van der Rohe (1948–51). These lesser buildings, the Time-Life, Equitable Life Assurance and J.C. Penney Buildings, all mundane walls of glass upon thin sticks, had a cheapening effect on the style of the neighborhood, which was only relieved by the construction of the Columbia Broadcasting Building (see p. 235).

4. So prodigious was Kahn's output that no thorough inventory of his work exists. I am indebted to Professor Grant Hildebrand, author of *Designing for Industry, The Architecture of Albert Kahn* (Cambridge, Mass.: The MIT Press, 1974), for his kind letter to me of January 9, 1976. In it, he points out that the American Can Company was a client of the Kahn firm and ventures the opinion that "the odds are" that the Portland building came from its drafting rooms.

5. See Wayne Andrews, *Architecture in New England; A Photographic Survey* (Brattleboro, Vermont: The Stephen Greene Press, 1973), p. 198 below.

CHAPTER 7
THE ARCHITECTURE OF MAINE'S SCHOOLS

1. *Records of the Governor and Company of the Massachusetts Bay in N. E.*, vol. II (Boston: The Press of William White, 1853), Nov. 11, 1647.

2. Kermit S. Nickerson, *150 Years of Education in Maine* (Augusta: State of Maine Department of Education, 1970), p. 8.

3. *Ibid.*, p. 8.

4. *Ibid.*, p. 9.

5. William Corthell, *The Twenty-third Annual Report of the State Superintendent of Common Schools* (Augusta: Sprague, Owen, and Nash, 1877), p. 15.

6. John D. Bardwell in NRHP nomination, Old Schoolhouse, York, Aug. 8, 1972.

7. Earle G. Shettleworth, Jr. and Frank A. Beard in NRHP nomination, Alna School, April 4, 1975.

8. Frank A. Beard and Earle G. Shettleworth, Jr. in NRHP nomination, Day's Ferry Historic District, Aug. 29, 1974.

9. Ava Chadbourne, *History of Maine Education* (Lancaster, Pa., 1936), pp. 112–113 (hereafter cited as Chadbourne, *History*).

10. Josiah Pierce, *History of Gorham, Maine* (Portland, Maine: Foster & Cushing, 1862), p. 164.

11. Ruth Arline Wray, "History of Secondary Education in Cumberland and Sagadahoc Counties," *The Maine Bulletin*, XLIII, No. 1 (August, 1940), p. 28.

12. Denys Peter Myers, *Maine Catalog* (Augusta, 1974), pp. 59–60.

13. *Ibid.*, p. 60.

14. According to a copy of the deed dated 12 October 1833 and witnessed the following April, provided kindly by Mrs. Ruth G. Bennock, Registrar of Deeds of Hancock County, these two buildings should be dated in 1834–35 (clapboard), and 1837–38 (brick). This information contradicts that given in the *Maine Historic Resources Inventory* (Augusta, Maine, revised ed., 1975), p. 80. It now appears from a conversation with Earle G. Shettleworth, Jr. that the late date given one of these buildings in the *Inventory* is an error resulting from a mistaken notation of information. This mistake will be corrected in the forthcoming 1976 edition of the *Maine Historic Resources Inventory*.

15. Earle G. Shettleworth, Jr., *Maine Historic Preservation Commission Inventory, 1974* (Augusta, 1974), p. 85 (hereafter cited as Shettleworth, *Inventory*).

16. *Ibid.*, p. 77.

17. Mary Ellen Chase, *A Goodly Heritage* (New York: Henry Holt and Co., 1932), p. 267.

18. Shettleworth, *Inventory*, p. 85.

19. *Ibid.*, p. 82.

20. *Ibid.*, p. 82.

21. *Ibid.*, p. 81.

22. Ben Butler, Natalie Butler and Donald W. McKeen, *Zephaniah Builds a Schoolhouse—Among Other Things* (Farmington, Maine, 1975), p. 64.

23. Henry Barnard, *School Architecture or Contributions to the Improvement of School-Houses in the United States,* 2nd ed. (New York, 1849), p. 6.

24. Chadbourne, *History*, pp. 164–165.

25. Shettleworth in NRHP nomination, New Gloucester Historic District, June, 1974.

26. Chadbourne, *History*, pp. 324–326.

27. *Public Laws of Maine*, 1909, Chap. 88, Sec. 1.

28. "Learning Center at Kent's Hill," *Maine Architecture and Construction,* 1, No. 3, (July/August 1968), p. 11.

29. "Topsham's Octagonal School," *Maine Architecture and Construction,* 1, No. 4, (Sept./Oct. 1968), pp. 8–10.

30. Kevin Ryan and James M. Cooper, *Those Who Can, Teach* (Boston, 1972), pp. 470–471.

CHAPTER 8

MAINE LANDSCAPES

1. Bar Harbor was named "Eden" until 1918; see Samuel Eliot Morrison, *The Story of Mount Desert Island* (Boston, 1960), p. 77.

2. The sensitive and dramatic siting of Maine towns is a key to its landscape beauty and variety; for example, Lubec, perched above contending tides, is a white-clapboard version of Mont-Saint-Michel.

3. If the cause of this exclusive preference is baffling, the results of establishing a street-tree monoculture are disastrous. Countless American Main Streets in the East and Mid-West have been denuded by the Dutch elm disease. This generation, with its sadly gained foresight, should match the great planting effort of the past but with diversity in its choice of species.

4. A row of carriage sheds is adjacent to the South Congregational Church, Kennebunkport (1824).

5. Denys Peter Myers, *Maine Catalog*, Historic American Buildings Survey (Augusta, Me.: Maine State Museum, 1974), pp. 66–67.

6. Warren Manning was a founder of the American Society of Landscape Architects.

7. *Portland, A Publication of Greater Portland Landmarks Incorporated,* Martin Dibner, ed., architectural text by Patricia McGraw Pancoast (Portland, 1972), p. 217 (hereafter cited as Dibner/Pancoast, *Portland*).

8. Frank A. Beard and Earle G. Shettleworth, Jr., in NRHP Nomination, Mount Hope Cemetery District, December 4, 1974. Information was also kindly provided by H. S. Burrill, Jr.

9. Earle G. Shettleworth, Jr., "Developers Plotted Facets of Boston for Frontier City," *Bangor Daily News*, September 22, 1975, p. 13.

10. Pancoast in Dibner/Pancoast, *Portland*, p. 101 makes interesting comments on the interplay of materials and details in the townscape.

11. Professor Charles Beveridge, who with Professor Charles McLaughlin, is preparing Olmsted's papers for publication, kindly provided information about an interesting correspondence between Olmsted and Sara Orne Jewett relating to this project; he also gave details regarding Olmsted's post-Civil War mood.

12. See Charles Eliot, *Charles Eliot, Landscape Architect* (Cambridge, Mass., 1902), pp. 308–15, for poetic and far-sighted impressions of the Maine coast.

13. According to Roderick Nash, *Wilderness and the American Mind* (New Haven, 1969), p. 91, "The wilderness of Maine shocked Thoreau. . . ."

14. *Ibid.*, pp. 141–42, an account of Joseph Knowles' trip as "Adam" in the Maine backwoods in 1911, and the resultant furor.

15. Poland Spring House, built in 1876, had three lakes, greenhouses, acres of gardens, cottages, a golf course, a sewage plant, etc.

16. Hancock Point (a village resort developed by several professors at the turn of the century), in achieving all the comforts and style of Bar Harbor without its absurd extravagance, is a distillation of these validities.

17. Richard Saltonstall, Jr., *Maine Pilgrimage* (Boston, 1974), p. 58 (hereafter cited as Saltonstall, *Maine*).

18. Much material relating to Beatrix Farrand was courteously provided by Mr. Robert Patterson, Mr. Charles Savage, and particularly by Mrs. W. B. Dickson Stroud, whose personal recollections proved invaluable.

19. Capability Brown's reply to the query, "When would he do Ireland?" was supposed to have been, "I haven't finished England yet!" referring to his re-design of its landscapes.

20. All information, letters, obituaries and recollections relating to Hans Heistad were provided through the courtesy of his daughter, Mrs. G. H. Kononen.

21. This unique beach house should be restored and could serve surrounding communities as a focus for activities relating to the incomparable site (a hilltop meadow, only briefly utilized for blueberry harvesting).

22. See Paul Shepard, *Man in the Landscape* (New York, 1967), pp. 117–18 for a celebration of the garden.

23. Since the Kebo Valley Club was founded in Mount Desert Island in 1887, one hundred courses have been built; with summer camps and ski resorts, they account for a considerable amount of landscaped open space in the state.

24. Many came from the liquidation of the Bar Harbor Nursery stock. This firm was one of the few commercial growers in Maine, though the industry has recently become more active.

25. Dr. Clapp is credited with introducing several hardy species to Maine, expanding the palette of designers (largely restricted to the spruce-hardwood association plants). These introductions include the redbud, katsura tree, carolina hemlock, Japanese dogwood, red pine, metasequoia, and various lindens.

26. Designs for Maine projects include those by: Clarke and Rapuano (New York City) for Gould Academy; Sasaki Associates (Watertown, Massachusetts) for the Maine Way Development in Portland; The Architects Collaborative (Cambridge, Massachusetts) for Maine National Bank Plaza in Portland; Myron Lamb (Limerick, Maine) for Brooklawn Memorial Park, Portland; Wolcott Andrews (Wiscasset, Maine) for Lincoln County Courthouse, Wiscasset; and Moriece and Gary (Portland, Maine) for the Westbrook Urban Renewal Project.

27. According to Elmer Crockett, Mrs. Bok stipulated that the work be accomplished with horse-drawn equipment and ordinary workingmen's tools, to insure the hiring of local crews.

28. Fletcher Steele was the designer of "Naumkeag," one of America's most celebrated gardens, at Stockbridge, Massachusetts.

29. See Ralph H. Hayden, "Ladies and Libraries" (typescript, Camden Library, 1931 [?]), p. 6, who quotes from Mrs. Bok's dedication.

30. Dibner/Pancoast, *Portland*, p. 101.

31. For a discussion of Portland's ambiance and factors (natural and planned) which might limit urban sprawl, see Saltonstall, *Maine*, pp. 233–34.

32. The Beaver Cove second-home development at Moosehead is one of the few developments designed by landscape architects, Moriece and Gary of Portland.

33. Snowmobiles, now numbering more than 70,000 in the state, have no place in a park which is to "forever be left in its natural wild state and forever kept as a sanctuary for wild beasts and birds," as Baxter stipulated.

34. Cleveland Amory, *The Last Resorts* (New York, 1952), p. 328.

35. Saltonstall, *Maine*, p. 208.

36. *Ibid., passim*.

37. These regulations have involved critical areas such as land within 250 feet of any shoreline; "wild lands," dividing these into protection, management and development districts, under the administration of a Land Use Regulation Commission; and all new "developments" exceeding twenty acres, which are placed under the jurisdiction of a Board of Environmental Protection.

38. The extensive and beautiful interior wood work for Louis Kahn's distinguished Exeter Academy Library (1970) was executed by a Maine firm whose grateful

owner transported his factory force to New Hampshire to see their work after its installation.

39. E. F. Schumacher, *Small is Beautiful* (New York, 1973), *passim*. Sophisticated technologies, largely unworkable in the "third world," may also be undesirable for Maine. This is an inspired discussion of alternative choices for development.

Glossary

This Glossary includes architectural terms that may be unfamiliar to some readers. Terms of the kind that are in normal common usage, eg., roof, banister, shutter, have been omitted. The editor is grateful to Denys Peter Myers, William B. Miller and Richard M. Candee for contributing most of the following definitions.

Abacus	The uppermost member of division of a capital.
Acroterion	An upright ornament placed above the apex or at the outer edge of a pediment.
Amphiprostyle	Having columns in front of both ends.
Anta	A pier that constitutes one boundary of a porch.
Antefix	An upright ornament along the eaves of a roof.
Anthemion	A symmetrical pattern of honeysuckle or palm leaves in a radiating cluster.
Architrave	The molding around a door or window. The lowest of the three elements composing an entablature.
Ashlar	Masonry composed of squared blocks of stones.
Attic	A low wall or story above the cornice of a facade.
Balloon frame	A frame composed of numerous light studs nailed to horizontal sills and plates.
Baluster	A small column; in a series called a balustrade, supporting a handrail or coping.
Bargeboard	A board, often carved or ornamentally cut, attached along the edge of a gable roof.
Barrel vault	Ceiling cover of semi-circular section.
Batter	A slope, as of the outer side of a wall, that recedes from bottom to top.
Bay	A portion of wall containing a door or window, or a section of wall marked off by vertical elements.
Beading	A narrow, half-rounded molding. Any narrow strip of trimming.
Belt course	A continuous projecting horizontal element marking the division between stories.
Berm	A narrow shelf or path along the top of a bank.
Block work	Wood scored or cut to resemble masonry.
Board and batten siding	Exterior sheathing composed of vertical boards with their joints covered by narrow vertical strips of wood.
Bolection molding	A molding of unusually large and broad convex projection often used to cover the joint between different surface levels.

Bracket	A projecting member, generally formed of scroll shapes, supporting an overhang. When used to support a cornice, called Console or Modillion.
Broken pediment	A pediment whose slopes are not continued upward until they meet at the apex.
Buttress	A stabilizing mass of masonry resisting outward pressures from vaults and walls.
Cavetto cornice	A cornice with a concave soffit, Egyptian in origin. A large molding of ninety-degree concave curve from vertical wall to horizontal overhang.
Cella	The enclosed rectangular core of a Greek or Roman temple.
Chamfer	A diagonal cut or bevel.
Chancel	The section of a church reserved for altar, clergy and choir.
Chimney girt	A horizontal member spanning between front and rear posts and beside a chimney stack; it supports either a summer beam or the ends of the floor joists.
Clerestory	The windowed upper portion of a wall or construction used for light and ventilation.
Closed string	Stairs in which a slanted board conceals the ends of the steps.
Coffer	A decorative sunken panel in a soffit, ceiling, dome or vault.
Collar beam	A horizontal tie between opposite roof rafters.
Colossal order	An order whose columns rise the full height of a facade wall that is more than one story high.
Common bond	Brick laid up with headers only every seven or so courses.
Composition	A hard material consisting of resin, whiting and glue, premolded into mantelpieces, cornices, architraves, etc., often of imported origin. Sometimes called "compo" or "London putty."
Console	A decorative bracket, often of elongated S-shape.
Corinthian order	The most ornate of the three classical orders of architecture, characterized by a slender fluted column having an elaborate bell-shaped capital decorated with acanthus leaves.
Cornice	A horizontal or sloping molded projection crowning a building or wall. The molding where the walls and ceiling of a room join.
Cove	A curved surface forming a junction between a ceiling and wall. A concave molding.
Crenelated	Having open spaces at regular intervals; or decorative trim of battlement form.
Cross gable roof	A roof having three or more gables so that their ridges meet at the center to form a T or a cross.
Crosset	A projection at the corner of an architrave or panel.
Cupola	A small decorative structure at the top of a building.
Dentil	One of a series of small rectangular, tooth-like, blocks forming a molding or projecting beneath a cornice.
Denticulated	Having dentils.
Distyle	Having two columns.
Distyle in antis	Having two columns between antae.
Doric order	The oldest and simplest of the three classical orders of architecture, char-

acterized (in its Greek form) by heavy fluted columns with plain saucer-shaped capitals and no bases.

Dormer	A window unit inserted into, and usually projecting from, a sloping roof.
Dovetail	A woodworking joint tapered along one or more sides.
Drip stone or drip molding	A projecting molding over an arch or opening; also known as hood molding.
Ear	A projection at the corner of an architrave or panel.
Egg and dart	A decorative molding composed of alternating egg-shaped and dart-like forms in a continuous row.
Entablature	The upper section of a classical order, composed of architrave, frieze, and cornice.
Entablature block	A discontinuous section of an entablature.
Entasis	Swelling or convexity in the shaft of a column or at the outer edges of a pilaster.
Fan	A semi-circular or elliptical wooden panel, usually louvered, over a front door.
Fan-light	A semi-circular or elliptical window over a front door.
Fielded panel	A panel whose surface projects to or beyond the plane of its stiles.
Flanker	An outbuilding (usually one of a pair) attached to, or flanking the side of a main block.
Flemish bond	Bricks laid in rows of alternating headers and stretchers.
Flute	One of a series of long parallel grooves, usually with rounded inner surfaces, incised on the shaft of a column.
Flying staircase	Stairs of which the principal flight (to a landing) is freestanding.
Frieze	A plain or decorated horizontal band between the architrave and cornice of an entablature.
Gable	The triangular upper portion of an end wall to carry a pitched roof.
Gambrel roof	A ridged roof having two slopes on each of its two long sides, the lower slopes have the steeper pitch.
Garrison	A building in which soldiers or militia are housed. Colloquially, a domestic building improved for defense by its inhabitants.
Gazebo	A small open garden house, usually of ornate design; sometimes called summer house.
Gravel stop	Metal flashing attached to a roof to protect its edge from water penetration, and to prevent its gravel surface from falling over its edge.
Gutta	One of a series of small peg-shaped ornaments below the metopes of a Doric entablature.
Half timber	Construction which exposes wooden members, with the interspaces filled and plastered.
Hammerbeam	The joining of exposed beams to form a truss.
Hexastyle	Having six columns.
Hip	The external angle formed by the meeting of two adjacent slopes of a roof.
Hip roof	A roof having four sides of equal slope.
Howe truss	A wooden bridge truss with single diagonals extending across two panels

	and vertical wrought-iron tension members. First patented by William Howe in 1840.
Ionic order	An order of classical architecture characterized by column capitals with opposed volutes.
Jetty	An overhanging storied wall of a building.
Joists	Horizontal timbers laid parallel between summer beam and plates or between spanning beam and girts to support the boards of a floor.
Keyblock	A wooden ornament in the shape of a keystone at the top of an arch or in the middle of a flat arch.
Keystone	The central wedge-shaped stone of an arch that locks the others together.
Lancet window	A tall narrow window terminating in a pointed arch; associated with the Gothic Revival.
Lappet	When used as eaves trim, one of a series of wooden flap-shaped pendants.
Light	Something that admits light. A pane of glass.
Long truss	A wooden truss with two diagonals in each panel and a king (A-form) truss over the center panels. First patented by Stephen H. Long in 1830.
Mansard roof	A roof having two slopes on all four sides, with the lower slope steeper than the upper one. Frequently associated with the Second Empire style of French origin.
Module	The size of a selected part of a structure by which the other parts are determined; used as a basis to standardize or govern the design of a part of a building.
Meander pattern	The Greek fret or key pattern, deriving its name from Maiandros, a Phrygian river noted for its windings.
Metope	One of the spaces between the triglyphs of a Doric frieze.
Modillion	An ornamental bracket used in series under the cornice of the Corinthian, Composite or Roman Ionic orders.
Monitor	A raised portion of a roof with windows along its sides.
Mortise	A cavity, usually rectangular, prepared to receive a similarly shaped projection, or tenon, to fasten two structural elements together.
Obelisk	A single squared and tapering shaft, ending in a pyramid point; Egyptian in origin.
Octastyle	Having eight columns.
Ogee	A double curve in the shape of a very elongated S. An arch with two such curves meeting in a point.
Open string	Stairs in which the stringpiece, or slanted support, does not conceal the ends of the steps.
Paddleford truss	A wooden Long truss without the central king (A-form) truss.
Palladian window	A unit composed of an arched window flanked by narrow vertical rectangular windows, derived from a motif much used by the Italian architect Andrea Palladio (1518–1580).
Pantheon dome	A low saucer-shaped dome with a stepped base like that of the Roman Pantheon.
Parapet	A low protective wall or railing along the edge of a roof, balcony, or similar structure.

Patera	A circular floriform ornament; a rosette.
Pavilion	A section of a building projecting beyond the plane of the main mass.
Pediment	A broad triangular gable bounded by an entablature cornice and the raking cornices of the roof.
Pent roof	A narrow roof with a single slope at approximately second-floor level.
Pentastyle	Having five columns.
Peripteral	Having columns on all four sides.
Piazza	Roofed but open appendage to the side of a house.
Pier	A square or rectangular pillar; a vertical supporting member.
Pilaster	A shallow rectangular column with capital and base set against a wall.
Pilaster respond	A pilaster placed directly to the rear of a column.
Pilaster strip	A projecting pilaster-like element lacking capital and base.
Plate	The horizontal timber capping exterior studs and posts as well as supporting the rafters.
Plinth	A block or slab (or its imitation in wood) serving as the pedestal for an architectural element or ornament.
Podium	A wall or block serving as the base to support an architectural element.
Portico	A porch-like appendage usually at the front of a building; it consists of its own roof and supports.
Prostyle	Having columns across the front only.
Pseudo-peripteral	Having columns partially along each side to give the effect of a peripteral building.
Pulvinated frieze	A frieze having a convex or cushion-like, profile.
Purlin	Horizontal member(s) of the roof parallel with the plate, supported by principal rafters and supporting either common rafters or vertical roofing boards.
Pylon	Large gateway to an Egyptian temple.
Quoin	A stone (or its imitation in wood) marking the corner of a building. When superposed, quoins form a pattern of alternating long and short blocks.
Rafter	One of a pair of roof timbers sloping from the wall plate to the ridge.
Raking cornice	A slanting cornice, as over a gable or pediment.
Reveal	The side of an opening within the depth of a wall, or the depth from the inner face of a chimney up to the wall plane.
Ribbon bracket	A small, thin bracket of C-scroll shape set in close series under a cornice.
Ridge	The horizontal line formed by the junctions of two rafters, sometimes joined by a horizontal member termed a ridge pole.
Rosette	A boss or knob carved in the shape of a flower.
Rustication	Masonry with the blocks beveled at the edges to accentuate the joints, or a wooden imitation of such masonry.
Segmental arch	A low arch formed by the arc of a curve subtended by a chord.
Shiplap	Wooden sheathing in which the boards are joined (by rabbeting) so that the lower edge overlaps the upper edge of the next.
Soffit	The underside of a structural component such as a beam, arch, staircase, cornice, or lintel.

Spandrel	The triangular space between the left or right exterior curve of an arch and the rectangular framework surrounding it.
Spanning beam	An intermediate horizontal timber between girts, often acting as a summer beam or a tie-beam between rafters at their base.
Stop flute	A flute with the bottom third or so filled in.
String course	An element like a belt course, but thinner.
Stripped classic	Architecture that adheres to classical proportions but eliminates details such as capitals and bases.
Stud	An intermediate vertical member of a wooden frame.
Summer beam	An intermediate horizontal spanning timber supporting the ends of joists.
Swan's neck pediment	A broken pediment the right and left portions of which have elongated S-curve outlines.
Tenon	A projection on the end of a timber shaped for insertion into a mortise.
Tetrastyle	Having four columns.
Trabeated	Having horizontal beams or lintels rather than arches.
Transom	A small rectangular window above a door. Colonial and Greek Revival entrance transoms were fixed, not hinged.
Treenail	A wooden peg which swells when wet, used to fasten timbers at mortise and tenon joints.
Triglyph	An ornament in a Doric frieze composed of a projecting block having three parallel vertical channels on its face.
Tudor arch	An arch of rather flat curve.
Wainscot	The paneling of an interior wall, often referring only to the lower quarter or third of a wall.

Abbreviations and Selected Bibliography

Abbreviations and general works useful in all periods

Antiques = *The Magazine Antiques*

Dibner/Pancoast, *Portland* = *Portland, A Publication of Greater Portland Landmarks Incorporated*, Dibner, Martin, ed.; architectural text by Pancoast, Patricia McGraw; historical text by Demar, Josephine H. Portland, 1972.

Green, Samuel M. *Exhibition of Maine Architecture from the 17th Century to the Civil War*. [catalog] Waterville: Art Department of Colby College, [1945].

Hitchcock, Henry-Russell. *American Architectural Books*. Minneapolis: University of Minnesota Press, 1946 and 1962.

Hitchcock, Henry-Russell. *Architecture—Nineteenth and Twentieth Centuries*. Baltimore, Md.: Penguin Books, 1958.

Isaacson, Dorris, ed. *Maine—A Guide 'Down East'*. Rockland, Maine: Courier-Gazette, Inc., 1970.

Myers, *Maine Catalog* = Myers, Denys Peter. *Maine Catalog*, Historic American Buildings Survey. Augusta, Maine: Maine State Museum, 1974.

NRHP Nomination = National Register of Historic Places, Nomination forms. On file in Washington, D.C. and at the Maine Historic Preservation Commission, Augusta.

OTNE = Old-Time New England

Shettleworth, *Bangor Inventory* = Shettleworth, Earle G., Jr. *Bangor Historic Resources Inventory*. Augusta: Maine Historic Preservation Commission, 1975.

Shettleworth, *Maine Inventory* = Shettleworth, Earle G., Jr. *Maine Historic Resources Inventory*. Augusta: Maine Historic Preservation Commission, 1974.

Shettleworth, Earle G., Jr. *The Builder's Guide—an Exhibition of Architectural Books, 1554–1920*. [catalogue] Waterville; Colby College Art Museum, 1969.

Whiffen, Marcus. *American Architecture Since 1780. A Guide to the Styles*. Cambridge; M.I.T. Press, 1969.

Chapter 1. The Earliest Settlements

Biggar, H. P., ed. *The Voyages of the Sieur de Champlain, Book I: Acadia and New England.* Vol. 1. Toronto: The Champlain Society, 1922.

Bourque, Bruce. "Comments on the Late Archaic Population of Central Maine." *Arctic Anthropology*, XII, No. 2 (1976), pp. 35-45.

Brasser, T. J. C. "Group Identification Along a Moving Frontier." In *Proceedings of the 38th International Congress of Americanists.* Vol. 2, p. 262. Stuttgart-München, 1968.

Davis, Ronald B.; Bradstreet, Theodore E.; Stuckenrath, Robert Jr.; and Borns, Harold W. Jr. "Vegetation and Associated Environments During the Past 14,000 Years Near Moulton Pond, Maine." *Quaternary Research*, 5 (1975), pp. 435-465.

Kingsbury, Isaac and Hadlock, Wendell S. "An Early Occupation Site, Eastport, Maine." *Massachusetts Archaeological Society Bulletin*, XII, No. 2 (1951), pp. 22-26.

MacDonald, George F. "Debert: A Palaeo-Indian Site in Central Nova Scotia." *Anthropology Papers*, No. 16. Ottawa: National Museums of Canada, 1968.

Ritchie, William A. *The Archaeology of New York State.* New York: Natural History Press, 1965.

Sanger, David. "Prehistory of Passamaquoddy Bay: A Summary." *Bulletin of the Maine Archaeological Society*, 11, No. 22 (1971), pp. 14-19.

Sanger, David. "Cow Point: An Archaic Cemetery in New Brunswick." *Mercury Series*, No. 12. Ottawa: National Museums of Canada, 1973.

Sanger, David. "Culture Change as an Adaptive Process in the Maine-Maritimes Region." *Arctic Anthropology*, XII, No. 2 (1976), pp. 60-75.

Sanger, David and MacKay, Robert G. "The Hirundo Archaeological Project: Preliminary Report." *Man in the Northeast*, No. 6 (1973), pp. 21-29.

Thwaites, R., ed. "Lettre du P. Biard." In *Travels and Explorations of the Jesuit Missionaries in New France*, p. 41. Cleveland, 1896.

Chapter 2. The Architecture of Maine's Settlement

Augusta. Maine State Archives. Twinbly, Ida F., compiler. "Typescript of the Early Town Records of Biddeford from 1653 to 1733." Microfilm. Augusta, 1906.

Banks, Charles E. *History of York, Maine,* 3 vols. reprinted in 2. Baltimore, Md.: Regional Publishing Co., 1967.

Banks, Charles E. "New Documents Relating to the Popham Expedition, 1607." *Proceedings of the American Antiquarian Society*, N.S. 30, Part I (1929), pp. 309-15.

Baxter, James Phinney. *Sir Ferdinando Gorges and His Province of Maine*, vol. II. Boston, 1890.

Baxter, James Phinney, ed. *The Trelawney Papers*. Documentary History of the State of Maine, vol. III. Portland, 1884.

Bourne, Edward Emerson. "Garrison Houses, York County." *Collections of the Maine Historical Society*, vol. VII. Bath, Maine, 1876, pp. 111–113.

Candee, Richard M. "A Documentary History of Plymouth Colony Architecture, Part III." *OTNE*, LX, No. 2 (Fall, 1969), pp. 37–53.

Candee, Richard M. "Merchant and Millwright." *OTNE*, LX, No. 4 (Spring, 1970), pp. 131–149.

Carey, George. "Fort St. George Historical Research." Unpublished report for the Maine State Parks and Recreation Department, 1966.

Carroll, Charles F. *The Timber Economy of Puritan New England*. Providence: Brown University Press, 1973.

Documentary History of the State of Maine, vol. V, Baxter, James Phinney, ed. Portland: Maine Historical Society, 1897.

Dunnack, Henry E. *Maine Forts*. Augusta, Maine, 1924.

Farries, K. G. and Mason, M. T. *The Windmills of Surrey and Inner London*. London, 1966.

Forman, Benno M. "Mill Sawing in Seventeenth Century Massachusetts." *OTNE*, LX, No. 4 (Spring, 1970), pp. 110–130.

Exeter City Library, Devonshire, England. Thomas Gorges Manuscript Notebooks. Typescript by Robert E. Moody.

Hadlock, Wendell S. "Recent Excavations at DeMont's Colony, St. Croix Island, Maine." *OTNE*, XLIV, No. 4 (Spring, 1954), pp. 93–99.

Harrington, J. C. "Preliminary Archaeological Explorations on St. Croix Island, Maine." Typescript report and evaluation, National Park Service, North East Region, Philadelphia, Pa., July 30, 1951.

Hubbard, William. *A Narrative of the Indian Wars in New England. . . .* Worcester, Mass., 1801.

Lane, Gardiner. "An Archaeological Report on Excavations Carried Out at Sabino Head in Popham Beach, Maine—The Site of Fort St. George 1607–1608 A.D." Unpublished report for the Maine State Parks and Recreation Department, 1966.

Eliot, Maine. Collection of Joseph W. P. Frost. Daybook and ledger of William Pepperrell, Sr. and Jr., 1717–1721.

Provincial and Court Records of Maine, 4 vols. Portland, Maine, 1932–1964.

Provincial Papers of New Hampshire, 9 vols. Concord, New Hampshire, 1867–76.

Records and Files of the Quarterly Courts of Essex County, Massachusetts, vol. I. Salem, Massachusetts, 1911.

Riley, Edward M. "Brief History of Saint Croix Island." Typescript, National Park Service, North East Regional Office, Philadelphia, Pa.

Savage, James, ed. *History of New England, 1630–1649*, vol. I. [Contains journal of John Winthrop.] Boston: Phelps & Farnham, 1825.

"The Diary of Samuel Sewall, 1674–1700." *Collections of the Massachusetts Historical Society*, vol. V. Boston, 1886.

Shurtleff, Harold. *The Log Cabin Myth*. Reprint. Gloucester, Mass. 1967.

Thayer, Henry O., ed. *The Sagadahoc Colony, Comprising the Relation of a Voyage to New England. . . .* Portland, Maine, 1892.

Williamson, W. D. *History of the State of Maine*, vol. II. Hallowell, Maine, 1832

Winterthur, Delaware. Henry F. DuPont Winterthur Museum. Joseph Downs Manuscript and Microfilm Collection. Building contract between Francis Moore, John Watts and Edward Hutchinson, March 23, 1714/15.

York. *Deeds*, 10 vols. Portland, Maine, 1887–94.

Chapter 3.   Colonial Architecture

Connally, Ernest Allen. "The Cape Cod House: an Introductory Study." *Journal of the Society of Architectural Historians*, XIX, No. 2 (1960), pp. 47–56.

Cummings, Abbott Lowell. *Architecture in Early New England*. Sturbridge, Massachusetts: Old Sturbridge Village, [1974].

Glassie, Henry. *Pattern in the Material Folk Culture of the Eastern United States*. Philadelphia: University of Pennsylvania Press, 1969.

Howells, John Mead. *The Architectural Heritage of the Piscataqua*. New York: Architectural Book Publishing Company, [1937].

Keune, Russell V. and Replogle, James. "Two Maine Farmhouses." *Journal of the Society of Architectural Historians*, XX, No. 1 (1961), pp. 38–39.

Park, Helen. "A List of Architectural Books Available in America before the Revolution." *Journal of the Society of Architectural Historians*, XX, No. 3 (1961), pp. 115–130.

Strawberry Banke, Inc. *Architecture Near the Piscataqua*. Portsmouth, 1964.

Chapter 4, Part 1.   The Federal Style

Benjamin, Asher. *The American Builder's Companion. . . .* Boston: Etheridge and Bliss, 1806.

Elwell, Edward H. *Portland and Vicinity*. Portland: W. S. Jones and Loring, Short and Harmon, 1876. Reprint ed., Greater Portland Landmarks, Inc., 1975.

Kimball, Fiske. *Domestic Architecture of the American Colonies and of the Early Republic*. New York: Charles Scribner's Sons, 1922. Reprint ed., Dover Publications, 1966.

Kirker, Harold. *The Architecture of Charles Bulfinch*. Cambridge, Mass.: Harvard University Press, 1969.

Pain, William. *The Practical House Carpenter. . . .* Boston: William Norman, 1796.

Pierson, William H. *American Buildings and Their Architects*. Vol. I. The Colonial and Neoclassical Style. New York: Doubleday, 1970.

Shipman, William D. *The Early Architecture of Bowdoin College and Brunswick, Maine.* Brunswick, Maine: Brunswick Publishing Co., 1973.

Work Projects Administration. Federal Writer's Program. *Portland City Guide.* Portland: Forest City Printing Company, 1940.

Chapter 4, Part 2.   The Greek Revival

Benjamin, Asher. *The Builder's Guide.* . . . Boston: Perkins & Marvin, 1839.

Benjamin, Asher. *The Practical House Carpenter.* . . . Boston: R. P. & C. Williams and Annin & Smith, 1830.

Benjamin, Asher. *The Practice of Architecture.* . . . Boston: The author and Carter, Hendie & Co., 1833.

Dictionary of American Biography. New York: Charles Scribner's Sons, 1928– , vol. XIV, pp. 254–55.

[Eliot, William Havard]. *A Description of Tremont House.* Boston: Gray & Bowen, 1830.

Work Projects Administration. Federal Writer's Project. *Portland City Guide.* Portland: Forest City Printing Company, 1940.

Fowler, Orson Squire. *A Home for All; or, The Gravel Wall and Octagonal Mode of Building.* New York: Fowler and Wells, 1848.

Green, Samuel M. "The Architecture of Thomaston, Maine." *Journal of the Society of Architectural Historians,* X, No. 4 (1951), pp. 24–32.

Green, Samuel M. "Thomas Lord, Joiner and Housewright." *Magazine of Art,* 40, No. 6 (October, 1947), pp. 230–35.

Hamlin, Talbot [Faulkner]. *Greek Revival Architecture in America.* New York: Oxford University Press, 1944.

Hills, Chester. *The Builder's Guide.* . . . Hartford: D. W. Kellogg & Co., 1834.

A History of Public Buildings Under the Control of the Treasure Department. Washington: Government Printing Office, 1901.

Kirker, Harold. *The Architecture of Charles Bulfinch.* Cambridge, Mass.: Harvard University Press, 1969.

McLanathan, Richard B. K. "Bulfinch's Drawings for the Maine State House." *Journal of the Society of Architectural Historians,* XIV, No. 2 (1955), pp. 12–17.

Morrison, John H. *History of American Steam Navigation.* New York: Stephen Daye Press, [1958].

New York. Columbia University, Avery Architectural Library. Rogers, Isaiah. Diaries, manuscripts.

Retting, Robert Bell. *Guide to Cambridge Architecture: Ten Walking Tours.* Cambridge: MIT Press, [1969].

Schmidt, Carl F. *The Octagon Fad.* [Scottsville, N.Y.: Carl F. Schmidt], 1958.

Shaw, Edward. *Civil Architecture.* . . . Boston: Shaw and Stratton, 1830.

Shaw, Edward. *Rural Architecture.* . . . Boston: James B. Dow, 1843.

Shettleworth, Earle G., Jr. "Benjamin Dean imprinted his design on city." *Bangor Daily News*, September 15, 1975, p. 15.

Shettleworth, Earle G., Jr. "Greek Temple Style Survives here in Art School, Funeral Home." *Evening Express* (Portland, Maine), August 14, 1965.

Shettleworth, Earle G., Jr. "A Mark Upon the Land—The Life and Work of Charles D. Lawrence, A Mid-Nineteenth-Century, Fairfield, Maine, Builder." *OTNE*, LVIII, No. 2 (Fall, 1967), pp. 31–48.

Shettleworth, Earle G., Jr. "Pond designs in 1830's left mark on Bangor." *Bangor Daily News*, November 24, 1975, p. 19.

Smith, Oliver P. *The Domestic Architect: Comprising a Series of Original Designs for Rural and Ornamental Cottages. . . .* Buffalo: Derby & Co., 1852.

Smith, Philip Chadwick Foster. "The Metamorphosis of East India Marine Hall." *Historic Preservation*, 27, No. 4 (October-December, 1975), pp. 10–13.

Thompson, Slason. *A Short History of American Railways*. Addendum B. Chicago: Bureau of Railway News and Statistics, 1925.

Upjohn, Everard M. *Richard Upjohn, Architect and Churchman*. New York: Columbia University Press, 1939.

[Vickery, James B.] *An Illustrated History of the City of Bangor, Maine 1769–1969*. Bangor, 1969.

Chapter 4, Part 3   The Architecture of the Maine Shakers

Andrews, Edward Deming. *The People Called Shakers*, revised ed. New York: Dover Publications, 1963.

Dodd, Eugene M. "Functionalism in Shaker Crafts." *Antiques*, XCVIII, No. 4 (October, 1970), pp. 588–93.

Hopping, D.M.C. and Watland, Gerald R. "The Architecture of the Shakers." *Antiques*, LXXII, No. 4 (October, 1957), pp. 335–39.

Johnson, Theodore, E. *Hands to Work and Hearts to God: The Shaker Tradition in Maine*. Brunswick: Bowdoin College Museum of Art, 1969.

"A Note from the Shaker Parent Ministry." *The World of Shaker*, IV, No. 2 (Summer, 1974), p. 3.

Péladeau, Marius B. "The Shaker Meetinghouses of Moses Johnson." *Antiques*, XCVIII, No. 4 (October, 1970), pp. 594–99.

Péladeau, Marius B. "The Shakers of Maine." *Antiques*, CVII, No. 6 (June, 1975), pp. 1144–53.

Chapter 5, Part 1.   Revival Styles of Maine Architecture

Anthony, Alfred Williams. *Bates College and Its Background*. Philadelphia, 1936.

Clark, Kenneth. *The Gothic Revival*. London, 1928.

Clifford, Angela Godfrey. *Cliff Cottage, 1847–1947.* Bangor, Maine, 1947.

Downing, Andrew Jackson. *The Architecture of Country Houses.* New York: D. Appleton & Co., 1850.

Drisko, George W. *History of Machias.* Machias, Maine, 1904.

Elwell, Edward H. *Portland and Vicinity.* Portland: W. S. Jones and Loring, Short and Harmon, 1876.

Fitch, James Marston. *American Building—The Historical Forces That Shaped It,* 2nd ed. Boston, 1966.

Gardiner, Robert Hallowell. *Early Recollections of Robert Hallowell Gardiner, 1782–1864,* Robert Hallowell Gardiner, II, ed. Hallowell, 1936.

Gillon, Edmund V. Jr. and Lancaster, Clay. *Victorian Houses—A Treasury of Lesser-Known Examples.* New York: Dover Publications, 1973.

Greason, Polly [Mrs. A. L.]. "The Johnson House." Unpublished paper, University of Maine, Portland-Gorham, 1974. On file at Historic Preservation Commission, Augusta.

Greenough, Horatio. *Form and Function,* Harold A. Small, ed. Berkeley, California, 1947.

Hamlin, Talbot Faulkner. *Benjamin Henry Latrobe.* New York, 1955.

Hawthorne, Nathaniel. *The American Notebooks,* Claude M. Simpson, ed. Columbus, Ohio, 1972.

Kouvenhoven, John A. *Made in America.* New York, 1948.

Larkin, Oliver W. *Art and Life in America,* revised ed. New York, 1960.

Littlefield, Ada Douglas. *An Old River Town . . . History of Winterport, Maine.* New York, 1907.

Merrill, Georgia Drew. *History of Androscoggin County, Maine.* Boston, 1891.

Scully, Vincent J., Jr. *The Shingle Style and the Stick Style,* revised ed. New Haven, Conn., 1971.

Shettleworth, Earle G., Jr. "Henry Rowe's Structures Were Outstanding." *Evening Express* (Portland), September 4, 1965, p. 16.

Shettleworth, Earle G., Jr. "U. S. Seamen Had to Pay 20¢ a Month to Get Hospital Care," *Evening Express* (Portland), August 2, 1967, p. 32.

Shettleworth, Earle G., Jr. "Benjamin Deane." *Bangor Daily News,* September 15, 1975, p. 15.

"Summer Chapels in Maine." *The Northeast* [a publication of the Episcopal Diocese of Maine], 8, No. 6 (July, 1961), pp. 4–20.

Upjohn, Everard M. *Richard Upjohn, Architect and Churchman.* New York: Columbia University Press, 1939 and Da Capo Press, 1968.

[Vickery, James B.] *An Illustrated History of the City of Bangor, Maine 1769–1969.* Bangor, 1969.

Williamson, Joseph. *History of the City of Belfast,* completed and edited by Alfred Johnson. 2 vols. New York, 1913.

Chapter 5, Part 2. Turn-of-the-Century Architecture

Hatch, Louis C. *Maine: A History*. 3 vols. New York: The American Historical Society, 1919.

Lawrence, Ellis F. "John Calvin Stevens." *Architecture* (New York, July, 1932), pp. 1–6.

Olmsted, Frederic Law. *Report and Advice of the Development and Improvement of Cushing's Island, Maine*. Privately printed, Portland?, 1883.

Price, Bruce. *A Large Country House*. New York: William T. Comstock, 1886.

Scully, Vincent J., Jr. *The Shingle Style*. New Haven: Yale University Press, 1955.

Sheldon, George W. *Artistic Country Seats*. New York: D. Appleton, 1886–87.

Stevens, John Calvin and Cobb, Albert Winslow. *Examples of American Domestic Architecture*. New York: William T. Comstock, 1889.

Sturgis, Russell. *The Works of Bruce Price*. New York: The Architectural Record Company, 1899.

Wilcox, Mark M. "John Calvin Stevens, the Development of Ordered Complexity Within the Shingle Style." Unpublished undergraduate study, Brown University, 1975.

Chapter 5, Part 3. Industrial and Commercial Architecture

Candee, Richard M. "The Design of the Mills, the Plan for the City." Typescript, Lewiston Public Library, 1973.

Elder, Joseph G. *History of Lewiston*. Lewiston, Maine, 1882.

Grindle, Roger L. *Quarry and Kiln: The Story of Maine's Lime Industry*. Rockland, Maine: Courier: Gazette, Inc., 1971.

Johnson, Roger R. "Samuel Batchelder, 1784–1879." Typescript, Biddeford Economic Improvement Commission, 1971.

Johnson, Roger R. "Economic History of Biddeford, Maine." Typescript, Biddeford Economic Improvement Commission, 1971.

Leitman, Eva M. "An Historic Perspective of the Franklin Company's Role in the Development of Early Lewiston, Maine." Typescript, Lewiston Public Library, undated.

Péladeau, Marius B. *Adventures in Maine History*. Lewiston, Maine: Maine League of Historical Societies and Museums, 1976.

Shettleworth, Earle G., Jr. "Nineteenth Century Lewiston, An Architectural View." Typescript, Lewiston Public Library, 1973.

Smith, David C. *A History of Lumbering in Maine, 1861–1960*, University of Maine Studies, No. 93. Orono, Maine: University of Maine Press, 1972.

Thompson, Slason. *Short History of American Railways*. Chicago, 1925.

Turner, Augustus R. *Souvenir Program of the One Hundredth Anniversary of the City of Lewiston*. Auburn, Maine, 1895.

"Auburn Central Fire Headquarters and Emergency Operations Center." *Maine Architecture and Construction*, 4, No. 5 (Spring, 1972), pp. 18–19.

Bayer, Herbert: Gropius, Ise; and Gropius, Walter. *Bauhaus, 1919–1928*. New York: The Museum of Modern Art, 1938.

Blake, Peter. *Marcel Breuer: Architect and Designer*. New York: Architectural Record and The Museum of Modern Art, 1949.

Bletter, Rosemarie Haag and Robinson, Cervin. *Skyscraper Style; Art Deco New York*. New York: Oxford University Press, 1975.

"Bowdoin College Library." *Architect and Builder* [Brunswick, Maine], 1, No. 1 (December, 1964), pp. 8–11, 14.

"Bowdoin Senior Center." *Architect and Builder* [Brunswick, Maine], 1, No. 1 (December, 1964), p. 4.

"Bowdoin's New Gymnasium." *Architect and Builder* [Brunswick, Maine], 1, No. 4 (December, 1965), pp. 7, 8.

"Casco Bank—New Monument on the Square." *Maine Architecture and Construction*, 4, No. 1 (January-February, 1971), pp. 8–11, 24, 25.

"Casco Bank's Waterfront Fort." *Maine Architecture and Construction*, 4, No. 4 (July-August, 1971), pp. 14–16.

"Church by Woodward Reflects Modern Trend." *The Maine Builder* [Brunswick, Maine] (November-December, 1961), pp. 6–7.

"Cluster Homes." *Maine Architecture and Construction*, 4, No. 7 (August-September, 1972), pp. 12–13.

"Cooper Milliken—An Architectural Profile." *Maine Architecture and Construction*, 4, No. 4 (July-August, 1971), p. 13.

"An Educational Use of Wood." *Maine Architecture and Construction*, 1, No. 5 (November-December, 1968), pp. 11–13.

Giedion, Siegfried. *Space, Time and Architecture*. Cambridge, Mass.: Harvard University Press, 1963.

Hilberseimer, L. *Mies van der Rohe*. Chicago: Theobald, 1956.

Hildebrand, Grant. *Designing for Industry, The Architecture of Albert Kahn*. Cambridge, Mass.: The M.I.T. Press, 1974.

Hitchcock, Henry-Russell, and Johnson, Philip. *The International Style: Architecture Since 1922*. New York: W. W. Norton & Co., 1932. Reprint, New York, 1966.

Hitchcock, Henry-Russell. *In the Nature of Materials, the Buildings of Frank Lloyd Wright, 1887–1941*. New York, 1942.

"Homes with a View." *Maine Architecture and Construction*, 1, No. 1 (March, 1968), pp. 12–15, 25.

"Industry and Education, U.M.O.'s Chemical Engineering Complex." *Maine Architecture and Construction*, 4, No. 2 (March-April, 1971), pp. 20–21.

Jeanneret, Charles-Edouard [Le Corbusier]. *Towards a New Architecture*. London: Architectural Press, 1927. Reprint, New York: Praeger, 1960.

Jordy, William H. *American Buildings and Their Architects*; vol. 3, Progressive and Academic Ideals at the Turn of the Twentieth Century. Vol. 4, The Impact of European Modernism in the Mid-Twentieth Century. Garden City, N. Y.: Doubleday, 1972.

"Krumbhaar and Holt, An Architectural Profile." *Maine Architecture and Construction*, 4, No. 3 (May-June, 1971), pp. 12–13.

"Lewiston's Canal National Bank." *Maine Architecture and Construction*, 3, No. 4 (November-December, 1969), pp. 12–13, 24.

Mumford, Lewis, ed. *Roots of Contemporary American Architecture*. New York: Grove Press, 1959.

Nelson, George and Wright, Henry. *Tomorrow's House*. New York: Simon and Schuster, 1945.

Nelson, George. *Living Spaces*. New York: Whitney (*Interiors* Library), 1952.

"New Housing at Pine Tree Camp." *Maine Architecture and Construction*, 1, No. 2 (May, 1968), 14–15, 32, 33.

"New Industries on the Maine Scene." *The Maine Builder* [Brunswick, Maine] (June, 1958), p. 14.

"A New Look at Colby." *Maine Architecture and Construction*, 1, No. 1 (March, 1968), pp. 6–11, 26, 27.

"Nine Buildings Win 1972 Library Awards." *Maine Architecture and Construction*, 4, No. 6 (June-July, 1972), pp. 19–24.

"Oak Point Summer Houses." *The Maine Builder* [Brunswick, Maine] (October-November, 1960), pp. 16–18.

"Osteopathic Hospital, Portland, Maine." *Maine Architecture and Construction*, 4, No. 5 (Spring 1972), pp. 12–13.

"Planning the Place of Worship." *The Maine Builder* [Brunswick, Maine] (October-November, 1960), pp. 11–13, 24.

"Planning Tomorrow's Schools." *The Maine Builder* [Brunswick, Maine] (June, 1960), pp. 11, 22.

Plowden, David. *Bridges. The Spans of North America*. New York: Viking, 1974.

"Redington North Year-round Resort Living." *Maine Architecture and Construction*, 1, No. 6 (January-February, 1969), pp. 11–14, 32.

"Residential Designs, House in Amherst, Mass. by Cooper Milliken." *The Maine Builder* [Brunswick, Maine] (April, 1960), p. 21.

Rudofsky, Bernard. *Streets for People; A Primer for Americans*. Garden City, New York, 1969.

Saarinen, Eliel. *Search for Form*. New York: Reinhold Publishing Corp., 1948.

"St. Peter's Church, Manset." *Maine Architecture and Construction*, 1, No. 5 (November-December, 1968), pp. 16, 17, 27.

Scully, Vincent. *Frank Lloyd Wright*. Masters of World Architecture Series. New York: Braziller, 1960.

Scully, Vincent. *The Shingle Style Today or the Historian's Revenge*. New York: Braziller, 1974.

"School Expansion Programs." *The Maine Builder* [Brunswick, Maine] (April, 1960), pp. 10–16.

"Schoolroom Progress U.S.A." *The Maine Builder* [Brunswick, Maine] (December, 1957), pp. 15–22.

"Schools Across the State." *The Maine Builder* [Brunswick, Maine] (September-October, 1961), pp. 14–15.

"Second Annual Building Perspective." *The Maine Builder* [Brunswick, Maine] (March-April, 1961), pp. 8–17.

"Shorefront Residence in York." *Maine Architecture and Construction*, 1, No. 2 (May, 1968), pp. 20–23.

Speyer, A. James. *Mies van der Rohe*. Chicago: The Art Institute, 1968.

"A Star is Born. St. Matthew's in Hampden." *Maine Architecture and Construction*, 4, No. 4 (July-August, 1971), pp. 9–11.

"State of Maine Library—Museum—Archives." *Maine Architecture and Construction*, 4, No. 5 (Fall, 1971), pp. 6–10, 26.

"Sugarloaf Condominiums." *Maine Architecture and Construction*, 4, No. 1 (January-February, 1971), pp. 18, 19.

"Summer Houses." *Maine Architecture and Construction*, 2, No. 3 (September, 1969), pp. 16–21.

"Telstar Regional High School." *Maine Architecture and Construction*, 2, No. 2 (July-August, 1969), pp. 8–11.

"Topsham's Octagonal School." *Maine Architecture and Construction*, 1, No. 4 (September-October, 1968), pp. 8–10, 26.

"The Total Concept in a Physical Education—Athletic Complex." *Maine Architecture and Construction*, 1, No. 2 (May, 1968), pp. 24–29, 34.

"Two Important Buildings in One City." *Maine Architecture and Construction*, 4, No. 5 (Spring, 1972), pp. 9–11.

"Union Mutual's New Home in the Country." *Maine Architecture and Construction*, 4, No. 2 (March-April, 1971), pp. 4–7.

Venturi, Robert. *Complexity and Contradiction in Architecture*. New York: The Museum of Modern Art, 1966.

Wright, Frank Lloyd. *The Future of Architecture*. New York, 1953.

Wright, Frank Lloyd. *A Testament*. New York, 1957.

"Year-round Vacation Home in West Bethel." *Maine Architecture and Construction*, 1, No. 5 (November-December, 1968), pp. 14, 15, 27.

Chapter 7. The Architecture of Maine's Schools

Bardwell, John D. NRHP Nomination, Old Schoolhouse, York. August 8, 1972.

Beard, Frank A. and Shettleworth, Earle G. Jr. NRHP Nomination, Day's Ferry Historic District. August 29, 1974.

Barnard, Henry. *School Architecture or Contributions to the Improvement of School-Houses in the United States*. 2nd ed. New York, 1849.

Butler, Ben; Butler, Natalie; and McKeen, Donald W. *Zephaniah Builds a Schoolhouse—Among Other Things*. Farmington, Maine, 1975.

Chadbourne, Ava. *History of Maine Education*. Lancaster, Pa., 1936.

Chase, Mary Ellen. *A Goodly Heritage*. New York: Henry Holt and Co., 1932.

Corthell, William. *The Twenty-Third Annual Report of the State Superintendent of Common Schools*. Augusta: Sprague, Owen, and Nash, 1877.

"Learning Center at Kent's Hill." *Maine Architecture and Construction*, 1, No. 3 (July-August, 1968), p. 11.

Nickerson, Kermit S. *150 Years of Education in Maine*. Augusta: State of Maine Department of Education, 1970.

Pierce, Josiah. *History of Gorham,* Maine. Portland, 1862.

Records of the Governor and Company of the Massachusetts Bay in New England, vol. II. Boston: The Press of William White, 1853.

Ryan, Kevin and Cooper, James M. *Those Who Can, Teach*. Boston, 1972.

Shettleworth, Earle G. Jr. NRHP Nomination, New Gloucester Historic District. June, 1974.

Shettleworth, Earle G. Jr. and Beard, Frank A. NRHP Nomination, Alna School. April 4, 1975.

"Topsham's Octagonal School." *Maine Architecture and Construction*, 1, No. 4 (September-October, 1968), pp. 8-10.

Wray, Ruth Arline. "History of Secondary Education in Cumberland and Sagadahoc Counties." University of Maine Studies, 2nd series, No. 51. *The Maine Bulletin*, XLIII, No. 1 (August, 1940), 1-153.

Chapter 8.   Maine's Landscapes

Amory, Cleveland. *The Last Resorts*. New York, 1952.

Angier, C.; Colby, R. E.; Kimball, T. H.; and Mark, L. *A Citizen's Report on Back Cove*. Privately printed, Portland, 1972 for Maine Audobon Society.

Bangor City Planning Department. *Bangor, Maine, Comprehensive Plan Summary*. Bangor, 1974.

Beard, Frank A., and Shettleworth, Earle G., Jr. NRHP Nomination, Mount Hope Cemetery District. December 14, 1974.

Bliss, M. D. "An Attempted Evocation of a Personality." *Landscape Architecture*, XLIX, No. 4 (1959), pp. 218-24.

Brown, Lenard E. *Acadia National Park, History, Basic Data*. Washington, D.C.: U. S. Department of the Interior, 1971.

Bureau of Parks and Recreation, Maine Department of Conservation. *An Outline of the Priorities for the Acquisition of Land for State Park Purposes*. Augusta, 1975.

Bureau of Parks and Recreation, Maine Department of Conservation. *A Short History*. Augusta, 1975.

Butcher, Russ and Butcher, Pam. "Carriage Roads and Bridges of Acadia National Park." *Down East Magazine* (August, 1972), pp. 52-55; 87.

Crane, J. "Garden Potter." *Down East Magazine* (September, 1958), pp. 26-29.

Crowe, Sylvia. *Garden Design*. New York: Hearthside Press, Inc., 1959.

Dorr, George B. *Acadia National Park, Its Growth and Development.* 2 vols. Bangor, Maine: Burr Printing Co., 1948.

Eliot, Charles. *Charles Eliot, Landscape Architect.* Cambridge, Mass.: Riverside Press, 1902.

Eliot, Charles W., 2nd. *The Future of Mount Desert Island.* Bar Harbor, Maine: Bar Harbor Village Improvement Association, 1928.

Garvin, James L. NRHP Nomination, Isles of Shoals. May 16, 1974.

Gothein, Marie Luise. *A History of Garden Art.* 2 vols. London and Toronto: J. M. Dent and Sons Ltd.; New York: E. P. Dutton & Co., 1928.

Hayden, Ralph H. "Ladies and Libraries." Typescript, Camden Public Library, 1931?.

Hill, Albert F. "The Vegetation of the Penobscot Bay Region, Maine." *Proceedings of the Portland Society of Natural History*, III, Part 3 (1923), pp. 305–438.

Hyland, Fay and Steinmetz, Ferdinand H. *The Woody Plants of Maine.* Orono, Maine: University of Maine Press, 1944.

Jellicoe, Susan and Jellicoe, Godfrey. *Modern Private Gardens.* New York: Abelard and Schuman, 1968.

Lacognata, Esther. *The Role of the States in Guiding Land Use Decisions.* Augusta, Maine: Land Use Regulation Commission, 1974.

Laverty, Dorothy Bowler. *Millinocket, Magic City of Maine's Wilderness.* Freeport, Maine: Bond Wheelwright Co., 1973.

Laws, Carl H. *The Saco River Corridor.* Cornish, Maine, 1973.

Lovering, Frank W. "Watering Places of the Gay Nineties." *Down East Magazine* (September, 1959), pp. 16–19.

Maine State Planning Office. *Revised Planning and Zoning Statutes in Maine.* Augusta, 1975.

McHarg, Ian L. *Design with Nature.* Garden City, N.Y.: Doubleday, 1969.

Nash, Roderick. *Wilderness and the American Mind.* New Haven: Yale University Press, 1969.

Newton, Norman T. *Design on the Land; the Development of Landscape Architecture.* Cambridge, Mass.: Harvard University Press, 1971.

Olmsted, [Frederic Law Jr.]; Olmsted, [John Charles]; and Eliot, [Charles]. *Landscape Architects' Report on the Improvement of Back Cove.* Brookline, Mass., May 27, 1896.

Patterson, R. W. "Beatrix Farrand, 1872–1959, An Appreciation of a Great Landscape Gardener." *Landscape Architecture*, XLIX, No. 4 (1959), pp. 216–18.

Roper, Laura Wood. *FLO, a Biography of Frederick Law Olmsted.* Baltimore, Md.: Johns Hopkins University Press, 1973.

Saltonstall, Richard, Jr. *Maine Pilgrimage.* Boston: Little Brown and Co., 1974.

Schumacher, E. F. *Small is Beautiful.* New York: Harper Torch Books, 1973.

Shepard, Paul. *Man in the Landscape.* New York: Alfred A. Knopf, 1967.

Shettleworth, Earle G., Jr. "Developers Plotted Facets of Boston for Frontier City." *Bangor Daily News*, September 22, 1975, p. 13.

Siller-Neagle, M. "Maine's House of Entertainment, Appledore." *Down East Magazine* (July, 1963), pp. 34–37.

Tree, C. "Calendar Islands Prove 225 Short During 3 Hour Cruise." *Boston Sunday Globe*, July 14, 1974, pp. 70–71.

Todd, Frederick, *et al. Comprehensive Land Use Plan for Plantations and Unorganized Townships of Maine, Policies Plan*. Augusta, Maine, 1974.

Watts, May Theilgaard. *Reading the Landscape*. New York: Macmillan, 1957.

Wherry, Edgar T. *Wild Flowers of Mount Desert Island, Maine*. The Garden Club of Mount Desert, 1928.

Zube, Ervin H., ed. *Landscapes, Selected Writings of J. B. Jackson*. Amherst, Mass.: University of Massachusetts Press, 1970.

Index

All Maine buildings are listed under their towns so that the Index may serve visitors to different localities and persons interested in local history. Figure numbers are in italics.

Orders, classical. *See also* Columns; Pilasters
Corinthian, 50, 70, 101, 126, 133, 136, 172, 175
Doric, 46, 59, 66, 79, 82, 98, 100, 106, 107, 108, 110, 111, 114, 115, 116, 118, 121, 124, 126, 128, 129, 130, 132, 134, 135, 136, 137, 257
Ionic, 77, 91, 101, 110, 112, 115, 116, 117, 118, 121, 122, 124, 125, 126, 127, 130, 132, 135, 136, 137, 170, 198
superposed, 124
unclassical adaptations of, 125–6, 127, 130, 132–3, 136, 137
Orland Methodist Church, 114
Orff, George W., architect, 217
Orono
Treat, Nathaniel, House, 130
University of Maine, 226, 275, 283
University of Maine, Newman Center, 248
University of Maine original campus plan, 263, 268, *124*
Washburn, Governor Israel, House, 135–6
Whitney, Thomas, House, 127
Ottowa House. *See* Cushing's Island
Ovens, 61, 115, 134
Overhangs, 28, 30, 32, 33, 34, 36, 94
Overlock, James (1813–?), builder-architect, 98, 135
Owls Head Light, 94
Oxford
Congregational Church, 152
mill, 214
Oxford County Jail. *See* Paris Hill

— P —

Packard, Isaac, housewright, 63, 294 n.8
Paddy, William, sawmill owner, 25
Pain, James, 295 n.10
Paint, exterior, 53, 155, 161, 164–5, 188
Paint, interior, 53, 57
Painting, interior ornamental and mural, 50, 167, 203, 208
Pain, William, 82, 295 n.10
Pain, William, *The Practical House Carpenter*, 77
Palermo, Dinsmore Mill, 214
Palisades, 17th-century, 19, 20, 28, 30, 33. *See also* Indian, prehistoric, palisaded villages; Fortifications and defensive buildings
Palladian motif, 202, 208. *See also* Windows, Palladian
Palm Beach, Fla., 271
Palmer, Asa B., House. *See* Bath
Palynology, 5, 286, n.4
Pancoast, Patricia McGraw, 307 n.36, 312, n.10
Panic of 1837, 266
Paper mills and companies, 214, 216, 265, 278

Parapets, 100, 101, 115, 116, 121, 133, 160, 208
Paris, Hill, 74, 75
Oxford County Jail, 91
Rawson, Samuel, House, 75
Parker, Carl Rust, landscape architect, 201
Parker, Israel, Belfast builder, 180
Parks, city and town, 214, 215, 266, 268, 275, 277
Parks, national, 268, 275, 280–81
Park setting of houses, 77, 82, 158, 160, 201, 265
Parks, state, 223, 275, 281–2
Parquet, 162
Parris, Alexander (1780–1852), architect, 70, 72, 75, 97, 107, 295 n.4
Parsonsfield, 84
Parsons-Bourne House. *See* Kennebunkport
Parsons, Isaac, first and second, Houses. *See* New Gloucester
Partitions, moveable, 49, 64
Partridge, Jesse, House. *See* Portland (Stroudwater)
Partridge, Rhoda, House. *See* Portland
Pascal, John and Alexander, builders, shipwrights, 117
Patterson, Robert, landscape architect, 313 n.18
Paty, Thomas, sawmill owner, 25
Pavilions, 63, 74, 87, 91, 92, 98, 100, 111, 112, 133, 137, 208, 257, 274, 277
Peacock Tavern. *See* Gardiner vicinity
Peaks Island, Underwood Park, 268, *125*
Pearson, Moses, house carpenter, 53
Peck, Bradford, *The World a Department Store*, 211
Pediments
arched, 61
swan's neck, 50, 53
triangular, 46, 51, 59, 62, 77, 87, 91, 92, 93, 99, 110, 111, 112, 114, 118, 120, 121, 132, 135, 136, 137, 202
Pejepscot Paper Mill. *See* Topsham
Pemaquid, Harrington Meetinghouse, 46
Pemaquid, 17th-century colony and fort, 19, 28
Pemaquid Light, 94
Penney, J.C., Building, New York, 309 n.3
Penobscot Valley, 97
Penobscot County, 219
Pent roofs, 135
Pepperrell, Lady, House. *See* Kittery
Pepperrell, William, first and second, Houses. *See* Kittery
Pepperrell, William (Jr.), Sir, 44, 50
Pepperrell, William, Sr., landowner, 43, 49
Percy and Small Shipyard. *See* Bath
Peripteral houses, 121
Perkins, Abner, House. *See* Kennebunkport
Perkins, Elizabeth, House. *See* York
Perkins, Homestead. *See* Newcastle
Perkins, Isaiah, House. *See* York
Perkins, Tristram, House. *See* Kennebunkport
Peters, Russell, House. *See* Bangor

Steele, Fletcher, landscape architect, 277, 314 n.28
Stein House, Saint-Cloud, France, 237
Stetson, George K., House. *See* Bangor
Stevens, John, Boston architect, 175
Stevens, John Calvin I (1855–1940), architect, 182, 184, 186–9, 192–4, 196–9, 201–03, 205–06, 208–09, 259, 268, 307 n.28
Stevens, John Calvin I, House. *See* Portland
Stevens, John Calvin II (1908–), architect, 187, 306 n.18
Stevens, John Howard (1879–1958), architect, 187, 201, 208
Stevens, Paul Stratton, architect, 187
Stick Style, 166, 182, 187, 205
Stone construction, 43, 49, 155, 158, 160, 164, 166, 167, 189, 196, 202, 205, 274, 280. *See also* Granite; Ashlar
Stone trim, 181, 187, 196, 208, 219, 230. *See also* Granite trim
Storehouses, 15, 16
Storer, Ebenezer, House. *See* Portland
Stoves
    cast-iron cooking, 115, 133, 134
    cast-iron, fireplace ("chill chasers"), 115, 130, 132, 134, 136
    Shaker, 59
Stowe, Harriet Beecher, 166
Strathglass Park. *See* Rumford
Streets, grid system of, 265
Strong, suspension bridge, 219–20
Stubbins, Hugh, and Associates, architects, 233, 245
Sturdivant Hall. *See* Hebron Academy
Sturgis, Russell, 205
Sugarloaf development, 278. *See also* Carrabasset Valley
Sullivan, Granite (Old Salt) Store, 102
Sullivan, Louis, architect, 228, 230, 249
Sullivan, Louis, style of, 211
Summer colonies, 192–3, 269, 271, 280
Sumner, Thomas Waldron (1768–1849), architect, 107
Sunday School movement, 111
Susquehanna Tradition, 6
Swedenborgian Church. *See* Bath
Sylvester, Isaac, House. *See* Freeport
Synagogues, 248

—T—

Tallman, Henry, House. *See* Bath
Tandy, Harold, House. *See* Hampden Highlands
Tarbell, Eaton W., architect, 236, 249, 250
Tate, George, House. *See* Portland (Stroudwater)
Tate, George, royal mast agent, 50
Taverns and inns, 39, 49, 51, 54, 57, 58, 59, 62, 92. *See also* Hotels
Teacher's Cove Site, 10, 6

Teak trim, 233
Temple-fronted buildings, 98, 99, 107, 108, 110, 112, 114, 116, 118, 119, 122, 124–7, 134, 136
Tenements, 216
Terra cotta trim, 188, 230, 259
Textile mills, 93, 214, 215, 222, 239–40
Thatcher Hotel. *See* Biddeford
Thaxter, Celia, author, 269
Thayer, Abbott, artist, 208
Theobald, Capt., House. *See* Richmond
Thing, Capt. Abraham, House. *See* Hallowell
Thomas, Mr. and Mrs. Arthur, 303 n.57
Thomas, Clara Fargo, House. *See* Seal Harbor
Thomas School of Dance, 168
Thomaston, 97, 222
    Dragon Cement Plant, 241
    Henderson, Capt. William, House, 135
    Keith, William R. (Howard Seymour), House, 118
    "Montpelier," 74, 75, 77
    Ranlett, Capt. Charles, House, 135
    Robinson, Edward, House, 83
    Ruggles, John, House, 75, 83
    St. John Baptist Episcopal Church, 166, 180
    Thompson, Benjamin, architect, 245, 247
    Thompson, Nathaniel Lord, House. *See* Kennebunk
Thoreau, Henry David, 223, 266, 313 n.13
Thornton Academy. *See* Saco
Tile sheathing, 233
Time-Life Building, New York, 309 n.3
Togus, Veterans Administration Hospital, 230
Tontine Hotel. *See* Brunswick
Topsham
    bank, 101
    Cone, John A., Elementary School, 262, *119*
    Holden-Frost House, 75
    Hunter, John, Tavern, 59
    Pejepscot Paper Mill, 214, 216
    Porter, Benjamin, House, 77, 92, *33, 34*
    Walker-Wilson House, 79
Tower, Ashley B., architect, 224
Towers, modern, 244. *See also* Office blocks, slabs and towers
Towers, revival and turn-of-the-century, 164, 172, 178, 180, 188, 196, 202, 206, 208, 211, 215
Towle, John D., architect, 174
Town halls, 89
Town meetings, buildings for, 46, 87, 89
Town plans by landscape architects, 275, 277, 278
Townsend Plan for Kennebec Valley, 283
Trabeated construction, 101, 102, 106, 107
Tracery, 110, 127, 154
Trade, European with Indians, 3, 12, 14, 18, 20
Tram cars, 266. *See also* Trolleys
Transitional style, Federal to Greek Revival, 93, 124–5, 128, 136